Intergovernmental Transfers in Federations

STUDIES IN FISCAL FEDERALISM AND STATE–LOCAL FINANCE

Series Editor: Jorge Martinez-Vazquez, *Regents Professor of Economics and Director, International Center for Public Policy, Andrew Young School of Policy Studies, Georgia State University, USA*

This important series is designed to make a significant contribution to the development of the principles and practices of state–local finance. It includes both theoretical and empirical work. International in scope, it addresses issues of current and future concern in both East and West and in developed and developing countries.

The main purpose of the series is to create a forum for the publication of high-quality work and to show how economic analysis can make a contribution to understanding the role of local finance in fiscal federalism in the twenty-first century.

Titles in the series include:

The Political Economy of Inter-Regional Fiscal Flows
Measurement, Determinants and Effects on Country Stability
Edited by Núria Bosch, Marta Espasa and Albert Solé-Ollé

Decentralization in Developing Countries
Global Perspectives on the Obstacles to Fiscal Devolution
Edited by Jorge Martinez-Vazquez and François Vaillancourt

The Challenge of Local Government Sizes
Theoretical Perspectives, International Experience and Policy Reform
Edited by Santiago Lago-Peñas and Jorge Martinez-Vazquez

State and Local Financial Instruments
Policy Changes and Management
Craig L. Johnson, Martin J. Luby and Tima T. Moldogaziev

Taxation and Development: The Weakest Link?
Essays in Honor of Roy Bahl
Edited by Richard M. Bird and Jorge Martinez-Vazquez

Multi-level Finance and the Euro Crisis
Causes and Effects
Edited by Ehtisham Ahmad, Massimo Bordignon and Giorgio Brosio

Fiscal Decentralization and Budget Control
Laura von Daniels

The Future of Federalism
Intergovernmental Financial Relations in an Age of Austerity
Edited by Richard Eccleston and Richard Krever

Fiscal Decentralization and Local Finance in Developing Countries
Development from Below
Roy Bahl and Richard M. Bird

Federalism in China and Russia
Story of Success and Story of Failure?
Alexander Libman and Michael Rochlitz

Local Accountability and National Coordination in Fiscal Federalism
A Fine Balance
Charles R. Hankla, Jorge Martinez-Vazquez and Raúl Alberto Ponce Rodríguez

Intergovernmental Transfers in Federations
Edited by Serdar Yilmaz and Farah Zahir

Intergovernmental Transfers in Federations

Edited by

Serdar Yilmaz

Lead Public Sector Specialist, Governance Global Practice, World Bank

Farah Zahir

Senior Economist, Governance Global Practice, World Bank

STUDIES IN FISCAL FEDERALISM AND STATE–LOCAL FINANCE

Cheltenham, UK • Northampton, MA, USA

Published by
Edward Elgar Publishing Limited
The Lypiatts
15 Lansdown Road
Cheltenham
Glos GL50 2JA
UK

Edward Elgar Publishing, Inc.
William Pratt House
9 Dewey Court
Northampton
Massachusetts 01060
USA

A catalogue record for this book
is available from the British Library

Library of Congress Control Number: 2019951902

This book is available electronically in the **Elgar**online
Economics subject collection
DOI 10.4337/9781789900859

ISBN 978 1 78990 084 2 (cased)
ISBN 978 1 78990 085 9 (eBook)

Typeset by Servis Filmsetting Ltd, Stockport, Cheshire

Printed and bound by CPI Group (UK) Ltd, Croydon, CR0 4YY

Contents

Contributors

Roy W. Bahl Jr is Regents Professor and Dean Emeritus at Georgia State University, USA and Professor Extraordinarius at the University of Pretoria, South Africa. From 1968 through 1971, Dr Bahl was an economist with the Fiscal Affairs Department of the International Monetary Fund. Then, he was the Maxwell Professor of Political Economy at Syracuse University, USA, where he directed the Metropolitan and Regional Research Center and the Metropolitan Studies Program. He serves as a consultant to various World Bank departments, the International Monetary Fund, the Asian Development Bank, the Lincoln Institute of Land Policy and to the United Nations.

Jamie Boex is a Senior Fellow at the Duke Center for International Development (DCID), USA and has extensive experience in public sector finance, fiscal decentralization, intergovernmental (fiscal) relations and local governance reforms in developing and transition countries around the world. Working with organizations such as the World Bank, United Nations Development Programme (UNDP), United States Agency for International Development (USAID) and numerous bilateral development agencies and research organizations, Jamie has contributed to policy reforms in over twenty countries around the world.

Howard A. Chernick is Professor Emeritus at the Department of Economics, Hunter College, the City University of New York, USA and a board member of the Institute for Taxation and Economic Policy. In 2015 he was awarded a Fulbright specialist grant for study in Paris. He has published in the areas of fiscal federalism, urban public finance and anti-poverty policy. Selected writings include the articles 'Fiscal Effects of Block Grants for the Needy: An Interpretation of the Evidence' (1998) and 'The Impact of the Great Recession and the Housing Crisis on the Financing of America's Largest Cities' (2011) and, as editor, *Resilient City: The Economic Impact of 9/11* (Russell Sage, 2005).

Jonathan Coppel is a Commissioner with the Australian Productivity Commission. Prior to his appointment, Jonathan was Head of the OECD G20 Sherpa office. In Australia he has held senior management positions at the Reserve Bank and started his career at the Commonwealth

Treasury. Jonathan has taught at the World Trade Institute's Mile Masters Programme in International Law and Economics and the Paris, Sciences Po Institute. He has a Master's in economics and management from Columbia University, New York, a Bachelor's in economics (Honours) from the Australian National University and is a graduate of the Australian Institute of Company Directors.

Bernard Dafflon was the Chief Economist at the Ministry of Local Affairs in Fribourg, Germany (1977–91) and full-time Professor of Public Economics at the University of Fribourg (1991–2013). He has worked as an international consultant on decentralization policies and reforms in a number of developed and developing countries. He is an expert on fiscal federalism, local public finance and environmental policies.

Julian Folgar is an economist at the World Bank Group. Julian works on various analytical projects including macro-fiscal areas, fiscal federalism and debt sustainability. He received his undergraduate degree in economics from the Buenos Aires University (UBA), Argentina, and is about to complete his Master's degree in economics at UBA. He worked as a consultant in macro-fiscal policy in the private sector, for the Congress of Argentina, and for various international organizations (International Labour Organization (ILO) and United Nations Economic Commission for Latin America and Caribbean (CEPAL)). He also teaches public sector economics at the UBA.

Marcelin Joanis holds a PhD in economics from the University of Toronto and is currently a Full Professor of Economics at Polytechnique Montréal and the Vice-President for Research of the Center for Interuniversity Research and Analysis on Organizations (CIRANO), Canada. He also serves as the Director of the Research Group on Globalization and Management of Technology (GMT) at Polytechnique Montréal. A specialist in public economics, political economy and fiscal federalism, he has published articles in, among others, *Fiscal Studies*, the *Journal of Development Economics, Public Choice, Economics and Politics* and *Applied Economics*, as well as several edited volumes and book chapters. He has also worked as an economist at Finance Canada and Quebec's Commission on fiscal imbalance and as a Professor of Economics at the Université de Sherbrooke.

Marco Larizza is a Senior Public Sector Specialist in the Governance Global Practice at the World Bank. He is a contributing author of the World Development Report 2017 'Governance and the Law'. His most recent work focuses on transparency and anti-corruption initiatives in Latin America and the Caribbean. Marco served as Visiting Fellow at the

Center for Latin American Studies, Georgetown University, USA and the Centre for Democracy and Conflict Resolution, University of Essex, UK. He has published journal articles, book chapters and policy reports on comparative democratization, human rights, the political economy of decentralization and public service reforms. He received his PhD and MA in political science from the University of Essex, UK and his MA in development economics from the University of Bologna, Italy.

Jorge Martinez-Vazquez is Regents Professor of Economics and Director of the Cluster of Public Finance Centers at the Andrew Young School, Georgia State University, USA. He has published over twenty books and numerous articles in academic journals, such as *Econometrica* and the *Journal of Political Economy*. He has advised federal and state agencies in the US and over ninety countries and is the recipient of numerous prizes and awards.

David Savage is a specialist in local service delivery, intergovernmental relations and urban public finance. He has served as a Commissioner on the Financial and Fiscal Commission, worked for the World Bank in South Asia and the South African National Treasury on urban development, service delivery and institutional restructuring issues and is most recently the former Program Manager of the Cities Support Program in the South African National Treasury. He holds Master's degrees in public administration from the London School of Economics and in Urban and Regional Planning from the University of Cape Town.

Bob Searle worked at the Commonwealth Grants Commission (CGC) in Australia for 30 years, the last ten as the CEO. Since leaving the CGC, he has worked as a consultant on decentralization and intergovernmental financial relations, mainly for the World Bank. Bob has assisted in developing the fiscal transfer system in several post-conflict African countries and has also worked in Central and South-East Asia and the Pacific.

Paul Smoke is Professor of Public Finance and Planning and Director of International Programs at the New York University Robert F. Wagner Graduate School of Public Service, USA. His policy and research interests include the political economy of public sector reform, especially decentralization, intergovernmental fiscal relations and service delivery, as well as urban and regional development planning. He has published in numerous journals and has authored or edited several books on decentralization and local governance. Professor Smoke teaches courses on public finance, development planning, governance and development assistance. He has worked in many countries, especially in Africa and Asia, and with a wide range of development partners.

Paul B. Spahn is Professor Emeritus of Goethe University, Frankfurt am Main, Germany. After retirement in 2005, he served as Macro Fiscal Advisor to the Minister of Finance and Treasury of Bosnia and Herzegovina, became the founding Executive Director of the House of Finance in Frankfurt and was Commissioner to the Government of Wales. A former Vice-President of the University of Frankfurt, Professor Spahn has held several visiting professorships across the world, has published widely in scholarly and policy-oriented journals and has provided expert advice to more than seventy government and parliamentary organizations worldwide.

François Vaillancourt is a Fellow at CIRANO and an Emeritus Professor (economics), Université de Montréal, Canada. He has published extensively in three areas of public policy: intergovernmental financial relations (IGFR), economics of language and language policy and compliance costs and complexity of taxation. He has been a Fulbright Scholar and a visitor in universities in Australia, Belgium, France, UK and USA. He has done extensive consulting work on language economics issues and on IGFR, the latter for governments in Canada and for international organizations (African Development Bank (AFD), International Monetary Fund (IMF), OECD, UNDP, World Bank).

Lorena Viñuela is a Senior Public Sector Specialist with the Governance Practice in the Eastern Europe and Central Asia ECA region. She worked previously with the Latin America and Caribbean Region and Public Sector Anchor Unit. Her work focuses on public financial management, intergovernmental fiscal relations and service delivery in multi-level governments. Prior to joining the World Bank, she worked at the Inter-American Development Bank's Research Department and for EuropeAid's AL-Invest Program. She has published several articles, books and book chapters on decentralization, political economy, public investment management and natural resource wealth management.

Deborah L. Wetzel is currently the Director of Regional Integration for the Africa and Middle East North Africa Regions of the World Bank. She has previously been Senior Director for the Governance Global Practice, Director of Strategy and Operations for the Middle East North Africa Region, Country Director for Brazil and Chief of Staff to the President at the World Bank. Over the years she has worked and written on intergovernmental finance issues in a range of countries including Brazil, Hungary, Russia and Ukraine, among others.

Serdar Yilmaz is a Lead Public Sector Specialist at the World Bank. He has broad experience in the related areas of fiscal decentralization, public expenditure management, subnational governance, and governmental accountability. Throughout his twenty-year tenure at the World Bank, he has provided technical assistance and contributed to policy reforms in low- and middle-income countries in Africa, Eastern Europe and Central Asia, the Middle East and East Asia regions. In addition to his task management responsibilities, Serdar makes original contributions to the literature.

Farah Zahir is currently a Senior Economist in the Governance Global Practice, South Asia Region, at the World Bank. She is a seasoned macro-economist and public policy specialist and a prolific writer on fiscal policy and macroeconomic management and fiscal decentralization. Her core areas of expertise have been fiscal policy and growth, statistics and fiscal federalism. Farah has led several large and complex lending operations of the Bank in India on decentralization and statistics. She has been a member of various high-level Government of India committees on decentralization and service delivery, and has worked in several countries besides India.

Foreword

Politicians, officials, scholars, students and citizens in many countries have been exposed to a litany of apparently opposing abstract labels in recent years: globalization versus nationalism, capitalism versus socialism, equity versus growth, private versus public, free market versus state control, centralization versus decentralization, and so on. These broad and vague concepts are often discussed not only as though they represent a clear choice between polar opposites, but also as if everyone knows exactly what they mean and understands them in exactly the same way. Because none of these assumptions is valid, all too often public discourse about the critical policy questions obscured by such labelling degenerates into little more than name calling. This book contributes to improving one of these debates, that on centralization versus decentralization, by casting the light of reasoned discussion on the often-contentious issue of intergovernmental transfers. In doing so, it demonstrates clearly why – as with many policy issues – the best solution is almost always context-specific and seldom simply or easily generalized: the problems hidden behind such labels as decentralization may be universal in scope, but the solution for any particular country usually needs to be carefully tailored to fit each situation.

There are few, if any, simple 'one-size-fits-all' designs for public policy in any area. To understand intergovernmental fiscal transfers in any country, for example, one must first understand the complex and often changing institutions and conditions that shape taxation, spending, and intergovernmental fiscal relations more generally. Because each country has its own history, political setting and economic conditions, every transfer system is different and transfer reform is always and everywhere an exercise in the art of political economy, requiring both familiarity with the considerable technical complexities required to design efficient and effective transfers and sensitivity to the realities of the relevant political, institutional and economic context. Whether novice or expert, all who attempt to navigate these difficult waters – whether trying to develop a better system or simply to understand why there are so often conflicting views about the design and effects of intergovernmental transfers – can learn much from this book.

In addition to the ten countries specifically singled out for study in this volume, the impressive set of authors included here draw on their prior experience in an even wider set of countries as well as on the growing theoretical and empirical literature focusing on the intergovernmental fiscal issues which underlie, shape and are in turn shaped by transfer systems. As this book (and the literature cited) shows, there is seldom any clearly 'best' way to design and implement intergovernmental transfers. The basic problems – vertical and horizontal imbalances, regional disparities in resources and capacity, poverty and inequality, coping with cyclical and other instabilities, balancing growth and equity, delivering basic public services effectively and equitably, damping down separatist tendencies – may exist to some extent in every country. But both the importance attached to each of these issues and the extent to which any feasible transfer may alter outcomes usually depends so much on specifically local factors that it is difficult to identify any simple scheme that will fit all seasons in all countries.

Successful transfer reforms are thus likely to continue to be tailor-made rather than simply cut-and-paste jobs based on someone's book of best practices. There are, of course, best practices that can be learned about how to approach reforming intergovernmental fiscal relations and the efficacy of different solutions in different circumstances. Would-be reformers, like students trying simply to understand what is going on, will find here both some master classes on questions that should be – but seldom are – asked and a number of careful examinations of how and why this or that approach seems to have worked to at least some extent in some circumstances, while failing in others. There is much more to be learned, but, as this book shows, we have already learned much.

Richard Bird
June 2019

Acknowledgements

The editors gratefully acknowledge the assistance of the following people, who reviewed the manuscript:

James Alm, Professor and Chair, Department of Economics, Tulane University, USA.

Richard M. Bird, Professor Emeritus of Economic Analysis and Policy, University of Toronto, Canada.

Giorgio Brosio, Professor of Public Economics, University of Turin, Italy.

William Dillinger, Former Lead Public Sector Specialist, World Bank.

Robert D. Ebel, Former Lead Economist, World Bank.

William F. Fox, Randy and Jenny Boyd Distinguished Professor, University of Tennessee, Knoxville, USA.

Guy Gilbert, Professor, École normale supérieure Paris-Saclay, France.

Andrew Reschovsky, Professor Emeritus of Public Affairs and Applied Economics, University of Wisconsin–Madison, USA.

Alain Schönenberger, Professor, Université de Neuchâtel, Switzerland.

Enid Slack, Director of the Institute on Municipal Finance and Governance, University of Toronto, Canada.

D.K. Srivastava, Chief Policy Advisor, Ernst and Young.

Trevor Tombe, Associate Professor, University of Calgary, Canada.

Mehmet Serkan Tosun, Barbara Smith Campbell Distinguished Professor of Nevada Tax Policy, University of Nevada, Reno, USA.

Timothy Stephen Williamson, Senior Public Sector Specialist, World Bank.

1. Introduction to the volume

Serdar Yilmaz and Farah Zahir

1.1 BACKGROUND

This book intends to contribute to the definition of the frontiers of research in vertical and horizontal imbalances (VFI) in federations. It also looks ahead for opportunities and challenges and subsequent needs for future research and development. Whereas the second section of the volume includes theoretical and methodological contributions, much of the book is devoted to case studies that illustrate important policy or methodological lessons.

The most important lesson to be learned from the book is that there is no single or best way of addressing vertical and horizontal imbalances. That is because each country is different and policy objectives of intergovernmental transfers are different. More importantly, transfer system design in a country is a response to specific conditions that exist at that particular time in history.

The book is divided into four sections. After this brief introduction, the second section covers conceptual issues of principles of VFI and public finance and political economy considerations in addressing them. Then, the next three sections analyse how different federations address VFI.

1.2 CONCEPTUAL ISSUES

Much of the earlier literature on fiscal federalism revolved around studying departures from a model fiscal system whereby intergovernmental transfers played a benevolent role. However, in the 21st century, the federations seem to be recalibrating their fiscal architecture to address the needs of pluralistic communities and their large populace. More recently, the system of intergovernmental transfers is more actively used for restoring a balance in sharing of resources between the states (and local governments) and the national government for improving development outcomes. The chapters in the second section of the book delve into the various theoretical aspects of VFI and political economy considerations in designing a transfer system in addressing them. The second chapter by Bahl offers explanations 'for why countries set up their grant systems in so many different ways, and to offer a set of principles that might enable low- and middle-income countries to do a better job with achieving the objectives they have set for their transfer systems'. The third chapter by Yilmaz and Zahir surveys the first-generation theory of fiscal federalism and the second-generation 'to summarize the theoretical conceptualization of intergovernmental transfer design . . . to present a case for the importance of political economy considerations in designing and analysing intergovernmental transfers systems'. The fourth chapter by Dafflon and Vaillancourt puts forward a fascinating reading of how the theory of fiscal equalization is an elusive goal for practitioners.

1.3   MATURE FEDERATIONS

A federation is a political union of partially or fully self-governing provinces, states or regions under a central/federal government. In a mature federation, the self-governing status of the constituent units, as well as the division of power between them and the central/federal government, is typically constitutionally entrenched and may not be altered by a unilateral decision of either party. The second section of the book focuses on five mature federations: Germany, United States, Canada, Switzerland and Australia. In this group of federations, sovereign power is formally divided between the federal government (centre) and the constituents of the federation (second tier) which retain some degree of control over its internal affairs. In mature federations, concurring sovereignties exist between the centre and constituent units of the federation, with full taxing and expenditure powers for each tier.

In Germany, each of three levels of government is autonomous in their expenditure and revenue responsibilities. Chapter 5 analyses the German equalization system which is characterized as one of the most generous ones in the world. The pending 2020 reforms in the intergovernmental transfer system have brought much anxiety among the stakeholders. According to Spahn, it is 'unlikely that the setup of the German financial constitution will change dramatically given that the majority of states, that exert strong legislative voting powers through the second chamber of parliament, are still at the receiving end of the scheme'.

The US, on the other hand, has a chaotic intergovernmental system with the judiciary playing a major role. In the US, Medicaid is the most important federal grant to states. Since its enactment, the Affordable Care

Act has been subject to several lawsuits. In Chapter 6, Chernick presents the intergovernmental grant system in the US which has a very high degree of conditionality. According to him, '[o]f the 1,714 authorized grant programs as of 2012, the vast majority are relatively narrow categorical grants, authorized for specific purposes'.

Unlike the US, in Canada the federal-provincial relationship is less confrontational. The federal government has the responsibility for standard sovereign functions, such as defence, foreign relations and monetary policy, and provinces are responsible for delivery of social services, such as health, education and welfare as well as infrastructure services. In Chapter 7, Joanis and Vaillancourt present the key aspects of fiscal federalism in this one of the oldest federations in the world. The chapter focuses on a contentious issue of how to incorporate provincial natural resource revenues into the equalization programme.

In the next chapter, Dafflon shows the constitutional and institutional complexities of VFI in Switzerland. Chapter 8 lays out the complex public finance arrangements to achieve national equalization through both revenue and expenditure equalization in the Swiss federation.

The last two chapters in this section are devoted to Australia. The six states in Australia, the original six British colonies, came together to form the Commonwealth, much like the US. Therefore, states have strong constitutional protection. However, the assignment of expenditure responsibilities and revenue capacities presents a large vertical imbalance question. In Chapter 9, Searle presents the complex architecture of Australian intergovernmental grant system and its institutional backbone. In the next chapter, Coppel examines the economic impacts of horizontal fiscal equalization (HFE) in Australia. He argues that HFE is functioning reasonably well, achieving a high degree of fiscal equality. However, he highlights the need for tax reforms, particularly for efficient taxation and extraction of mineral and energy resources. As the extraction activities are not evenly distributed across the country, the design of grants has distortionary effects on state level policies, much like Canada. He argues that '[i]f Western Australia raised royalties on iron ore, it would lose close to 90 per cent of the additional revenues to other states'.

1.4 EVOLVING FEDERATIONS

The third section of the book is devoted to evolving federations: Brazil, Argentina and India. In this group of federations, the balance of power between the centre and the constituent unit is evolving over time. As it stands today, the political and economic powers are concentrated in the centre. In these countries, the centre has the constitutional authority to circumvent the powers of a constituent unit government. Furthermore, the centre has the constitutional authority to suspend a constituent government or create new constituent units. India, for example, got its newest 29th state in Telangana in 2014. In Brazil, which has experienced both the federal and the unitary state in its history, the latest state, Tocantins, was created in 1988 for mainly administrative reasons.

Chapter 11 provides an overview of Brazil's system of intergovernmental transfers and reviews three performance-based transfer programmes. Wetzel and Viñuela provide a critical review of the Bolsa Familia programme, that provides grants to both states and municipalities for administering one of the largest social protection programmes and performance-based transfers in Ceara and Rio de Janeiro states.

Argentina is an evolving federation with territorial heterogeneity. In Chapter 12, Larizza and Folgar describe the inequalities across provinces as huge. In their words, Argentina has 'areas as rich as developed nations, and provinces as poor as low middle-income countries'. At the heart of the Argentinian intergovernmental system are an automatic revenue-sharing scheme ('coparticipación') and discretionary transfers to address these inequalities. The conclusion of the chapter is that the system needs reforming 'to simplify its design and align it with international best practices to better achieve three fundamental objectives: closing the vertical gap, closing the horizontal gaps and promoting sectoral objectives'.

Chapter 13 reviews the evolving role of the Finance Commission in the world's largest federation, India. Zahir 'traces the history of the Finance Commissions in India over last two and a half decades in shaping the intergovernmental transfer system in India'. According to her, the Finance Commissions, a constitutional body established every five years to make recommendations to the government on intergovernmental transfers, shape and recalibrate 'the Indian federalism from time to time . . . in providing continuity that has been critical to the unity of the country'.

According to Martinez-Vazquez, India has 'an elaborate and complex system of resource transfers to the states'. In Chapter 14, he provides reform options for India's transfer system by drawing from international experience with the design and implementation of transfers systems.

1.5   UNITARY FEDERATIONS

The last section of the book covers unitary federations: Kenya and South Africa. In a federation sovereignty is shared between the centre and the constituent units of the federation, whereas in a unitary country sovereignty rests with the central government. However, in unitary states autonomous self-governing regions may exist by the sufferance of the central government. We call these countries unitary federations. While federations are created by an agreement (Constitution) between the centre and a number of independent/autonomous regions, unitary federations are often created through a process of devolution, where the centre agrees to grant autonomy to regions that were previously entirely subordinate.

In Chapter 15, Boex and Smoke describe how Kenya, a unitary state, established a highly devolved system with the 2010 Constitution. They argue that 'Kenya's path towards devolution has in some ways been a "political" success'. However, they caution that transforming devolution into development outcomes requires ensuring 'the development and use of an appropriate intergovernmental fiscal framework'. They seem to have faith in the Commission of Revenue Allocation to do just that.

Chapter 16 reviews the trajectory of intergovernmental fiscal reforms in South Africa since the end of the apartheid era. Savage characterizes the country as a 'unitary state with federal characteristics'. The Constitution establishes three interdependent and interrelated spheres of government. As far as the transfer system is concerned, Savage argues that the recent reforms have created momentum in establishing a functioning performance-based transfer system.

1.6 CONCLUDING THOUGHTS

The best transfer system is the one that achieves the policy objectives set beforehand. The measurement of VFI is a scientific exercise; however, addressing them is a political choice. This book presents resource materials for researchers, practitioners, policymakers and students willing to understand the choices made by different countries against the overarching principles of needs, equity and efficiency for sharing of resources. The various chapters capture empirical, theoretical and methodological contributions, as well as case studies that illustrate important policy or methodological lessons for future work.

PART I

Conceptual Issues

2. The architecture of intergovernmental transfers: principles and practice in low- and middle-income countries

Roy W. Bahl Jr

2.1 INTRODUCTION

There is an economic science to the design of intergovernmental transfers, thanks to the effort spent by scholars in questioning the impacts of transfers on market efficiency (Yilmaz and Zahir, Chapter 3). But there is also an art. Practitioners have spent considerable effort trying to develop efficient, equitable and politically acceptable intergovernmental transfer structures from what is often a poor database. And there is a political economy dimension, where elected officials, bureaucrats and civil society have worked hard to turn the final design of transfers to their self-interest. While much has been learned from all of this (Bahl and Bird, 2018), a 'model' design for intergovernmental transfers has not emerged.

The goals in this chapter are to explain why countries end up structuring their grant systems in so many different ways, and to offer a set of principles that might help with improving the practice. We draw on reviews of the practice and more specifically on the experiences in countries described in the chapters in this book.[1]

This chapter begins with a discussion of the normative guidelines for structuring transfers, comments on the reasons for so much variation in the practice and describes the architecture of intergovernmental transfers. We then turn to a general evaluation of the most commonly used vertical and horizontal revenue sharing regimes, and to the important question of equalization. The focus is on the practice in low- and middle-income countries, and on what might be taken from the development of transfer systems in industrial countries. A concluding section offers a retake on the principles of good design of intergovernmental transfer systems.

2.2 NORMATIVE GUIDELINES AND THE ARCHITECTURE OF INTERGOVERNMENTAL TRANSFERS

The primary missions of an intergovernmental transfer system include covering some portion of the vertical fiscal imbalance and limiting fiscal disparities to some acceptable level. But these objectives can also be addressed with expenditure and revenue assignments, and changes in the structure of governance. Under each intergovernmental fiscal arrangement, transfers play a different role and are structured differently to accommodate that role. Universal norms are not easily found.

The fiscal culture also matters in the choice that governments make about their intergovernmental fiscal structures. Almost every country faces reform options that are just not starters. China finances almost all subnational government (SNG) expenditures with transfers and does not have a strong equalization programme (Bahl et al., 2014). Neither does the German system depend on SNG taxing autonomy, but its transfer system features significant equalization (Spahn, Chapter 5). Both countries are willing to accept the absence of incentives to mobilize local revenues, and with a weak model of accountability by elected local officials. On the commitment to a national minimum service level, there is more solidarity in Australia and Germany than in other industrialized countries reviewed here (Dafflon and Vaillancourt, Chapter 4). The US is committed to preserving subnational fiscal autonomy and competitive federalism. It does not use untied federal grants for fiscal equalization (Chernick, Chapter 6).

In this context of variation in the practice, the architecture of every intergovernmental transfer regime answers three questions, that is, (a) how the divisible pool for total grants is decided, (b) how this pool of funds is distributed across eligible subnational governments, and (c) how much autonomy SNGs will be given in making expenditure decisions. The more common methods of determining the divisible pool (the vertical share) are described in the columns of Table 2.1, and the methods of distributing this divisible pool (horizontal sharing) are presented in the rows.[2]

2.3 VERTICAL SHARING

Most countries determine the vertical share by one or both of two methods: a defined sharing of central government tax revenues, and/or a discretionary allocation in the annual central government budget.

Table 2.1 The architecture of intergovernmental transfers

	Vertical sharing	
Horizontal sharing	Specified share of national or state government tax	Annual budgetary decision
Origin of collection (derivation)	A	n.a.
Formula	B	E
Cost reimbursement (matching)	C	F
Ad hoc	D	G

Notes:
For definitions of forms A–G, see text.
n.a. = not applicable.

Sources: Adapted from Bahl and Linn (1992) and Bahl and Bird (2018, p. 290).

The Size of the Vertical Share

In theory, the vertical fiscal imbalance is the difference between (a) the amount that SNGs can raise from own-revenue sources if they exert a 'normal' revenue effort and (b) the amount they must spend to provide a 'minimum' level of the government services that have been assigned to them (Bahl and Bird, 2018, pp. 282–5). The gap for all subnational government in the country is:

$$GAP = \sum_i (\tilde{E}_i - \tilde{R}_i) \qquad (2.1)$$

where
$\tilde{R}_i$ = the revenue raised from own sources at normal effort by local government i
$\tilde{E}_i$ = the amount of expenditure needed to provide a minimum level of assigned services in local government i.

The targeted vertical share (VS) – the share of central taxes allocated to subnational transfers – is then:

$$VS = \frac{\alpha(GAP)}{CR} \qquad (2.2)$$

where α is the affordability parameter, that is, the per cent of the financing gap that the central government commits to cover with the transfer system, and CR is the total amount of revenues raised by the central government from current sources.

Few low- and middle-income countries explicitly use such a model in deciding on their vertical shares, or even attempt to define exactly what they mean by 'normal tax effort' or 'minimum service provision'. Most decisions on vertical shares are constrained by present levels of SNG expenditures with adjustments relying on a few crude indicators combined with intuition about expenditure needs, and a good sense of the political economy and the slack in the central government budget. Countries tend not to move too far from current levels of SNG expenditures in changing their vertical shares. Interestingly, the Indian Finance Commission awards have increased the vertical share by only about four percentage points of total taxes over the past 15 years (Zahir, Chapter 13).

Some industrial countries have developed approaches to determining the vertical share that are similar to the theoretical model described above. The vertical share for Canada's equalization grant is determined as a sum of provincial entitlements (Joanis and Vaillancourt, Chapter 7). However, in Australia, there apparently has been little interest in restructuring inter-governmental transfers to address the underlying issues regarding vertical fiscal imbalance (Searle, Chapter 9).

Shared Taxes

The shared tax approach is used in many low- and middle-income coun-tries, but the specific practice varies widely in terms of which taxes are shared and the size of the sharing rate. Indonesia shares 26 per cent of all taxes with SNGs, the Philippines 40 per cent, Pakistan 57 per cent and Mexico 20 per cent. In other countries, the sharing rate varies by tax. For example, China shares 40 per cent of income taxes and 50 per cent of value added taxes with provincial governments. Only 15 per cent of Kenya's revenues are mandated to be shared with SNGs.

The practice is similarly varied in the industrial countries. Australia shares goods and services tax (GST) collections with SNGs, Germany and Switzerland share 50 and 13 per cent of income taxes, respectively, with states (lander and cantons) and Japan uses a complicated system of revenue sharing with different sharing rates for several taxes. It is difficult to find a 'common' practice (Kim et al., 2010).

The advantages of this approach in low- and middle-income countries depend on whose glasses one is looking through, and on the specifics of the tax sharing programme that is in place. SNGs as a class can ben-efit from the shared tax approach, because it could give them access to a broad-based and income-elastic tax base which their central government or their constitution oftentimes denies them. The tax sharing approach is transparent, usually stable enough over time to allow fiscal planning by

SNGs and can involve less 'gaming' of Congress to give them a larger share than is the case for a discretionary allocation made by government in the annual budget. To gain these benefits, however, SNGs must accept some of the drawbacks to tax sharing, including vulnerability to changes in central government tax policy. And, unless tax sharing rules are enshrined in the constitution, they can be lowered by the central government.

There also are drawbacks to vertical sharing from the point of view of the central government. In particular, budget management and fiscal policy are made more difficult because SNGs are guaranteed a revenue entitlement.

The Discretionary Budget Approach

The other possibility for determining the vertical share is with discretionary allocations made as part of the budget process. Under this approach, the central government and/or the Congress can determine that a particular expenditure programme, or all SNG expenditures, will be funded by an intergovernmental transfer for the coming fiscal year (or for multiple years). The discretionary budget approach is part of the vertical sharing regime in most low- and middle-income countries. In Kenya, for example, the vertical share for the major intergovernmental transfer programme ('equitable shares') is determined as part of the annual Division of Revenue Act. It is subject to a lower limit of 15 per cent of total national revenues, and may be changed annually (Boex and Smoke, Chapter 15). South Africa takes a similar approach in regulating transfers to subnational governments through the national budget process.

A major advantage of the discretionary budget approach is that it allows specific central programmes to be terminated when they are no longer needed or are no longer meeting their objectives. Sometimes a sunset law is imposed, requiring a thorough review of the programme as a requirement for renewal.

Vertical shares that are established as discretionary budget allocations raise a number of issues. Three are particularly important to note. First, grant programmes tend to be owned, often by a line ministry, and so they may have a champion with enough political clout to keep them in play, even if their effectiveness is questionable. Or, if the champion does not have significant influence, a grant programme might find itself endangered, even if it is meeting its objectives. This raises the unfortunate prospect of viable programmes being discontinued midstream for political or administrative reasons (Shah, 2013). The South African system guards against this problem by managing intergovernmental transfers with a three-year rolling cycle medium-term expenditure framework (MTEF) (Savage, Chapter 16).

A second issue is that grant programmes funded in this way can proliferate in numbers and can lead to significant administrative and compliance costs. The US conditional grants system includes 1714 separately authorized programmes, equivalent in amount to about 17 per cent of all federal spending (Chernick, Chapter 6). Third, the discretionary approach usually supports grants that carry conditions about how the money will be spent and diverts local budgets from the outcomes that voter-consumers at the local level might have preferred. Searle (Chapter 9) argues that this has led to a steady reduction over time in the autonomy of state governments.

When the vertical share for any major intergovernmental grant programme in the country is revisited annually by an elected Congress, it is at risk of being heavily influenced by political factors, as may now be the case in Kenya (Boex and Smoke, Chapter 15).

Mixed Models

Because countries are trying to do so many different things with their intergovernmental transfer system, they often use both of these approaches to vertical sharing. The tax sharing approach seems more suited for general purpose aid for SNGs in decentralized countries, because it gives recipients a more or less guaranteed base and tends toward untied grants. The annual budget approach seems especially suited for conditional grants or special purpose assistance, because these programmes can be more short-lived and lend themselves better to earmarking for individual programmes.

Still, the practice varies widely as the following few examples illustrate.

- India directs intergovernmental transfers to the states with vertical shares based on recommendations made by the Finance Commission, which convenes every fifth year. Parallel to this is a set of 'centrally sponsored schemes', which are multiyear programmes where the funding is decided every year at the time the budget is made (Zahir, Chapter 13; Martinez-Vazquez, Chapter 14; Mathur, 2012).
- China finances provincial and local government budgets with shared income and value added tax collections. But it also funds numerous conditional grant schemes with annual allocations, though the revenue importance of these has been trending downward (Bahl et al., 2014).
- The vertical share in Kenya is determined annually by Congress, but subject to a constraint that it must be at least 15 per cent of national government revenues (Boex and Smoke, Chapter 15).

- The vertical share for Canada's Health transfer programme is funded through a budget allocation that is indexed to a three-year moving average of GDP. The funding for the Social Transfer programme was last set in 2009 and is indexed at 3 per cent per year. The vertical share for equalization grants is determined, bottom up, by provincial entitlements (Joanis and Vaillancourt, Chapter 7).
- At the canton level in Switzerland, the share of revenues received as intergovernmental transfers is 6 per cent from shared federal taxes, 4 per cent from federal equalization, 13 per cent from federal subsidies and specific grants-in-aid, and 7 per cent are contributions of communes for shared competencies (Dafflon, Chapter 8).
- Under Argentina's co-participation programme, total transfers to subnational governments are equivalent to about 70 per cent and are allocated as shared taxes. The remaining 30 per cent are a set of transfers authorized by special laws (Larizza and Folgar, Chapter 12).
- Australia's transfer system is about equally divided between discretionary conditional grants and unconditional grants. The growth in untied grants is pegged to national consumption tax revenues, and the growth in conditional grants is pegged to general price increases.

2.4   HORIZONTAL SHARING

Horizontal sharing, the second dimension of the architecture of an intergovernmental transfer, is the method by which the central government divides the vertical share among the eligible subnational government units. In practice, countries seem to have followed one or more of four approaches to horizontal sharing: derivation, formula, cost reimbursement, and ad hoc distributions.

Derivation

The derivation approach (Type A in Table 2.1) distributes a shared national tax among SNGs according to where the tax is collected. For example, in China, 50 per cent of domestic value added tax (VAT) collections and 40 per cent of income tax collections in each province are kept by the province where it was collected. The appeal to this approach is that it returns national government tax collections to urban areas where the investment may yield greater returns, and it finances intergovernmental transfers with more efficient central government taxes.

The most contentious feature of derivation-based sharing is that regions with a stronger economic base will receive more transfer revenue than poorer ones. This reinforces the disparities in the quality of public services and infrastructure that already are better in many regions with a stronger economic base. Paradoxically, countries that use the derivation approach often adopt an equalization transfer to offset the advantages given to the rich provinces. For example, Germany shares 50 per cent of income taxes on a derivation basis, but mostly erases the advantage of higher income states with a sharing of the VAT and a horizontal sharing regime among the states that is equalizing (Spahn, Chapter 5). Switzerland shares 13 per cent of federal income tax collections with cantons on a derivation basis, but also has a significant equalization programme (Dafflon, Chapter 8).

Formula Grants

The formula approach (Types B and E in Table 2.1) is probably the most widely used method of horizontal sharing in low- and middle-income countries. An appealing feature of a formula grant is that it offers the possibility of building equalization features into the distribution of transfers. The richer subnational governments might be less enthusiastic about the formula approach since they are home to most of the tax base and may receive less of the transfer pie.

A formula can offer transparency, simplicity and objectivity. But these advantages are not always achieved. Particularly in low- and middle-income countries, data are limited and finding a transfer formula that will do the job is often a stretch. The goal of simplicity is also hard to hold to, in part because well-intentioned 'social engineers' often lobby to insert additional variables into the formula to achieve some particular effect. Horizontal transfer formulae can become complicated to a point where support for them can be eroded. Coppel sees the Australian system as 'fiendishly complicated' (Chapter 10), the Argentinean system has long been referred to as a 'labyrinth' (Larizza and Folgar, Chapter 12) and fully understanding the Swiss approach is no easy matter. Most horizontal distribution formulae use indicators that reflect fiscal capacity and expenditure needs. The obvious proxy for fiscal capacity is a broad measure of the potential tax base such as regional or local GDP, or better yet, bases of SNG taxes, but many developing countries do not have good measures of either.

The expenditure needs focus is also common. Many countries have landed on the goal of giving the formula 'common sense elements' that the general population can identify with, for example, the higher cost of providing public services in more remote Indonesian provinces, or the special needs of Indian rural local governments with heavy concentrations of poverty, or simply the belief that population size is a good indicator of expenditure needs. In the end, the variable used to take account of the needs-resources gap is rough justice at best.

While there are common elements to the formulae in low- and middle-income countries, the approaches taken vary a great deal. Brazil's intergovernmental transfers are structured with different sharing rates for each tax, and extensive earmarking. The long-term trend has been to move toward a formula-based distribution of transfers (Wetzel and Viñuela, Chapter 11). Mexico's unconditional transfers are distributed under eight different heads, each with a different formula; and Ethiopia's includes 14 indicators of expenditure needs and fiscal capacity. Over 90 per cent of South Africa's transfers to provincial governments are allocated on a basis of population size, health care needs and education sector needs (Savage, Chapter 16). In the first six years of the operation of Kenya's equitable shares grant, Congress has prepared two horizontal distribution formulae. More than 80 per cent of the revenues are distributed according to population size, equal shares and poverty (Boex and Smoke, Chapter 15).

There is also variation in the approach taken in the industrial countries in this sample. Canada's health and social transfers are allocated across provinces on an equal per capita basis (Joanis and Vaillancourt, Chapter 7). The VAT transfer is distributed across states in Germany on a per capita basis (Spahn, Chapter 5). The horizontal sharing formulae for the equalization grants in Switzerland and Australia are structured to close the gap between resources and needs. The Swiss revenue capacity equalization fund is distributed by a representative tax approach, and the two expenditure equalization components by formula (Dafflon, Chapter 8).

Cost Reimbursement and Matching Grants

Cost reimbursement grants (Types C and F in Table 2.1) usually are earmarked for a particular function. The practice with respect to cost reimbursement grants is varied, both in terms of the objectives sought and the structure of the grants. In Nepal a conditional grant funds the salaries of central government employees that were transferred to the newly formed local governments. Another justification is to compensate for an activity that the centre fears the subnational government cannot afford, or for which the central government feels some degree of responsibility, for example, medical assistance to low-income families in the US, or compensation for the abolition of a local tax. The cost reimbursement approach may also be used to support programmes of the line ministries, for example, matching grants for India's rural development schemes.

Ad hoc Transfers

Finally, some intergovernmental transfers are distributed on an ad hoc basis
by the legislature or by the central government (Types D and G in Table
2.1). Ad hoc grant programmes exist in most countries and are roundly
criticized for their lack of transparency and susceptibility to corruption.
But they survive because they are a way for the central government or the
Congress to build their support base.

One version of ad hoc grants would have subnational governments
compete for funding from a special pool of funds, with the higher-level
government choosing those projects to be funded. Ad hoc grants may also
take the form of emergency (off-budget) year-end bailouts for regions in
trouble, or special support to troubled regions. Some countries, like India,
have given legislators an allocation to be spent at their own discretion. The
discretionary grants used in the Argentine transfer system, which could be
used as conditional transfers to attack specific sectoral objectives, in practice
are used as a tool of political bargaining (Larizza and Folgar, Chapter 12).

2.5   EQUALIZATION

It would be rare to find an intergovernmental transfer system in a low- or
middle-income country that does not include equalization as a prominent
goal for its intergovernmental transfer system. Yet, research in this area
suggests that many low-income countries do not do a very good job with
narrowing fiscal disparities or favouring poor regions with their distribution of transfers.[3]

Many explanations might be offered for this policy failure. Central
governments and parliaments do not begin the design of an equalization
programme with a precise statement of the ultimate objective, usually avoid
the guaranteed minimum service level question, work with inadequate data
and rarely monitor outcomes. In the end, a rough justice approach is taken,
with an equalization variable included in the grant distribution formula to
reflect the general level of economic and service level well-being of local
populations.

Dafflon and Vaillancourt (Chapter 4) argue that the approach has
been flawed and call for a 'second generation' approach that better inte-
grates expenditure needs and revenue capacity factors into the horizontal
equalization approach. Martinez-Vazquez (Chapter 14) makes a similar
argument with reference to equalization transfers in India.

In fact, the approach to equalization taken by the countries in this volume
show a good deal of variation. The South African equitable shares grant is

distributed among local governments according to a formula that provides enough funding for provision of basic services to poor households (Savage, Chapter 16). During the first five years of the devolution in Kenya, the horizontal allocation formula distributed considerably greater resources to the undeveloped and less (densely) populated counties (Boex and Smoke, Chapter 15). On the other hand, the co-participation transfers in Argentina do not show a significant impact on regional re-distribution (Larizza and Folgar, Chapter 12). While the education and health transfers in Brazil favour lower income states, the minimum supported levels are low, and wide dispari-ties among the states continue to exist (Wetzel and Viñuela, Chapter 11).

The experience with equalization in the industrial countries studied here brings some good lessons, though the transferability is limited because the context is so different than in low- and middle-income countries. Industrial countries tend to have a clearer policy to define what they want from their equalization system, and they have a longer experience with intergovern-mental transfer regimes. The existing level of fiscal disparities tends to be less, better data are available with which to develop creative formulae, and the fiscal culture is more likely to accept a complicated regime of intergov-ernmental fiscal transfers. But, like the lower income countries, they must balance the gains from equalization with political considerations.

Most of these countries attempt equalization on both the revenue capac-ity and expenditure needs dimensions of the budget. Though Canada is committed to equalization, and its basic approach to fiscal capacity equalization is consistent with good international practice, its efforts in this direction have weakened in recent years (Joanis and Vaillancourt, Chapter 7).

Swiss cantons receive about 30 per cent of revenues from intergovern-mental transfers, but equalization transfers account for only about 4 per cent (Dafflon, Chapter 8). The system of equalization transfers adopted in Switzerland in 2008 includes three separate components: revenue capacity equalization, expenditure needs equalization, and a transition fund to accommodate those burdened by the shift to the new system.

The intergovernmental transfer system in Germany is structured to achieve horizontal fiscal balance. The national VAT is distributed among the states according to population, and state government revenues are reallocated among the states according to fiscal capacity (Spahn, Chapter 5). In Australia, the distribution of untied grants to the states is managed by the Commonwealth Grants Commission (CGC). In 2010, the equaliza-tion objective was redefined to say that state governments should receive funding such that, after allowing for material factors affecting revenues and expenditures, each would have the fiscal capacity to provide services and the associated infrastructure at the same standard, if each made the same effort to raise revenue from its own sources and operated at the same level of efficiency (Searle, Chapter 9).

The US is the outlier in this group in that it has no general purpose equalization grants. The approach to equalization is to subsidize SNG provision of merit goods, using matching or block grants. Overall grant distributions have moved toward favouring rich states because of their higher Medicaid expenditures (Chernick, Chapter 6).

Evaluations of the impacts of the intergovernmental transfer system are more common in industrial countries, in fact it is legally required in the Swiss system (Dafflon, Chapter 8). There is a system in place to manage and evaluate horizontal fiscal equalization in Australia, though it now may involve the national treasury as well as the CGC.

The fiscal capacities of German and Australian states are significantly levelled by vertical and horizontal transfers (Spahn, Chapter 5, and Coppel, Chapter 10). Australia is the only OECD country that takes the objective of fully eliminating disparities in fiscal capacity (Coppel, Chapter 10). In the Swiss system, seven cantons with taxable capacity above the national average contribute to the equalization pool, and post-distribution, all cantons are levelled at 85 per cent of the national average (Dafflon, Chapter 8). The extent to which the expenditure needs formulae contribute to equalization are less clear.

2.6 CONCLUSIONS: GUIDELINES FOR STRUCTURING HORIZONTAL AND VERTICAL SHARING

No single 'model' regime for intergovernmental transfers has emerged from the practice in low- and middle-income countries. This is partly because these governments have shaped their intergovernmental fiscal systems in different ways, partly because they do not have the data to develop a proper approach, and partly because they do not have the political mandate to make the sweeping and sensitive changes that might be necessary. But even within this wide variation in the practice, there are some more or less universal principles that can help guide the practice. These are outlined below.

1. The place to begin in designing (or reforming) an intergovernmental transfer regime is with a policy outlining the objectives that the government wants to achieve. 'How much vertical fiscal balance and how much equalization is desired, what incentives will be imbedded in the system, and how much autonomy will be released to the SNGs' are the

kinds of questions that will be answered by government with its policy and its laws.

2. The intergovernmental transfer system should be designed, or reformed, in a context of the overall system of intergovernmental finance. Expenditure and revenue assignment, and capital finance, all will impact the choices made for the best design of the grant regime.

3. The maintenance of the intergovernmental transfer regime is as important as the design of its architecture. Governments could greatly benefit from an intensive review of the system, carried out periodically by an apolitical, professionally staffed research cell. Governments should redouble their efforts to provide a database that can support the work of the evaluation unit.

4. There is no one best way to structure the vertical share of intergovernmental transfers. In fact, some valuable diversity comes from using both the shared tax and the discretionary budget approach. Tax sharing is well suited to support general expenditure programmes for subnational governments in that it can provide access to a broad and income-elastic tax base, and it tends not to carry spending conditions. The annual budgetary approach to vertical sharing fits conditional grants and special purpose transfers because of their special conditionalities and monitoring requirements. While they can be structured as multiyear programmes, they should be structured to face a sunset at which time their continuation would depend on a full evaluation.

5. The right choice for horizontal distributions depends on the objectives the government has set down for its grants system. The derivation approach puts the funds back to the richer places where presumably the greatest return can be received from the transfer, but it favours rich subnational governments to such an extent that a significant equalizing transfer programme is necessary to undo the equity damage. Many low- and middle-income countries pair a shared tax approach to vertical sharing with a formula approach to horizontal sharing.

6. Formula systems for horizontal sharing should follow the objectives laid out in government policy. They should be monitored regularly and changed as better data become available or when the formula becomes compromised by political considerations.

7. Intended and unintended incentives are present in almost all intergovernmental transfer systems and should be reviewed periodically to understand their effectiveness and impact.

8. The equalization component of intergovernmental transfers should be subjected to comprehensive, regular review. The benchmark for evaluation should be the government's policy statement about the goals of equalization.

NOTES

1. This chapter draws heavily from Bahl and Bird (2018), Chapter 7, where there is a more in-depth and comprehensive discussion of this topic, and where more extensive referencing is provided.
2. This taxonomy of intergovernmental transfers was first developed in Bahl and Linn (1992) and was enhanced and upgraded in Bahl and Bird (2018, p. 290).
3. For reviews on this, see Bahl and Bird (2018) and Mathur (2012). For a more positive view about the effectiveness of second-best solutions, see Boex and Martinez-Vazquez (2007).

REFERENCES

Bahl, Roy and Richard Bird (2018) *Fiscal Decentralization and Local Finance in Developing Countries: Development from Below* (Cheltenham, UK and Northampton, MA, USA: Edward Elgar Publishing).

Bahl, Roy and Johannes Linn (1992) *Urban Public Finance in Developing Countries* (New York: Oxford University Press).

Bahl, Roy, Chor-Ching Goh and Baoyun Qiao (2014) *Reforming the Public Finance System to Fit a More Urbanized China* (Beijing: China Financial and Economic Publishing House).

Boex, Jameson and Jorge Martinez-Vazquez (2007) 'Designing Intergovernmental Equalization Transfers with Imperfect Data: Concepts, Practices and Lessons' in Jorge Martinez-Vazquez and Bob Searle (eds), *Fiscal Equalization: Challenges in the Design of Intergovernmental Transfers* (New York: Springer), pp. 291–344.

Kim, Junghun, Jørgen Lotz and Niels Jorgen Mau (eds) (2010) *General Grants versus Earmarked Grants Theory and Practice: The Copenhagen Workshop 2009* (Albertslund: Korea Institute of Public Finance and Danish Ministry of Interior and Health).

Mathur, Om Prakash (2012) 'Intergovernmental Transfers in Local Government Finance: Decentralization and Strengthening of Local Authorities', Report submitted to UN-Habitat, Nairobi.

Shah, Anwar (2013) 'Grant Financing of Metropolitan Areas: A Review of Principles and Worldwide Practices' in Roy Bahl, Johannes Linn and Deborah Wetzel (eds), *Financing Metropolitan Governments in Developing Countries* (Cambridge, MA: Lincoln Institute of Land Policy), pp. 213–42.

3. Issues in intergovernmental fiscal transfers: public finance and political economy considerations

Serdar Yilmaz and Farah Zahir

3.1 INTRODUCTION

Intergovernmental transfers[1] are an essential component of intergovernmental fiscal arrangements.[2] They play a prominent role in subnational finances in both federal and unitary countries.[3] Thus, the design of an intergovernmental transfer system is of great importance for efficiency and equity of local public service provision and the fiscal health of subnational governments. Intergovernmental transfers, including grants, shared taxes, revenue sharing, subsidies and subventions, are used to pursue a variety of public policy objectives in different countries.

The design of the intergovernmental transfers in many countries is influenced by the traditional public finance theories which emphasize their role in correcting vertical and horizontal imbalances. This so-called first-generation theory (FGT) of fiscal federalism has an efficiency-centred view of policy. The FGT refers to a normative theory in which the main elements are well established (Oates 1972; Gramlich 1977). Intergovernmental transfers are viewed as economic policy tools to correct imperfections. However, the first-generation theory assumed that decision makers are benevolent actors who would intervene to provide public goods efficiently (Weingast 2014; Oates 2005; Inman and Rubinfeld 1997). A second generation of thinking (SGT) in the fiscal federalism literature recognizes that public officials have divergent interests and they are not necessarily benevolent actors who seek to maximize public interests (Weingast 2009; 2014). The SGT focuses on the political economy implications of transfers and pays attention to the institutional and political incentives that induce or constrain the behaviour of officials as they interact within and across the tiers of government. The second-generation literature sees intergovernmental transfers as a potentially tempting target for rent-seeking politics. The SGT is particularly mindful about the potential distortionary effect of intergovernmental transfers on the internal economic union of a country.

The FGT and SGT complement each other. According to Weingast (2009: 290), the FGT 'studies the optimal design of fiscal institutions in the context of welfare maximization with respect to incentives of political officials. [SGT] extends and adapts [FGT] lessons to the context of incentives and self-interested political officials'. In terms of intergovernmental transfers, the SGT builds on the normative lessons of the FGT and focuses on the incentive structure of the transfers to foster local economic development. It highlights the importance of local revenue generation which enhances accountability of local politicians to their citizens and 'the incentives to provide market-enhancing public goods' (Weingast 2009: 290). In terms of the design properties of a transfer system, the SGT strongly suggests the use of step functions 'to provide subnational governments with higher marginal incentives to foster local economic prosperity' (Weingast 2009: 290).

The main purpose of this chapter is to survey the FGT and SGT literature to summarize the theoretical conceptualization of intergovernmental transfer design and empirical analyses in specific country contexts. It aims to present a case for the importance of political economy considerations in designing and analysing intergovernmental transfer systems. After this brief introduction, we begin this chapter by describing the evolution in thinking about fiscal federalism. We then discuss the purposes of intergovernmental transfers with an emphasis on incentives. Finally, we conclude with some broad lessons about designing intergovernmental fiscal systems for effective service delivery.

3.2   THE EVOLUTION OF THEORY IN FISCAL FEDERALISM

The traditional public finance theory prescribes expenditure and revenue assignments between levels of government and the design of transfer systems and subnational debt on the grounds of efficiency, equity and macroeconomic stability. These prescriptions are expressed as the four pillars of an intergovernmental system in a country – expenditure assignment, revenue assignment, intergovernmental transfers/grants and subnational debt/borrowing (Bird 2000). For efficiency reasons, lower tier governments should provide public goods and services that benefit local consumers, and which their residents prefer, given that the tastes for goods are local-specific, and local authorities may have more accurate information about what their citizens want (Tiebout 1961). Higher tier governments should provide goods that are non-excludable, meaning those goods that a non-paying individual cannot be prevented from enjoying – for example, national defence. In terms of revenues, efficiency considerations suggest that the most buoyant sources of taxes, that is, those based on income, can be collected at the centre more easily and at lower economic costs than at subnational level. And intergovernmental transfers are a prescription to remedy the resulting vertical and horizontal imbalances after the assignment of service delivery responsibilities and taxing powers to the levels of government. In cases where the provision of local goods generates externalities, the centre handles the issue by providing subsidies or transfers to internalize the benefits (Oates 1972). And, for reasons of intergenerational equity, subnational governments should use borrowing for infrastructure investments.

It is important to realize that these four components of an intergovernmental system are highly interdependent, and transfers are just one component of the system. Therefore, the design of a transfer system cannot be separated from the design and evolution of the broader intergovernmental fiscal system. Of course, each of these components of the system must be very well linked to broader fiscal policy and service delivery objectives.

The design of an intergovernmental system has come under intense questioning by the SGT. While accepting the basic premises of the traditional public finance analysis in designing an intergovernmental system, the SGT puts strong emphasis on giving own source revenue powers to subnational governments.[4] It underlines the importance of horizontal competition between subnational governments for economic efficiency and argues for refrainment of the central level from interfering in subnational taxing and spending decisions. It regards central fiscal interventions as distortionary policy instruments that inhibit the development of a competitive and efficient intergovernmental system. According to the SGT analysis, central interventions create incentive compatibility problems by inducing subnational spending, amassing unsustainable deficits, and perpetuating their dependence on the centre for more support (McKinnon and Nechyba 1997).[5] In addition, the SGT literature warns about the dangers of soft budget constraint,[6] highlighting disincentives created by transfers for subnational governments to pay attention to their expenditures and make prudent fiscal decisions. The literature also warns about the so-called common pool problem (Rodden 2003; Oates 2005; Rodden and Wibbels 2002) – the potential adverse incentives created by transfers.[7] If the design of a transfer system symbolizes fiscal dentistry,[8] subnational governments will have incentives for opportunistically shifting their overspending costs and excessive borrowings to the centre. In that sense, transfers create a moral hazard by insuring fiscally reckless behaviour. In fact, the literature presents the Argentine and Brazilian fiscal crises of the 1980s and 1990s as examples of fiscal recklessness (Rodden 2012). The SGT prescribes market-based and rule-based institutional mechanisms that would create hard budget constraint (Ter-Minassian 1997). Market-based institutional mechanisms involve the establishment of an efficient market together with an intergovernmental system in which subnational governments have autonomous taxing and expenditure powers. Rule-based institutional mechanisms are laws that prohibit deficits, severely limit borrowings, provide for credible no-bailout and minimal intergovernmental transfers, and allow for subnational bankruptcy (Burret and Feld 2014; McKinnon and Nechyba 1997; Oates 2005; Skeel 2011; Ter-Minassian 1997).

3.3   THE PURPOSES OF INTERGOVERNMENTAL TRANSFERS

Traditional public finance theories suggest that intergovernmental transfers can serve a useful purpose in aligning subnational incentives to national public welfare, while the SGT literature highlights the potential detrimental impact on economic performance through rent-seeking. The rent-seeking arguments stem from Brennan and Buchanan's (1980) work where they argue that governments are net surplus maximizers (Leviathan thesis).[9] In this line of thinking, intergovernmental transfers create dependency and discourage subnational governments for competition. Thereby, transfers create an environment for rent-seeking for bureaucrats' own benefit. The empirical literature provides some evidence to support this argument.[10]

The traditional public finance theory and literature focus mostly on static effects of intergovernmental transfers dealing with the question of designing a system to achieve a minimum standard of service delivery across subnational jurisdictions – horizontal equity. Whereas the SGT puts emphasis on growth effects of fiscal federalism design, particularly the impact of intergovernmental transfers on revenue mobilization at the subnational level. The most critical aspect of an intergovernmental transfer system is not the issue of who gives them or who gets them but its effect on the efficiency of public service provision as well as achieving fiscal equity and macroeconomic stability (Bird and Smart 2001). The large spread of literature on intergovernmental transfers presents theoretical arguments on how to achieve these objectives. In this section, we organize the discussions around four major objectives of intergovernmental transfers. We discuss public finance and political economy considerations in achieving these objectives:

1. Closing the vertical gap, in other words to improve revenue adequacy;
2. Addressing horizontal fiscal inequalities – interjurisdictional redistribution;
3. Financing spatial spillovers;
4. Meeting national goals, objectives and priorities.

3.3.1 Closing the Vertical Gap

Revenue and expenditure assignments give rise to vertical and horizontal fiscal imbalances within a nation's intergovernmental finances. Vertical fiscal imbalance is the disparity between revenue sources and expenditure needs of the aggregate of subnational governments. Vertical fiscal imbalance exists when there is no broad correspondence between the expenditure responsibilities assigned to each level of government and the fiscal resources available to them to carry out those responsibilities at some prescribed minimum level. For the most part, tax collection is the responsibility of central government as it collects taxes at a lower cost than the subnational governments.

The most common source of vertical imbalance is the lack of own revenue sources at the subnational level. Intergovernmental transfers are typically designed to redress this vertical imbalance. However, it is very important to properly estimate the vertical gap as 'increased transfers might muddle rather than clarify the link between taxes and benefits, which increases the likelihood of fiscal illusion' (Rodden 2003: 706). There are at least two other ways to close the vertical imbalance gap, such as increasing the revenue-raising ability of subnational governments (raising own revenues) and/or reducing the expenditure responsibilities of subnational governments (reducing subnational expenditures). Addressing the vertical gap problem through only transferring more resources to subnational governments can easily have adverse incentive effects on subnational behaviour. Increasing revenue autonomy of subnational governments, rather than increasing transfer revenues, will also help strengthening Wicksellian connection of the cost of service delivery and revenues to finance them.[11] However, subnational taxation comes at a cost as well. Subnational taxation can easily lead to tax competition or tax exporting, which creates inefficiencies. In addition, subnational governments can easily use their taxation power in order to affect the composition of their population.

The FGT takes subnational governments' revenues as given and tries to formulate a transfer model to increase revenues for expenditures. Efficiency considerations highlighted in the FGT suggest that the central government is best positioned to collect more taxes at a lower cost and then transfer the resources to subnational governments to close at least a portion of the vertical gap. On the other hand, the SGT emphasizes own source revenue generation by subnational governments as a way to strengthen accountability linkages to citizens, to provide market-enhancing local public goods and services and minimize corruption (Rodden 2003; Singh and Srinivasan 2006; Carega and Weingast 2003). The SGT literature suggests that subnational governments need to keep a big chunk of own revenues. Otherwise, the increase in the retention rate of the centre will have an adverse impact on the revenue-raising efforts of subnational governments. In order to show these adverse impacts, Carega and Weingast (2003) calculate the retention rate in Mexico. The low retention rate of 23.3 per cent coincided with the poor performance of the Mexican economy in 1995. In contrast, the retention rate in China during the high growth period of 1981–92 was 89 per cent (Jin et al. 2005).

The SGT examines the effects of transfers on incentives for revenue-raising and responsible spending. The concerns in the SGT literature stem from negative incentives created by transfers on subnational revenue mobilization.[12] According to Weingast (2009: 284), the SGT logic suggests that the design of transfer should 'lower the tax burden on the economy and limit tax competition and following the [SGT] fiscal incentive approach, transfer systems should reward subnational governments that foster local economic growth'. The SGT literature suggests that federations can simultaneously achieve 'horizontal equalization, preventing tax competition, and ensure high marginal incentives – by designing transfer by non-linear functions' (Weingast 2009: 284). The policy recommendation to provide incentives to subnational governments in closing the vertical gap is to design a transfer system with a step function which allows wealthier subnational jurisdictions to keep a proportion of revenues above a certain level (Weingast 2009).

Vertical imbalance persists in almost all countries for three reasons (Bahl and Bird 2018): first, central governments are unwilling to devolve more revenue-raising powers to subnational governments, like in China or Egypt. Second, subnational governments have very limited capacity to finance even a minimum level of services without support from the centre, like Nepal. Third, some of the subnational expenditures generate spillovers.

A generic representation of the vertical gap measure in mathematical notation is

$$VG^i = \left[\sum_{j=1}^{R} (t_j^s B_j^i) \right] - \left[\sum_{k=1}^{z} (c_k^g E_k^i) \right] \qquad (3.1)$$

where VG^i is the vertical gap in subnational government i. The first bracket is revenue-raising ability of subnational government i. In the first bracket,

B^i_j is the tax base for revenue item j in i and t^s_j is the standard tax rate for item j. The total number of revenue items is R ($j = 1 \ldots R$). The second bracket represents the total costs of expenditure responsibilities of the subnational government i. In the second bracket E^i_k denotes expenditure item k in i and c^s_k is the standard cost of expenditure item k. The total number of expenditure items is Z ($k = 1 \ldots Z$).

Therefore, the total vertical gap in country A is equal to the sum vertical gap across subnational governments:

$$VG^A = \sum_{i=1}^{n} VG^i \qquad (3.2)$$

where VG^A is the sum vertical gap in all subnational governments in country A. In other words, the vertical gap amount is 'total pool of funds to be allocated to subnational governments . . .' (Bahl and Wallace 2007: 205). However, this notation of vertical gap in designing an intergovernmental transfer system 'is more easily conceptualized than it is measured . . .' (Bahl and Wallace 2007: 206). There are two major assumptions in this notation: (i) subnational governments exert a normal level effort to collect revenues; and (ii) subnational governments provide an acceptable level of services. It is always difficult to define these concepts. If transfer revenues are directly linked to the actual amount of revenues collected, subnational governments have incentives to underperform in the collection. It is quite difficult to measure whether subnational governments make an acceptable level of effort to exploit revenue bases available to them. More importantly, when subnational governments become dependent on transfers, their incentive to exploit their own revenue base weakens (Weingast 2009). On the expenditure side, the definition of acceptable is subject to interpretation – acceptable to whom? It is impossible to come up with an individual utility function to estimate an aggregate level at the subnational level. As Bahl and Bird (2018: 284) suggest 'since the public generally has little idea of the real tax price of local public goods in any case, the demand for local government services is always likely to outweigh the capacity (or willingness) at any level to finance them'.

There is only a handful of countries trying to estimate the vertical gap according to the notation presented.[13] Even then, these countries are partially successful at using this approach. In many federations, the application of the vertical gap measure concentrates only on the revenue side which makes the total elimination of vertical imbalance a challenging task. In Canada, for example, the system focuses only on the revenue-raising ability of subnational governments.

Total elimination of vertical imbalance is an impossible task since some degree of mismatch between expenditure needs and revenue capacity is

unavoidable. The difficulty of elimination of vertical imbalance is related
to its estimation, which requires detailed information about local governments' expenditure needs and revenue-raising capacity and effort. The
lack of reliable information related to both the expenditures and revenues
of subnational governments are the most important technical constraints
in designing an effective intergovernmental transfer system to close the
vertical gap. In addition, central governments need information about
local preferences to estimate the optimal amount of Pigouvian subsidies to
address interjurisdictional spillovers (Oates 2005).

Even if there is an abundance of data and information, it is still a
challenging task to include politically accepted expenditure norms and a
fair estimate of the revenue capacity of subnational units in estimating
vertical imbalance (Alm and Martinez-Vazquez 2002). The fairness of the
allocation is widely questioned by subnational governments in the systems
that use the formula-based method. In some cases, the central government
takes away part or all of surplus revenues, giving the subnational governments no incentives to optimize their own revenues. Even supposing the
decision makers find a way to overcome the issues raised above to estimate
the optimal amount for closing the vertical gap, there are at least two other
issues they need to attend to going forward. First, the dynamic nature of
intergovernmental finance requires keeping an eye on revenue adequacy
and buoyancy. Second, the affordability of the vertical gap financing.

Revenue adequacy and buoyancy
In designing a transfer system to close the vertical gap, it is important to
secure revenue adequacy to generate sufficient resources for subnational
governments, and to reduce distortions in the allocation of resources
and increase fairness. Revenue adequacy refers to availability of revenues
to cover the cost of service delivery. A transfer system provides revenue
adequacy when it ensures that subnational governments have enough
resources to cover expenditure needs. The assessment of revenue adequacy
needs to be conducted to understand changes in intergovernmental
finances. A good example is the abolition of octroi in India. When the
Indian federal government decided to abolish octroi, it had a negative
impact on the vertical gap as octroi was a source of state revenues. In
order to compensate for the loss in revenue adequacy, the government has
decided to allocate a percentage of goods and sales tax revenues to states.

However, the estimation of vertical gap should be a dynamic process
providing ability to subnational governments to continue with the provision of services. In order to guarantee a certain quality and quantity of
subnational services, revenues should grow as much as the expenditure
needs. Buoyancy of the transfer system refers to the growth of the

transferred resources with the expenditure needs of subnational governments. The term buoyancy must be defined in a relative sense: revenues are buoyant when they grow at the rate necessary to allow local governments to finance their services over time. Thus, a system has appropriate buoyancy if revenue growth is at the same rate as expenditure growth. Revenue growth should be at the same rate as the desired expenditure growth. Alternatively, buoyancy can be measured by the growth in revenues relative to the growth in GDP. Thus, a buoyancy coefficient of one indicates that revenues grow at the same rates as GDP, a coefficient of less than one is evidence of revenues growing more slowly than the economy, and a coefficient of greater than one shows that revenues are growing faster than the economy. Regardless of the measurement method, low buoyancy means that a revenue system that is adequate today will be inadequate in the future, since revenue growth will not keep pace with expenditure needs. The buoyancy of revenue systems comes from a combination of growth in tax base, such as through improvements in tax administration, and rate increase.

Affordability
In designing a transfer system to close the vertical gap, it is important to recognize budget constraints and macroeconomic stability at the centre. The intergovernmental transfer programmes that try to address expenditure needs should particularly pay attention to budget constraints at the central level. These programmes must also estimate the extent to which expenditure needs can be covered by available resources (Bahl and Wallace 2007). Closing the vertical gap will ultimately be a bargain over what subnational governments need and what the central government can afford (Bahl and Wallace 2007). In Australia (Chapter 9), Searle notes, the size of the Commonwealth's wallet seems to have by far the greatest influence on what is done and how it is done.

3.3.2 Addressing Horizontal Fiscal Inequalities

The second objective of intergovernmental transfers is to minimize horizontal imbalance. According to Dafflon and Vaillancourt (in this volume, Chapter 4), there are five possible origins of horizontal fiscal inequalities: three outside the control of subnational governments and two in the fiscal preferences of subnational jurisdictions. They identify the three possible origins outside of subnational governments as the capacity to raise (tax) revenues, the expenditure needs, and the net residual which is expressed as 'needs minus capacity'. The other two are related to local preferences for expenditures and taxes, therefore, they need not be compensated by any kind of equalization or transfer payment (Dafflon and Vaillancourt Chapter 4).

Subnational provision of services and subnational taxation invariably make it impossible to provide a comparable level of public services at a comparable level of taxation in all jurisdictions. In all countries, subnational jurisdictions have dissimilar needs and the cost of public service provision differs across them. Jurisdictions with more elderly, for example, will allocate resources to healthcare services, and jurisdictions with more school-age children to education. In addition, the cost of per unit service provision might differ across jurisdictions due to geography, wage differentials and other factors. On the revenue side, differences in tax bases across jurisdictions generally require different rates to generate same level per capita revenue. These forces are the main reason for net fiscal benefits – the net benefits accrue to identical households in different jurisdictions. Net fiscal benefits are the source of potential inefficiency and inequality. Individuals would move to jurisdictions where they maximize net fiscal benefits. Therefore, there would be inefficient allocation of labour across jurisdictions due to the fiscally induced migration. However, if individuals with identical income do not migrate despite differences in net fiscal benefits, there will be horizontal inequality: individuals with identical income will be treated differently in different jurisdictions (Boadway 2007).

Intergovernmental grants can be an effective instrument to avoid fiscally induced migration and to minimize horizontal inequalities arising from differences in fiscal capacity across subnational jurisdictions.[14] They help to achieve efficiency in labour allocation and horizontal equity by providing additional resources to subnational governments for comparable levels of public services at comparable tax rates. In countries like Germany, interjurisdictional redistribution is the main purpose of the equalization transfer system. For instance, Spahn in Chapter 5 concludes,

> In Germany (like in Canada) the focus of equalization is on taxable capacity only, with little or no concern for specific burdens. As the tax law is uniform throughout Germany (except for some limited discretion of municipalities to vary their tax rates), there is no need to standardize taxable capacity among regions (as in Canada), because effective tax collections can be considered to reflect the regional variations of tax potentials.[15]

At first glance, addressing fiscal inequalities seems an easy task. Once the extent of fiscal inequalities is measured, a decision needs to be made in terms of how much of the interregional inequality needs to be eliminated. Then an equalization formula should be designed to address the issue. However, measuring fiscal capacity is not an easy task. To begin with, there is a controversy surrounding its measure. The application of the fiscal capacity measure in some countries, such as Canada, concentrates only on the revenue side (see details in Chapter 7, Joanis and Vaillancourt). The treatment of the fiscal capacity concept solely as the revenue-raising ability of subnational governments can be observed in the academic world as well (Martinez-Vazquez and Boex 1997a; 1997b).

On the expenditure side, the overriding concern in designing an equalization transfer system is to ensure that subnational governments provide similar bundles of necessary public services to all citizens at comparable tax rates. Dafflon (Chapter 8) argues:

> In the Swiss context, expenditure needs equalization is exclusively vertical. The theoretical argument is that horizontal equalization exists where beneficiaries of services in low-costs-low-needs jurisdictions accept a tax-price supplement (that is, more expensive public services) in order to subsidize public services in high-costs-high-needs jurisdictions. This would distort the relative tax prices of subnational public services and result in allocative inefficiency and wrong incentives in deciding service levels.

Australia is the only OECD country that seeks to fully eliminate disparities in fiscal capacity for both revenue and expenditure between sub-national governments (Coppel, Chapter 10). It enables all states to provide the average national level of services and mostly adjusts for material structural disadvantages that are out of states' control. The principle of fiscal equalization is strongly supported. To achieve this goal, most governments design equalization transfer systems focusing on either equalization of the capacity of local governments to provide certain levels of services or equalization of the performance of local governments. Bird and Smart (2001) criticize the performance approach on the grounds that central governments' policy preferences are dominant and 'there is clearly no agreement on either the desirability or the effects of general intergovernmental transfers intended to achieve this goal'. They also point out the fact that, if capacity issue is given little consideration, performance approach awards local governments that do not try to raise their own revenues. If fiscal capacity is measured accurately, which is not an easy task due to the reasons mentioned earlier, intergovernmental transfers would create very little incentives for local governments' revenue-raising restraint.

Although the FGT sees equalization transfers as a necessary tool to prevent relatively rich regions attracting more investments at the expense of poorer regions, the SGT literature argues against full equalization. According to the SGT literature, full equalization discourages subnational governments from pursuing policies to promote economic development to expand the tax base as it takes away the revenue gains from economic growth (Weingast 2009). Weingast recommends bringing all subnational fiscal capacity to a certain level rather than full equalization by using step functions; so that subnational governments have 'marginal incentives to foster local economic prosperity' by retaining a certain percentage of revenue derived from their own tax base (Weingast 2009: 290).

3.3.3   Spatial Spillovers

A third objective of intergovernmental transfers is to correct for interjuris-dictional spillovers. Some local government services' benefits (or costs) extend beyond the borders of the locality. In case of positive spillovers, local governments may be unwilling to provide an efficient level of certain services if they believe that people who reside outside their locality will enjoy many of the resulting benefits.[16]

Bird and Smart (2002) highlight three potential complications in deter-mining the size of spillovers: (i) the matching rate for the central government might decline if externalities decline with the increase in expenditures; (ii) the rate might also vary across jurisdictions if there is a higher local price elasticity of demand for the spillover generating service in some areas; and (iii) if local fiscal capacities are not fully equalized a uniform matching rate would discriminate against poorer subnational jurisdictions.

Because of these complications empirical studies on the outcome of matching grants to address spillovers find mixed results. In the US context, Inman (1988) suggests that the intergovernmental grant programmes do a very poor job of making subnational governments internalize spillovers. Similarly, Chernick (2000) finds that the fiscal incentive packages provided by the federal government to states to induce social welfare spending have limited impact.

In the developing world, designing a matching grant programme is even more challenging because of the lack of information. Designing a sector specific matching grant programme requires a clear specification of the level of service to be provided in addition to fairly accurate and up-to-date per unit cost of service provision.

3.3.4   National Goals, Objectives, and Priorities

Intergovernmental transfers can be an important instrument for national governments to achieve broader national goals, objectives and priorities. Here we discuss the issue of macroeconomic priorities.

Macroeconomic stabilization by risk sharing
From a national perspective intergovernmental transfers fulfil a risk-sharing or stabilization function (von Hagen 2007). When different regions

are subject to different economic shocks, intergovernmental transfers can serve as an insurance to provide financial resources for addressing adverse impacts of economic downturn. Zahir (Chapter 13) notes that disentangling the redistribution, stabilization, and risk-sharing roles of fiscal transfers is complicated in India as centre-state fiscal transfers are believed to affect all roles simultaneously. Regional risk sharing through intergovernmental transfers stabilizes regional business cycles (von Hagen 2007).[17] To the extent that economic shocks have an adverse impact on personal incomes and household consumption, subnational governments are exposed to risks as their tax revenues will be impacted.[18] According to von Hagen (2007: 108), '[c]hanneling income from prosperous regions to regions in distress can help attenuate asymmetries in the cyclical fluctuations of regions within a country, producing more even economic development across regions'.

Von Hagen (2007) argues that intergovernmental transfers, especially equalization transfers, may also act as a stabilization factor when economic shocks are lasting. Transfers can be instrumental in facilitating fiscal adjustments, including regional wage and price adjustments, to a region's specific asymmetric shocks. Transfer systems can facilitate adjustment by providing relief to reduce the fiscal pain. In addition, transfers can act as a built-in stabilizer by augmenting aggregate demand in economic shock affected regions.[19]

Political economy considerations, however, suggest that risk-sharing arrangements give incentives to subnational governments in devising risk avoidance strategies. Perrson and Tabellini (1996) show that subnational governments have little incentive to raise local taxes in order to finance programmes to alleviate the negative impact of economic shocks elsewhere. Similarly, Baretti, Huber and Lichtblau (2002) suggest that, if regional insurance transfer payments are tied to tax revenues collected by subnational governments, it will lead to reduced tax effort.

3.4   CONCLUSION

Traditional public finance considerations are the raison d'être for intergovernmental transfers. However, this chapter has argued that considering political economy issues in designing intergovernmental transfers is equally important to promote equal access to services for all citizens. Evidence from the literature suggests that imperfections in political markets have huge bearing on intergovernmental resource allocations. Boex and Smoke note, in Chapter 15, Kenya's path towards devolution has in some ways been a 'political' success. The basic elements of the county government systems have been defined and are being implemented. The extent to which devolution has led to improved service delivery and governance outcomes, however, is far less self-evident. Zahir (Chapter 13) further reiterates the point that the attempt to use states as 'laboratories for experimenting with what programs work best' had both political and economic ramifications in India. In the last two decades in India there has been a general trend towards coalition governments with a number of states and local representatives now participating in politics at the centre. In addition, the 73rd and the 74th Constitutional Amendments in 1992 had incentivized grassroots level politicians to rise above the petty politics of local and state level and occupy a space at the centre. Poor regions tend to have less informed citizens on public policies and they are less likely to participate in political process. Given this evidence, it is important to come up with institutional arrangements that secure broad-based representation in the sharing of intergovernmental resources. For instance, Chernick in Chapter 6 points out that the US grants system distributes large amounts of fiscal resources to incentivize states and their localities to provide services to the poor and enhance their capital stocks. While there is some modest fiscal equalization, interstate and intrastate differences in spending for redistribution and education, both between and within states, remain substantial.

The SGT literature suggests several remedies to address the political economy imperfections in designing an intergovernmental system. First, it suggests using market economy institutions to address some of the adverse selection issues. For example, creating efficient credit markets will improve subnational governments' fiscal performance as credit market ratings have a bearing on the cost of borrowing. Similarly, creating efficient land markets is an important disciplining factor on subnational finances through local property values. Second, it suggests strengthening fiscal institutions which have a bearing on subnational fiscal behaviour. The existence of a stable and clear system of taxation, for example, creates the Wicksellian connection between revenues and the cost of local services. Third, the SGT literature suggests using constitutional or legislative restrictions to provide constraints on fiscally irresponsible behaviour (see details, for example, in Wetzel and Viñuela, Chapter 11; Larizza and Folgar, Chapter 12). For instance, the existence of balanced-budget requirements and limitations on borrowing as well as the existence of public bankruptcy laws can promote fiscally prudent decision-making.

Finally, an analysis of intergovernmental transfer design must also recognize the importance of institutional arrangements for managing the system. There are two different institutional arrangements to minimize the political influence: formula-based transfers and establishing independent agencies to decide on the distribution of transfer resources. The evidence from literature is mixed. In the South African intergovernmental fiscal framework (Savage, Chapter 16) the primary transfer to subnational government is the unconditional, constitutional entitlement known as the 'equitable share'. This is distributed to provinces and municipalities through the Provincial Equitable Share (PES) and the Local Government Equitable Share (LGES), both of which are formula-based allocations that are distributed without conditions. Worthington and Dollery (1998) present evidence from Australia which suggests that formula-based transfers are less prone to political influence as opposed to transfers which are not subject to strict formulae.[20] Similarly in India, Khemani (2003) finds evidence that political agents play a big role in the distribution of general purpose federal transfers, whereas the distribution of transfers by independent Finance Commission is less subject to political interference.[21]

NOTES

1. The term 'transfers' is often used to refer to a number of different kinds of public finance arrangements, including grants, subsidies, tax sharing and cost-reimbursement. In this chapter, we use all these terms interchangeably to refer to transfers of funds from central government to subnational governments.
2. The direction of a transfer mechanism can encompass all levels of government, such as central to provincial, provincial/state to local, directly central to local or even national to supra national (like the EU).
3. We use the term 'subnational' to encompass all governments below the central level.
4. On the issue of own revenues, the FGT is concerned about tax distortions and inefficiencies introduced by decentralized revenue-raising. In addition, the FGT is also apprehensive about potential tax competition among subnational governments. Whereas the SGT perceives tax competition as beneficial by reining in excessive spending by subnational governments. Tax competition is a particularly relevant issue in federations where subnational governments use broad-base taxes that overlap with federal taxes because of harmonization of tax bases.
5. A case in point is the changes in borrowing by Spain's Autonomous Communities (AC) in 2015. When they got into financial distress during the recent Spanish financial crisis, due to a high level of borrowing, the central government's Autonomous Financing Fund (FFA in Spanish) came to their rescue. For more on the issue, please see Caixa Bank (2018).
6. The concept of soft budget constraint was initially coined by Kornai (1980; 1986) to highlight perpetual bailing out of public enterprises with state funds. Loss-making public enterprises were able to count on financial assistance from state coffers, an expectation that defined the behaviour of their top management. Later, the concept was applied to subnational governments (Kornai et al. 2003).
7. Rodden (2003: 697) describes the potential negative impact of transfer revenues as 'breaking the link between taxes and benefits, mere expenditure decentralization might turn the public sector's resources into a common pool that competing local governments will attempt to overfish'.
8. Bird (1993) defines fiscal dentistry as gap-filling, suggesting that subnational governments with larger deficits receive larger transfers.
9. Brennan and Buchanan have developed a body of theory where they present government as a revenue-maximizing Leviathan, which can be constrained by a constitution.

This constitution places definite limits upon the tax base. They believe that a tax constitution is required to restrict governments which have propensity to tax and spend.

10. Grossman (1994), for example, argues that the per capita amount of intergovernmental transfers in the US is correlated with party similarity, size of state bureaucracy and size of state Democratic Party majority, suggesting that the transfer decisions are politically driven. Sorensen (2003) finds that lobbying activities of local governments have an impact on the amount of intergovernmental transfers in Norway. Borck and Owings (2003) show that in California proximity to the state capital is an important factor in determining the amount of transfer resources going to counties. Feld and Schaltegger (2005) find that in Switzerland fiscal referendums lead to lower levels of intergovernmental transfers suggesting that voters serve as a hard budget constraint. Sole-Olle and Sorribas-Navarro (2008) show that partisan alignment has a sizeable positive effect on the amount of transfer revenues coming to municipalities in Spain. Sorens (2016) presents evidence from the United States that subnational spending financed by federal dollars leads to higher subnational and overall government debt and spending.

11. Theoretical considerations suggest that transfer revenues exert an incentive effect on the tax effort of subnational governments. Buettner (2006) tests these theoretical predictions using a large panel data of German municipalities and his empirical findings suggest that the volume of transfer revenues reduces tax effort.

12. Evidence from empirical studies provides a convincing case of the disincentive effects of intergovernmental transfers on local tax effort in different countries. For the German equalization transfers, Buttner (1999) and Baretti et al. (2002) report a similar negative effect on local revenues. In the context of India, Naganathan and Sivagnanam (2000), Rajaraman and Vasishtha (2000) and Panda (2009) present similar evidence. In the case of China, Liu and Zhao (2011) provide considerable evidence of disincentive effects of transfers on local tax revenue generation. For Ghana, Mogues and Benin (2012) find that transfers have a depressing effect on local revenues. In an empirical analysis, Bravo (2010) finds negative effects of intergovernmental grants on local revenues in Chilean municipalities. Similarly, Canavire-Bacarreza and Espinoza (2010) show that conditional transfers negatively affect property tax collection in the State of Sinaloa in Mexico.

13. In the 1980s, the United States Advisory Commission on Intergovernmental Fiscal Relations developed a methodology to incorporate the expenditure side of public finances into the vertical gap concept (ACIR 1986; 1990a; 1990b). However, this methodology was never applied to the estimation of actual federal transfers to states.

14. However, it is important to avoid eliminating differences in net fiscal benefits arising from regional choices in the mix of public services (Boadway 2007). According to Sing and Srinivasan (2006: 8), the concept of equalization is 'eminently sensible if there is a social consensus on what should be included in the set of services to be provided by the government and at what level'.

15. A uniform state tax regime is, of course, immune against horizontal tax competition among states in a legal sense. However, there could be incentives for the states to relax their tax administration in an effort to attract and foster economic activities in their jurisdiction. Such incentives are to be expected if the shortfall of revenue from lenient tax administration is fully compensated through equalizing grants, which is true for a number of states in Germany. Although there has been suspicion of leniency in some instances, it is, of course, difficult to prove in practice. The redistribution effects following the primary allocation of taxes will also induce lenient states (strategical reasons, administrative inertia, weaker tax compliance where authorities are seen to be lenient) to go on with their practice since they may make up 92 per cent of the difference through equalization.

16. Tertiary education and transportation service provision are two good horizontal spending externality examples. In both cases interjurisdictional spillovers could easily generate disincentives for subnational governments to invest in the sector.

17. If the design of the transfer operates as an insurance mechanism over the business cycle, then transfer revenues can reduce the procyclicality of subnational government

resources. However, if transfers are subject to typical political pressures to increase spending when in a boom, transfers can exacerbate the procyclicality of expenditures.
18. On the expenditure side, subnational governments might have to bear additional expenses for programmes on soup kitchens, shelters and food banks to take care of needy citizens during economic turmoil.
19. von Hagen (2007: 113) suggest that '[t]axing the prospering region and giving the proceeds to the region in distress restores aggregate demand there and reduces aggregate demand in the taxed region'.
20. In Australia, intergovernmental transfers are recommended by an independent Commonwealth Grants Commission to the federal government.
21. There is a growing recognition of the relevance of political agency models in explaining incumbent behaviour. Besley and Burgess (2002) use this approach to study how politicians respond to shocks in India under the spotlight of the media. They observe that state governments where the difference in the seats held by the two major parties is smallest also appear to have more responsive governments. India's sluggish performance from independence through the early 1990s reflects its centralized federal system, where the central government made most of the important policy decisions (compromising subnational autonomy) and imposed some restrictions on the movement of goods across states (prevented a common market). Democracy provides an obvious value to citizens when it allows them to make choices over competing visions about policy and to throwing out bad local officials. Yet the tragic brilliance mechanism – the threat by the centre of withholding substantial revenue or policy benefits from localities that support the opposition – perverts elections by preventing citizens from exercising freedom of expression and choice (Weingast 2007).

REFERENCES

ACIR (United States Advisory Commission on Intergovernmental Fiscal Relations). (1986). *Measuring State Fiscal Capacity: Alternative Methods and Their Uses*. Information Report M-150. Washington, DC: ACIR.
ACIR (1990a). *Representative Expenditures: Addressing the Neglected Dimension of Fiscal Capacity*. Information Report M-174. Washington, DC: ACIR.
ACIR (1990b). *State Fiscal Capacity and Effort*. Information Report M-170. Washington, DC: ACIR.
Alm, J. and Martinez-Vazquez, J. (2002). 'On the Use of Budgetary Norms as a Tool for Fiscal Management'. Working Paper. Georgia State University, International Studies Program, Atlanta.
Bahl, R. and Bird, R. (2018). *Fiscal Decentralization and Local Finance in Developing Countries*. Cheltenham, UK and Northampton, MA, USA: Edward Elgar Publishing.
Bahl, R. and Wallace, S. (2007). 'Intergovernmental Transfers: The Vertical Sharing Dimension'. In Jorge Martinez-Vazquez and Bob Searle (eds). *Fiscal Equalization Challenges in the Design of Intergovernmental Transfers*. New York: Springer, pp. 205–49.
Baretti, C., Huber, B. and Lichtblau, K. (2002). 'A Tax on Tax Revenue: The Incentive Effects of Equalizing Transfers, Evidence from Germany'. *International Tax and Public Finance* **9** (6): 631–49.
Besley, T. and Burgess, R. (2002). 'The Political Economy of Government Responsiveness: Theory and Evidence from India'. *The Quarterly Journal of Economics* **117** (4): 1415–51.

Bird, R.M. (1993). 'Threading the Fiscal Labyrinth: Some Issues in Fiscal Decentralization'. *National Tax Journal* **46** (2): 207–27.

Bird, R.M. (2000). 'Intergovernmental Fiscal Relations: Universal Principles, Local Applications'. International Studies Program Working Paper 00-2. Andrew Young School of Policy Studies, Georgia State University, Atlanta.

Bird, R. and Smart, M. (2001). 'Intergovernmental Fiscal Transfers: Some Lessons from International Experience'. Paper prepared for Symposium on Intergovernmental Transfers in Asian Countries: Issues and Practices, Asian Tax and Public Policy Program, Hitosubashi University, Tokyo, Japan, February 2001.

Bird, R. and Smart, M. (2002). 'Intergovernmental Fiscal Transfers: International Lessons for Developing Countries'. *World Development* **30** (6): 899–912.

Boadway, R. (2007). 'Grants in a Federal Economy: A Conceptual Perspective'. In Robin Boadway and Anwar Shah (eds). *Intergovernmental Fiscal Transfers Principles and Practice*. Washington DC: World Bank, pp. 55–74.

Borck, R. and Owings, S. (2003). 'The Political Economy of Intergovernmental Grants'. *Regional Science and Urban Economics* **33** (2): 139–56.

Bravo, J. (2010). 'The Effects of Intergovernmental Grants on Local Revenue: Evidence from Chile'. Documentos de Trabajo 393. Instituto de Economia. Pontificia Universidad Católica de Chile. Accessed 17 February 2019 at https://www.sociedadpoliticaspublicas.cl/archivos/BLOQUE1/Descentralizacion/El_efecto_de_las_transferencias_intergubernamentales_en_el_ingreso_local.pdf.

Brennan, G. and Buchanan, J.M. (1980). *The Power to Tax: Analytical Foundations of a Fiscal Constitution*. Cambridge, UK: Cambridge University Press.

Buettner, T. (2006). 'The Incentive Effect of Fiscal Equalization Transfers on Tax Policy'. *Journal of Public Economics* **90** (3): 477–97.

Burret, H.T. and Feld, L.P. (2014). 'A Note on Budget Rules and Fiscal Federalism'. *CESifo DICE Report: Journal for Institutional Comparisons* **2** (1): 3–11.

Buttner, T. (1999). 'Regional Stabilization by Fiscal Equalization? Theoretical Considerations and Empirical Evidence from Germany'. ZEW Discussion Papers No. 99-23. Accessed 17 February 2019 at ftp://ftp.zew.de/pub/zew-docs/dp/dp2399.pdf.

Caixa Bank (2018). *Monthly Report Economic and Financial Market Outlook Number 422*. Accessed 15 March 2019 at http://www.caixabankresearch.com/en/2018-04-01-000000.

Canavire-Bacarreza, G. and Espinoza, N.G.Z. (2010). 'Fiscal Transfers a Curse or Blessing? Evidence of Their Effect on Tax Effort for Municipalities in Sinaloa, Mexico'. Andrew Young School of Policy Studies Research Paper Series Working Paper 10-30. Georgia State University, Atlanta.

Carega, M. and Weingast, B.R. (2003). 'Fiscal Federalism, Good Governance and Economic Growth in Mexico'. In Dani Rodrik (ed.). *Search of Prosperity: Analytic Narratives on Economic Growth*. Princeton University Press: Princeton, pp. 399–438.

Chernick, H. (2000). 'Federal Grants and Social Welfare Spending: Do State Responses Matter?' *National Tax Journal* **53** (1): 143–52.

Feld, L.P. and Schaltegger, C.A. (2005). 'Voters as a Hard Budget Constraint: On the Determination of Intergovernmental Grants'. *Public Choice* **123** (1–2): 147–69.

Gramlich, E.M. (1977). 'Intergovernmental Grants: A Review of the Empirical Literature'. In W.E. Oates (ed.). *The Political Economy of Fiscal Federalism*. Kentucky: Lexington Books, pp. 274–94.

Grossman, P.J. (1994). 'A Political Theory of Intergovernmental Grants'. *Public Choice* **78** (3–4): 295–303.

Inman, R.P. (1988). 'Federal Assistance and Local Services in the United States: The Evolution of a New Federalist Order'. In H. Rose (ed.). *Fiscal Federalism*. Chicago: University of Chicago Press, pp. 33–78.

Inman, R.P. and Rubinfeld, D.L. (1997). 'Rethinking Federalism'. *Journal of Economic Perspectives* **XI** (4): 43–64.

Jin, H., Qian, Y. and Weingast, B.R. (2005). 'Regional Decentralization and Fiscal Incentives: Federalism, Chinese Style'. *Journal of Public Economics* **89** (9–10): 1719–42.

Khemani, S. (2003). 'Partisan Politics and Intergovernmental Transfers in India'. Policy Research Working Paper No. 3016. World Bank, Washington, DC.

Kornai, J. (1980). *Economics of Shortage*. Amsterdam: North-Holland Publishers.

Kornai, J. (1986). 'The Soft Budget Constraint'. *Kyklos* **39** (1): 3–30.

Kornai, J., Maskin, E. and Roland, G. (2003). 'Understanding the Soft Budget Constraint'. *Journal of Economic Literature* **41** (4): 1095–136.

Liu, Y. and Zhao, J. (2011). 'Intergovernmental Fiscal Transfers and Local Tax Efforts: Evidence from Provinces in China'. *Journal of Economic Policy Reform* **14** (4): 295–300.

Martinez-Vazquez, J. and Boex, L.F.J. (1997a). 'An Analysis of Alternative Measures of Fiscal Capacity for the Regions of the Russian Federation'. International Studies Program Working Paper 97-4. Andrew Young School of Policy Studies, Georgia State University.

Martinez-Vazquez, J. and Boex, L.F.J. (1997b). 'Fiscal Capacity: An Overview of Concepts and Measurement Issues and Their Applicability in the Russian Federation'. International Studies Program Working Paper 97-3. Andrew Young School of Policy Studies, Georgia State University.

McKinnon, R. and Nechyba, T. (1997). 'Competition in Federal Systems: The Role of Political and Financial Constraints'. In John Ferejohn and Barry R. Weingast (eds). *The New Federalism: Can the States be Trusted?* Stanford: Hoover Institution Press, pp. 3–61.

Mogues, T. and Benin, S. (2012). 'Do External Grants to District Governments Discourage Own Revenue Generation? A Look at Local Public Finance Dynamics in Ghana'. *World Development* **40** (5): 1054–67.

Naganathan, M. and Sivagnanam, K.J. (2000). 'Federal Transfers and Tax Efforts of States in India'. *The Indian Economic Journal* **47** (4): 101–10.

Oates, W.E. (1972). *Fiscal Federalism*. New York: Harcourt Brace Jovanovich.

Oates, W.E. (2005). 'Toward a Second-Generation Theory of Fiscal Federalism'. *International Tax and Public Finance* **XII** (4): 349–73

Panda, P.K. (2009). 'Central Fiscal Transfers and States' Own-Revenue Efforts in India: Panel Date Models'. *The Journal of Applied Economic Research* **3** (3): 223–42.

Perrson, T. and Tabellini, G. (1996). 'Federal Fiscal Constitutions: Risk Sharing and Redistribution'. *Journal of Political Economy* **104** (5): 979–1009.

Rajaraman, I. and Vasishtha, G. (2000). 'Impacts of Grants on Tax Effort of Local Government'. *Economic and Political Weekly* **35** (33): 2943–8.

Rodden, J. (2003). 'Reviving Leviathan'. *International Organization* **57** (4): 695–729.

Rodden, J. (2012). 'Market Discipline and U.S. Federalism'. In Peter Conti-Brown and David A. Skeel (eds). *When States Go Broke: The Origins, Context, and Solutions for the American States in Fiscal Crisis*. New York: Cambridge University Press, pp. 123–45.

Rodden, J. and Wibbels, E. (2002). 'Beyond the Fiction of Federalism: Macroeconomic Management in Multitiered Systems'. *World Politics* **54** (4): 494–531.

Singh, N. and Srinivasan, T.N. (2006). 'Federalism and Economic Development in India: An Assessment'. SCID Conference on the Challenges of Economic Policy Reform in Asia, Stanford University, 1–3 June 2006.

Skeel, D.A. (2011). 'Give States a Way to Go Bankrupt: It's the Best Option for Avoiding a Massive Federal Bailout'. *California Journal of Law and Public Policy* **3** (2): 1–6.

Sole-Olle, A. and Sorribas-Navarro, P. (2008). 'The Effects of Partisan Alignment on the Allocation of Intergovernmental Transfers: Difference-in-Difference Estimates for Spain'. *Journal of Public Economics* **92** (12): 2302–19.

Sorens, J. (2016). 'Vertical Fiscal Gaps and Economic Performance: A Theoretical Review and an Empirical Meta-analysis'. Mercatus Working Paper. Mercatus Center at George Mason University, Arlington, VA.

Sorensen, R.J. (2003). 'The Political Economy of Intergovernmental Grants: The Norwegian Case'. *European Journal of Political Research* **42** (2): 163–95.

Ter-Minassian, T. 1997. 'Decentralization and Macroeconomic Management'. IMF Working Paper 97-155. International Monetary Fund, Washington, DC.

Tiebout, C. (1961). 'An Economic Theory of Fiscal Decentralization'. In National Bureau Committee for Economic Research (ed.). *Public Finances: Needs, Sources, and Utilization*. Princeton, NJ: Princeton University Press, pp. 79–96.

von Hagen, J. (2007). 'Achieving Economic Stabilization by Sharing Risk within Countries'. In Robin Boadway and Anwar Shah (eds). *Intergovernmental Fiscal Transfers Principles and Practice*. Washington, DC: World Bank, pp.107–29.

Weingast, B.R. (2007). 'Second Generation Fiscal Federalism: Implications for Decentralized Democratic Governance and Economic Development'. Accessed 17 February 2019 at https://web.stanford.edu/~jrodden/weingast.pdf.

Weingast, B.R. (2009). 'Second Generation Fiscal Federalism: The Implications of Fiscal Incentives'. *Journal of Urban Economics* **65** (3): 279–93.

Weingast, B.R. (2014). 'Second Generation Fiscal Federalism: Political Aspects of Decentralization and Economic Development'. *World Development* **53** (1): 14–25.

Worthington, A. and Dollery, B. (1998). 'The Political Determination of Intergovernmental Grants in Australia'. *Public Choice* **94** (3/4): 299–315.

4. The practice of fiscal equalization: a political economy clarification*

Bernard Dafflon and François Vaillancourt

4.1 INTRODUCTION: THE RATIONALE FOR EQUALIZATION[1]

Most federal and decentralized States experience fiscal imbalance, vertical and horizontal, and have found it necessary to correct both. In a decentralized setting, vertical imbalance results from the fact that, in most cases, major buoyant taxes such as personal or corporate income taxes or consumption taxes are tax fields that belong to the federal or central government, while costly labour intensive functions, such as health, education and social services have usually been assigned to sub-national governments (SNGs thereafter; they can be regional or local) for reasons of proximity and preferences (Watts, 2008, p. 103). Vertical imbalance can be solved by re-assigning taxation and functions, or, with those unchanged, through financial transfers from the centre to the SNGs.

The origin of horizontal imbalance is different. First, federal or decentralized countries do not have perfectly homogenous regions; indeed, their more or less decentralized arrangements are put in place because of this lack of homogeneity. Thus, sub-national financial capacities depend on both the revenue bases legally accessible to SNGs and the territorial distribution of those bases. Needs vary according to the particular preferences of the SNG residents; but they also depend on geographic, demographic and socio-economic factors. They are further determined by legal (but not only) requirements as to the type of mandatory public services that SNGs must provide. And unit costs of publicly provided goods and services can vary between SNGs due to factors such as weather or topography. Second, no matter how carefully functions and revenues are decentralized at a point in time (say when writing or amending the Constitution) with the objective of matching expenditures and taxation, their paths differ over time causing disparities in decentralized budgets of SNG units.

Equalization is the usual answer to horizontal imbalance. It refers to attempts made at the reduction of fiscal differences among SNGs by monetary transfers. Two initial questions arise with respect to implementing equalization schemes. (i) What sort of 'solidarity' among SNGs is accepted and acceptable and who decides on this? More solidarity would clearly mark a trend towards standardization in the delivery of core local public services, instead of leaving SNGs provide local-specific services, assuming the consequences in terms of tax levels, under the constraint of the potential mobility of users/taxpayers. In the case of federal countries, examples of substantial solidarity between SNGs are Australia and Germany, of less solidarity Canada and Switzerland and of little solidarity the United States. (ii) Where to draw the line between local preferences and mandatory local public services? As Boex and Martinez-Vazquez (2007, p. 293) put it: 'Without a clear demarcation line separating specific standards of services from an overall envelope of expenditures, perceptions of what may be a need can easily escalate to completely unaffordable expenditure levels'.

For practitioners, the theory of fiscal equalization is elusive. There is no core programme; it is mainly derived from the theory of grants-in-aid. There are several ways to consider SNGs' 'capacity' or 'needs'; the distinction between expenditures/costs/needs equalization is blurred. This is not surprising. Equalization is first and foremost a question of redistributive justice among SNGs; this is to ensure the equal or similar treatment of residents of a country wherever they live. Thus, equalization is pervaded with value judgements that cannot be easily explained by economic theory. Questions such as 'how much' the 'rich' jurisdictions should contribute to equalization and 'how much' the 'poor' can claim, the estimation of the degree of capacity – financial, fiscal or tax capacity – together with the evaluation of the amount to be paid or received are closely – though not exclusively – related to the concept of 'solidarity'. This concept can vary between individuals, political parties and so on often with payers being inclined to less generosity than beneficiaries. Thus, politicians have as much to say as economists in policy implementation. Yet, in politics, 'fiscal equalization' is very often poorly defined (elusive), but overused because of its ambiguity which is precisely a political rhetorical resource.

Confronted with this multiplicity of approaches, the purpose of this chapter is to offer a benchmark for the economic and political examination of equalization policies in different countries. When reading papers about international experiences with equalization schemes, we most often encounter a descriptive and careful analysis of the institutional process aimed at some form of fiscal equalization. It is, however, very difficult to compare one national experience to another due to the absence of an analytical yardstick. Yet, in the architecture and design of equalization for any country, the same questions and the same problems always arise. The objective in this chapter is to list the main issues in a sequential, comprehensive and coherent way so that one can more easily compare national experiences about the fundamental architecture of equalization, although not in all its operational details.

The chapter is divided into five sections. The first one briefly summarizes the literature on equalization, not to give a full overview, but to highlight milestone contributions to the political economy of interregional solidarity. The second section examines and explains the possible origins of disparities or differences in the public finance position of SNGs. Disparities are equalizable, differences not. The third section points out the changes in the policy objectives from first- and second-generation models: when first introduced, explicit equalization either ignored expenditure needs equalization (Canada, 1957) or would mix revenue and expenditure needs in one single formula (Australia, 1934; Switzerland, 1959). The lack of expenditure equalization made reaching the goals of equalization impossible, while the intertwining of the two objectives unduly complexified matters. It is now clear that for proper outcomes to be attained, expenditure needs equalization cannot be ignored; and revenue equalization and expenditure needs equalization must be addressed explicitly by themselves, yet in complementary fashion. The fourth section presents a comprehensive and coherent listing of the key issues in equalization policy. The last section proposes a synopsis of possible determinants of disparities that can be used to guide the design of the architecture of equalization policies.

4.2 SOLIDARITY AND EQUALIZATION: A SUMMARY OF THE LITERATURE

This first section presents a summary, not a survey, of the literature on equalization in order to introduce step by step the main arguments leading from solidarity between SNGs, a political concept, to equalization, its economic/fiscal counterpart that makes the concept operational, with the main obstacles and difficulties that implementation faces.

In his seminal pieces on equalization, Buchanan (1950, 1952) argues for a similar treatment not of SNGs but of individuals, wherever they reside in a country, in terms of fiscal residual or net fiscal benefit (that is, the value of public goods and services provided minus the tax cost). He updated these pieces 50 years later without much change (Buchanan, 2002).

In response to Buchanan, Scott (1950) argues that equalization from rich to poor regions means that the latter can offer public services at an incorrect price to their residents. This creates a distortion in the allocation of resources between regions and slows down labour mobility. Workers in the poor region benefit after equalization from more public services than what they could afford with their own resources, reducing maximization of national output. Buchanan (1952) replies by arguing that equalization reduces inefficient migration.

Buchanan and Goetz (1972) argue that since migrants do not take into account that their movement increases the per capita fiscal price in their region of origin, reduces it in their region of destination while perhaps creating congestion in it, equalization internalizes social costs and is thus desirable. Boadway and Flatters (1982) synthesize the arguments of efficiency and equity in the debate on equalization. Since net fiscal residuals in SNGs are not zero when the user-pay principle does not apply, there are two possibilities for correcting this: adjustment for individuals through central taxes (as proposed by Buchanan) or equalization between SNGs with higher and lower net fiscal residuals.

Von Hagen (2000) analyses equalization as a type of insurance against shocks to the economy of SNGs. Today's rich SNGs in terms of resources and with little or no needs can become poor tomorrow because of globalization, changes in demand or technological obsolescence. Equalization helps alleviate these shocks. Thus, a rich SNG may well want to contribute to equalization, knowing that one day it may draw benefits from this programme.

While these papers do not explicitly examine the link between resources and needs equalization, it is clear that key dimensions of equalization have not been agreed to among scholars. They can be summarized as follows:

- The fiscal residual is with respect to individual taxpayers. Some argue for replacing equalization by transfers to individuals. The argument is that otherwise rich taxpayers in poor SNGs benefit from both kinds of equalization.
- Migration is not only by individuals but can also be carried out by firms to benefit from tax competition/public subsidies. Thus, some ask why resource equalization should allow SNGs to lower tax burdens for firms. This may be appropriate if the tax burdens before equalization were substantially higher in poor SNGs (to finance adequate public services) leading to an inefficient use of immobile resources.
- Expenditure equalization often accounts for social costs and congestion associated with urban areas. Reducing these costs through expenditure equalization may lead to urbanization over an optimal level. In these situations, corrective transfers should intervene within the concerned territories and not through a nationwide equalization policy.

In the late 2000s, the pertinence of equalization was not so much debated; it was accepted that 'fiscal equalization transfers are conceptually justified on grounds of fiscal efficiency and regional fiscal equity' (Shah, 2008, p. 35). The discussion was on operational issues (OECD, 2007). It is important to note that equalization in practice does not consider the individuals as Buchanan did, but only the SNGs as jurisdictions and territories. Whereas revenue equalization had been largely accepted, most often in the form of an RTS (Representative Tax System), the more debated question is whether expenditure need equalization is worth doing. The first practical (operational) issue is identifying the origin of fiscal disparities. Whether equalization is desirable depends on the functions and revenue sources devolved to SNGs, their population average size, geographical and territorial diversity, urban/rural, mountain divide (Kim and Lotz, 2008). Table 4.1 addresses these variables.

4.3 FISCAL DISPARITIES VERSUS DIFFERENCES

A typical textbook explanation of fiscal disparities is that 'fiscal disparities arise because the capacity to raise revenue to finance publicly provided services relative to the amount needed to provide a standard package of public services varies across jurisdictions' (Ladd, 1999, p. 123). In this definition, resources are balanced against a 'standard package' of local public services. Thus, we can identify three possible origins of fiscal disparities: the capacity to raise (tax) revenues, the expenditure needs, or the net residual which is expressed as 'needs minus capacity'. Still this remains too vague to allow drawing the policy-relevant frontier line between 'differences' that result from local choices and 'disparities' which have exogenous causes.

Yet the literature is not very abundant on this distinction; only a few contributions to the political economy of equalization tackle this issue;[2] we do this in Table 4.1. It distinguishes three possible origins of fiscal disparities (A, B and C) outside the control of SNG authorities and two origins of differences in the fiscal position of decentralized government units (D and E). Items A and E relate to the revenue side; A concerns the potential tax bases at the disposal of SNGs (something that can be approximated by an RTS, as we shall argue later) and E corresponds to the tax arrangements that are possible at the local level given the flexibility of the legal system of taxation, notably between various forms of taxes and the mix of taxation and user charges. Items B to D refer to local expenditure functions. Classes B and C group the conditions of provision of local public services; only class D is about local preferences in public service provision. Differences

Table 4.1   Possible origin of fiscal disparities/differences

---

A. Differences in the access to resources (Oakland, 1994). It takes two forms:
    (i) differences in the income and wealth of community residents, or (ii)
    differences in communal property and/or natural resource endowment. Also:
    differences in SNGs' taxable resources (Smart and Bird, 1996; Dafflon,
    1995); tax bases (Gilbert, 1996); taxable resources per head (King, 1997);
    economic position and opportunity (Dafflon and Vaillancourt, 2003);
    territorial distribution of the unequal tax bases (Bird and Vaillancourt, 2007)
B. The amount of mandatory public goods that the SNGs must provide for
    exogenous reasons (Gilbert, 1996); needs per head (King, 1997). Also: (i)
    differences in the number of units of standardized service required per capita
    owing to demographic reasons: age structure, different participation rates
    in social programmes by persons of different ages (Bird and Vaillancourt,
    2007), the socio-demographic composition of the population (Break, 1980;
    Reschovsky, 2007); (ii) the fact that some populations are more costly to serve
    than others (Oakland, 1994)
C. Cost differences due to input-output relationship (Break, 1980, cited in
    Shah, 1996). Also: (i) cost differences per unit of mandatory public goods,
    quantity and composition of input that is necessary for producing the public
    service (Dafflon, 1995; King, 1997; Dafflon and Vaillancourt, 2003); (ii) cost
    differences due to the natural conditions of service areas, for example, due
    to climatic or geographic features, density, distance or other environmental
    factors (Break, 1980) or (iii) differences in labour cost across regions (on
    the basis of real private sector wages, Bird and Vaillancourt (2007)); (iv)
    economies of scale in the service provision (Dafflon, 1995; Dafflon and
    Vaillancourt, 2003)
D. Differences due to specific tastes of residents in the various SNGs or to
    policy decisions at the local level (Break, 1980). Local preferences either for
    optional services or for quantities or quality above the minimum standard
    level in the provision of mandatory services (Dafflon, 1995; Gilbert, 1996;
    Dafflon and Vaillancourt, 2003)
E. Local preferences among different forms of taxes and between taxation and
    user charge (Inman and Rubinfeld, 1996)

Sources: Adapted from Dafflon (2007), Dafflon and Mischler (2008).

under D and E result from local preferences and hence they need not be
compensated by any kind of equalization or transfer payment.

Table 4.1 establishes the fundamental distinction between disparities and
differences. Disparities A, B and C are outside the influence and the policy
choices of SNGs and should be equalized. Differences D and E depend on
local own decisions and should not be compensated. Table 4.1 also identifies the possible origins of disparities; these can be used as indicators in the

needs equalization formula. If this rationale for equalization is accepted, the next and immediate question is whether revenue and expenditure needs equalization should be integrated into one or run in parallel fashion.

But is this economic approach readily accepted? How do politicians deal with equalization issues? Will they worry about the distinction between disparities and differences? Many times, these distinctions are used by politicians to obtain support from their local voters. In Table 4.1 situations D and E would not be compensated through equalization transfers. But in politics, politicians at all government tiers impress upon policymakers the need to compensate for differences in SNGs preferences. In practice political interference in equalization – or in domains related to equalization – is frequent. States are asked to compensate for differences in local preferences; providing block grants to local bodies for meeting service delivery deficits is in a loose sense supporting local preferences for the provision of particular services. With respect to situation D above, one might argue, for example, that the higher costs of a sprawled municipality arise from policy choices to encourage, or at least not discourage, urban sprawl. Equalization should not reward those municipalities that make no effort to reduce sprawl and, as a result, have higher costs. Yet, Yilmaz et al. (2012, p. 126) illustrate the conceptual difficulties to distinguish between impossible economies of scale or reluctance to cooperate, and between genuine cost disparities versus X-inefficiencies. From this perspective, any policy of expenditure-based equalization is a tremendous challenge.

Also, since equalization is the operational design of interstate solidarity, and solidarity is an ethical and social concept, the frontier between the economic rationale for equalization and political strategy is more a grey zone than a demarcation line. Thus, in the following sections we do not assert what should be done, but the objective is to list in a sequential and coherent way the practical issues which should be answered.

4.4 FIRST- AND SECOND-GENERATION EQUALIZATION

Equalization policies introduced in the 1970s or before (we call it 'first-generation equalization' thereafter) either neglected expenditure needs or when addressing both combined revenue and expenditure disabilities in one measurement formula. Today experts (for example, see Koller et al., 2012) recommend separate but parallel and coordinated treatment of these items.

Table 4.2 presents the two types of equalization, both in terms of what they have in common and in terms of what distinguishes them. This facilitates identifying the links between resources and expenditures equalization. Table 4.2 presents the situation of a constituent unit or a subnational government relative to other SNGs. For example, cell ① (i)–(a) (upper left corner) describes an SNG with resources per inhabitant higher than average and also expenditures per inhabitant higher than average.

Two (strong) hypotheses can be presented in a simplified version of Table 4.2. First, if one accepts that there is no disparity in the revenue raising capacity of SNGs, columns (a) and (c) can be ignored. Thus, all SNGs are supposed to benefit from the 'average' resources and the only issue is the relative positions of SNGs in expenditure needs/costs equalization (cells ②, ⑤ or ⑧). Second hypothesis: if one accepts that there is no disparity in expenditure needs/costs between SNGs, then lines (i) and (iii) can be ignored. All SNGs are supposed to have the same 'average' position in expenditure needs/costs. Thus, only revenue equalization is necessary, which correspond to cells ④, ⑤ and ⑥.

Yet, we strongly suspect that these two hypotheses do not correctly mirror the possible positions of SNGs. With different evolutions in taxation and decentralized functions, the practical economy of equalization is nowadays faced with four additional situations: SNG units with: (i) high tax potential and higher expenditure needs ①; (ii) high tax potential low needs ⑦; (iii) low tax potential high needs ③; and (iv) low tax potential low needs ⑨. Equalization that concerns revenue sources only is half the story and does not encompass the situations described above. And a unique formula combining tax potential and expenditure needs cannot answer the four situations. The complementarity of revenue equalization and expenditure needs equalization must be taken into account. We call it 'second-generation equalization'.

These four situations apply to regional-local equalization as well as to federal-regional equalization: the argument that some SNGs have resources above average but also needs and/or costs above average is also true in large metropolitan areas. The logic and the key issues (Table 4.2) are the same, but the implementation must be adapted to local circumstances (especially the local characteristics and determinants of equalization – Table 4.3).

In first-generation equalization, we observe three situations:

(1a) Equalization does not account for differences in needs or costs: it is assumed that needs or costs are identical (*average level*) for all SNGs. In this case, the equalization of resources is horizontal, from ④ to ⑥ and thus financed by SNGs for SNGs. One then focuses on potential resources (line (ii)), with horizontal equalization taking some resources from SNGs with potential resources (tax base) above average ④ to redistribute them to SNGs with a resource potential below average ⑥. This could be done by specific budget lines in SNG budgets or by a redistribution of SNG taxes collected by the central government.

Table 4.2   Foundations of equalization SNGs relative position

Equalization of → ↓		Resources (tax potential)		
		Superior (a)	Average (b)	Weak (c)
Expenditures Needs/costs	Strong (i)	①	②	③
	Average (ii)	④	⑤	⑥
	Weak (iii)	⑦	⑧	⑨

Source: Authors.

A first alternative (1b) is vertical equalization of resources. In that case, the central government finances equalization from its budget. The practical question, that needs a political answer, is who are the SNGs that benefit: those with resources potential below average ⑥ only or all SNGs ④⑤⑥ – which dampens the impact of resources equalization? The central equalization fund comes from federal revenues collected in all SNGs; thus, considered together, economic agents who are federal tax payers and residing in SNGs with higher potential resources than average contribute more than all economic agents residing in SNGs with below average potential.[3] Thus with vertical equalization, there is de facto some horizontal equalization between rich SNGs and poor SNGs. A second alternative (1c) could be combining vertical and horizontal equalization; yet in this case, only SNGs in situation ⑥ would benefit – one does not see SNGs in ④ contributing to horizontal revenue equalization but benefiting from vertical transfers.

(2) In the case some SNGs have expenditure needs above average (strong, line (i)), equalization formulas help reduce costs differences with respect to a target cost or to account for excess needs compared to the average of SNGs. Differences in resources are set aside or it is assumed that SNGs' resources are equal (average, column (b) of Table 4.2). Group ② SNGs benefit from expenditure equalization, while those in groups ⑤ or ⑧ do not.

Expenditure needs/costs equalization can only be vertical to be efficient. Horizontal equalization would mean that beneficiaries of services in a low-cost (need) jurisdiction would accept a tax-price supplement (that is, more expensive public services) in order to subsidize public services in other, high-cost (need) SNGs. This would distort the local tax price of public services and result in allocative inefficiency. This was noted by Yilmaz et al. (2012): 'First, for those public services that are financed through user charges, if the "price" does not reflect benefit, consumers will face false price signals.' But they add that:

Second, when the difference between SNG choices, X-inefficiencies and genuine disparities is not clear, SNGs might indulge in strategic behavior with the aim of placing themselves in a more favorable equalizing position (in this case, higher costs and more needs). Vertical needs equalization can be set on expenditure standards that eliminate functions based on the benefit principle for their financing and that ignore SNGs potential strategies, but this adds to complexity.

(3) Some first-generation equalization formulas combine the two types of equalization (Swiss cantons, 1959–2007, Yerly 2013). In that case the focus is on cases ② and ③.

Thus, first-generation equalization addressed ④⑤⑥ for resources, ignoring needs and costs; ② for expenditures, ignoring differences in revenue; or ②③ for combined formulas. Issues ①⑦⑧⑨ are not relevant.

Second-generation equalization accounts separately yet simultaneously for resources and expenditures. It recognizes the fact that it is more common, particularly in urban areas, to have SNGs with resources above average but also needs or costs (or both) above average. First-generation equalization formulas do not take this situation into account.

When second-generation equalization includes both equalization of resources and expenditures, this should be done according to our judgement using different formulas, coherent and coordinated. Different (unmixed) since the reference bases are not of the same type. For resources, evaluating the potential relies on differences in comparable tax/revenue bases with identical definitions yielding a monetary measure. The RTS which dates back in its original form to the 1960s is an example of this approach (Smart and Bird, 1996 for Canada; ACIR, 1962 as a proposal not implemented for the USA).[4] For expenditures, we use for calculations differences in 'needs' yielding a relative measure of needs not expressed in monetary values. For resources equalization, standardized tax rates are used, while for expenditures equalization normative costs or needs are used. Coherence of the two parts of a full equalization system results from the fact that: (i) both equalizations use a base x indicator approach; (ii) both use a representative system with potential values, not real ones; (iii) when more than one tax is used for resource equalization and more than one variable for expenditures equalization, weights are required in both based on an analytical approach and not as a result of political bargaining between governments. This is preferable to equalizing fiscal gaps, the difference between expenditure needs and revenue raising capacity, since it makes the process clearer.[5]

In the literature, Ahmad and Craig (1997) examine how to implement both types of equalization without linking them. Yilmaz, Vaillancourt and Dafflon (2012) combine three indicators of equalization to calculate full equalization. Expenditure equalization is divided into needs and cost differences. This is done to highlight analytically the difficulty of measuring differences in costs.

In general, work linking the two types of equalization does not examine the determinants of these two types of equalization and their interaction; we do the latter in section 4.6 of this chapter. Dafflon (2012) presents a synthesis of the linkages of these two kinds of equalization; the same author (2007, 2015) shows that equalization of resources and expenditures equalization (needs variables) can be simultaneous, are complementary and can be formulated in a coherent fashion. The model put forward by Dafflon avoids previous difficulties by not using as a measure of needs service benchmarks; rather variables determining needs (proportion of school-aged children into total population for schooling needs, for example) are used, being transparent and statistically verifiable indicators, avoiding central government interference in SNG decisions.

4.5   KEY ISSUES

We can now turn to the key issues associated with the design of an equalization system. With the second-generation equalization, both revenue equalization and expenditure equalization must be considered. Three issues must be addressed: (i) measuring disparities A, B, and C in Table 4.1 in order to construct the appropriate synthetic indicators; (ii) the choice of the equalization formulas that cover all relevant situations from Table 4.2; and (iii) the importance (amount) and origin of the funds allocated to equalization. These three issues must be addressed in a parallel fashion. They are summarized in Table 4.3.

Measurement issues are the domain of experts, while who receives and how much is allocated are political choices. Thus, in step one, using technical advice on the most relevant (from an economic perspective) taxes and tasks the final choice of revenue (tax) sources and the selection of tasks included in equalization should be left to politicians, after their characteristics and specificities have been clarified by experts. In step two, the construction of the formula should be left to experts, but the operational choice of the appropriate formulas after simulation remains with politicians since their equalization effects vary from one formula to the other. Also, in step three, the importance and the institutional anchoring of the funds is political: it represents the status and extent of solidarity between SNGs.

Table 4.3   Key issues of equalization

Issues/steps	Resources	Needs/costs
1. Measuring disparities	Measure of tax potential: ● What revenue (tax) sources to include in the measure? ● What are the tax bases (normed, average?) and ● What reference rates (normed, average?) to be considered for the '*Representative Tax System*' (RTS)? ● Should natural resources be included? If yes, how are they measured (stock or flow)? ● Construction of an indicator of tax potential for each source used ● Find appropriate weights to calculate a global indicator of RTS	Evaluation of needs and costs using norms: ● What specific tasks (spending items) are included? ● What are the causal indicators (explanatory variables) of disparities? And can they form a '*Representative Expenditure* [needs/costs] *System*' (RES)? ● Construction of an indicator of relative needs/costs for each task examined ● How to calculate a synthetic indicator of expenditures [needs/costs] RES? Find the appropriate weights according to the specific task included in the evaluation
2. Choose an equalization formula	● Vertical, horizontal, mixed ● If vertical, selection of the SNG receiving transfers ● If horizontal, the average delineates beneficiary and contributing SNG ● Formula: proportional (linear) or progressive ● Simulation of various formulas	● Must be vertical ● Selection of SNG receiving transfers: needs/costs above average? ● Formula linear or progressive ● Simulation of various formulas
3. Determine the envelope for equalization?	Possibilities are: ● % of one or more taxes ● In the law ● In the annual or pluriannual (3 years? 5?) budget	Possibilities are: ● % of one or more taxes or ● proportion related to revenue equalization ● In the law ● In the annual or pluriannual (3 years? 5?) budget

Sources: Authors, drawing on Dafflon (2007, pp. 31 ss); Yilmaz et al. (2012, pp. 120–26).

4.6 ECONOMIC CHARACTERISTICS AND DETERMINANTS OF EQUALIZATION OF RESOURCES, NEEDS AND COSTS

This last section focuses on the interaction between the regional economic characteristics and the determinants of equalization. A key point is that SNGs with (tax) revenue capacity higher than average often will have higher unit costs that they can self-finance[6] – a situation that is ignored by first-generation equalization.

As noted in Table 4.3, once equalizable disparities have been identified the next step is the measurement of these disparities. One way of doing this is to prepare a list of factors that can lead to differences in resources, needs or unit costs between SNGs. This is done in Table 4.4, where we examine one by one the impact of diverse characteristics; one by one since some characteristics are mutually exclusive. Columns (a) and (b) present how the relative position of SNGs with respect to each of 16 demographic, economic, topographic and so on characteristics can have an impact on its revenue base (column (c)), its needs for public services (d) and the unit cost of those public services thus affected (e). Table 4.4 shows (combined analysis of columns (a) and (e)) that the most common determinant of higher unit costs is the cost of labour. Capitalization in the price of land of regional (geographic) rents also plays a role.

The list of 16 elements in Table 4.4 was prepared by the authors drawing on their past work in numerous countries and on their knowledge of various transfer formulas.[7] This list is fairly complete but most likely not exhaustive since specific societal factors are present in every country. The inferred impacts between the characteristics of SNGs and various equalizations result either from typical equalization formulas or from the use of production and cost functions and supply and demand on input markets. Thus, a higher labour productivity due to working in resource extractive industries results in higher remuneration in the private labour market[8] that has a knock-on effect on the public labour market and thus public costs. The exact impact depends on similarities and differences between the two kinds of labour and substitution elasticities between labour and other inputs in the production functions of private goods and services and of publicly produced goods and services. Also, in general, a higher tax base is linked to higher unit costs for a given SNG. This is a type ① (Table 4.2) situation that first-generation equalization ignores.

Table 4.4 Regional characteristics and determinants of equalization

Characteristics varying between SNGs (a)	Relative position of SNG$_i$ with respect to all SNGS (b)	Impact on fiscal potential per inhabitant (c)	Impact on needs per inhabitant (d)	Impact on the unit cost of public services (e)
Population:				
1. Size and density	SNG$_i$ has a larger population than the average SNG	Economies of agglomeration that can increase productivity and thus the tax base	Higher demand for public services linked to density (police, fire fighting, parking, green spaces)	Reduction of the unit cost of services of a public good type or with important scale economies
2. Younger population	SNG$_i$ has a higher proportion of school-aged children in total population than in the average SNG	May reduce somewhat average earnings per adult if some parents withdraw temporarily from labour force. Small impact	Needs are higher for school-related inputs such as buildings and perhaps school transportation (depends on population density)	Scale economies possible (school infrastructure)
3. Older population	SNG$_i$ has an older population than the average SNG	Variation in the tax base (pension rather than labour income), and in the tax treatment of income (age exemption . . .); tax base in SNG$_i$ perhaps lower than average	Older population → higher specific needs leisure, culture (65+) specialized care (80+)	Unit cost per user the same for specific services (health)

4. Sicker population	SNG_i has a sicker population than the average SNG due to past industrial activity, endemic diseases or heredity	Illness can result in lower productivity and thus lower earnings	Sicker population will require more and perhaps specialized healthcare	Unit cost per user the same for specific services (health)
5. Schooling level	SNG_i has a better schooled labour force than the average SNG	Since labour productivity increases with schooling, the tax potential (labour income) is higher in SNG_i than the average SNG	Better schooled population → less crime, better health, less needs for some services. But higher demand for cultural services	If schooling level is higher → private wages are higher, increasing the unit cost of public services (higher wages in SNG_i → higher cost per hour of input)
6. Migrant composition	SNG_i has a larger proportion of its population born abroad than the average SNG	Human capital of migrant workers may be less productive for part of their work life leading to lower earnings	Specific integration services (civics, education) may be required	Unit costs of general public services may be higher if additional time is required to provide contextual information
7. Linguistic composition	Typical SNG is homogeneous while SNG_i has four language groups (say 40-30-20-10%)	No impact except if returns to language skills varies	Specific services for minorities (linguistic competencies for some services such as education, health, justice)	Four linguistic groups in SNG_i reduce scale economies if all languages used, increasing unit cost

Geography and territory:

8. Area	SNG_i larger than average SNG	None	Needs for more roads, transportation systems	If population is distributed uniformly per km² in each SNG, then some public services cost more in SNG_i

Table 4.4 (continued)

Characteristics varying between SNGs (a)	Relative position of SNG_i with respect to all SNGS (b)	Impact on fiscal potential per inhabitant (c)	Impact on needs per inhabitant (d)	Impact on the unit cost of public services (e)
9. Topography	SNG_i has a more rugged terrain (hills, mountains) than the average SNG	None	More rugged terrain can create special needs (twisting roads, protection against avalanches)	SNG_i faces higher unit costs than average for some public services (roads, tunnels)
10. Climate and/or natural attractivity	SNG_i is a nicer place to live than the average SNG (climate, beauty, water side, and so on)	Land rent in SNG_i higher than in average SNG	Climate differences leads to different needs: snow removal/ protection against tropical storm	Services with land inputs will be more expensive
11. Geographic position	SNG_i has the sole/major harbour of the country	Higher import/export taxes do not impact SNG_i tax base but tax potential higher due to associated economic activities (truck stops, custom brokerages . . .)	Port and transport infrastructures are needed: centrally or SNG provided?	No impact on unit costs except drop in transport costs of imported inputs into public services due to lower transport costs
Natural resources:				
12. Quality of agricultural soil	Soil in SNG_i is more fertile than in the average SNG	Tax potential of farmers higher in SNG_i	Possible impact on sectoral government interventions	Higher agricultural revenue leads to capitalization in land prices; public services with land input may cost more

13. Non-renewable natural resources present	SNG$_i$ has more petroleum or mining assets	Tax potential, direct and indirect, is higher	May require more infrastructures, need for environmental protection	If natural resources increase private sector productivity and thus wages, this could increase unit cost
Economic context:				
14. Historical economic advantage	SNG$_i$ has head offices, research centres or philanthropic foundations linked to past economic activity	Higher tax potential except if special tax regime	No impact	No impact on unit cost except if high demand for office space leads to higher rents paid in public sector
15. Regulatory economic advantage	SNG$_i$ benefits from a national protection in specific economic sectors such as finance or communications	Higher tax potential fiscal if regulation creates monopolistic rents	No impact	Possible impact on labour unit cost
16. Strength of unions	Unions in SNG$_i$ are more powerful than elsewhere	Wages are higher, profits lower; uncertain impact on tax base (business avoids SNG$_i$)	Possible impact on demand for services for workers	Higher unit cost if impact of private sector wages on public wages

Source: Authors.

4.7   CONCLUSION

This chapter contributes to the analysis of equalization by:

- distinguishing in Table 4.1 public finance disparities that have to be compensated through equalization because their origins fall outside the SNGs' choices, from differences that arise from own choices;
- presenting in Table 4.2 the nine possible combinations of expenditure needs and resources of SNGs' interaction between possible levels of resources and theoretical arguments for equalization;
- listing in three steps in Table 4.3 the key issues associated with the design of an equalization system, parallel and coherent for reducing (tax) revenue and expenditure needs disparities;
- examining in Table 4.4 plausible relationships between 16 demographic, geographic (including natural resources) and economic characteristics of SNGs, on the one side, and resources, needs and cost elements of equalization, on the other side. Additional characteristics not addressed by the authors should be analysed in similar form.

The theoretical literature shows that it is not as easy to equalize expenditures as it is to equalize revenues (Reschovsky, 2007; Yilmaz et al., 2012). The difficulties come from: (i) identifying the functions that would be selected for equalization; (ii) distinguishing expenditures that result from the standards set by the federal government that oblige SNGs from expenditures resulting from their own choices; and (iii) solving the problem of measuring needs or unit costs precisely. We also demonstrate the necessity of running simultaneously and in a coherent way revenue and expenditure needs equalizations when there is a strong relation between higher tax potential and higher expenditure needs or unit costs of public services.

Finally, how the politicians deal with equalization issues needs to be explored in greater detail; they are unlikely to care much about the distinction between disparities and differences. Good political inputs are needed for good equalization but good politics leading to re-election may conflict with this; thus, good equalization is an elusive concept, but it remains worth striving for.

NOTES

*   Thanks to Guy Gilbert, Andrew Reschovsky, Enid Slack, Serdar Yilmaz and Farah Zahir for their comments and suggestions on an earlier version of this chapter.

1. Dafflon and Vaillancourt (2003) were among the first economists to give a formal presentation of equalization setting out the issues for operational purposes. This approach was updated and further developed in Yilmaz et al. (2012). For a more complete presentation on the equalization issues and a survey of the existing literature, see Dafflon (2007, 2012); Dafflon and Mischler (2008).
2. For example, in *The Oxford Handbook of State and Local Government Finance* (Ebel and Petersen, 2012), only 12 pages (Yilmaz, Vaillancourt, Dafflon) out of 982 pages are devoted to the equalization issue. First contributions on the origin of disparities and differences in SNGs' public finance in an equalization perspective are noted in Table 4.1.
3. Residents with the same high income pay the same federal income tax in rich or poor SNGs. But since it is likely that more residents with high income live in rich SNGs (A in Table 4.1), rich SNGs contribute more to the federal financing of equalization through the federal current budget. Thus, vertical revenue equalization indirectly includes horizontal effects.
4. In these two papers, the SNGs' per capita entitlement in a revenue category is equal to its per capita tax base deficiency in the category, relative to a per capita standard for the category, multiplied by the calculated national average tax rate for the category. Yet, according to Bahl (1972, footnote 2) 'The term RTS in no way connotes any model system selected on purely normative ground. The adjective "representative" is used here instead of "average" only because of tradition'. In the normative model, the assessment of the tax bases is identical for all SNGs, whereas the tax rates considered are not calculated on the average SNGs' tax effort but based on an identical tax rate schedule. In a piggyback tax system for SNGs, the reference for measuring the tax disparities in the individual SNG would be the per capita tax base standard and the tax rate schedule fixed in the law, fully – 100 per cent – considered).
5. For more on this concept see Chernick and Reschovsky (2015).
6. Calculations by the authors for Canadian provinces using revenue capacity from Courchene (2013, T1) and a cost index by Gusen (2012) show a 0.86 positive correlation. Similarly, there is a 0.94 correlation between revenue capacity and wage indicators of Australian States, using data from the Commonwealth Grants Commission (2015 – Main Report Table 2, p. 5 for revenue capacity and Figure 6, p. 92 for wage costs). For Switzerland, the correlation coefficients present the right sign, but are not significant (chapter on Switzerland in this volume).
7. A tentative list is given in Bird and Vaillancourt (2007). For a detailed technical description of certain variables in Table 4.4, see Dafflon and Mischler (2008) and Dafflon (2012). For a practical detailed exposé of the three-steps method described in Table 4.3 and its components in Table 4.4, see www.fr.ch/Scom/sommaire/perequation-financière-intercommunale.
8. Higher wages in extractive industries may reflect in part the risk of workplace accidents; this is not accounted for in equalization calculations.

REFERENCES

ACIR (1962), 'Measures of state and local fiscal capacity and tax effort', The Advisory Commission on Intergovernmental Relations, October, M-16, accessed 11 March 2019 at https://library.unt.edu/gpo/acir/Reports/information/M-16.pdf.

Ahmad, E. and J. Craig (1997), 'Intergovernmental transfers', in T. Ter-Minassian (ed.), *Fiscal Federalism in Theory and Practice*, International Monetary Fund, Washington, DC, pp. 73–107.

Australian Government, Commonwealth Grants Commission, 'Fiscal Equalisation', accessed 12 September 2019 at https://www.cgc.gov.au/about-us/fiscal-equalisation.

Bahl, R.W. (1972), 'A representative tax system approach to measuring tax effort in developing countries', *Staff Papers (International Monetary Fund)*, **19** (1), 87–124.

Bird, R. and F. Vaillancourt (2007), 'Expenditure-based equalization transfers', in J. Martinez-Vazquez and B. Searle (eds), *Fiscal Equalization: Challenges in the Design of Intergovernmental Transfers*, Springer, New York, pp. 259–89.

Boadway, R. and F. Flatters (1982), 'Efficiency and equalization payments in a federal system of government: a synthesis and extension of recent results', *Canadian Journal of Economics*, **15** (4), 613–33.

Boex, J. and J. Martinez-Vazquez (2007), 'Designing intergovernmental equalization transfers with imperfect data: concepts, practices, and lessons', in J. Martinez-Vazquez and B. Searle (eds), *Fiscal Equalization: Challenges in the Design of Intergovernmental Transfers*, Springer, New York, pp. 291–343.

Break, G. (1980), *Financing Government in a Federal System*, The Brookings Institution, Washington, DC.

Buchanan, J.M. (1950), 'Federalism and fiscal equity', *American Economic Review*, **40** (4), 583–99.

Buchanan, J.M. (1952), 'Federal grants and resource allocation', *Journal of Political Economy*, **60** (3), 208–17.

Buchanan, J.M. (2002), 'Fiscal equalization revisited', accessed 11 March 2019 at http://www.iedm.org/files/011025.

Buchanan, J.M. and C.J. Goetz (1972), 'Efficiency limits of fiscal mobility: an assessment of the Tiebout model', *Journal of Public Economics*, **1** (1), 25–43.

Chernick, H. and A. Reschovsky (2015), 'The fiscal health of U.S. cities', in R.M. Bird and E. Slack (eds), *Is Your City Healthy? Measuring Urban Fiscal Health*, Institute on Municipal Finance and Governance, Toronto, pp. 83–117.

Commonwealth Grants Commission (2015), 'Report on GST revenue sharing relativities 2015 review: volume 1', Australian Government, Canberra, accessed 7 March 2019 at www.cgc.gov.au/sites/g/files/net5366/f/documents/2015%20Review%20Report/Report/R2015%20Report%20-%20Volume%201%20-%20Main%20Report.pdf.

Courchene, T.J. (2013), 'Surplus recycling and the Canadian Federation addressing horizontal and vertical fiscal imbalances', Mowat Centre, accessed 3 March 2019 at https://mowatcentre.ca/surplus-recycling-and-the-canadian-federation.

Dafflon, B. (1995), *Fédéralisme et solidarité*, Institute of Federalism, University of Fribourg, Series Études et Colloques 15, Helbing & Lichtenhahn, Basle and Fribourg.

Dafflon, B. (2007), 'Fiscal capacity equalization in horizontal fiscal equalization programs', in R. Boadway and A. Shah (eds), *Intergovernmental Fiscal Transfers: Principles and Practice*, Public Sector, Governance and Accountability Series, The World Bank, Washington, DC, pp. 361–96.

Dafflon, B. (2012), 'Solidarity and the design of equalization: setting out the issues', *eJournal of Tax Research*, **10** (1), 138–64.

Dafflon, B. (2015), 'Analyse de performance de la péréquation intercommunale dans le canton de Fribourg', Rapport à l'intention de la Direction des institutions, de l'agriculture et des forêts, Canton de Fribourg, Suisse, accessed 3 March 2019 at www.fr.ch/Scom/sommaire/perequation-financière-intercommunale/rapports des experts.

Dafflon, B. and P. Mischler (2008), 'Expenditure needs equalisation at the local level: methods and practice', in J. Kim and J. Lotz (eds), *Measuring Local*

Government Expenditure Needs, Danish Ministry of Social Welfare, Copenhagen and Korea Institute of Public Finance, Seoul, pp. 213–40.

Dafflon, B. and F. Vaillancourt (2003), 'Problems of equalisation in federal systems', in R. Blindenbacher and A. Koller (eds), *Federalism in a Changing World: Learning from Each Other*, McGill-Queen's University Press, Kingston, pp. 395–411.

Ebel, R.D. and J.E. Petersen (eds) (2012), *The Oxford Handbook of State and Local Government Finance*, Oxford University Press, New York.

Gilbert, G. (1996), 'Le fédéralisme financier: perspectives de microéconomie spatiale', *Revue Économique*, **47** (2), 311–63.

Gusen, P. (2012), 'Expenditure need: equalization's other half', Mowat Center, accessed 3 March 2019 at https://mowatcentre.ca/wp-content/uploads/publications /46_expenditure_need.pdf.

Inman, R.F. and D.L. Rubinfeld (1996), 'Designing tax policy in federalist economies: an overview', *Journal of Public Economics*, **60** (3), 307–34.

Kim, J. and J. Lotz (eds) (2008), *Measuring Local Government Expenditure Needs*, Danish Ministry of Social Welfare, Copenhagen and Korea Institute of Public Finance, Seoul.

King, D. (1997), 'Intergovernmental fiscal relations: concepts and models', in R.C. Fisher (ed.), *Intergovernmental Fiscal Relations*, Kluwer, Dordrecht, pp. 19–58.

Koller, A., D. Thürer, B. Dafflon, B. Ehrenzeller, T. Pfisterer and B. Waldmann (2012), *Principles of Federalism: Guidelines for Good Federal Practices – A Swiss Contribution*, Dike Publishers, Zurich.

Ladd, H.F. (1999), 'Fiscal disparities', in J.J. Cordes, R.D. Ebel and J.G. Gravelle (eds), *The Encyclopedia of Taxation and Tax Policy*, The Urban Institute, Washington, DC, pp. 123–35.

Oakland, W.H. (1994), 'Recognizing and correcting for fiscal disparities: a critical analysis', in J.E. Anderson (ed.), *Fiscal Equalization for State and Local Government Finance*, Praeger, Westport, pp. 1–19.

OECD (2007), 'Fiscal equalisation in OECD countries', OECD Network on Fiscal Relations across Levels of Government, Paris, accessed 13 March 2019 at https:// www.oecd.org/ctp/federalism/39234016.pdf.

Reschovsky, A. (2007), 'Compensating local governments for differences in expenditure needs in a horizontal fiscal equalization program', in R. Boadway and A. Shah (eds), *Intergovernmental Fiscal Transfers: Principles and Practice*, Public Sector, Governance and Accountability Series, The World Bank, Washington, DC, pp. 397–424.

Roy-César, Edison (2013), 'Canada's equalization formula', Library of Parliament, accessed 13 September 2019 at https://lop.parl.ca/sites/PublicWebsite/default/ en_CA/ResearchPublications/200820E#a1.

Scott, A.D. (1950), 'A note on grants in federal countries', *Economica*, **17** (64), 416–22.

Shah, A. (1996), 'A fiscal need approach to equalization', *Canadian Public Policy: Analyse de Politiques*, **22** (2), 99–115.

Shah, A. (2008), 'Fiscal need equalization: is it worth doing? Lessons from international practices', in J. Kim and J. Lotz (eds), *Measuring Local Government Expenditure Needs*, Danish Ministry of Social Welfare, Copenhagen and Korea Institute of Public Finance, Seoul, pp. 35–60.

Smart, M. and R. Bird (1996), 'Federal fiscal arrangements in Canada: an analysis of incentives', *Proceedings of the Annual Conference on Taxation Held under the*

Auspices of the National Tax Association, Tax Institute of America, Washington DC, vol. 89, pp. 1–10; also accessed 7 March 2019 at http://homes.chass.utoronto.ca/~msmart/wp/cits.pdf.

Von Hagen, J. (2000), 'Fiscal policy and intra-national risk sharing', in G.D. Hess and E. van Wincoop (eds), *Intranational Macroeconomics*, Cambridge University Press, Cambridge, pp. 272–94.

Watts, R.L. (2008), *Comparing Federal Systems*, third edition, Institute of Intergovernmental Relations, McGill University Press, Montreal and Kingston.

Yerly, N. (2013), 'The political economy of budget rules in the twenty-six Swiss cantons: institutional analysis, preferences and performances', PhD thesis, Faculty of Economics and Social Sciences, University of Fribourg, Switzerland.

Yilmaz, S., F. Vaillancourt and B. Dafflon (2012), 'State and local government finance: why it matters', in E. Ebel and J.E. Petersen (eds), *The Oxford Handbook of State and Local Government Finance*, Oxford University Press, New York, pp. 105–35.

PART II

Intergovernmental Transfers in Mature
Federations

5. The German model of addressing vertical and horizontal fiscal imbalances

Paul B. Spahn

5.1 INSTITUTIONAL SETUP OF THE MODERN GERMAN FEDERATION

Today's Germany consists of 16 states (*Länder*) with their own constitutions, which are entrenched in the federation as sovereign entities. Local governments enjoy budget autonomy, but are subject to policy constraints determined by their respective state. As a concession to German history there are three city-states, Hamburg and Bremen – the 'Hanse cities' – and Berlin, which introduces minor asymmetries into intergovernmental fiscal relations since these states execute local government function as well.

In order to achieve similar or equivalent living conditions and homogeneity of policies, there must be uniform – typically centralized[1] – guiding principles for the whole nation. This by itself introduces a new type of asymmetry at the vertical level.

While other federations such as the United States or Canada accept concurring sovereignties at various levels, with full taxing and expenditure powers for each tier, the German model of federalism can be characterized as asymmetrical power-sharing among tiers of government. In this different paradigm, the federation (apart from its exclusive competencies such as foreign affairs and defence) sets out a general framework for policymaking for all *Länder* (and eventually municipalities), while the latter implement and administer such policies within the general framework. The historic roots of this form of power-sharing can also be found in the German Reich where the states (and municipalities) had already had a long tradition of public administration that the centre could build upon, while the Reich itself had no comparable infrastructure on its own (excepting the structures for its newly acquired exclusive responsibilities such as defence).

The vertical sharing of powers is as follows:

- The federation exercises
  - Exclusive powers conferred to the federation by constitution (e.g. defence, foreign policy, citizenship);
  - Concurrent powers, where both federal and state governments may act or intervene, but the federal rule overrides the states if in conflict (e.g. civil law, labour legislation, public welfare).
- The sovereign states control
  - All residual powers (e.g. education, culture, police, hospitals).

As a rule, legislation is typically centralized in Germany (federal) where the states, as said, inject their voice conjointly through the vote by the state house (Bundesrat). However, the administration or implementation of laws and their enforcement as well as public service delivery are almost entirely decentralized. Formerly the federation had the power to legislate an incomplete 'framework', which the states had to complete by state legislation. This led to conflicts because the federal power to legislate was not well determined. Framework legislation was hence abolished in 2006.[2]

Homogeneity of policies is also fostered at the national level through the voting mechanism for the national parliament (Bundestag), which follows the model of proportional representation while excluding all parties that fall below 5 per cent of the vote. This provision tends to neutralize extremist and factional parties, which had once played a key role in ruining the Weimar democracy. This mechanism represents another example of asymmetric institutions designed to foster homogeneity and ultimately symmetry of outcomes at the national level.

Although the political landscape has varied quite considerably during the history of the Federal Republic of Germany – with new entrants in parliament such as the greens, the former communists, and, more recently, a nationalistic party – the political system and its institutions are relatively robust, relying heavily on consensus-forming according to the preferences of the median-voter. He or she will ultimately determine the pace of politics at the national level, and the states and municipalities are being compelled to implement and administer such policies within a common national framework. Collective decision-making in the Bundesrat is another mechanism to form consensus.

The limited policy discretion at lower tiers of government, and the 'emptiness of the agenda' of state parliaments combined with the inability of states to use own tax instruments, is exacerbated by a host of intergovernmental transfers that are all destined to foster national homogeneity and similarity of living conditions. It begins with the formula apportionment of the jointly appropriated value added tax (VAT) onto regions (mainly population based and highly equalizing); it proceeds through the horizontal redistribution of resources among states according to the Equalization Law (*Finanzausgleich*); and is completed through a number of asymmetrical vertical grants by the federal government in favour of some 'needy states' however defined. This interregional solidarity is pushed to a point where the average command of public resources per capita is now very close to the national average per capita.[3]

5.2   THE MAIN TRAITS OF THE GERMAN FINANCIAL ARRANGEMENTS

Intergovernmental revenue allocation follows four steps in Germany:

- First, the Constitution assigns own resources, including shared revenues, to each layer of government (*revenue allocation*).
- Second, the VAT shares are gauged in a way to align aggregate revenue with aggregate expenditures for each layer of government (*vertical fiscal balance*).
- Third, the allocation of resources to states aims at achieving *horizontal fiscal balance*. In this regard there are two distinctive mechanisms:
  a) The aggregate VAT share is distributed predominantly on the basis of population, which is implicitly equalizing (*equalization effects of VAT*); and then
  b) State revenues are reallocated among jurisdictions in line with their fiscal capacities (*explicit horizontal equalization*, or *Finanzausgleich* in a narrow sense).
- Fourth, the federation completes horizontal equalization by supplying supplementary funds to selected states according to legislation (*asymmetrical vertical compensations*).

5.2.1   Revenue Allocation

It is consistent with the nature of German fiscal federal arrangements that taxes are not only uniform but also shared. This is true for all major taxes representing about three-quarters of total revenue (including the main municipal tax, the *Gewerbesteuer*).

The sharing of tax revenues is illustrated in Figure 5.1. Revenue from exclusive state taxes is only three per cent of the total; municipalities collect local taxes that represent about nine per cent of all taxes. The majority of all taxes is collected conjointly as shared taxes that ought to be passed on through redistributive mechanisms. This leads not only to a jumble of political responsibilities; it also tapers financial autonomy through the

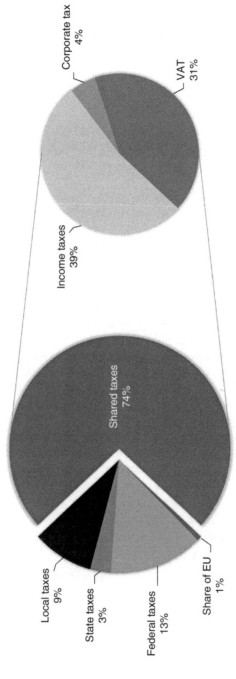

Source: Author's calculation from the Federal Ministry of Finance.

Figure 5.1 The structure of assigned and shared taxes in Germany, 2017

packaging of tax policy and a mix-up of joint financing schemes. These limitations at the fiscal edge are now widely considered to narrow state sovereignties in particular. They tend to blur political accountability and restrain the principle of subsidiarity.

5.2.2   Vertical Fiscal Balance

5.2.2.1   Gauging the VAT share

The federal and *Länder* shares of corporate tax and income tax are invariably laid down in the Constitution (the Grundgesetz – GG). The vertical sharing of key taxes in Germany is depicted in Table 5.1. Half of the revenue from income taxes is allocated to both the federation and the states – with municipalities participating in the share of personal income taxes. This rule is technically simple, even as to their horizontal apportionment, which follows the derivation principle,[4] except for the wage tax that is allocated according to the residence of the taxpayer.

However, the allocation of VAT can, and will, be flexibly adapted to vertical fiscal imbalances between the federal government, the *Länder* and the municipalities. Hence VAT sharing plays the decisive role in establishing vertical fiscal balance. It aims at correcting differences in financial strength (without, however, fully offsetting them); at supporting financial self-responsibility of the states; and at securing 'fairness' among the federation and its constituent states. Indeed, the states' shares have moved considerably, notably increasing after unification. This reflects the need to reach consensus with the old states on the incorporation of the new states into the intergovernmental fiscal machinery. A compromise was found only at the expense of the federal share in VAT.[5]

The vertical equalization among the federation and the states through VAT sharing is based on article 106, sections 3–9 of the Constitution, and a federal law requiring the consent of the Bundesrat governs the allocation

Table 5.1   The vertical distribution of shared taxes, 2017

	Income tax	Corporate tax	VAT
Federation	42.5%	50%	≈ 49.7%
States	42.5%	50%	≈ 48.3%
Local governments	15.0%	–	≈ 2.2%
Allocation criteria:	*Derivation*		*¾ population* *¼ 'frail' states*

Sources: Constitution, and Ministry of Finance.

of its proceeds. The Constitution presumes that it is possible to define 'necessary expenditures' at both levels – state and federal governments – and to achieve a 'fair compensation' (*billiger Ausgleich*) between them (article 106, section 3). Technically, this is approximated by calculating 'coverage ratios' (*Deckungsquoten*), which represent the arithmetical ratio of income (excluding income from loans) to expenditure (excluding expenses for repayments) for each level of government in the aggregate. The coverage ratios are then used to determine resulting gaps and hence the aggregate claims on VAT between tiers of government.

According to the objectives of the Constitution, and to the way VAT is calculated to cover potential vertical gaps in financing, there is no 'vertical fiscal imbalance' in Germany as exists in other federations with exclusive tax assignments (such as Australia or Canada). This may be considered an advantage, although the political and technical implementation of this constitutional rule is fraught with problems and always subject to dispute.

5.2.2.2 Equalizing effects of VAT

It is important to note that the derivation and residency principles for allocating taxes to lower-tier governments play up economic imbalances that may exist among them. This is true in particular for personal and corporate income taxes in Germany. However, the VAT share is not allocated according to derivation, but predominantly by the number of inhabitants. In addition, states with below-average tax revenues receive so-called supplementary VAT shares. These allocation rules mitigate the differences of fiscal capacity among regions. Although this can be considered a first step towards horizontal equalization, this interpretation is officially rejected in Germany since the VAT share constitutes 'own revenue' of the states; it is not considered a vertical federal grant with equalizing effects (as in Australia, for instance).

As to the horizontal allocation of VAT, three-quarters of VAT is apportioned to the states according to population in a first instance. The other quarter is reserved for those states that are considered 'financially frail'. They receive supplementary transfers from VAT in order to bring their fiscal potential up to at least 92 per cent of the average of total state taxes per capita.[6]

The implicit redistribution effects of VAT sharing are often underestimated. When considering only the new states of the East (without Berlin), their initial tax potential was only 8.9 per cent of the national average, but reached a level of 13.3 per cent of the national average including VAT revenues in 2016. It implies that Eastern states acquire roughly 60 per cent more VAT per capita than their Western counterparts.

The equalizing effects of the VAT sharing process are indeed extensive.

They reduce the (unweighted) standard deviation for own state revenues per capita of 28.5 per cent before VAT to 7.2 per cent after VAT. Although the population-based allocation of VAT has significant levelling effects, this is officially not considered part of the *Finanzausgleich* in Germany since the VAT shares represent own state revenue in a legal sense.

5.2.3   Horizontal Fiscal Balance

5.2.3.1   Equalization 'philosophies'

Whatever approach is taken to establish horizontal fiscal balance in a nation, there must be clear procedures and firm criteria that govern equalization. At the international level, interregional equalization schemes have adopted varying philosophies.

- In the United States, for instance, an explicit regional redistribution programme is nonexistent, but there are implicit redistribution effects resulting, for instance, from the workings of a progressive national income tax. Also, there are regional asymmetries entrenched in the multitude of federal programmes entailing either transfers to persons, or specific-purpose or block grants to regional jurisdictions. However, the regional pattern of redistribution will fluctuate in accordance to variations in the local 'take-up' rate of such grants, in particular for cost-sharing programmes.
- At the other extreme, Australia has put in place an explicit and ambitious equalization scheme that underpins the distribution of goods and services tax (GST) revenue to the states and territories. In establishing a point of reference for such a scheme, Australia does not only attempt to evaluate detailed standardized taxing powers of her states, but also standardized expenditures adjusted for needs and costs differentials among jurisdictions.
- In Germany (like in Canada) the focus of equalization is on taxable capacity only, with little or no concern for specific burdens. As the tax law is uniform throughout Germany (except for some limited discretion of municipalities to vary their tax rates), there is no need to standardize taxable capacity among regions (as in Canada), because *effective* tax collections can be considered to reflect the regional variations of tax potentials.[7]

5.2.3.2   Explicit horizontal equalization (*Finanzausgleich*)

In addition to the implicit redistribution effects of joint taxes, in particular of VAT, there is an explicit regional equalization programme that is working horizontally among states in a 'brotherly fashion' (*Finanzausgleich*, or equalization proper). Indeed, this scheme leads to a horizontal redistribution of resources among the states without federal interference (except for legislation and administration). It is the logical consequence for a situation where there is no vertical fiscal imbalance. Where such imbalances do exist – as in Australia in favour of the Commonwealth, or in the European Union (EU) in favour of the member states – regional equalization schemes would typically be implemented in the form of vertically asymmetrical per capita grants (downwards in Australia, upwards in the EU). In the absence of vertical imbalance, however, regional equalization must be arranged horizontally among the participating states. Germany is distinctive in having created such a system among states,[8] which is, of course, based on a federal law governing the mechanics of the scheme with uniform rules.

The definition of differentials in tax capacities requires a benchmark. It is found in a standardized 'equalization yardstick' (*Ausgleichsmesszahl*) for state fiscal potentials, which is roughly the average tax revenue per capita, including VAT, multiplied by the population for each state. The procedure is, however, more complex. In particular it comprises an asymmetric bias in favour of city-states, whose populations are weighted by a factor of 1.35 (compared to 1.0 for the other states), and other special provisions.[9]

The equalization yardstick is compared with the effective financial situation of each state, and the gap is subsequently equalized according to a formula. States below the average (*ausgleichsberechtigte Länder*) receive a compensation that is to be financed, in progressive steps, by the states above the average (*ausgleichspflichtige Länder*). The sum of payments received always equals the sum of disbursements; the scheme is thus a complete clearing mechanism. In the interest of the fiscal autonomy and sovereignty of the states, the differences in state fiscal capacities are only partially increased or reduced by financial equalization.

The size of the compensation payments to fiscally weaker states depends on the amount by which their financial capacity per (fictitious) inhabitant falls below the average financial capacity per inhabitant. A linear-progressive compensation schedule is used to calculate by how much the difference from the average is partially topped-up. Similarly, the size of the adjustment amounts that fiscally stronger states have to pay depends on the amount by which their per capita financial capacity exceeds the average fiscal capacity per inhabitant. The difference from the average is skimmed off partially using a progressive 'tariff' (*Ausgleichstarif*).[10]

5.2.3.3 Asymmetrical vertical compensations

In a final step, there is a corrective of the distribution of public resources in the form of asymmetrical vertical grants by the federal government: so-called supplementary federal grants (*Bundesergänzungszuweisungen*).

They exhibit both vertical and horizontal equalization effects. Such transfers according to article 107(2) of the GG have been widely used after unification, while they were almost insignificant before. They were also decisive in establishing consensus among the various jurisdictions with the aim of compensating the formerly socialist Eastern states.

Two types of federal supplementary grants are to be distinguished: (i) general federal supplementary grants to cover the general financial requirements of all underperforming states in the amount of 77.5 per cent of the deficits remaining after the implementation of the *Länder* fiscal equalization system (at 99.5 per cent of the equalization yardstick). All states receive this type of gap-filling grant to varying degrees. (ii) Moreover, 10 states out of 16 receive 'special-needs' federal grants to relieve them of the costs of 'political management' (*politische Führung*), and the new Eastern states as well as some Western counterparts receive federal grants in compensation of 'special burdens', for example, higher unemployment.

The federal grants have met criticism not only by economists, who tend to stress the inefficiencies of 'softening' budget constraints, but also by politicians and lawyers – and specifically the Constitutional Court – who stress the excessive redistribution effects of this type of grant. The Constitution had reserved such forms of asymmetrical vertical intervention by the federal government for exceptional circumstances (such as unification, for instance); there was no intention to use them as regular instruments for 'filling gaps' in the budgets of a majority of states.

5.2.3.4   Comprehensive allocation and distribution effects

The importance by volume of each of the three steps of horizontal equalization is shown in Table 5.2.

If the equalizing effects of the various steps of resource allocation and distribution are combined, measured in terms of deviations from their averages in per cent, the picture in Figure 5.2 is obtained.

Table 5.2   Volume of redistributed resources, 2016

VAT (only supplement payments)	*Finanzausgleich* equalization 'proper'	Federal supplementary grants
In billions of euros		
15.3	10.6	9.9
In per cent of total fiscal capacity		
4.6%	3.2%	3.0%

Source: Bundesministerium der Finanzen (2017).

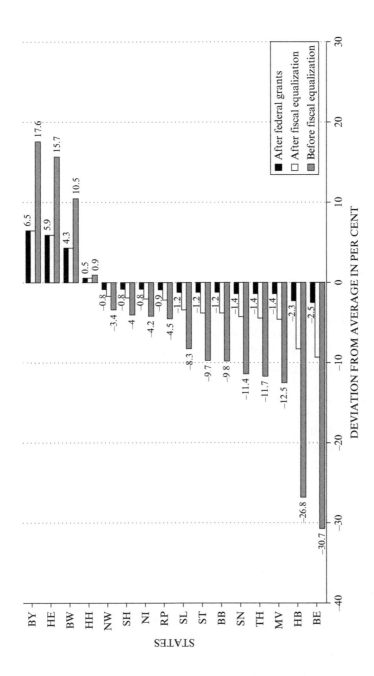

Sources: Federal Ministry of Finance (2017); own representation.

Figure 5.2 Horizontal distribution effects of VAT allocations, of fiscal equalization and of federal supplementary grants in 2017

The figure shows that the equalization fund is 'sponsored' by three larger Southern states (Bavaria, Baden-Württemberg and Hessen) and the city-state of Hamburg. All other states benefit from the scheme at varying degrees.

5.2.4 Solidarity versus Efficiency

While interjurisdictional solidarity through equalization facilitates consensus within an intergovernmental framework, and has achieved a high degree of homogeneity in policy outcomes, this is not without political and economic costs. The redistributive process among states and among the federation and lower tiers of government breaks the link that should exist between expenditure decisions and their financing. This reduces the accountability of policymakers, and diminishes the influence citizen-voters can exert on politicians. Moreover, the German states lose any interest in developing their own tax bases, for instance through more effective tax administration or better economic policies. In a formal sense, inter-regional solidarity tends to reduce the financial autonomy of states even further – which is severely curtailed by the Constitution anyway. This jeopardizes the independence of their budgeting, and hence of policies. Moreover, equalization arrangements that put high penalties on any excess fiscal capacity relative to the national average tend to encourage inefficient budget behaviour, especially if combined with federal grants that effectively bail out non-performing governments.

The analysis of the implicit marginal burden inherent in the combined system of interstate equalization poses the question, how much of a ficti-tious increment of own revenues of a state will ultimately remain at the disposition of that state? Conversely, what would the implicit marginal burden on incremental own revenue be? If a state is guaranteed a mini-mum, and if that state's resources fall below that minimum, any increment of own resources is virtually 'taxed' or diverted through the system of equalization. This explains the lack of interest of such states in developing their own tax base.

Figure 5.3 indicates the high degree of implicit marginal burdens on own taxes inherent in the German system of intergovernmental finance. It depicts 'marginal retention rates' for selected taxes, that is, it shows what a state will keep from any amount of additional tax collected in its jurisdiction.

If, for instance, a state makes an explicit effort to increase its tax revenue, say, of the corporate tax through better tax administration, most of it will be lost through redistribution among states. Hamburg is in the privileged position to keep at least 26.6 per cent of the additional corporate tax collected, a maximum. Neighbouring Bremen retains only 0.7 per cent. For wage taxes, the marginal retention rates vary between about 33 and 7

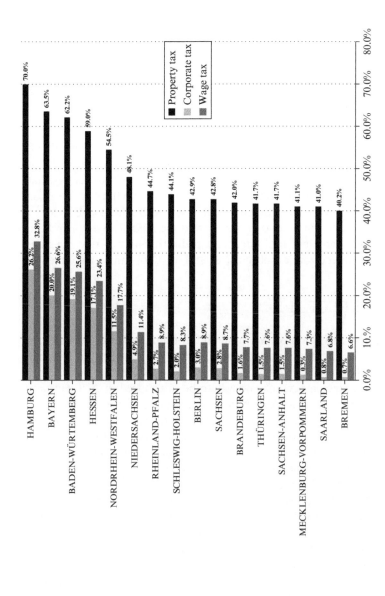

Sources: Wissenschaftlicher Beirat (2015); own calculations and representation.

Figure 5.3   Marginal retention rates in per cent for selected taxes collected by a state

per cent. Of course, there is little incentive to increase tax collections under these circumstances.

The marginal retention rates are highest for the local property tax, but even this tax, which is acclaimed to be an ideal local tax because of its immobile tax base and hence full local incidence, exhibits severe 'leakages' in Germany. From additional property tax, municipalities retain only between 70 and 40 per cent according to the state they are in. The rest is 'taxed' through equalization.

A further aspect of the system is related to potential moral hazard by state authorities. A transfer system that takes actual revenue and expenditures into account, such as the federal supplementary grants, favours irresponsible budget behaviour. Subnational governments are almost invited to carry budget deficits, since they can expect, through the principle of intergovernmental solidarity, to receive compensating grants to a large degree. Hence, a state can spend more than corresponds to its original fiscal capacity, knowing, or confiding in, that the community of states or the federal government will ultimately bail it out. Although it is difficult to prove such behaviour in practice, it is true that the *Finanzausgleich* and the federal grants soften any hard budget constraint that may exist at the state level. This entails economic inefficiencies and waste of public resources.

5.3   THE REFORM 2020

The financial constitution of Germany did not remain without challenge. In particular two of the larger contributors to the scheme, Bavaria and Hesse, have asked for a verdict of the Constitutional Court on the arrangements in 2013. Since a new scheme was to be introduced in 2020 anyway, there was a broad discussion that produced a number of reform proposals, inter alia from the Scientific Council at the Federal Minister of Finance.[11]

The Council called for greater transparency of intergovernmental finance, for mitigating disincentives in revenue policy through higher retention rates, and the inclusion of all local taxes conjointly with a reduction of the progressivity of the compensation tariff for *Finanzausgleich*. Since the reform of the federal fiscal equalization system is made more difficult by the limited ability of the states to generate their own revenues, a reform was also expected to ensure greater revenue autonomy. To strengthen tax autonomy, the Council proposed in particular a limited surcharge on income tax or property tax.

The reform, decided in June 2017, brought some marginal changes avoiding more comprehensive systemic changes to the system. From 2020 on,

- The VAT allocation mechanism will be consolidated and simplified.
- The compensation tariff will be fixed at a uniform 63 per cent of the deficits or surpluses relative to average national financial capacity.
- The share of municipal taxes to be incorporated is raised from 64 to 75 per cent.
- The tariff of the general federal supplementary grants is raised in favour of financially weak states.
- The scope of special-needs federal supplementary grants is extended, and partly increased.

So, the reform 2020 of the German financial constitution does not touch upon the fundamentals of the system, but simplifies (VAT allocations), extends (higher share of municipal taxes; federal supplementary grants) and also reduces the scale of progressivity. Like after unification, agreement among the states was once again reached by the federal government tossing in additional own resources. However, the federal government also acquired more constitutional powers than before.

The Constitution stipulates the 'creation of equivalent living conditions' in Germany, and a comparable performance of tasks in the case of different economic conditions among states. This is to be achieved by vertical and horizontal equalization as discussed. However, the new rules from 2020 onwards are unlikely to noticeably counteract the increasing inequality in the distribution of general funds and total available revenues.

> The new financial equalization system also falls short in terms of transparency. Many special regulations and new interdependencies between the Federal Government and the *Länder* are creating new systemic dependencies. And it can be assumed that the federal government will let its more powerful position vis-à-vis the *Länder* be felt.[12]

Finally, it is unlikely that the setup of the German financial constitution will change dramatically given that the majority of states, which exert strong legislative voting powers through the second chamber of parliament, are still at the receiving end of the scheme.

5.4 LOCAL FINANCES

5.4.1 Municipal Own Revenue

German local governments possess an autonomous status under federal and state legislation. This status is guaranteed by the Constitution (art.

28, s 2): 'The municipalities must be guaranteed the right to regulate all affairs of the local community under their own responsibility within the framework of the law. . . . The guarantee of self-administration also includes the principles of financial self-responsibility . . .'. The municipalities are responsible for all tasks rooted in the local community (principle of universality).

As to their own resources, municipalities control the property tax, the trade tax (*Gewerbesteuer*, a tax on business profits) and local excise duties and expense taxes. The structure of local revenues in Germany is depicted in Figure 5.4.

While own resources of municipalities constitute a significant part of their aggregate revenue, their grants dependency remains relatively high on average (40 per cent of total revenue). In addition to grants, municipal finances benefit from the direct sharing of state taxes such as the personal income tax (15 per cent of total tax), the capital yields tax (12 per cent) and the VAT (2.2 per cent), and the obligatory indirect sharing of *Länder* revenues from income tax, corporate tax and turnover tax in accordance with the respective state legislation. Conversely, the municipalities must share the trade tax with their state and the federation in a standardized form using a complex algorithm and differentiated parameters. Of course, there are large discrepancies in local revenue among states and, within states, among municipalities. One important political indicator for Germany is the relative fiscal capacity between Western and Eastern states, which was roughly 100:78 per capita in 2016.

A large part of municipal taxes is derived from the property and trade taxes, where local revenue autonomy is expressed through optional municipal tax rate setting (on a nationally standardized tax base to be assessed by their respective state). Obviously, there is a large variation of tax rates among German municipalities (see Table 5.3).

Of course, differences in local tax rates entail horizontal tax competition among jurisdictions, except for the property tax where the tax base is immobile. In particular, differences in trade tax rates may have a significant impact on locational decisions of firms. If an enterprise has permanent establishments in several municipalities, or if the permanent establishment extends over the territory of several municipalities, the tax assessment amount is distributed to an individual municipality on the basis of payroll.

As discussed before, a certain portion of the (standardized[13]) trade tax is shared with the federal and state governments. This, together with the inclusion of municipal taxes in the interstate equalization formula, leads to a significant 'confiscation' of own resources through redistribution even for classical local taxes such as the property tax (see Figure 5.4). So, the German local tax system is far from being neutral as to the allocation of

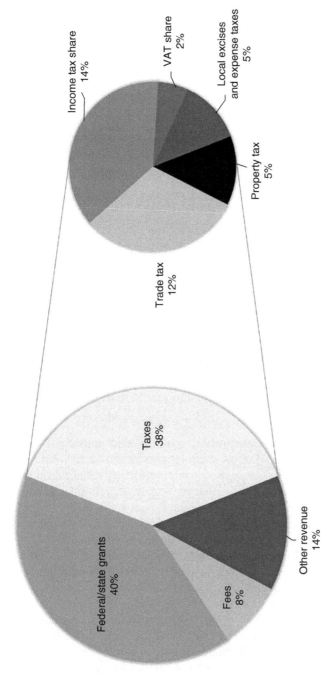

Income tax share
14%

VAT share
2%

Local excises
and expense taxes
5%

Property tax
5%

Trade tax
12%

Taxes
38%

Other revenue
14%

Fees
8%

Federal/state grants
40%

Sources: Deutscher Städtetag (2017); own calculations and representation.

Figure 5.4 The structure of German municipal revenues, 2017

*Table 5.3   The variation of tax rates (*Hebesätze*) among German municipalities**

	Property tax A	Property tax B	Trade tax
Lowest	100%	100%	200%
Highest	690%	700%	900%
Average	343%	377%	369%
Coefficient of variation	6.7%	7.5%	5.9%

Note: * Excepting outliers. The tax rate is uniform and incorporated in the taxable base. The *Hebesatz* (leverage ratio) allows the increase of that rate implicitly.

Sources: Statistische Ämter des Bundes und der Länder (2017); own calculations.

own revenue. This is true in particular for the trade tax where municipalities compete for investors through attractive rates.[14]

5.4.2   Grants and Intermunicipal Equalization

The basis of the municipal equalization system is found in article 106, paragraph 7 of the GG:

> From the state share of the total revenue of joint taxes, a percentage to be determined by the state legislation shall flow to the municipalities and associations of municipalities. Moreover, the state legislation determines whether and to what extent the revenue of the state taxes accrues to the municipalities (associations of municipalities).

Article 107(2) of the Constitution requires that municipal financial resources be equalized to allow them to provide standard local services. However, since the responsibility for intermunicipal equalization rests in the hands of the state, it follows that the various intermunicipal equalization systems vary to a considerable degree.

Typically, however, there are asymmetrical vertical state grants that complement the municipalities' own resources in each state.[15]

This is effected through an equalization fund (*Verbundmasse*) destined to support local governments, whose volume is determined by the annual state budget. It corresponds normally to a share of state taxes, the state share of joint taxes, and of transfers. As a rule, the fund is split into separate subfunds for different categories of local government (cities, counties (*Kreise*), municipalities). From the fund (or sub-funds), a percentage determined by a formula is assigned to each municipality (*Schlüsselzuweisungen*).

To determine this percentage, the tax potential (*Steuerkraftsumme*) of each municipality is examined. In doing so the tax potential is normalized by using standard (average) tax rates for local taxes since tax rates may differ. Normalization is to avoid penalizing (rewarding) local governments whose tax rates are above (below) the average. The fiscal capacity (*FC*) per capita of the municipality is then compared with financial needs (*FN*) per capita.

- If *FN* > *FC* then the municipality is entitled to equalization payments.
- If *FN* < FC then the municipality will not receive transfers, but usually does not have to pay either (except in Brandenburg and Schleswig-Holstein).

The resulting 'gap' is not fully equalized. Equalization transfers may cover between 50 and 90 per cent of the fiscal gap.

All federal states assume that the demand for public services does not grow proportionally with the size of a municipality. Instead, larger cities provide infrastructure and related services (including for the surrounding area) that smaller cities do not have: public transport, schools, clinics, museums, theatres – that grow disproportionately with the size of the municipality. They also have greater responsibilities in social protection to cope with: the unemployed and other transfer recipients such as migrants are often concentrated in the cities, and facilities and services to cope with their needs must be made available. Municipal financial equalization, which is based on a per capita financial requirement, takes this into account by giving greater weight to the population figures of larger cities (*Einwohnerveredelung*).

Finally, some states also account for special needs (*Sonderbedarfe*) such as culture, transportation of pupils, and so on, and for area size, in particular for rural counties. In other *Länder* social burdens are taken into account, for example, on the basis of the number of unemployed. Also, in most Länder the needs-measurement figure is fictitious; it is not based on actual financial needs, but determined in such a way that the *Verbundmasse* provided for in the *Land* budget is actually exhausted by all the municipalities of the respective type.

In the state of Hessen, for example, the municipal equalization fund consists of about a quarter of the state resources from income tax, corporate tax, VAT, motor vehicle tax, property transactions tax and the state share of the municipal trade tax (*Gewerbesteuer*). Its size depends on an analysis of financial needs in the past to establish vertical fiscal balance in a similar vein as for federal-state relations. However, there are additional constraints to be observed.

Table 5.4   Specific transfers from the Land *Hessen to its municipalities*

Specific recurrent transfers	Specific capital transfers
● Expenditures for schools (incl. student care) ● Social expenditures ● Alleviation of the burden from labour market reform ● Local care for children and youths ● Subsidies for kindergartens and for care of the under 3-year-olds ● Recurrent cost of public transportation ● Theatre, libraries, museums, music schools, culture ● Maintenance of roads, interest subsidies for special investments	● General investment (lump sum) ● Construction of roads ● Public transportation ● Institutions for old-age care ● Village refurbishment and renovation ● Water and sewage plants ● Hospitals

In Hessen, the State Court of Justice, with its ruling of 21 May 2013, has specified two levels of financial resources to be observed for each municipality: the 'minimum financial envelope' must be calculated in such a way that the municipalities (i) can perform their compulsory tasks; and (ii) are able to fulfil a minimum of voluntary tasks. This level of funding must be ensured by the state irrespective of a municipality's financial capacity. The lynchpin of the resource distribution is, after all, the assumed financial requirements of the municipalities. Its determination is often complex and complicated, and is often at the centre of court disputes.

In addition to general revenue in the form of equalization payments, municipalities may also receive transfers for specific municipal functions. These are given for both recurrent and investment purposes. Examples of these functions are given in Table 5.4.

In addition to these conventional instruments, many *Länder* have set up their own programmes to support structurally indebted municipalities, for which they have found imaginative names (e.g. 'protective umbrella' or 'strengthening pact'). Finally, there are always support programmes and special allocations outside regular municipal equalization, in particular the co-financing of municipal projects.

5.4.3   Cost Sharing and Incentives

There are a very limited number of programmes where the federation (via the state) may co-finance local government activities indirectly. According to article 104b of the Constitution the federation may grant financial aid to the *Länder* for particularly significant investments by the *Länder* and the municipalities (associations of municipalities) in order (i) to prevent a disturbance of the macroeconomic equilibrium; (ii) to balance different economic strengths; or (iii) to promote economic growth. However, it may only provide such funding where it has legislative powers; all objects and measures that fall within the competence of the state are not eligible for funding.

However, the federal government can grant the states financial assistance for nationally important investments by financially weak local governments in the area of municipal education infrastructure (art. 104c). Also, the area of urban renewal and development remains a mixed-funded investment area, to which the federal government can provide financial assistance to be specified in the budget. Previously, the federal government had also responsibility for municipal transport financing (in part) and the promotion of housing, yet these responsibilities have been transferred to the states through a reform on federalism in 2006. The corresponding federal grants continue, but will no longer be earmarked for a specific purpose, and their use was consigned to the budgetary autonomy of the states. The aim was to strengthen state autonomy more generally. However, the states will pass on some of these resources to municipalities in the form of co-financing or matching grants.

Local mass transportation is an area in which the federal government had taken interest by supporting integrated local transport systems and creating incentives for internalizing regional spillovers and fostering inter-municipal cooperation. For this purpose, federal legislation had provided financial aid to the states to improve the conditions for municipal mass transportation (*Gemeindeverkehrsfinanzierungsgesetz*). However, this co-financing was criticized as blurring political accountabilities and setting wrong incentives. In 2007 co-financing between the federation and state governments was hence terminated by the Law on Disentanglement (*Enflechtungsgesetz*), except for some areas (such as regional economic development) that are enumerated in articles 91a-c of the Constitution.

Yet co-financing local mass transportation through matching grants remains a powerful instrument at the state level. Matching grants are probably the only financial instrument with positive incentives in Germany. While this author has advocated for intergovernmental joint financing in the past,[16] it is doubtful whether this kind of incentivizing is appropriate in all circumstances.

Where the matching share of the state is too high (as in the case of mass transportation: 70 per cent of construction costs in Hessen), there is a risk that projects are carried through only because of the grant, and for little other reasons. This may be different where the share is to compensate vertical spillover effects that are measurable.

Performance-based transfers among government do not exist in Germany, which fully respects the sovereignty of states and the financial autonomy of municipalities. Paternalistic financial instruments such as grants based on performance indicators do not fit in such an environment. It is difficult enough to conceive intergovernmental finances in a way to keep the system reasonably incentive-neutral, for example to avoid implicit penalties for making an extra effort in raising taxes through better administration and collection. Given the high degree of interstate redistribution through equalization and the provisions that govern municipal finances this modest goal remains unrealistic in Germany.

NOTES

1. Indeed, centralizing such principles is the rule, but uniform or analogous principles can also be established through horizontal coordination among states. In Germany this is achieved in conferences of state ministries and conforming treaties among governments. One prominent example is the cooperation in education and culture through the Kultusministerkonferenz.
2. The concept was, however, influential on European legislation, which has the instrument of 'directives'. It requires member states to achieve a particular result without dictating the means of achieving it.
3. More precisely: a mainly population-driven equalization yardstick.
4. The horizontal distribution of business taxes is not without problems, however. The regional allocation of the corporate and the local business taxes adopt formulae to count for firms with multiple regional activities (*Zerlegungsgesetz*). The formulae are mainly based on wages (for the producers and distributors of energy: on capital). The same is true for the local business tax (*Gewerbesteuergesetz*).
5. It should be noted, however, that the federal government was partially compensated by higher federal taxes (in particular on mineral oil) and by a federal 'solidarity' surcharge on the income tax.
6. State taxes are defined in paragraph 7(1) Finanzausgleichsgesetz (FAG).
7. A uniform state tax regime is, of course, immune against horizontal tax competition among states in a legal sense. However, there could be incentives for the states to relax their tax administration in an effort to attract and foster economic activities in their jurisdiction. Such incentives are to be expected if the shortfall of revenue from lenient tax administration is fully compensated through equalizing grants, which is true for a number of states in Germany. Although there has been suspicion of leniency in some instances, it is, of course, difficult to prove in practice. The redistribution effects following the primary allocation of taxes will also induce lenient states (strategical reasons, administrative inertia, weaker tax compliance where authorities are seen to be lenient) to go on with their practice since they may make up 92 per cent of the difference through equalization.
8. In Switzerland, the cantons also participate in a horizontal revenue equalization scheme complementary to the vertical confederation-canton equalizing scheme.
9. The equalization yardstick also accounts for tax revenues of the state's municipalities (at 64 per cent). The weighting procedure for the population is ruled in paragraph 9(2) FAG for the states, and in paragraph 9(3) FAG for local governments. For local taxes,

of which municipalities can vary the tax rate, an average national tax rate is used to standardize revenue. The differential weights for city-states and larger municipalities can be interpreted as accounting for some 'agglomeration costs' of larger jurisdictions. The higher weighing of population (between 102 and 105 per cent) for local taxes of the Eastern states Mecklenburg-Vorpommern, Brandenburg and Sachsen-Anhalt is motivated by their sparse population.

10. To ensure the sum of the adjustment amounts corresponds with the sum of the adjustment payments, the adjustment amounts are either increased or decreased by a corresponding percentage.
11. See Wissenschaftlicher Beirat (2015).
12. See Holler and Nürnberger (2017); own translation.
13. In particular, differences in municipal tax rates are evened out to ensure that high taxing municipalities do not have to share their individual tax 'effort' with higher-level jurisdictions (incentive neutrality).
14. It should be noted, however, that revenue from trade tax, which is also very sensitive to the business cycle, is not the only decision parameter for local decision makers. Most municipalities would value the location of firms probably more under the aspect of job creation and job security.
15. There is hence no 'brotherly' horizontal equalization at the municipal (except for Brandenburg and Schleswig-Holstein).
16. Spahn (2015).

REFERENCES

Bundesministerium der Finanzen (2017). 'Bund/Länder-Finanzbeziehungen auf der Grundlage der Finanzverfassung', BMF-Dokumentation (Oktober), Berlin.
Bundesministerium der Finanzen (2018). 'Ergebnisse des Finanzausgleichs 2017', Monatsberichte (März), Berlin.
Deutscher Städtetag (2017). 'Gemeindefinanzbericht', Berlin/Cologne.
Holler, Franziska and Henrik Nürnberger (2017). 'Neuer Finanzausgleich: Geld für die Länder, Macht für den Bund', *Public Governance: Zeitschrift für öffentliches Management*, Institut für den öffentlichen Sektor e.V., pp. 14–15.
Spahn, Paul Bernd (2015). 'Contract federalism', in Ehtisham Ahmad and Giorgio Brosio (eds), *Handbook of Multilevel Finance*, Cheltenham, UK and Northampton, MA, USA: Edward Elgar Publishing, pp. 144–60.
Statistische Ämter des Bundes und der Länder (2017). 'Hebesätze der Realsteuern', Düsseldorf.
Wissenschaftlicher Beirat (2015). 'Reform des bundesstaatlichen Finanzausgleichs: Gutachte des Wissenschaftlichen Beirats beim Bundesministerium der Finanzen', 1/2015, May, Berlin.

6. The United States grant system*

Howard A. Chernick

Intergovernmental grants form an important part of the system of public finances in the US. In 2017, 17 per cent of federal government outlays were grants to state and local governments ($675B), under some 1,700 separately authorized programmes (Keegan 2012).[1] In 2016, 30 per cent of total state revenues came from the federal government, while 33 per cent of local government revenues came from grants, mainly from their states. This chapter discusses the major features of the US system of intergovernmental grants and assesses the effectiveness of this important allocation of fiscal resources in our federal system of government.[2]

The chapter has five sections. The first section describes the general features of the US grant system. Section 6.2 assesses the effectiveness of grants in addressing horizontal fiscal disparities – fiscal equalization – and the countercyclical role of grants. The equalization discussion considers federal aid to states and cities, and state grants to localities. Section 6.3 discusses the fiscal politics of grants-in-aid, focusing on the geographical distribution of grants. Section 6.4 considers the fiscal response of state and local government to the receipt of grants, including a section on capital grants. A final section 6.5 summarizes the main points.

6.1   GENERAL FEATURES OF THE US GRANT SYSTEM

A.   Aggregate Amounts

Figure 6.1 shows the amount of grants, both as a share of the federal budget and as a share of GDP, from 1960 to 2017. The grant percentage went from 7.6 per cent in 1960 to 15.5 per cent in 1980, fell back to 11 per cent in 1990, rose to almost 17 per cent in 2011, and has remained at that level since 2011. As a share of GDP, grants followed a similar pattern, rising in post-recessions periods, and falling somewhat during recovery periods. In 2017 federal grants equalled 3.5 per cent of GDP, greater than any year other than 2011.

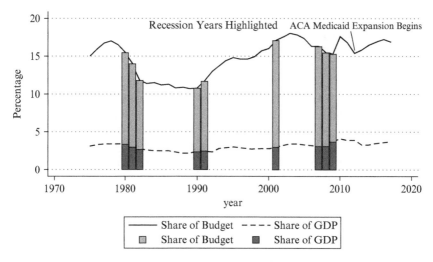

Source: OMB, Federal Budget History, Table 12.1.

Figure 6.1   Federal grants as share of federal budget and GDP 1975–2017

By function, the dominant feature is the increasing share of grants for health, from 44 per cent in 2000 to 60 per cent in 2018. Next is income security, declining from 24 per cent to 15 per cent. Transportation's share has hovered around 10 per cent over this period, while the aggregate category of education, employment, training, and social services dropped from 13 to 9 per cent. Community and regional development grants were about 4 per cent.

The Office of Management and Budget (OMB) divides grants into payments to individuals, that help pay for income transfers, physical capital investment, and other. The major payments to individuals are for health insurance for low-income people (Medicaid), income security and nutrition, while the major capital investments are for highways and public transportation. There has been a rapid increase in the share going to individuals, reaching 76 per cent in 2017, and a parallel decline in the capital investment share, going from almost half of federal grants in 1960 to less than 12 per cent.

B.   Grant Characteristics

Grants can be distinguished in terms of conditionality, the fiscal terms on which funds are provided, the distribution mechanism and the requirements imposed on grant recipients. Highly conditional aid, called categorical grants, is for narrowly defined purposes, for example to hire additional police in a city. Block grants represent an intermediate degree of conditionality, with grant recipients allowed broad discretion in determining the uses of the grants. Examples are grants for urban development and welfare spending. Unconditional grants are provided without programmatic or functional area restrictions. Grants may be matching – recipient governments have to pay a share of the costs – or lump-sum. Matching grants, in turn, may be open-ended – the granting level of government matches any eligible expenditures – or closed ended, that is, matched only up to some maximum grant level. Grants may have maintenance-of-effort (MOE) requirements, requiring recipients to maintain prior levels of spending. Formula grant amounts are awarded on the basis of legislatively determined formulae. Project grants are awarded to a subset of eligible grant recipients based on a competitive application process (Keegan 2012).

Of the 1,714 authorized grant programmes as of 2012, the vast majority are relatively narrow categorical grants, authorized for specific purposes. Most categorical aid is distributed as project grants, but formula grants dominate in terms of dollars. In 2009, 84 per cent of grant dollars were distributed under the ten largest formula grant programmes (GAO, 2009). The distributional criteria for both formula and project grants are the outcome of legislative bargaining, both within particular congressional committees and across the entire legislature.[3]

Since at least the 1960s, when the number of categorical grant programmes increased substantially as part of the Great Society initiative, there has been concern about the complexity and administrative unwieldiness of the categorical grant structure. Complaints arise both from local officials, who object to the lack of control over such funds and the interference in their own budgetary prerogatives, and from Congress, which has questioned the efficacy of having so many separate programmes. There have been periodic efforts to reduce this complexity, by folding numerous categorical programmes into block grants.[4] Despite repeated efforts to simplify the grant system, small categorical aid programmes have proved to be quite durable. Categorical aids are able to develop strong, albeit narrow, constituencies of providers, beneficiaries and legislators, while providing a greater measure of federal control over use of the funds than for block grants (Weingast et al., 1981). Because the use of grants is narrowly defined, and frequently earmarked for capital investment, categorical grants (at least in appearance) are less fungible with own-source revenues than broader purpose grants. Hence, they appear to be more effective at actually inducing spending on particular purposes.[5]

Narrow categorical aids also enable the federal government to enlist recipients as agents in introducing new or innovative services or delivery modes (Schultze, 1974, Aaron, 1985). Under this model, it is appropriate for the higher-level government to finance most of the grant (high matching rates), and to place strict limits on the total amount of aid.

In contrast, block grants, because they are diffuse in purpose, fail to develop powerful constituencies, and become more vulnerable to budgetary pressures at the granting level. Because block grants tend to be larger in amount, they are almost always distributed by formula, reducing the role of bureaucratic or legislative discretion in the award of grants. Typically lacking binding matching requirements, and broad in the allowed use of funds, it is easier for recipient governments to substitute grants for own resources. Most federal countries, the US included, go through periodic cycles of increased then decreased categorization of grants. As the restrictions on local policy choices grow, resistance to categorical grants rise. However, when replaced by broader block grants, constituency and legislative support tends to wane, leading to reintroduction of categorical aids.[6]

By far the largest grant programme is Medicaid, which provides healthcare to low-income children and families. Federal outlays in 2017 were equal to $375B, more than half of all grant dollars. The Medicaid programme will be discussed in section 6.2.A of this chapter. Other major programmes are the highway grant programme ($44B), Child nutrition ($22B), rental assistance ($20.6B), Education Aid for the Disadvantaged ($16.2B), Family Assistance ($16B), Special Education ($12.5B) and Urban Mass Transportation ($12B). Smaller programmes include Children and Family services, Foster Care and Adoption, Food Assistance, Community Development, and Child Care and Social Services. Disaster relief fluctuates widely from year to year.[7]

A major goal of federal aid to state and local governments is to provide assistance to low-income individuals and families. The largest grant categories, for health and income assistance, are for means-tested benefit programmes. The two biggest grant programmes in education are for aid to poor school districts (Title 1), or for assistance in meeting the high costs of educating students with disabilities. The biggest grant from the Department of Housing and Urban Development is for rental assistance to low-income families. Grants for economic development, such as the Community Development Block Grant, are intended to promote development in the poorer areas of cities.

C. Grants and Tax Expenditures

Grants are just one component of the fiscal relationship between the federal government and subnational governments.[8] Tax expenditures under the federal income tax, equal to almost 20 per cent of federal grants, also provide important subsidies to state and local governments. In 2017, the largest of these tax expenditures were the deductibility of individual state and local taxes ($101B), and the exclusion of interest on general obligation bonds of states and localities ($26B) (Joint Committee on Taxation, 2018). The Tax Cut and Jobs Act of 2017 (TCJA) capped state and local tax deductions (SALT) at $10,000, reducing them by nearly 75 per cent. While the merits of SALT deductibility are subject to debate, the politics of the TCJA cap clearly reflect an intentional shift in federal tax burdens from low to high tax states.[9] For many of the direct grant programmes, there are also parallel tax expenditures, for example low-income housing credits for community development.[10]

6.2 FISCAL EQUALIZATION UNDER THE FEDERAL GRANTS SYSTEM

A common goal of intergovernmental aid is to offset differences in fiscal capacity or expenditure need among lower-level governments, using unconditional grants with no matching requirements. However, while variation among US states in capacity and need are wide and growing (Yilmaz et al., 2006), fiscal equalization is not a primary feature of the US grant system.[11, 12]

A. Equalization at the Federal Level

At the federal level, the US relies on categorical aid, typically with matching requirements, to provide assistance to particular target populations or areas.[13] The most important categorical programme is the open-ended matching grant for Medicaid. The federal government matches eligible state expenditures using a formula known as the Federal Medical Assistance Percentage (FMAP). The FMAP is inverse to a state's per capita personal income (as measured by the average of the three most recently available years of data), relative to national per capita income, with lower and upper bounds of 50 and 83 per cent. The formula is

$$FMAP = 1 - \left[\frac{(statepci)^2}{(nat'lpci)^2} \right] * 0.45, \ 0.5 < FMAP < 0.83^{14} \qquad (6.1)$$

Evidence suggests that the price incentive under the matching grant has been successful in inducing increased spending on healthcare for the poor (Carlino and Inman, 2016). However, despite highly favourable matching rates for low-income states, adequacy varies widely across states (Holahan, 2003).

While the Medicaid formula does not take direct account of differences in need across states, to the extent that per capita income is negatively correlated with the percentage of the population eligible for services, the variable matching rate goes some way towards addressing differential needs. Fiscal bargaining between states and the federal government over the effective matching rate has also been used, though unevenly, to compensate for differential costs.[15, 16]

The income factor in the FMAP provides a measure of risk sharing as states' relative economic positions change over time. However, the lower bound of 50 per cent mitigates the degree of fiscal equalization in the distribution of federal funds. Over time the distribution of federal Medicaid funds has shifted towards the richer states, despite the favourable matching rates enjoyed by poorer states, suggesting that for higher income states income effects outweigh price effects. The lower bound on the matching rate is crucial in this regard. If the relative income of states at the 50 per cent lower bound increases, there is no additional price effect to offset the increased demand for medical services for the poor that accompanies increased fiscal resources. An enhanced FMAP (30 per cent above the regular FMAP) is also used to distribute funds under the Children's Health Insurance Program (SCHIP), which provides capped funding for health insurance for children who are not Medicaid-eligible but live in low-income families.[17]

The Affordable Care Act (2010) represents the latest effort to expand health services for low-income persons, providing coverage up to 138 per cent of the Federal Poverty Line. Given the budgetary pressure on states from rapid growth in traditional Medicaid spending, (almost) full federal financing of the expansion was a necessary condition for the bill's passage. As of this writing, 36 states had accepted the expansion, with a number of the 14 non-expansion states likely to do so in the near future.

With the exception of Medicaid, all major grant programmes are capped in total amount, with distributions based on population and a variety of other criteria. Highway funds are distributed based on population and road miles, with minimum amounts for small states.[18] Urban transportation funds are based on population and passenger miles. School subsidies, community development, social services and child care block grants use poverty counts. Capital programmes have high matching rates, but are capped in amount. Minimum grant constraints and grandfathering of prior levels of aid tend to push block grants and capped matching aid towards equal per capita distributions across states.

Gordon et al. (2016) evaluate grant distributions using the fiscal gap approach, defined as the difference between revenue capacity plus federal grants, and expenditure need. States with the largest negative gaps are concentrated in the South, while Northeastern states show the largest positive fiscal positions. Operationally, equalization is undermined by matching and MOE requirements, grant-minimums and hold-harmless provisions, even as economic and fiscal conditions change.

B.   Equalization at the State Level

Fiscal equalization, while not a primary feature of the federal grant system, is important at the subnational level. Between 2012 and 2016 about 37 per cent of local general revenue came from intergovernmental grants. Grants from states make up almost 90 per cent of that aid, with the remainder from the federal government.[19]

In 2016, 60 per cent of all state aid was for elementary and secondary education, comprising 47 per cent of local education revenues (US Census Bureau, 2016). Federal aid provided 8 per cent of school revenues. The major trend in state aid in the US has been an increase in the state share of education finance, and the incorporation of equalization criteria in the distribution of aid to local schools.[20] Before the 1970s, state aid was typically distributed to local school districts on a per pupil basis. Because property, the base for the main local revenue source, is unequally distributed, even aid distributed on a per pupil basis is equalizing as compared to local financing. Evans et al. (1997) find that, under the impetus of a number of court decisions, state aid for education became more equalizing over time.[21] The General Accounting Office (GAO, 1998) found an average state equalization effort of 62 per cent in 1997, where 100 per cent would imply that each school district could attain the statewide spending per pupil with an average fiscal effort.[22] Notably, equalization was increased more by increasing the state share of total financing then by greater targeting of state aid to poorer districts. However, the degree of equalization differed substantially across states. Federal aid, though small relative to total funding (7 per cent), was highly targeted to poor students, and increased spending on poor students by 77 per cent. For a sample of 149 big US cities, Chernick and Reschovsky (2018) found that education aid was by far the most equalizing of all categories of state aid, but the range across states was substantial.[23, 24]

While state aid is equalizing, direct federal aid to cities is positively correlated with local tax capacity (Chernick and Reschovsky, 2018). This pattern does not appear to be due to differences in poverty rates, but instead may reflect the greater ability of richer cities to negotiate the administrative procedures for obtaining federal aid, and enhanced ability to satisfy matching or MOE requirements (Chernick, 1979).[25]

C. Grants as Countercyclical Fiscal Instruments

An important role of intergovernmental grants-in-aid is to offset fiscal contractions of state and local governments during economic downturns. Almost all states and localities are subject to annual balanced budget rules. While these rules vary in their degree of stringency (Bohn and Inman, 1996), they nonetheless imply that recession-related decreases in tax revenues and increases in expenditure needs force spending cuts and/or tax increases, thus exacerbating recessions. Increased federal grants can help to offset contractionary fiscal behaviour on the part of states while protecting vital public services.

Figure 6.2 shows grants as a share of state general revenues from 1992 to 2011, with an increase in the federal share in the aftermath of each downturn. The increase reflects both an increase in federal grants and a decrease in state tax collections. Countercyclical fiscal relief has both automatic and discretionary components. The automatic component comes from recession-related increases in spending on programmes for the needy, mainly for Medicaid, and the automatic increase in federal matching funds which results. The automatic feature of open-ended matching grants constitutes an important risk-sharing mechanism during cyclical downturns.

There have also been a variety of discretionary countercyclical federal grant programmes. In the mid 1970s, several billions of dollars of

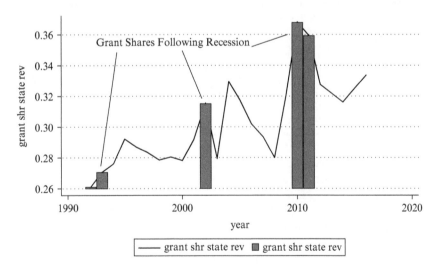

Source: U.S. Census Bureau, Annual Survey of State Government Finances, various years.

Figure 6.2   Federal grants as share of state general revenues

supplemental aid went to states and local governments. In 2003 and 2004 some $20B was allocated to states, half on a per capita basis, and half in enhanced Medicaid funding. Responses in both periods have been criticized as being both for being poorly targeted in terms of need, and lacking in timeliness, with funds arriving after the recessions had already ended (GAO, 2004).

Fiscal relief to state and local governments in the aftermath of the Great Recession dwarfed any of the prior amounts post-World War II. The bulk of the $300B in funds was earmarked for the two largest categories of state and local spending, health and education, $90B for Medicaid, and $100B for education. The remaining funds went for assistance to low-income families ($18B), for unemployment compensation ($39B) and for infrastructure spending ($58B).

In contrast to the timing problem of prior countercyclical fiscal assistance programmes, in which funds typically arrived too late, fiscal relief to states under the American Recovery and Reinvestment Act of 2009 (ARRA) was delivered on a relatively timely basis. However, the rapid drawdown of ARRA funds to states after 2011 can be criticized as happening too fast. Not only was the drop in state tax revenue in the Great Recession the sharpest since the Depression, but the recovery has also been the slowest. In 2015, six years after the official end of the recession, fiscal pressure on states and cities remained severe. For example, in large cities the two most important sources of local government revenue, the property tax and state aid, were only slightly higher in 2015 than they were in 2000 (Chernick and Reschovsky, 2018).[26]

In both the 2001 and 2007–09 recessions, enhanced Medicaid matching rates were used as a vehicle for fiscal relief. In 2003, the Medicaid matching rate (FMAP) was increased by 2.95 percentage points for five quarters. From 2009 to 2011, the federal matching rate was increased by at least 6.2 percentage points for all states, with additional matching rate supplements for high unemployment states, and a hold-harmless provision in matching rate adjustments for states whose relative income had increased.[27] Given the size of the Medicaid programme, a temporary increase in the federal matching rate has proved to be an efficacious way to increase federal support to states during recessions.

A uniform increase in the federal matching share makes the increase in federal Medicaid payments proportional to the amount of prior state spending. This approach sidesteps the difficult political issue of winners and losers in the distribution of incremental assistance. In 2009, the variation in matching rate enhancement based on differences in the increase in unemployment was small relative to the uniform increase. As a consequence, more than a third of relief payments went to the five states with the largest Medicaid enrolments (Kaiser Commission on Medicaid and the Uninsured, 2011). The Medicaid relief Act included an MOE requirement to prevent states from tightening eligibility standards. Even with this requirement, the recession-induced pressure on Medicaid spending in most states was less than the amount of extra funds provided.[28] This allowed states to divert substantial portions of the increased federal aid into general revenue, which could be used to offset reductions in tax revenues. Despite the importance of fiscal relief under the enhanced Medicaid match, Carlino and Inman (2017) find that the price reduction was still much more effective than lump-sum federal aid in terms of countercyclical stimulus per dollar of federal aid.[29]

The other major share ($100B) of Great Recession fiscal relief for states was for elementary and secondary education. States were awarded about $60B based on school age and overall population, with the funds distributed to local school districts using each state's basic state formula for school aid. An additional $10B was allocated to supplement education aid for low-income students. In response to the pressure on local resources, local education agencies were allowed to use their supplemental Title I appropriation to satisfy the MOE requirement.

Initial research on the efficacy of the Great Recession fiscal relief package suggested that most of the funds went into state balances (Cogan and Taylor, 2012). However, Carlino and Inman (2017), using a much longer panel of data, find that the enhanced Medicaid match was effective at releasing resources for low-income individuals that otherwise would have been spent on medical care. Leduc and Wilson (2013) find a strong stimulus effect for increased aid for highways under the ARRA. While there was a sharp increase in direct federal grants to cities from 2009 to 2011, this increase was more than offset by declines in city tax revenues and state aid.

6.3   THE POLITICS OF GRANTS

A.   Geographical Distribution Patterns

In 2010, per capita federal grant amounts vary widely across states. High grant states include some small population states – Montana, North and South Dakota and Wyoming – high spending states in the northeast – New York, Vermont and Maine – and very poor states – Mississippi and Louisiana. The four lowest grant states were Virginia, Nevada, Colorado and Utah. Florida and Texas also received a relatively small amount of aid on a per capita basis. The basic patterns were similar in 2017 (Rockefeller Institute, 2018).

The geographic distribution of grants depends on the formula criteria, and matching requirements. Population is a key factor, though grants for education, community development, social services and child care also take account of the number of children in poverty (GAO, 2005, 2009). Penner (1979) argues that the geographic distribution of grants was roughly equal on a per capita basis. Grants favouring poor states were offset by minimum constraints favouring small states, and greater 'pull-in' of funds by wealthier states for discretionary project grants and open-ended matching grants. The differential growth of Medicaid spending by state since the early 1980s has tended to undo this per capita balance, favouring states with high percentages of the population enrolled in Medicaid and/or relatively generous benefit packages. The Affordable Care Act has reinforced this trend.[30]

An alternative way to look at grant distributions is as a share of state revenue. In 2016, on average 32.6 per cent of state revenues came from federal grants (Tax Foundation, 2019). The most dependent states have high concentrations of poverty, high Medicaid matching rates and limited tax collections.[31] The least dependent states get relatively low Medicaid grants, while states in the middle have levels of taxation high enough to offset high levels of Medicaid spending.[32]

B.   Broader Perspectives on Intergovernmental Fiscal Flows

Grants are only one component of the fiscal flows between central and subnational governments. Another important component is direct federal spending, particularly for national defence. Whether intentional or not, a case can be made that the US substitutes military spending for equalizing grants, using its exceptionally large national defence budget to redistribute resources to the poorest regions of the country. In 1997, per capita defence spending (prime contract awards plus compensation) was almost equal to grants ($762 versus $870) (GAO, 1998). Comparing spending by the four census regions, outlays for defence were equal to 4.5 per cent of income in the South, compared to an average of 2.8 per cent in the others, while per capita income in the South was 9 per cent lower than the rest of the country.[33, 34] This distribution reflects population-based rules, combined with strong support for military spending in the South, and the success of southern legislators in controlling key congressional committees (Carsey and Rundquist, 1998). These results suggest that if defence spending were included together with intergovernmental grants, the negative fiscal gaps for poor states found by Gordon et al. are likely to be substantially reduced or even eliminated.

An even broader perspective on fiscal flows is to include both taxes paid to the federal government and federal expenditures, to arrive at a 'balance of payments' estimate for each state. A recent study finds that the poorer the state, the larger the positive balance of payments (Schultz and Cummings, 2019). The main explanatory factor is differential federal income and payroll taxes by region.[35]

6.4   EFFECT OF GRANTS-IN-AID ON STATE AND LOCAL EXPENDITURES

The fiscal impact of grants may range from full substitution of grant for recipient dollars, to fully additive effects or even to stimulating state and local spending. Fiscal impacts are likely to vary over time, by type of grant (matching versus lump-sum), by the degree of conditionality (categorical versus block grant) and by the extent to which any MOE requirements are binding.

At the macro level, Figure 6.3 shows federal grants and state and local own revenues by year. Over most of the period from 1970 to 2017, both own revenues and federal grants increased in tandem.[36] During recession periods, particularly the years following the 2007–09 recession, federal grants increase as state–local revenues decline.[37] The overall pattern of grant supplementation reflects joint federal-state funding of Medicaid, the largest and fastest growing federal grant.

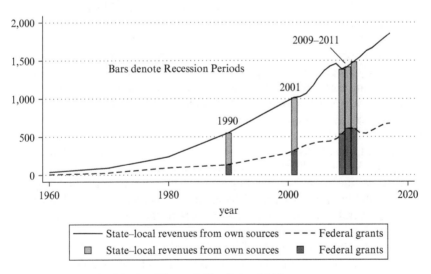

Source: OMB, Federal Budget History, Tables 12.1 and 14.1.

Figure 6.3   *Federal grants and state–local own-source revenues (billions of nominal $)*

An early paper by Gramlich and Galper (1973) found that state fiscal responses to unrestricted aid were approximately equally divided between spending increases, tax reductions and increases in state savings. Carlino and Inman (2016) find that a dollar increase in federal aid through higher federal matching rates leads to an additional 70 cents in spending for lower income households, with the rest of the response going to tax relief and an increase in state savings, at least partially funded by a reduction in other state spending.[38] By contrast, a dollar increase in project aid (largely for infrastructure and education) is equally divided between increased spending and increased public sector savings.

The long-run average annual rate of growth in Medicaid spending is striking, equal to 6.25 per cent per year from 1996 to 2019, and exceeding the average rate of increase in state revenues (Rudowitz et al., 2018). The increase is due to both increased enrolments and increased spending per beneficiary, particularly for the aged and disabled.[39] State dollars spent on Medicaid have gone from 12 per cent of own-source revenues in 2000 to 17 per cent in 2012, and remained since at that level.[40] The increase in Medicaid's share of state revenues has led to concern that Medicaid growth is crowding out other state spending areas, particularly education and other welfare spending.[41]

States' fiscal incentives for redistribution changed when Aid to Families with Dependent Children (AFDC) was converted to a block grant under the welfare reform Act of 1996. Because the amount of aid is fixed, states must bear the full cost of any increase in the welfare rolls, but realize the full savings from a decline in the rolls. States were constrained in how much they could reduce their own spending on cash assistance by MOE requirements, set in nominal dollars. The main state response to the Temporary Assistance for Needy Families (TANF) block grant has been to freeze or decrease cash assistance, by promoting a rapid reduction in the number of people getting assistance. When it was created in 1996, the federal TANF block grant was funded at $16.5B per year. It has remained at that nominal level since. While the lifetime limits on welfare receipt have clearly played a role, the decline in welfare spending suggests that the change from an open-ended matching grant to a fixed block grant has had a powerful effect in reducing overall spending on cash assistance to the poor, and in increasing inequalities across states (Ayala et al., 2017).[42]

A widely discussed effect of grants-in-aid is the so-called flypaper effect, under which the impact of a dollar of aid on recipient spending greatly exceeds the impact of a comparable increase in resident income (Inman, 2009). One explanation is that the fiscal terms on which the grant is awarded may be misidentified. Administrative discretion in the awarding of project grants may lead to greater amounts of aid awarded to jurisdictions that are more willing to match federal contributions (Chernick, 1979).

Knight (2002), using congressional representation as instruments to address endogeneity in the award of federal highway grants, finds that funds are disproportionately awarded to high demand states. Thus, he argues that highway grants substitute federal for state dollars, rather than increasing total spending. However, these results have been challenged by Leduc and Wilson (2013), and Fisher and Wassmer (2015), both of whom find substantial stimulus effects of augmented aid for highways as part of the ARRA recovery Act of 2009.

The fiscal impact of grants differs depending on the functional purpose of the grant, and the amount of recipient spending in that functional area. Gordon (2004) finds that, despite non-supplant regulations, over time, federal grants to cities displace local resources. In contrast, Chernick (2017) finds that each dollar of direct federal aid to cities – mainly for child care, social services and community development – is associated with more than a dollar of total spending increase. A dollar of state aid to cities leads to spending increases between 64 and 87 cents. Thus, both state and direct federal aid to cities appear to be mainly additive to local spending effort.

How can the various results regarding grant effects be reconciled? Because, for most grants, there is no matching at the margin, differential price effects are not likely to be important. However, another factor is the size of the grants relative to own spending. For example, education aid for the disadvantaged represents a small fraction of total local spending on education. Over time, it becomes difficult to enforce the non-supplant rules based on earlier spending levels, making grant dollars fungible with local dollars.

By contrast, direct federal aid to cities goes primarily for social services, and housing assistance. Under the pressure of the most recent recession, cities have cut back own spending in these particular functional areas, relying more and more on outside aid. Nonetheless, overall public spending may also be higher in cities that receive more aid.[43] The delivery mode for social services, with cities largely relying on contracting out to non-profits, may also affect the ability of cities to more rapidly adjust spending levels in response to changes in grant amounts.[44]

Capital grants are almost always closed ended categorical matching grants, with high federal matching rates.[45] Federal grants comprised 38 per cent of state and local capital spending on water and transportation in 2014, and 45 per cent of public transportation capital outlays (Mallett, 2018). Fisher and Wassmer (2015) find that state and local capital investment tends to show an increase in the years following recessions, as countercyclical federal grants are translated into increased spending. However, following the 2007–09 recession, the increase in federal grants for capital spending was not sufficient to offset the severe fiscal stress states and localities faced from the declining economy. Between 2009 and 2013, state and local capital outlays fell by 20 per cent (Fisher and Sullivan, 2016).[46]

Gramlich and Galper (1973) find that about half of what they term C grants (categorical grants with closed-end matching) increase spending, while the other half goes to tax relief. Fisher and Wassmer (2015) find a low elasticity of state/local capital expenditures with respect to federal grants, but a higher elasticity for stimulus funds following the Great Recession. Estimates of the fiscal impact of highway grants range from full displacement to actually stimulating spending from own resources. At the aggregate level, the high shares of federal monies in water and transportation suggest that capital grants in these functional areas may be displacing at least some state and local effort. Announcement effects, wherein the prospect of award of discretionary capital grants leads states or cities to defer projects, may also contribute to substitution.[47] However, state and local capital spending is sensitive to the business cycle, and augmented federal capital grants in periods of recession have clearly helped to maintain capital spending, or to reduce the magnitude of cuts.

6.5   CONCLUSION

Federal grants to states and localities are an important feature of federalism in the US, comprising 17 per cent of all federal spending in 2017 and 33 per cent of state general revenues. The share of funds that ultimately go to individuals, mainly for healthcare, has increased, while the share for capital expenditures has diminished sharply. Some 84 per cent of all grant money is awarded on the basis of congressionally determined formulae, though categorical project grants have been a persistent feature of the US grant system. Over time a number of categorical grants have been replaced by block grants, allowing greater leeway in the use of funds.

A principal goal of the US system is to provide a floor on support for the poor and reduce the incentives for a race to the bottom in redistribution, while still preserving subnational fiscal autonomy and competitive federalism, as these concepts are interpreted in the US tradition. Unlike most federalist countries, the US does not use untied grants for fiscal equalization. Instead, it subsidizes subnational provision of certain merit goods, using income-adjusted matching grants or block grants. Medicaid, expanded and incentivized with highly favourable matching rates under the Affordable Care Act (2010), and the Children's Health Insurance Program, set a floor on medical services for the poor, but still allows for wide variation in coverage and benefits across states. Though rapid growth in healthcare spending under Medicaid may lead to lower spending in other functional areas, the welfare implications of this shift are ambiguous, depending on programme effectiveness and the social value states assign to public spending on different groups.

Education is primarily a local function in the US, though almost half of all revenues come from state aid. The equalizing effect of state aid has increased over time, bolstered by an increase in state dollars and the incorporation of equalization criteria into state education formulae. Nonetheless, wide disparities both across and within states persist.

Grants play an important role as countercyclical fiscal instruments, increasing both in amount and in share of state revenues in times of recession and providing a buffer against reduced tax revenues and increased expenditure needs. Fiscal relief to states following the 2007–09 recession, through enhanced Medicaid matching rates and an increase in school aid, dwarfed any of the prior efforts following World War II. Research suggests that fiscal relief to states played an important role in maintaining services, enhancing capital investment and stimulating state economies.

Overall grant distributions have moved away from equal per capita towards favouring richer states, due to their higher Medicaid expenditures. However, as a share of state revenue, federal grants favour states with high concentrations of poverty and limited tax collections. Federal military expenditures in the US, almost equal in magnitude to grants-in-aid, tend to offset any tendency for grants to favour high-income states.

At the macro level, grants are roughly additive to own revenues, a direct result of the open-ended matching requirement for Medicaid. However, conversion from open-ended matching to fixed block grants for cash assistance has been accompanied by a sharp drop in spending, and an increase in interstate benefit differentials. The stimulus effect of other categorical aid varies depending on the size of the grant and the degree of specificity. The literature on substitution for capital grants is ambiguous, with results ranging from full to very little substitution.

The US grants system distributes large amounts of fiscal resources to incentivize states and their localities to provide services to the poor, and enhance their capital stocks. While there is some modest fiscal equalization, interstate and intrastate differences in spending for redistribution and education, both between and within states, remain substantial. One lesson is that federal attempts to induce spending on the poor must be accompanied by very strong financial carrots. Mandates alone are insufficient, and untied funds are ineffective. Capital grants, though politically salient, may in some cases lead to displacement of own state fiscal resources, suggesting that enhanced federal spending on infrastructure must be carefully designed to minimize the displacement effect. There is clearly a role for policy analysis in providing ongoing analysis of the effectiveness of each dollar spent on grants-in-aid.

NOTES

*   I would like to thank William Fox, Richard Bird, Serdar Yilmaz and Farah Zahir for helpful comments on earlier drafts.
1.   In 2008, the last year before the great recession (2007–09), over 15 per cent of the federal budget went for grants, which then comprised about 27 per cent of state and local own-source revenues. Between 2009 and 2011 the amount and budget share of federal grants were augmented by \$216B of stimulus funds to state governments and local school districts as part of the American Recovery and Reinvestment Act of 2009 (ARRA). In addition, beginning in 2014, the Affordable Care Act's federally funded expansion of eligibility for Medicaid, the programme of health insurance for low-income individuals.
2.   Gordon (2018) provides a concise review of the US grants system, and considers changes in distributional criteria to target the economic development of lagging regions.
3.   Knight (2005) finds evidence for the ability of proposal committee members to increase federal project grant allocations to their own congressional districts.
4.   One such example was the 1974 Community Development Block Grant (CDBG), which combined seven categorical grants into a single grant for community development.
5.   Theory suggests that the greater the degree of specificity of grant earmarking, the more likely is the grant to at least initially increase spending on that particular category. However, over time the fiscal impact of narrow categorical grants may diminish, if recipients are able to reduce spending in closely related categories of spending. Evidence on the fiscal response of recipient governments to earmarking is discussed in Section 6.4.
6.   See the discussion by Gillette (2004) on the role of categorical and block grants in Sweden.
7.   For example, spending was equal to \$5.3B in 2017, but rose to \$20B in 2018.
8.   While most federal grants are funded from general revenues, one of the largest grant programmes, for transportation, is funded by an earmarked tax on gasoline. The tax, currently at a rate of 18.3 cents per gallon, is used to pay for highway construction and mass transit projects.
9.   Arguments for allowing SALT deductibility, in terms of reducing interstate tax competition, offsetting differential costs of the public sector and encouraging subnational tax progressivity, are discussed in Chernick (2018).
10. Even more broadly, the federal government and the states must ultimately share the same tax base, and are thus in potential competition for tax revenues (Chernick and Tennant, 2010; Gordon and Cullen, 2012).
11. The ratio of per capita income of the five richest states to the five poorest states increased from 1.44 to 1.64 between 1980 and 2016.
12. In theory, the equalization grant could actually be negative for states with positive fiscal residuals, implying little or no net cost to the federal treasury. In this case, the grant would represent a pure horizontal transfer. For political (and legal) reasons, negative grants have never been used in the US.
13. The only such grant was general revenue sharing (GRS), enacted under President Nixon in 1972, and ended completely under President Reagan in 1986. In 1978, GSR made up about 9 per cent of total grants. The formula for distribution, which took into account both state income and fiscal effort, and was reflective of the need to build a broad coalition of support, meant that there was relatively little fiscal equalization under GRS (Sawicky, 2001). This result is consistent with the primary rationale for GRS, which was

not to offset differences in fiscal conditions between states or localities, but to address vertical fiscal imbalances between the federal government and the states (Heller and Pechman, 1967).

14. In 2019, 14 states are at the lower bound, while the highest federal share (Mississippi) is 74 per cent. In 2000, 11 states were at the lower bound, while the highest federal share was 76 per cent. While the poorest states have consistently received the highest federal shares since the FMAP was first instituted in 1961, the identity of a number of states at the lower bound has changed considerably.

15. Another factor in the expansion of Medicaid has been the maximization strategies employed by states to increase Medicaid funding. Since the 1990s, the federal share of Medicaid spending has grown more rapidly than the state share in certain states because the federal government helps to finance extra hospital spending for states with high levels of charity care. In the past, the Medicaid programme has allowed states to satisfy the matching requirement for this type of spending with a variety of special financing devices. These strategies have increased the overall Medicaid matching rate from 56 per cent to almost 60 per cent. One may view this process as part of the ongoing bargaining relationship between the federal government and the states, in which the states try to extract additional federal financing as the price for expanding coverage or services. In this interpretation, Medicaid maximization strategies are but one step in the historical evolution of the financing of health insurance for low-income individuals (Ku and Coughlin, 1992).

16. For example, Ohio was at 50 per cent in 1967, and is now at 63 per cent.

17. The programme has an MOE requirement for eligibility and spending, and an 88 per cent federal matching rate. Because funding is capped globally and for most states, there is typically no price reduction at the margin.

18. The federal matching rate is 80 per cent.

19. A portion of federal grants to states are 'passed through' to localities. Hence, the 5 per cent figure for federal grants to local governments understates the total fiscal impact of federal grants to local governments. It was not possible to get an overall estimate of the amount of pass-through aid. For the city of New York, budget data suggest that such aid is roughly equal to 5 per cent of total city revenues.

20. The equalization goal is typically reflected in aid programmes which make state funds a function of the gap between own property tax base and the average base, multiplied by the average property tax rate in the state. A number of states also include cost factors in the formulae.

21. They found that in 1992 equalization criteria removed almost half of the inequality in spending that would have occurred if aid were distributed on a per pupil basis.

22. To address cost differentials, the study uses a cost index for teachers in its calculations, but ignores cost differentials due to differences in the demographic composition of the student body. The resultant cost differences are quite important (Reschovsky, 1994).

23. The simple correlation between state aid and a representative tax system measure of city fiscal capacity was negative ($\rho = -0.32$), while other state aid was positively correlated with city fiscal capacity ($\rho = 0.23$).

24. Since 2000, both the negative correlation for state aid and the positive correlation for other types of state aid have increased. For example, in 2014 state aid's share of city spending on education was 85 per cent or more for the ten highest share cities, compared to less than 39 per cent for the ten lowest share cities. For the period 2000–14, the correlation between state aid and city fiscal capacity, not taking account of differences in expenditure need, was a negative 0.55 in Texas, 0.49 in New York, 0.28 in California, and a positive 0.03 in Florida.

25. This interpretation is strengthened by the finding that direct federal aid to cities is unusually stimulative, with an extra dollar of federal aid associated with more than an extra dollar of total spending (Chernick, 2017).

26. The main reason for the sharp decline in property tax revenues was the decline in home values that followed the bursting of the housing bubble in 2006 (Chernick et al., 2018).

27. The unemployment-based adjustment to the federal share was roughly half of the basic adjustment, with larger states tending to receive greater increases than smaller states.
28. Holahan and Garett (2009) find a strong relationship between changes in unemployment and expansion in the Medicaid rolls. However, Chernick and Reimers (2019) find only a very weak relationship between the increase in state unemployment rates from 2007 to 2010 and the overall increase in Medicaid spending. The same lack of a strong relationship holds for the increase in the percentage of the population below 200 per cent of the federal poverty line.
29. Carlino and Inman (2016) estimate that the 10 percentage point increase in the federal Medicaid matching share under the ARRA increased spending for poor families by about $70 for each $100 of federal spending. The added federal price incentive led to a reduction in other state spending, and an increase in government saving and tax relief.
30. Given the dominant role of Medicaid in the federal grant system, and the fact that the non-expansion states are on average poorer than the expansion states, the Supreme Court's decision to make Medicaid expansion optional has undoubtedly made the federal grant system less equalizing than before. At the time of writing, 14 states have declined to take the Medicaid expansion.
31. For the year 2009, I estimate an elasticity of taxes per capita with respect to personal income of about 1.0.
32. High share states include Mississippi and Kentucky, low share states include Virginia and Kansas, while middle share states include New York and California.
33. When one divides the US into nine census divisions, as opposed to four regions, high defence spending is concentrated primarily in 'Division 5' (Delaware, the District of Columbia, Florida, Georgia, Maryland, North and South Carolina, Virginia and West Virginia) as opposed to the other states in the South.
34. The distribution of defence spending can be addressed by regressing 1997 per capita defence spending by state on region and state per capita income.

$$\text{SPENDPC} = -1943 - 1096 \text{ (Northeast)} - 817(\text{Midwest}) - 265(\text{West}) \ 0.132 \text{ per capita personal income} \tag{6.2}$$

SPENDPC: Per capita amounts by State for Prime Contract Awards and Compensation, Department of Defense.
All variables are significant at the 5 per cent level or higher.
The omitted region in the above regression is the South, indicating that, controlling for income, average defence spending is almost $1,000 lower in the Northeast and the Midwest than in the South. The fact that per capita income has a positive effect on defence spending suggests that the concentration of defence spending in the South is not due to lower wages in that region.

35. By region, southern states tend to have relatively large positive balances, while states in the Northeast have the largest negative balances. The balance of payments results are primarily a result of the interaction between regional income disparities and graduated income taxation.
36. This visual picture is supported by regression analysis showing that for every dollar increase in federal grants, state–local revenues increased by $2.
37. The decline in state–local receipts reflects the sharp drop in tax revenues from a decline in state and local tax bases in the aftermath of a deep and prolonged recession, rather than a choice to decrease tax rates on a stable base (Dadayan and Boyd, 2013).
38. These estimates translate into an elasticity of welfare spending with respect to the price −0.43, within the range reported by Chernick (1998) for the AFDC programme.
39. The latter category now comprises two-thirds of all Medicaid spending.
40. Eight states spent more than 20 per cent of their own revenue on Medicaid, while five states spent less than 10 per cent.
41. Kane et al. (2005) find that Medicaid crowds out higher education spending. In a

comment, Inman (2005) argues that the instruments used by these authors are not valid, and that Medicaid spending represents a choice by states. Baicker (2001) finds that federal mandates to enhance Medicaid coverage have the effect of crowding out other types of welfare expenditures.

42. The spending reduction effect has been more powerful than predicted from analyses of the effect of variation in matching rates on welfare spending prior to TANF (Chernick, 1998).
43. Chernick and Reschovsky (2018) found that cities with higher fiscal capacity received more direct federal aid.
44. Adjustments in staffing levels for non-government agencies than for government employees are likely to be more rapid, as cities shift the risk underlying uncertain resource flows to the non-profits.
45. Capping the amount of grant dollars to any one recipient allows a spreading of federal resources among more recipients, thus increasing political support for the grant.
46. These cuts are similar to the patterns for large cities, where capital outlays declined by 19 per cent from their peak in 2009, the most of any category of city spending.
47. There has been some concern in the literature that federal funding of capital as opposed to operating expenses can lead to inefficiencies. Cromwell (1989) finds that federal capital grants for mass transportation have led to premature replacement of older buses by newer ones. However, the degree of inefficiency is not particularly large.

REFERENCES

Aaron, H. (2005). 'Comment on "Reforming U.S. Fiscal Arrangements," by Edward Gramlich.' In *American Domestic Priorities: An Economic Appraisal*, John M. Quigley and Daniel Rubinfeld (eds), 70–74. Berkeley, CA: University of California Press.

Ayala, L., E. Bárcena-Martín and J. Martínez-Vázquez (2017). 'The Unintended Distributional Costs of Devolution in the U.S. Welfare Reform.' International Center for Public Policy Working Paper Series, at AYSPS, GSU paper 1719, International Center for Public Policy, Andrew Young School of Policy Studies, Georgia State University.

Baicker, K. (2001). 'Government Decision-Making and the Incidence of Federal Mandates.' *Journal of Public Economics*, **82** (2), November, 147–94.

Bohn, H. and R. Inman (1996). 'Balanced Budget Rules and Public Deficits: Evidence from the U.S. States.' Carnegie-Rochester Conference Series on Public Policy, November.

Carlino, G. and R. Inman (2016). 'Fiscal Stimulus in Economic Unions: What Role for States?' *Tax Policy and the Economy*, **30** (1), 1–50.

Carsey, T. and B. Rundquist (1999). 'The Reciprocal Relationship between State Defense Interest and Committee Representation in Congress.' *Public Choice*, **99** (June), 455–63.

Chernick, H. (1979). 'An Economic Model of the Distribution of Project Grants.' In *Fiscal Federalism and Grants-in-Aid*, COUPE Papers on Public Economics 1, Peter Mieszkowski and William Oakland (eds), 81–103. Washington, DC: Urban Institute.

Chernick, H. (1998). 'Fiscal Effects of Block Grants for the Needy: An Interpretation of the Evidence.' *International Tax and Public Finance*, **5** (May), 205–33.

Chernick, H. (2018). 'The 2017 Federal Tax Cuts and Jobs Act: Its Impact on Massachusetts and New York.' *MassBenchmarks*, **20** (1), 11–17.

Chernick, H. and C. Reimers (2019). 'Medicaid Generosity and State Medicaid Outlays during the Great Recession.' Mimeo, Hunter College.

Chernick, H. and A. Reschovsky (2018). 'Measuring the Fiscal Health of U.S. Cities.' Mimeo, Lincoln Institute of Land Policy.

Chernick, H. and J. Tennant (2010). 'Federal-State Tax Interactions in the U.S. and Canada.' *Publius: The Journal of Federalism*, **40** (3), 508–33.

Chernick, H., S. Newman and A. Reschovsky (2018). 'The Effect of the Housing Crisis on the Finances of Central Cities.' In review, *Journal of Housing Economics*.

Cogan, J. and J. Taylor (2012). 'What the Government Purchases Multiplier Actually Multiplied in the 2009 Stimulus Package.' In *Government Policies and the Delayed Economic Recovery*, Lee Ohanian and John Taylor (eds), 85–114. Stanford, CA: Hoover Institution Press.

Cromwell, B. (1989). 'Capital Subsidies and the Infrastructure Crisis: Evidence from the Local Mass Transit Industry.' Federal Reserve Bank of Cleveland Working Paper Series, quarter 2. Accessed February 4, 2013. at http://www.clevelandfed.org/research/review/1989/89-q2-cromwell.pdf.

Dadayan, L. and D. Boyd (2013). 'State Revenue Report: State Tax Revenues Continue Slow Rebound.' Rockefeller Institute of Government, No. 90 (February). Accessed February 4, 2019, at http://www.rockinst.org/pdf/government_finance/state_revenue_report/SSR-90.pdf.

Dilger, R. (2018). 'Federal Grants to State and Local Governments: An Historical Perspective on Contemporary Issues.' CRS 7-5700. Accessed January 16, 2019, at https://fas.org/sgp/crs/misc/R 40638.pdf.

Fisher, R. and R. Sullivan (2016). 'Why is State and Local Government Capital Spending Lower in the New England States than in Other U.S. States?' New England Public Policy Center, Federal Reserve Bank of Boston. Policy Report 16-1.

Fisher, R. and R. Wassmer (2015). 'An Analysis of State and Local Government Capital Expenditure during the 2000s.' *Public Budgeting and Finance*, **35** (1), 3–28.

GAO (Government Accountability Office) (1998). 'Defense Spending: Trends and Geographical Distribution of Prime Contract Awards and Compensation.' GAO/NSIAD-98-195.

GAO (2004). 'Federal Assistance: Temporary State Fiscal Relief.' GAO-04-736R.

GAO (2005). 'Community Development Block Grant Formula: Targeting Assistance to High-Need Communities Could Be Enhanced.' GAO-05-622T.

GAO (2009). 'Formula Grants: Funding for the Largest Federal Assistance Programs Based on Census-Related Data and Other Factors.' GAO-10-263.

Gillette, C. (2004). 'Constraining Misuse of Funds from Intergovernmental Grants: A Legal Analysis.' In *Fiscal Federalism in Unitary States*, Per Molander (ed.), 101–22. Nowell, MA: Kluwer Academic Publishers.

Gordon, N. (2004). 'Do Federal Grants Boost School Spending? Evidence from Title I.' *Journal of Public Economics*, **88** (9–10), 1771–92.

Gordon, R. and J.B. Cullen (2012). 'Income Redistribution in a Federal System of Governments.' *Journal of Public Economics*, **96** (11–12), 1100–109.

Gordon, T. (2018). 'Harnessing the U.S. Intergovernmental Grant System for Place-Based Assistance in Recession and Recovery'. The Hamilton Project, Policy Proposal. September.

Gramlich, E. and H. Galper (1973). 'State and Local Fiscal Behavior and Federal Grant Policy.' *Brookings Papers on Economic Activity*, **1**, 15–65.

Heller, W. and J. Pechman (1967). 'Questions and Answers on Revenue Sharing.' In *Revenue Sharing and Its Alternatives: What Future for Fiscal Federalism?* Testimony to U.S. Joint Economic Committee, 107–22. Washington, DC: U.S. Government Printing Office.

Holahan, J. (2003). 'Variation in Health Insurance Coverage and Medical Expenditures: How Much is Too Much?' In *Federalism and Health Policy*, John Holahan, Alan Weil and Joshua Wiener (eds), 111–44. Washington, DC: The Urban Institute Press.

Holahan, J. and A. Garrett (2009). 'Rising Unemployment, Medicaid and the Uninsured,' Kaiser Commission on Medicaid and the Uninsured, Washington, DC (January).

Inman, R. (2005). 'Comment on Kane et al.' *Brookings-Wharton Papers on Urban Affairs*, 147–9.

Inman, R. (2008). 'The Flypaper Effect.' National Bureau of Economic Research Working Paper 14579.

Joint Committee on Taxation, U.S. Congress (2013). 'Estimates of Federal Tax Expenditures for Fiscal Years 2012–2017.' U.S. Government Printing Office 78-317, Washington: 2013 JCS-1-UU13. Accessed January 15, 2019 at https://www.jct.gov/publications.html?func=startdown&id=4504.

Joint Committee on Taxation, U.S. Congress (2018). 'Estimates of Federal Tax Expenditures for Fiscal Years 2017–2021.' May. JCX-34-18.

Kaiser Commission on Medicaid and the Uninsured (2011). 'Impact of the Medicaid Fiscal Relief Provision in the American Recovery and Reinvestment Act (ARRA).' October. Accessed June 13, 2018 at http://www.kff.org/medicaid/upload/8252.pdf.

Kane, T., P. Orszag and E. Apostolov (2005). 'Higher Education Appropriations and Public Universities: Role of Medicaid and the Business Cycle'. *Brookings-Wharton Papers on Urban Affairs*, 99–146.

Keegan, N. (2012). 'Federal Grants-in-Aid Administration: A Primer.' Congressional Research Service, Report for Congress 7-5700. 3 October.

Knight, B. (2002). 'Endogenous Federal Grants and Crowd-Out of State Government Spending: Theory and Evidence from the Federal Highway Aid Program.' *American Economic Review*, **92** (1), 71–92.

Knight, B. (2005). 'Estimating the Value of Proposal Power.' *American Economic Review*, **95** (5), 1639–52.

Ku, L. and T.A. Coughlin (1995). 'Medicaid Disproportionate Share and Other Special Financing Programs'. *Health Care Financing Review*, **16** (3), 27–54.

Leduc, S. and D. Wilson (2013). 'Are State Governments Roadblocks to Federal Stimulus? Evidence from Highway Grants in the 2009 Recovery Act.' Federal Reserve Bank of San Francisco, WP 2013-16.

Mallett, W. (2018). 'Federal Public Transportation Program: In Brief.' Congressional Research Service. 30 April. Accessed February 12, 2019 at https://fas.org/sgp/crs/misc/R42706.pdf.

Penner, R. (1979). 'Reforming the Grants System.' In *Fiscal Federalism and Grants-in-Aid*, COUPE Papers on Public Economics 1, Peter Mieszkowski and William Oakland (eds), 111–37. Washington, DC: The Urban Institute.

Reschovsky, A. (1994). 'Fiscal Equalization and School Finance.' *National Tax Journal*, **47** (1), 185–97.

Rudowitz, R., E. Hinon and L. Antonisse (2018). 'Medicaid Enrollment and Spending Growth: FY 2018 and 2019.' Kaiser Family Foundation. Accessed February 14,

2019 at https://www.kff.org/medicaid/issue-brief/medicaid-enrollment-spending
-growth-fy-2018-2019.

Sawicky, M. (2001). 'An Ideal whose Time has Returned: Anti-Recession Fiscal Assistance for State and Local Governments.' Economic Policy Institute. October. Accessed June 10, 2013 at http://www.epi.org/publication/bp116/.

Schultz, L. and M. Cummings (2019). 'Giving or Getting? New York's Balance of Payments with the Federal Government – 2019 Report.' Rockefeller Institute of Government. Accessed February 13, 2019 at https://rockinst.org/wp-content/uploads/2019/01/1-7-19b-Balance-of-Payments.pdf.

Schultze, C. (1974). 'Sorting Out the Social Grant Programs: An Economist's Criteria.' *American Economic Review*, **64** (2),181–9.

Tax Foundation (2019). 'Which States Rely the Most on Federal Aid?' Accessed February 13, 2019 at https://taxfoundation.org/federal-aid-reliance-rankings/.

U.S. Census (2017). 'Annual Survey of School System Finances.' 2017 Public Elementary-Secondary Education Finance Data, Table 1. Accessed February 15, 2019 at https://www.census.gov/programs-surveys/school-finances/data/tables.html.

U.S. Office of Management and Budget. 'Federal Budget History.' Accessed January 16, 2019 at https://www.whitehouse.gov/omb/historical-tables/.

Weingast, B., K. Shepsle and C. Johnsen (1981). 'The Political Economy of Benefits and Costs: A Neoclassical Approach to Distributive Politics.' *Journal of Political Economy*, **89** (4), 642–64.

Yilmaz, Y., S. Hoo, M. Nagowski, K. Rueben and R. Tannenwald (2006). 'Fiscal Disparities across States, FY 2002.' Urban Institute and the New England Public Policy Center at the Federal Reserve Bank of Boston, Washington, DC.

7. Federal finance arrangements in Canada: the challenges of fiscal imbalance and natural resource rents*

Marcelin Joanis and François Vaillancourt

INTRODUCTION

Federal arrangements in place at a point in time in a country are (given preferences and technology) the result of five factors: geography, history, demography, economics and politics. This chapter, which focuses on the intergovernmental finance arrangements in Canada, presents in its first part the key aspects of Canadian fiscal federalism. The second part provides a critical overview of some of the changes in Canadian fiscal federalism over the past three decades, with a focus on a debate on fiscal imbalance in the 1995–2005 period that still resonates in 2019. The third part focuses on current natural resources issues in Canadian federalism, examining: (1) the treatment of natural resource rents in equalization; (2) the difficulties over access to the sea for inland oil and gas; and (3) the taxation of carbon. The second of these three items illustrates how geography interacting with political agendas can create conflicts in a federation. The third one examines interaction between multilevel taxation, regulation of the environment and international environmental commitments; here geography, economics and politics interact with a multi-generational dimension in the background.

7.1 FISCAL FEDERALISM IN CANADA: A PRIMER

7.1.1 Demography, Economy and Institutions

Canada comprises ten provinces, three territories, numerous first nations but no national capital territory. Appendix Table 7A.1 presents key

109

characteristics of these 13 subnational governments (SNGs). Provinces account for 99 per cent of Canada's population and have substantially more autonomy than territories, especially in terms of financing.[1] Thus, throughout the chapter, we focus on the provinces.

Key facts (documented in Appendix Table 7A.1) about Canadian provinces include:

● Area-wise, Québec is the largest province followed by Ontario and British Columbia (BC);
● Population-wise, Ontario is the largest followed by Québec, with BC and Alberta fairly similar afterwards. Population is older in the Maritime provinces, Québec and BC;
● Alberta has the highest gross domestic product (GDP) per capita, almost twice that of Prince Edward Island (PEI). Petroleum production is concentrated in Alberta; and
● PEI is the province most dependent on federal transfers and BC, the least.[2]

Two institutional features should also be noted. First, Canada has a bicameral parliament but the appointed upper house (Senate) does not have the role of representing the regions. Second, while English and French are the official languages of Canada (Constitution Act of 1982), only 18 per cent of Canadians know both languages.[3] Francophones are concentrated in Québec, creating two fairly distinct labour markets in Canada.[4]

We now turn to a description of the key fiscal federalism arrangements.

7.1.2 Assignment of Spending/Regulatory Responsibilities and Taxation Powers

In terms of responsibilities, the federal government has the standard sovereign functions of defence, foreign affairs and money and banking. It is also responsible for telecommunications, broadcasting, non-road transportation, unemployment insurance, child benefits and old age pensions as well as immigration and agriculture (jointly with provinces). Provinces provide universal public health services, education, welfare, worker compensation and roads. Municipalities provide local services such as fire protection, roads, culture and sports, water and waste. Policing is provided by all three levels of government.

Turning to taxation, the federal government and Canadian provinces are constitutionally able to tax anything they want, except that international and interprovincial trade is not taxable by provinces. Natural resource rents are provincial revenues. Provinces can set their own tax base (definition of income, exemptions, deductions and so on), their own rates and collect their own taxes. In practice:

- Nine provinces (not Québec) use the federal Canada Revenue Agency (CRA) to collect their personal income tax (PIT), while eight (not Québec or Alberta) use it to collect the corporate income tax (CIT). To be able to use CRA services free of charge, provinces must use the federal definition of income but can set their own brackets (number, boundaries for the PIT) and their tax rates;[5]
- Five provinces (not Québec, the Prairie provinces and BC) use the services of the CRA to collect the Harmonized Sales Tax (HST), a joint federal-provincial value added tax (VAT) that combines the federal GST (Goods and Services Tax) and provincial taxes. Québec collects its own sales tax and the GST on behalf of the federal government.

7.1.3 Federal-Provincial Transfers

There are three major federal-provincial transfer programmes in Canada: equalization and the Canada Health and Social Transfers. Before turning to these main transfers, let us note that there also exists a diverse set of transfers that can be grouped under the label 'small transfers' (Vaillancourt, 2000).[6] These transfers are conditional grants for specific items such as social housing, agricultural income support and so on. Each is subject to specific cost-sharing conditions.

7.1.3.1 Equalization
Equalization was introduced in 1957 to facilitate the reintroduction by provinces of PIT, CIT and succession duties, levied by provinces before World War II, but 'rented out' to the federal government to finance the war effort. It is a Representative Tax System (RTS) formula with no needs or cost indicators. The main aspects are as follows.

Legal From 1957 to 1982, the programme was supported solely by a federal law. In 1982, as part of a package of constitutional changes, the principle of equalization was included in the Constitution as follows:

> Parliament and the government of Canada are committed to the principle of making equalization payments to ensure that provincial governments have sufficient revenues to provide reasonably comparable levels of public services at reasonably comparable levels of taxation. (The 1982 Canada Constitution Act, Section 36(2)[7])

The envelope and the allocation criteria are specified in federal legisla-
tion. The equalization programme has been formally reviewed a few times
(Gilbert and Vaillancourt, 2007); the last time was in 2004–06 (Expert
Panel on Equalization and Territorial Formula Financing, 2006).

Funding   Equalization in Canada is a vertical transfer, entirely funded
by the federal government from general revenues. Over the 1957–2019
period, the total amount of equalization has been most of the time determined as the sum of provincial entitlements. Thus, the allocation formula
has also been the envelope driver; this explains in part why it has been
changed several times over that period (Joanis, 2018). In some years an
aggregate amount (usually a cap, see below) has been implemented.

Allocation formula   In general, the following is calculated for each of the
tax bases in the formula:

$$
\begin{matrix} \text{Right} \\ \text{province } j \end{matrix} = \left[\left(\begin{matrix} \text{Fiscal capacity} \\ \text{standard} \end{matrix} - \begin{matrix} \text{Fiscal capacity} \\ \text{province } j \end{matrix} \right) * \begin{matrix} \text{Average} \\ \text{tax rate} \end{matrix} \right] * \begin{matrix} \text{Population} \\ \text{province } j \end{matrix}
$$

$$(7.1)$$

The sum of equalization rights for each of the sources gives the equalization payment that province *j* is entitled to receive for a given year. Provinces
for which the formula yields a negative amount do not need to pay; they
simply do not receive any equalization, that is, Canada has a gross equalization scheme.

The number of revenue sources included started at three in 1957 but
over time has increased to take into account all types of provincial revenues
(sales taxes, liquor revenues, gambling). Before 2007, equalization amounts
were calculated for each such source. Since then, five tax bases are used to
calculate equalization.

From 1957 until 1967, the fiscal capacity of the two richest provinces
(two out of Alberta, British Columbia and Ontario, varying over time) was
the standard except for 1962–63 (national average). In 1967, the standard
became the national average fiscal capacity. From 1982 to 2007, the standard was the average of five 'representative provinces' (Québec, Ontario,
Manitoba, Saskatchewan and British Columbia); in 2007, it reverted to
the national average.

Currently (2019), the total equalization payments are determined by the
following calculations:[8]

1. Calculate the two-year lagged, three-year weighted average (50 per cent weight for the nearest and 25 per cent for each of the two furthest) of non-resource fiscal capacity;
2. Calculate the same for resource fiscal capacity;
3. Calculate the equalization entitlements as the highest for each province with either zero or 50 per cent resource revenue inclusion;
4. Calculate the equalization of each province so that it does not exceed the Fiscal Capacity Cap (FCC, discussed below); and
5. Adjust the payments to each province to account for an overall (total) cap or floor on the sum of payments to provinces.

There can be important differences between the amounts calculated in step (3) with or without including 50 per cent of resource revenues. For example, Newfoundland is entitled to equalization with 0 per cent of resource revenues included but not with 50 per cent.

The FCC is different from fiscal capacity for equalization (FCE); both include 100 per cent of non-resource fiscal capacity (step 1 above) but FCE adds only 50 per cent of resource capacity (step 2), while FCC adds 100 per cent of resource capacity and equalization entitlements. The calculation of the FCC depends on the share of the population that receives equalization payments as follows:

1. When equalization-receiving provinces represent less than 50 per cent of the Canadian population, the FCC is determined by the total post-equalization per capita fiscal capacity of the lowest non-receiving province (usually Ontario); or
2. When equalization-receiving provinces represent more than 50 per cent of the Canadian population (which means Ontario is a receiving province), the FCC is determined as the average total post-equalization per capita fiscal capacity of all equalization-receiving provinces.

Turning to step 5, the aggregate equalization amount (AEA) that is the total cap or floor is set at $14,185 million for 2010–11[9] based on the total produced by the pre-AEA formula for the preceding year and with indexation applied (Finance Canada, 2008a); it is then indexed to the average growth of nominal GDP for the three calendar years preceding a fiscal year.[10]

If the AEA is a cap, then the (federal) *Minister* shall *determine the per capita reduction for a fiscal year* but if it is a floor *there* may *be paid to a province for that fiscal year an adjustment payment* (underlined by authors).[11] From 2009 to 2018, the AEA acted as a cap on equalization payments. For 2018–19 and 2019–20 it is acting as a floor. This possibility was noted by Nadeau (2014), predicted by Eisen et al. (2017) and well described by Tombe (2018b). Thus, in 2018–19, about 10 per cent of equalization payments are due to the adjustment payment. Ontario receives this payment even if it is not entitled to equalization since its total fiscal capacity would be below that of any equalization-receiving province without them, an upward adjustment based on the FCC concept. For 2019–20, this adjustment payment is only 2 per cent of equalization as Ontario no longer receives it. The federal minister of finance does not need to justify exceeding the floor; Tombe (2018b) argues that 'whether equalization does or doesn't have a floor is ultimately a policy question for the government'. It is also a political question; all receiving provinces were given more than they would have received otherwise and thus none complained.

7.1.3.2   Health and social transfers

History and legal aspects   The CHT and the CST were established in 2004 (Finance Canada, 2014). They replaced the Canada Health and Social Transfer (CHST) established in 1996, when the Established Programs Financing (EPF) and the Canada Assistance Plan (CAP) transfers were merged. The EPF had been created in 1977 as a block grant, replacing three separate cost-sharing federal transfers: (1) Post-Secondary Education; (2) Hospital Insurance and Diagnostic Services; and (3) Medical Care. The CAP financed welfare on a 50-50 cost sharing basis. The amount (base and growth) of the CHT and CST, both financed out of general federal revenues, is decided unilaterally by the federal government. It has been subject to various changes overtime.

The CHT requires the Medicare plan of a province to satisfy the criteria of the Canada Health Act, which are: Public administration; Comprehensiveness; Universality; Portability; Accessibility; Prohibition of extra-billing and of user charges. Madore (2003) presents in detail their exact meaning. Not respecting the prohibition requirement results in a reduction in federal transfers equal to the amount thus collected.[12] Provinces otherwise have great leeway in the organization, delivery and type of services provided (Health Canada, 2015).

Financing   Before 2014 the CHT resulted in a cash transfer to each province, calculated according to the level of the national per capita transfer set at the federal level, provincial population, and the value of tax points transferred to provinces in 1977. The use of transferred tax points in calculating cash transfers appears unique to Canadian fiscal federalism. Tax points in lieu of cash transfers, while first used in 1960, became important in 1966 when Québec was allowed to opt/contract out of major federal transfers, with the federal government reducing the amount of federal taxes it collects in that province, thus allowing Québec to collect more provincial PIT.[13] Thus, tax points refer to the tax room (measured as a percentage of taxable income) vacated by the federal government. Starting in 1977, the federal government considered the value of these tax points to be federal transfers, while the provinces treated them as own revenues. This created confusion as to the value of federal financing of CHST programmes. Since 2007 for the CST (Gauthier, 2012) and 2014 for the CHT, per capita cash transfers are the same for all provinces.

CHT calculations[14] The Canada Health Transfer is currently calculated in two parts:

1. Setting the size of the overall CHT envelope. The envelope was last reset in dollar terms in 2005;[15] it was indexed at 6 per cent per year from 2006–07 until 2017–18. Starting in 2017–18, the total CHT envelope grows in line with a three-year moving average of nominal GDP growth, with a minimum annual growth of 3 per cent.
2. Allocating the envelope to each province. CHT is allocated on an equal per capita basis across provinces.

CST calculations The Canada Social Transfer is calculated in two parts:

1. Setting the size of the overall CST envelope. The envelope was last reset in dollar terms in 2009;[16] it grows automatically by 3 per cent per year.
2. Allocating the envelope to each province. The CST is allocated on an equal per capita basis across all provinces.

7.1.4 Financial Flows

Table 7.1 presents the main financial indicators of relevance. It shows that:

* Federal transfers to other levels of government (essentially provinces) account for one-fifth of spending and of provincial revenues; this is about 3 per cent of GDP; and
* Equalization is about one-quarter of major transfers to provinces. The biggest transfer is the CHT.

Table 7.1 Federal government spending (total and by type) and provincial revenues, Canada, 2014–18

Year	Transfers to persons as % of federal spending	Transfers to other governments as % of federal spending	Direct + debt spending as % of federal spending	Total federal spending ($000000)	Provincial revenues ($000000)	Federal transfers as % of provincial revenues	Equalization ($000000)	CHT ($000000)	CST ($000000)
2014–15	27.0	22.3	50.7	282896	377941	18.0	16669	32113	12582
2015–16	27.8	22.1	50.1	298314	385695	19.0	17341	34026	12959
2016–17	29.1	22.0	48.9	312452	399542	20.0	17880	36068	13348
2017–18	28.2	21.2	50.6	332567	422459	19.0	18254	37150	13748

Note: In Canadian dollars ($).

Source: Finance Canada, *Fiscal Reference Tables* 7, 8, 9, 11 and 31–32 (accessed 19 September 2019 at https://www.fin.gc.ca/frt-trf/2018/frt-trf-18-eng.asp and accessed 19 September 2019 at https://www.fin.gc.ca/fedprov/mtp-eng.asp).

7.2 FISCAL IMBALANCE AND THE EVOLUTION OF CANADA'S FEDERAL-PROVINCIAL FISCAL ARRANGEMENTS[17]

The last three decades have seen a series of changes to Canada's main federal-provincial transfers, some of which were highlighted in the previous sections. This section provides a critical overview of some of these developments.

7.2.1 The Fiscal Imbalance Debate in the Late 1990s and Early 2000s

The introduction in equalization calculations of the five-province standard in 1982 and of a cap (new framework) on the total amount in 2004 were aimed at reducing the programme costs. The introduction of the CHST was accompanied by important (Laurent and Vaillancourt, 2004) unilateral cuts in health and social transfers[18] in the 1995 federal budget to facilitate achieving a balanced federal budget. Provinces could, in various proportions, reduce their spending, increase their taxes or borrow over the 1995–98 period. Yet, a few years later new federal programmes were reintroduced in the social policy field (Laurent and Vaillancourt, 2004) following the reappearance of federal surpluses. A historical look at federal spending initiatives shows that high federal revenues and potential surpluses are often accompanied by new cost-shared programmes, while drops in federal revenues are accompanied by cuts to the funding of these programmes leaving the provinces in the lurch.

Such changes led to the emergence of federal-provincial confrontation on 'fiscal imbalance' in the federation. Provincial demands at the time were reviewed by Quebec's Commission on Fiscal Imbalance (CFI), also known as the Séguin Commission.[19]

The CFI was mandated 'to identify and analyze the basic causes of the fiscal imbalance between the federal government and Québec'. Its final report (CFI, 2002, p. vii) states that:

> The fiscal imbalance between the government of Canada and the Québec government and, more generally, between the federal government and the provinces, stems essentially from three separate causes, namely imbalance between spending and access to sources of revenue, the inadequacy of intergovernmental transfers from the federal government to the provinces and the 'federal spending power'.

The main recommendations of the Séguin report were:

● To address vertical fiscal imbalance, the replacement of the CHST by a once-and-for-all tax-point transfer, either for the PIT or the GST;

- To address horizontal fiscal imbalance, changes to the equalization programme to make it a true RTS; and
- Various changes to the institutional framework of the federal-provincial fiscal arrangements, mainly to reduce the federal government's ability to make arbitrary changes.

These recommendations were guided by three 'principles of fiscal balance':

1. *Accountability principle:* each level of government must be accountable to its electorate for the decisions taken in its own constitutional fields of responsibility.
2. *Fiscal capacity principle:* each level of government must have the necessary financial resources to fulfil its own constitutional expenditure responsibilities.
3. *Autonomy principle:* each level of government must have the necessary decisional and budgetary autonomy in its own fields of constitutional responsibilities.

7.2.2   The Fiscal Arrangements after the Séguin Report

In 2004, the need was felt by both the federal government and the provinces to rethink the equalization programme once more. Two reports would eventually be produced, one by the Council of the Federation[20] and one by the federal department of Finance (the O'Brien taskforce).

The O'Brien report's main recommendations, all pertaining to the equalization programme, were:

- To simplify the RTS by reducing the number of tax bases used in calculating revenue capacity to five, one of which would be for natural resources;
- To adopt a ten-province standard; and
- To set the inclusion rate of natural resource revenues at 50 per cent.

While the O'Brien and Séguin reports agree on the ten-province standard, the 50 per cent inclusion rate for natural resource revenues in the O'Brien report can be seen as violation of the integral respect of the RTS defended by the Séguin report. Respecting the RTS integrally would treat all revenue sources in the same way and include them all fully (100 per cent) in equalization calculations. Yet, it represented a compromise with those advocating their full exclusion on the basis that natural resources are provincially owned according to the Constitution and thus yield private revenues.[21] However, since 2007, provinces now receive the highest amount of equalization based on calculations using either 50 or 0 per cent of natural resource revenues. This fulfils the Conservative Party's electoral promise to fully exclude natural resource revenues from the equalization formula.

Looking back, we can examine how the system of federal-provincial transfers meets the main recommendation of the CFI (Joanis, 2014):

1. Replacing the CHST by a transfer of tax points was not done; we now have the CHT and the CST;[22]
2. Replacing the five-province standard by the national average in equalization calculations is done;
3. Setting the total amount of equalization through the formula is not done: floors and ceilings are in place;
4. Full inclusion of natural resources is not in place, in part because of the Atlantic Accords (see Box 7.1); and
5. Unilateral changes in indicators can still be imposed by the federal government.

Generally speaking, the recommendations of the CFI have not been followed. In retrospect, it is interesting to note that issues pertaining to natural resources were almost entirely absent from the CFI report with the exception of a critique of the Atlantic accords. Since the most contentious issues in Canadian federalism in 2018–19 pertain to natural resources, we examine them in the next section.

7.3   NATURAL RESOURCES AND FISCAL FEDERALISM IN CANADA: CONTEMPORARY ISSUES

Three contemporary issues dealing with natural resources will be addressed here: (1) accounting for natural resource rents in equalization; (2) pipelines; and (3) carbon taxation.

7.3.1   Hydroelectric Rent: A Dissipated Resource?

A first contentious issue has to do with the way in which the equalization programme incorporates provincial revenues derived from various natural revenues. Revenues are used for this tax base while taxable capacity is used for the four other tax bases. Thus, there is a possibility of 'dissipated rents' for oil, natural gas and so on. However, the debate has focused on the dissipated rents associated with hydroelectric production.

BOX 7.1   THE ATLANTIC ACCORDS

There are three agreements commonly referred to as the Atlantic Accords:
The 1985 Atlantic Accord with Newfoundland-and-Labrador(I);
The 1986 Offshore Petroleum Resources Accord with Nova Scotia(II); and
The 2005 Offshore Arrangements with both provinces(III).
The two goals of the Accords are:

- To allow these two provinces to tax offshore resources as if they owned them (the federal government is the lawful owner); and
- To maintain for a set period, in whole or in part, equalization payments even if taxable capacity has increased.

(I) provided Newfoundland-and-Labrador with transitional protection, for a 12-year period beginning in 1999–2000, using a two-component formula:

- The *offset floor* component guarantees Newfoundland-and-Labrador a certain percentage (at least 85 per cent) of its total equalization and offset floor entitlement for the previous year; and
- The *phase-out* component provides additional protection against declines in payments, by guaranteeing a certain percentage of year-over-year declines in total equalization and offset floor payments. This percentage gradually declines over the 12-year period.

(II) provided Nova Scotia with transitional protection, for a 10-year period beginning in 1993–94, from reductions in equalization. A formula sheltered a declining percentage of offshore revenues from equalization over a 10-year period. In 2004, the government of Canada made payments to Nova Scotia to effectively reset the start of the 1986 Accord payments.
(III) The two Accords provide:

- 100 per cent protection from equalization reductions resulting from the inclusion of offshore revenues in the equalization programme for eight years (from 2004–05 to 2011–12) as long as the province receives equalization;
- An upfront payment in 2005 of $2.0 billion to Newfoundland and $830 million to Nova Scotia, made in 2005, to allow the province immediate flexibility to address its unique fiscal challenges. This is a pre-payment in respect of the new 100 per cent protection;
- In addition, this arrangement provides for a further eight-year extension if the province receives equalization in 2010–11 or 2011–12 and its per capita debt servicing charges have not become lower than that of at least four other provinces;
- During the second eight-year period, if the province no longer qualifies for equalization, it would receive transitional payments for two years: in the first year, this payment would equal two-thirds of the offset payments and in the second year one-third of the offset payments the province was entitled to the last year it received equalization; and

- The province could requalify for offsets and transitional payments if it again became eligible to receive equalization payments.

In our opinion, two key items to note are:

- Upfront payments to allow the province immediate flexibility to address its unique fiscal challenges (this is a pre-payment in respect of the new 100 per cent protection); and
- The link between per capita debt service charges and the length of the agreement.

Source: Authors, drawing on Finance Canada (2008b, 2008c).

The first proposal to account for these dissipated (uncollected) hydro-electric rent for equalization purposes is by Zuker and Jenkins (1984). They argue that: 'Because the benefits of lower electricity rates arising from low-cost hydro sites are not available to the residents of all provinces [. . .] fiscal benefits arising from hydro-electric consumption should be equalized in the same way as the benefits arising from the revenues on oil and gas and other natural resources' (p. 1). Courchene (2013, p. 10) takes this up 30 years later: 'it seems appropriate to act on the many recommendations to bring hydro-electricity rents more fully and formally into the equalization calculations for these provinces'. Feehan (2014, p. 18) also argues for this.

What is the evidence on the geographic disparities of hydroelectric rent? Line 13 of Appendix Table 7A.1 shows that the largest share of hydroelectricity is produced in Québec, with BC the next largest producer. Electricity prices are the lowest in Québec, followed by Manitoba and BC, and highest in PEI, at 2.5 times that of Québec for residential consumers.[23] In 2011 in Canada, 39 per cent of households use electricity as their main energy source for heating; in Québec, it is 85 per cent and in Alberta, 9 per cent.[24] So there is empirical support for rent dissipation occurring unequally between provinces.

There are two issues to be addressed to include it in the equalization formula. First, equalization in Canada is based on the RTS. 'Representative' is implemented as what is done by the provinces in various tax/revenue fields. For instance, gambling revenues were added in the 1970s after gambling became legal in Canada and provinces started offering various types of gaming. In the case of hydroelectricity, it appears that the representative behaviour of provinces is not to fully price hydroelectricity; why should a different criterion be used for this revenue source? This would be a first in Canadian equalization and would open the door to other judgement-laden choices. What would prevent arguing that a province with a higher payoff from gaming or lower markups from alcoholic beverages than other provinces is subsidizing these purchases (dissipating potential revenues), and therefore should see its taxable capacity adjusted upwards and its equalization payments downwards?

Second, this would treat revenues derived from one natural resource differently from all other resource revenues in the equalization formula, using notional rather than real prices and revenues. The price to be used is not always clearly stated by proponents of this approach, but Feehan (2014, p. 18) argues that 'the increased development of competitive wholesale electricity markets in North America has resulted in prices that can serve as indicators of the value of electricity [. . .]'. This would explicitly introduce in the Canadian equalization formula American prices; we are not aware of any national intergovernmental transfer formula, equalization or other, which has as an explicit parameter a foreign value. If one examines the pricing of provincial and foreign sales of electricity for the two largest producers of hydroelectricity for 2015, one finds an average domestic price per kilowatt of $0.064 for Québec and $0.094 for BC, while for exports one finds $0.056 and $0.035. Thus, there is no dissipated rent when real prices are used. One would also need to account for the fact that part of the dissipated rent results in higher economic activity and higher consumption of other goods and services that thus increase the tax base of dissipating provinces.

7.3.2   Pipelines

Alberta is a landlocked province that historically sent its petroleum products to Canadian and US refineries. The emergence of US shale oil since 2000 has dampened the price of petroleum in the US, while constraints on pipeline capacity have led to the use of rail shipping that is more expensive than pipelines. As a consequence, the price of Western Canada Select (WCS) is often lower than the West Texas Intermediate (WTI) price.[25] Thus, there has been a demand by Alberta for new pipelines, a federal government responsibility when they cross provincial or international borders.

Three pipelines from Alberta to the sea shore were under discussion in early 2015:

1. 'Northern Gateway': a new pipeline in the North of BC was blocked by the federal government in Fall 2016;
2. 'Trans Mountain' pipeline (TMP): an expansion of an existing pipeline in the south of BC was approved by the federal government in Fall 2016; and

3. 'Energy East': a new pipeline to Québec refineries and New Brunswick was dropped by Trans Canada Pipeline (TCP) in Fall 2017. This was linked to the acceptance by the Trump administration of the TCP Keystone project to ship to the US, reversing an Obama administration decision but Québec politicians were also strongly opposed.[26]

The TMP pipeline approval was, however, just a starting point since building it has not begun as of May 2019.[27]

The 2015–19 pipeline debate in Canada has thus seen:

- An attempt by one province, BC, to subvert federal powers on pipelines[28] through environmental regulations. In so far as the environment is a shared policy field, provinces do have a role to play in it but, in general, federal laws and regulations predominate given the doctrine of paramountcy.[29]
- An attempt by one province, BC, to obtain a share of natural resource royalty revenues earned by another province, Alberta, in exchange for a right of way for these resources. This was an unprecedented demand that was not acceded to and was abandoned. It would erect barriers to trade that do not seem to fit within a federal framework.
- A law to reduce access by one province, BC, to the natural resources of another one, Alberta. This law, entitled 'Preserving Canada's Economic Prosperity', would impose licencing requirements on firms exporting oil from Alberta; these licences could be used to deprive BC of oil and gasoline.
- Some political posturing to link the receipt of equalization payments to the approval of a pipeline. The Alberta government elected in April 2019 proposes to hold a referendum in 2021 on equalization, a constitutionally protected federal programme.

Overall, the Canadian federation has seen its degree of interregional solidarity challenged by the pipeline debates of the 2015–19 period.

7.3.3 Carbon Taxation

In 2015, the federal government of Canada signed the Paris accord on climate change.[30] Since environmental policy is a shared jurisdiction in Canada, its implementation is most easily attained by a combination of federal and provincial policies. The Pan-Canadian Framework on Clean Growth and Climate Change was adopted in December 2016. It states that:

> The federal government outlined a benchmark for pricing carbon pollution by 2018 [. . .] The goal of this benchmark is to ensure that carbon pricing applies to a broad set of emission sources throughout Canada and with increasing stringency over time either through a rising price or declining caps. The benchmark outlines that jurisdictions can implement (i) an explicit price-based system (a carbon tax or a carbon levy and performance-based emissions system) or (ii) a cap-and-trade system. (Environment and Climate Change Canada, 2016, p. 7)

The federal benchmark comprises the following elements (p. 50):

- 'For jurisdictions with an explicit price-based system, the carbon price should start at a minimum of $10 per tonne in 2018 and rise by $10 per year to $50 per tonne in 2022'.
- 'Provinces with cap-and-trade need [a system] that correspond[s], at a minimum, to the projected emissions reductions resulting from the carbon price that year in price-based systems'.
- 'Revenues remain in the jurisdiction of origin. Each jurisdiction can use carbon-pricing revenues according to their needs, including to address impacts on vulnerable populations and sectors and to support climate change and clean growth goals'.

And, of particular importance, there is a federal backstop: 'The federal government will introduce an explicit price-based carbon pricing system that will apply in jurisdictions that do not meet the benchmark. The federal system will be consistent with the principles and will return revenues to the jurisdiction of origin'.

Two provinces, Manitoba and Saskatchewan, refused to agree at that time. But since then, Ontario in June 2018[31] (following the election of a new government), Alberta in August 2018[32] (following the federal court judgment stopping TMP) and Manitoba in October 2018[33] (a political choice) have pulled out. As of 1 September 2019, the federal backstop thus applies in six provinces: PEI (a provincial choice), New Brunswick (since its provincial tax was deemed insufficient), Ontario, Manitoba, Saskatchewan and Alberta.[34] The money collected will be mainly (90 per cent) returned to taxpayers of the province through the federal income tax system. For 2019, this should be paid out in advance of collection since it will be returned in the spring when tax returns for 2018 are finalized (Mertins-Kirkwood, 2018). The amount known as the 'Climate Action Incentive Payments' will be the same for each household of a given size in a province but will vary between provinces ($248 in New Brunswick to $598 in Saskatchewan on average for 2019). It should, according to Finance Canada, on average exceed the cost incurred by a household (Finance Canada, 2018).

Saskatchewan, Ontario and Manitoba have all challenged the federal law through a reference to their respective Court of Appeals[35] as of 1 May 2019 with the Ontario and Saskatchewan courts deeming it constitutional in their respective judgments.[36]

The federal climate policy was introduced in part to counterbalance the approval of some pipelines. It is an innovative way to share a tax field,[37] although there is a precedent for using the federal tax return to compensate residents of specific provinces.[38]

7.4   CONCLUSION

This chapter has described key elements of the Canadian federation and of its fiscal federalism arrangements, then focused on recent developments related to natural resources. These developments reveal the political economy considerations that are at work in shaping the fiscal arrangements in a country with important horizontal imbalances in resource endowments across provinces.

Overall, the Canadian federal-provincial fiscal arrangements can be seen as being the result of an ongoing trade-off between three oft-conflicting objectives:

1. Respecting the equalization programme's constitutional principle;
2. Ensuring the political acceptability of all transfer programmes; and
3. Respecting the federal government's budget constraint.

Objective 1 implies no preferential treatment for natural resource revenues. Objective 2 has tended in recent years to limit redistribution of these revenues as a response to political considerations (mostly in the West). Objective 3 adds an additional limit to redistribution when horizontal fiscal imbalances become too important given the federal government's fiscal policy targets. The latter has arguably dominated the federal government's choices since the mid-1990s. With the centre of gravity of federal politics having shifted westward over the last decade, objectives 2 and 3 have aligned themselves as forces acting towards limiting the extent of redistribution through the equalization programme. In recent years, the pursuit of these two objectives appears to have been instrumental in weakening objective 1.

In sum, the main federal-provincial transfers in Canada achieve (limited) redistribution across provinces. While the Constitution mandates the federal government to provide equalization to 'ensure that provincial governments have sufficient revenues to provide reasonably comparable levels of public services at reasonably comparable levels of taxation', the 'social' transfers (CHT and CST) are essentially equal per capita across provinces. Beyond redistribution, they do not achieve other equity or efficiency related goals, nor do they take provincial needs into account. In the case of Canada, one could see the age structure of the population taken into account in equalization or, if not feasible, in the CHT as age differences (Appendix Table 7A.1) are one driver of differences in spending need between provinces.

Finally, we note that recent work by the Parliamentary Budget Office (2018) shows that: 'Current fiscal policy at the federal level is sustainable over the long term [. . .] (while) for the subnational government sector as a whole, current fiscal policy is not sustainable over the long term' (p. 2). The fiscal imbalance that the CFI documented in the early 2000s is thus alive and well as we enter the third decade of the twenty-first century.

NOTES

*   We thank the editors of this volume and Trevor Tombe for useful comments.
1. For more detail, see Finance Canada (2016a) and Finance Canada (2011).
2. Québec receives less cash transfer payments than other provinces as it occupies a larger portion of the personal income tax field, under the 'Québec abatement' scheme. Québec's cash transfers are reduced dollar for dollar against the yield of these tax points. This is worth about $4.5 billion for 2017 according to Finance Canada (2017). For a general presentation of this, see Finance Canada (2016b).
3. Statistics Canada data: accessed 19 September 2019 at https://www12.statcan.gc.ca/census-recensement/2016/dp-pd/hlt-fst/lang/Table.cfm?Lang=E&T=21&Geo=00.
4. Statistics Canada data (rounded numbers, mother tongue definition): accessed 19 September 2019 at https://www12.statcan.gc.ca/census-recensement/2016/dp-pd/hlt-fst/lang/Table.cfm?Lang=E&T=11&Geo=00.
5. CRA collects fees for 'non harmonized measures', that is provincial measures that differ from the federal ones. In 2017, CRA collected $112 million in fees from provinces and $113 billion of provincial tax revenues. Thus, fees account for 0.1 per cent of provincial revenues collected by CRA (Canada Revenue Agency (2018), pp. 26 and 30).
6. The total amount in 2017–18 was $9 billion according to the Public Accounts of Canada 2017–18 (Government of Canada (2018), Section 6). We subtract the Finance Canada amount from the total of transfers to obtain this number.
7. Enacted as Schedule B to the Canada Act 1982, (U.K.) 1982, c. 11, which came into force on 17 April 1982. This is the last legal intervention by the United Kingdom Parliament in the constitutional history of Canada. The first one was in 1867 (30 & 31 Victoria, c. 3. (U.K.)).
8. Following Tombe (2018a), we disaggregate step 1 from Nadeau (2014).
9. Paragraph 3.4(5) Federal-Provincial Fiscal Arrangements Act (R.S.C., 1985, c. F-8).
10. Fiscal year is 1 April–31 March for the federal and provincial governments in Canada.
11. Ibid., sections (7) and (8) respectively.
12. Totalling $47.5 million over the 1984–2018 period (Health Canada, 2019, p. 30).
13. In operational terms, this means that Québec residents calculate federal income tax

payable like all other Canadians (same exemptions, deductions, rates and so on) but reduce the amount of federal PIT to be paid by 16.5 per cent.

14. A historical perspective is found in Finances Québec (2017).

15. As follows: 24.1 (1) The Canada Health Transfer is to consist of a cash contribution equal to \$19 billion for the fiscal year beginning on 1 April 2005 (Federal-Provincial Fiscal Arrangements Act (R.S.C., 1985, c. F-8), accessed 19 September 2019 at https:// laws-lois.justice.gc.ca/eng/acts/F-8/page-12.html#h-26).

16. Paragraph 24.4 (1) The Canada Social Transfer is to consist of a cash contribution of \$10.537 billion for the fiscal year beginning on 1 April 2008, and (2) the product obtained by multiplying the cash contribution for the immediately preceding fiscal year by 1.03, rounded to the nearest thousand, for each fiscal year beginning after 31 March 2009 (accessed 19 September 2019 at https://laws-lois.justice.gc.ca/eng/acts/F-8/page-13. html#docCont).

17. This section and the conclusion are based on previously unpublished portions of the working paper version of Joanis (2018), which appeared in the working paper series of the School of Public Policy, University of Calgary (Joanis, 2014).

18. For more on the deficit-slaying 1995 budget, see Wobel (1995).

19. The Commission was presided over by Yves Séguin, who would go on to serve as minister of finance in Jean Charest's first (Liberal) cabinet. Though hardly an apolitical exercise – it was commissioned by Bernard Landry's Parti Québécois government – the report was well received in provincial circles across the country and would be an important building block of subsequent positions adopted by the Council of the Federation.

20. See http://www.canadaspremiers.ca/about/ (accessed 19 September 2019); this council has no legal role in federal arrangements in Canada.

21. The O'Brien report reviewed a series of other arguments in favour of an intermediate inclusion rate, including considerations related to the volatility of natural resource revenues and to the disincentive effect of equalization's 'tax-back' of revenues accruing from the development of the natural resource industries.

22. While the recommendations of the Séguin Commission were not implemented as such, the federal government reduced its GST rate from 7 per cent to 6 per cent then 5 per cent in the 2007–08 period, Québec increased its Québec Sales Tax rate by these 2 percentage points; it was the only province to occupy immediately this vacated tax room.

23. See Ontario Hydro (accessed 19 September 2019 at http://www.ontario-hydro.com/ electricity-rates-by-province) or Hydro-Québec (accessed 19 September 2019 at http:// www.hydroquebec.com/data/documents-donnees/pdf/comparison-electricity-prices.pdf).

24. Statistics Canada (2011).

25. *Oil Pricing*, accessed 19 September 2019 at https://www.nrcan.gc.ca/energy/oil-sands/18087; for a calculation of lost revenues, see Aliakbari and Stedman (2018).

26. Media source: Warren Mabee, 'What really Sank the Energy East Pipeline?', Canada's National Observer, accessed 19 September 2019 at https://www.nationalobserver.com/ 2017/10/20/analysis/what-really-sank-energy-east-pipeline.

27. The saga is detailed here: CBC, *Timeline: Key Dates in the History of the Trans Mountain Pipeline*, accessed 19 September 2019 at https://www.cbc.ca/news/canada/calgary/ timeline-key-dates-history-trans-mountain-pipeline-1.4849370.

28. Under the Canadian constitution, provincial powers include '92(10) Local Works and Undertakings other than such as are of the following Classes: [. . .] other Works and Undertakings [. . .] or extending beyond the Limits of the Province'.

29. See Surtees (2017) and Becklumb (2013).

30. Media source: CBC, *Canada Will Meet Climate Targets despite Emissions Gap: Environment Minister*, accessed 19 September 2019 at https://www.cbc.ca/news/politics/ emissions-gap-mckenna-2030-target-1.4563801.

31. Media source: Catherine McKenna, 'Ontario Cancelling Cap and Trade akin to Pulling out of Climate Framework', accessed 19 September 2019 at https://www.cbc.ca/news/ politics/ontario-federal-government-cap-trade-1.4734182.

32. Media source: CBC, 'Alberta Makes it Official: Bill Passed and Proclaimed to Kill

Carbon Tax', accessed 19 September 2019 at https://www.cbc.ca/news/canada/edmonton/alberta-carbon-tax-repealed-1.5162899.

33.   Media source: CBC, *'We Say No': Manitoba Defies Ottawa by Killing its Carbon Tax Plan*, accessed 19 September 2019 at https://www.cbc.ca/news/canada/manitoba/manitoba-carbon-tax-green-plan-1.4849128.

34.   See *Carbon Pricing in Canada*, accessed 19 September 2019 at https://en.wikipedia.org/wiki/Carbon_pricing_in_Canada.

35.   Provincial governments in Canada can ask their top provincial court (Court of Appeals) legal questions. In this case, the question is about the constitutionality of the federal law. The federal government can do the same by referring to the Supreme Court. There is no constitutional court or council in Canada to decide such questions.

36.   Media source: CBC, *Saskatchewan Premier Plans to Appeal Carbon Tax Decision to Supreme Court*, accessed 19 September 2019 at https://www.cbc.ca/news/canada/saskatchewan/carbon-tax-saskatchewan-appeal-1.5121414.

37.   Another innovative approach is the renting of the exclusive use of gambling taxation by Canadian provinces through a joint payment by their lottery authorities to the federal government (Desjardins et al., 2012).

38.   The federal government did that in 1978 when different provinces cut sales taxes in different ways. It sent a cheque to federal personal income tax filers residing in Québec in 1977 as it deemed its type of tax cut (industry-focused) inappropriate and thus not eligible for a revenue replacement payment to the provincial government (Dufour and Vaillancourt, 1982).

REFERENCES

Aliakbari, Elmira and Ashley Stedman (2018). 'The Cost of Pipeline Constraints in Canada', Fraser Institute. Accessed 22 September 2019 at https://www.fraserinstitute.org/sites/default/files/cost-of-pipeline-constraints-in-canada.pdf.

Becklumb, Penny (2013). 'Federal and Provincial Jurisdiction to Regulate Environmental Issues', background paper, Library of Parliament, Canada. Accessed 22 September 2019 at http://publications.gc.ca/collections/collection_2016/bdp-lop/bp/YM32-2-2013-86-eng.pdf.

Canada Revenue Agency (2018). *Departmental Results Report: Financial Statements, 2017–2018*. Accessed 22 September 2019 at https://www.canada.ca/content/dam/cra-arc/corp-info/aboutcra/dprtmntl-prfrmnc-rprts/2017-2018/2017-18-fnclstmnts-en.pdf.

Commission on Fiscal Imbalance (CFI) (2002). *A New Division of Canada's Financial Resources*, Final Report, Government of Quebec. Accessed 22 September 2019 at http://www.groupes.finances.gouv.qc.ca/desequilibrefiscal/en/pdf/rapport_final_en.pdf.

Courchene, T.J. (2013). 'Surplus Recycling and the Canadian Federation Addressing Horizontal and Vertical Fiscal Imbalances', Toronto Mowat Centre.

Desjardins, Étienne, Mélina Longpré and François Vaillancourt (2012). 'The Topsy-Turvy Sharing of the Gaming Tax Field in Canada, 1970–2010: Provincial Payments, Federal Withdrawal', CIRANO Scientific Series no. 2012-s21. Accessed 22 September 2019 at https://www.cirano.qc.ca/files/publications/2012s-21.pdf.

Dufour, Jean-Marie and François Vaillancourt (1982). 'Provincial and Federal Sales Taxes: Evidence of Their Effect and Prospect for Change', in W.R. Thirsk and J. Whalley (eds), *Tax Policy Options in the 1980s*, Toronto, Canadian Tax

Foundation, Tax Paper No. 66. Accessed 22 September 2019 at https://www2.cirano. qc.ca/~dufourj/Web_Site/Dufour_Vaillancourt_1982_CanTaxFoundation_Sales Tax.pdf.

Eisen, Ben, Joel Emes and Steve Lafleur (2017). 'Should Equalization Keep on Growing in an Era of Converging Fiscal Capacity?', Fraser Institute. Accessed 22 September 2019 at https://www.fraserinstitute.org/sites/default/files/should-equalization-keep-on-growing-in-an-era-of-converging-fiscal-capacity.pdf.

Environment and Climate Change Canada (2016). *Pan-Canadian Framework on Clean Growth and Climate Change.* Accessed 22 September 2019 at https://www. canada.ca/en/services/environment/weather/climatechange/pan-canadian-framew ork.html.

Expert Panel on Equalization and Territorial Formula Financing (2006). *Achieving a National Purpose: Putting Equalization Back on Track.* Accessed 22 September 2019 at http://publications.gc.ca/collections/Collection/F2-176-2006E.pdf.

Feehan, Jim (2014). 'Canada's Equalization Formula: Peering Inside the Black Box . . . and Beyond', research paper, School of Public Policy, University of Calgary, vol. 7, issue 24. Accessed 22 September 2019 at https://www.policyschool.ca/wp-content/uploads/2016/03/feehan-equalization.pdf.

Finance Canada (2008a). *Backgrounder: Protecting Transfers to Provinces and Territories.* Accessed 22 September 2019 at https://www.fin.gc.ca/n08/data/08-085_1-eng.asp.

Finance Canada (2008b). *Newfoundland and Labrador Offshore Arrangements.* Accessed 22 September 2019 at https://www.fin.gc.ca/fedprov/na-eng.asp.

Finance Canada (2008c). *Nova Scotia Offshore Arrangements.* Accessed 22 September 2019 at https://www.fin.gc.ca/fedprov/nsa-eng.asp.

Finance Canada (2011). *Territorial Formula Financing.* Accessed 22 September 2019 at https://www.fin.gc.ca/fedprov/tff-eng.asp.

Finance Canada (2014). *History of Health and Social Transfers.* Accessed 22 September 2019 at https://www.fin.gc.ca/fedprov/his-eng.asp.

Finance Canada (2016a). *Backgrounder on Territorial Formula Financing.* Accessed 22 September 2019 at https://www.fin.gc.ca/n16/data/16-024_1-eng.asp.

Finance Canada (2016b). *Quebec Abatement.* Accessed 22 September 2019 at https:// www.fin.gc.ca/fedprov/altpay-eng.asp.

Finance Canada (2017). *Quarterly Financial Report for the Quarter Ended September 30, 2017.* Accessed 22 September 2019 at https://www.fin.gc.ca/pub/qfr-rft/qfr-rft-2017-18-qt2-eng.asp.

Finance Canada (2018). *Fall 2018 Update: Estimated Impacts of the Federal Pollution Pricing System.* Accessed 22 September 2019 at https://www.canada.ca/en/environ-ment-climate-change/services/climate-change/pricing-pollution-how-it-will-work/ fall-2018-update-estimated-impacts-federal-pollution-pricing-system.html.

Finances Québec (2017). *The Québec Economic Plan: Health Funding – For a Fair Share of Federal Health Funding.* Accessed 22 September 2019 at http://www. budget.finances.gouv.qc.ca/budget/2017-2018/en/documents/Budget1718_Health. pdf.

Gauthier, James (2012). 'The Canada Social Transfer: Past, Present and Future Consideration', Library of Parliament, Canada. Accessed 22 September 2019 at https://lop.parl.ca/sites/PublicWebsite/default/en_CA/ResearchPublications /201248.

Gilbert, Guy and François Vaillancourt (2007). 'La péréquation financière au Canada et en France: mécanismes d'évaluation', *Revue française des finances publiques* (99), September, 75–92.

Government of Canada (2018). *Public Accounts of Canada, 2018*, vol. III. Accessed 22 September 2019 at https://www.tpsgc-pwgsc.gc.ca/recgen/cpc-pac/2018/pdf/2018-vol3-eng.pdf.

Health Canada (2015). *Canada Health Act: Annual Report 2014–2015*. Accessed 22 September 2019 at https://www.canada.ca/content/dam/hc-sc/migration/hc-sc/hcs-sss/alt_formats/pdf/pubs/cha-ics/2015-cha-lcs-ar-ra-eng.pdf.

Health Canada (2019). *Canada Health Act: Annual Report 2017–2018*. Accessed 22 September 2019 at http://publications.gc.ca/collections/collection_2019/sc-hc/H1-4-2018-eng.pdf.

Joanis, Marcelin (2014). 'The Politics of Chequebook Federalism: Can Electoral Considerations Affect Federal-Provincial Transfers?', Research paper, School of Public Policy, University of Calgary, vol. 7, issue 25.

Joanis, Marcelin (2018). 'The Politics of Chequebook Federalism: Can Electoral Considerations Affect Federal-Provincial Transfers?', *Public Finance Review* **46**(4), 665–91.

Laurent, Stephen and François Vaillancourt (2004). 'Federal-Provincial Transfers for Social Programs in Canada: Their Status in May 2004', Institute for Research on Public Policy, Working paper 2004-07. Accessed 22 September 2019 at http://irpp.org/wp-content/uploads/assets/research/canadian-federalism/new-research-article/wp2004-07.pdf.

Madore, Odette (2003). 'The Canada Health Act: Overview and Options', Library of Parliament, Canada, publication 94-4E. Accessed 22 September 2019 at http://publications.gc.ca/collections/Collection-R/LoPBdP/CIR/944-e.htm#dtherequirementstxt.

Mertins-Kirkwood, Hadrian (2018). 'Federal Carbon Tax Rebate a Pragmatic Solution to Political Impasse', *Behind the Numbers*. Accessed 22 September 2019 at http://behindthenumbers.ca/2018/10/23/federal-carbon-tax-rebate-a-pragmatic-solution-to-political-impasse/.

Nadeau, Jean-François (2014). '2014–2015 Federal Transfers to Provinces and Territories', Parliamentary Budget Office. Accessed 22 September 2019 at http://www.pbo-dpb.gc.ca/web/default/files/files/files/TransferPayments_EN.pdf.

Parliamentary Budget Office (2018). *Fiscal Sustainability Report*. Accessed 22 September 2019 at https://www.pbo-dpb.gc.ca/web/default/files/Documents/Reports/2018/FSR%20Sept%202018/FSR_2018_25SEP2018_EN_2.pdf.

Statistics Canada (2011). *Households and the Environment: Energy Use*. Accessed 22 September 2019 at http://publications.gc.ca/collections/collection_2013/statcan/11-526-s/11-526-s2013002-eng.pdf.

Surtees, Jeff (2017). 'Who's the Boss? Jurisdiction over the Environment in Canada', *Law Now*. Accessed 22 September 2019 at https://www.lawnow.org/whos-the-boss-jurisdiction-over-the-environment-in-canada/.

Tombe, T. (2018a). 'Final, Unalterable (and Up for Negotiation): Federal-Provincial Transfers in Canada'. Accessed 22nd September 2019 at https://econ.ucalgary.ca/manageprofile/sites/econ.ucalgary.ca.manageprofile/files/unitis/publications/1-9016260/Tombe_2018_CTJ_-_Transfers_in_Canada.pdf.

Tombe, T. (2018b). 'Unpacking Canada's Equalization Payments for 2018–19', School of Public Policy, University of Calgary. Accessed 22 September 2019 at https://www.policyschool.ca/unpacking-canadas-equalization-payments-2018-19/.

Vaillancourt, François (2000). 'Les transferts fédéraux-provinciaux au Canada,

1947–1998: évolution et évaluation', in *Les défis de la gouvernance à l'aube du XXIe siècle*, A. Downs and G. Paquet (eds), Montréal, Actes du Congrès 1999, ASDEQ, pp. 191–212.

Wrobel, Marion G. (1995). 'Budgets 1995: Federal and Provincial Efforts to Curb and Eliminate Deficits', Library of Parliament, Canada. Accessed 22 September 2019 at http://publications.gc.ca/Collection-R/LoPBdP/BP/bp400-e.htm#B.%20 Expenditure(Gov)txt.

Zuker, Richard and Glen Jenkins (1984). *Blue Gold: Hydro Electric Rent in Canada*, Ottawa: Economic Council of Canada. Accessed 19 September 2019 at http:// publications.gc.ca/collections/collection_2018/ecc/EC22-120-1984-eng.pdf.

APPENDIX

Table 7A.1   Key demographic and economic characteristics of Canadian provinces, 2015–17

		Canada	NFD	PEI	NS	NB	QUÉ
Area (km²)	(1)	9984670	405212	5660	55284	72908	1542056
Population ('000) 2016	(2)	35152	520	143	924	747	8164
Population density 2016	(3)	3.52	1.28	25.25	16.71	10.25	5.29
GDP ($000000) 2017	(4)	2137528	33074	6652	42715	36088	417173
GDP $ per capita 2017	(5)	60809	63639	46548	46248	48304	51097
Share of total area (%)	(6)	100	4.1	0.1	0.6	0.7	15.4
Share of total population 2016 (%)	(7)	100	1.5	0.4	2.6	2.1	23.2
Share of total GDP 2017 (%)	(8)	100	1.5	0.3	2.0	1.7	19.5
Share of total oil production 2017 (%)	(9)	100	5.3	–	–	–	–
Provincial/territorial government revenues ($000000) 2017	(10)	–	7079.00	1897.00	11528.00	9492.00	111470.00
Share of federal transfers (grants) in provincial/territorial revenues (%) 2017	(11)	–	23.0	37.3	34.1	33.5	20.4
Median age 2012	(12)	40.0	44.2	42.6	43.4	43.4	41.5
Share of total hydroelectric production 2017 (%)	(13)	100	9.1	0	0.2	0.7	51.5

Note: NFDL: Newfoundland-and-Labrador; PEI: Prince Edward Island; NS: Nova Scotia; QUÉ: Québec; ONT: Ontario; MAN: Manitoba; SASK: Saskatchewan; AL: Alberta; BC: British Columbia; YU: Yukon; NO: Northwest territories; NU: Nunavut.

Sources:
 1) https://en.wikipedia.org/wiki/List_of_Canadian_provinces_and_territories_by_area#Total_area (accessed 19 September 2019).
 2) Statistics Canada Population by broad age groups and sex, 2016 counts for both sexes, Canada, provinces and territories, 2016 Census – 100 per cent Data.
 3) (2)/(1).
 4) Statistics Canada. CANSIM Table 36-10-0222-01 Gross domestic product, expenditure-based, provincial and territorial, annual.
 5) (4)/(2).
 6), 7) and 8) Calculations using (1), (2) and (4) as inputs.
 9) https://www.nrcan.gc.ca/energy/facts/crude-oil/20064 (accessed 19 September 2019).
 10) and 11) Statistics Canada. CANSIM Table 10-10-0017-01 Canadian government finance statistics for the provincial and territorial governments.
 12) Text table 2.1 Population estimates, age distribution and median age as of 1 July 2012, Canada, provinces and territories Statistics Canada https://www150.statcan.gc.ca/n1/pub/91-215-x/2012000/t583-eng.htm (accessed 19 September 2019).
 13) Electric power, annual generation by class of producer Megawatt hours Annual CANSIM Table: 25-10-0020-01.

ONT	MAN	SASK	ALTA	BC	YU	NO	NU
1076 395	647 797	651 036	661 848	944 735	482 443	1 346 106	2 093 190
13 448	1 278	1 098	4 067	4 648	36	42	36
12.49	1.97	1.69	6.15	4.92	0.07	0.03	0.02
825 805	71 019	79 513	331 937	282 204	2 895	4 856	2 846
61 405	55 555	72 393	81 614	60 714	80 708	116 214	79 188
10.8	6.5	6.5	6.6	9.5	.8	13.5	21.0
38.3	3.6	3.1	11.6	13.2	0.1	0.1	0.1
38.6	3.3	3.7	15.5	13.2	0.1	0.2	0.1
–	0.9	11.7	80.7	1.4	–	–	–
140 816.00	15 482.00	14 090.00	44 990.00	51 179.00	1 298.00	2 112.00	2 069.00
17.3	26.0	17.5	16.1	16.8	84.0	74.0	80.9
39.8	37.6	37.1	36.1	41.4	39.4	32.1	24.7
10.2	9.2	0.9	0.5	17.5	0	0	0

8. Revenue and expenditure needs equalization: the Swiss answer*

Bernard Dafflon

8.1 INSTITUTIONAL BACKGROUND

Constitutional and organizational requirements of the vertical and horizontal equalization system in Switzerland are complex, with 26 cantons and 2212 communes,[1] where the population is unevenly distributed.[2] This complexity is mirrored in the public finance arrangements at the three government tiers (federal, cantonal, communal).

At the federal level, the legislative branch is organized in two chambers. The National Council has 200 members who represent the people. The larger the number of Swiss citizens in a canton, the more representatives it has in the National Council: from 35 representatives for the canton of Zürich (ZH) to 1 only for six cantons – Appenzell Innerrhoden (AI), Appenzell Ausserrhoden (AR), Glarus (GL), Nidwalden (NW), Obwalden (OW) and Uri (UR). The Council of States has 46 members representing all the cantons. Each canton has two representatives, except the half-cantons (AI, AR, Basel-Landschaft (BL), Basel-Stadt (BS), NW, OW), which have only one representative. Each canton decides how to elect its representatives. Both chambers have equal political powers: any federal law or decree must be accepted by a simple majority of votes in both chambers. Thus, the cantons' rights and prerogatives – including those of the smaller ones – are well protected.

In vertical relations, the federal government, the 'Confederation', must consider the possible consequences of its policy decisions on the cantons (article 45 of the Federal Constitution – thereafter Cst.), as well as on communes in the urban areas and in the mountainous regions (article 50 Cst.). Also, when harmonized norms or standards for a particular public service become a 'nationwide' issue, and in the absence of explicit constitutional provision, it can be dealt with by the cantons, instead of an adoption by the federal parliament (article 48 Cst.). Thus 'nationwide' norms are not the same as 'federal' norms. There are multiple (horizontal) agreements between the cantons (the so-called 'concordats'). These agreements cover the following areas according to article 48a of the Constitution: the execution of criminal penalties and measures; compulsory school education;[3] cantonal institutions of higher education (professional universities of applied sciences and universities); cultural institutions of supra-regional importance; solid waste management; waste water treatment; urban transport; advanced medical science and specialist clinics; institutions for the rehabilitation and care of invalids.

In the Constitution, fiscal democracy is organized around five principles (article 43a Cst.): subsidiarity, autonomy, horizontal cooperation, initiative and referendum. The principle of subsidiarity applies to both institutional and functional aspects of intergovernmental design. First, unspecified powers belong to the cantons: their fiscal sovereignty can only be limited by specific provision written in the Federal Constitution (article 42 Cst.). Yet, any change in the Constitution has to be accepted by the two federal chambers of equal power and requires a double majority of voters and cantons. Local or cantonal responsibilities can only be transferred to a higher level government if they require standardization to respond to major changes in behaviour or technology: for example, mobility of persons or economic activities, new technologies in the production and delivery of public services, or when horizontal cooperation is no longer feasible. Healthcare is a good example of this centralization trend.

When the Confederation prepares a new law or changes in the existing federal legislation, or initiates projects of substantial territorial impact, the cantons, political parties and interest groups are invited to express their views (article 147 Cst.). The same applies at the cantonal-communal level. The cantons have organized themselves horizontally in powerful 'Conferences of Cantonal Ministers', one for each sector. The Conferences act as strong negotiating partners. They participate in joint committees for proposing new federal policies and act as a partner with the federal government in promoting public policies decided at the federal level but implemented in and through the cantons. In public finance issues and fiscal equalization, the Conference of the Cantonal Ministers of Finance (the CCMF) plays a dominant role as no legislation would be adopted at the federal level without its prior consent.

At the federal level, initiative and referenda are also important tools of participative democracy, extensively used in public finance issues. Any 100,000 persons eligible to vote may, within 18 months of the official publication of their initiative, request a partial revision of the Federal Constitution in specific terms. Any parliamentary member, political group or permanent committee or any canton can submit an initiative to the Federal Assembly. Referendum is mandatory for an amendment to the Federal Constitution, the accession to supranational organizations, and emergency decrees that are not based on a provision of the Constitution (duration is limited to one year). Optional referendum is possible on the condition that, within 100 days of its official publication, any 50,000 persons eligible to vote or any eight cantons should request it. A referendum can be organized on federal laws and federal decrees if the Constitution or a law so requires. Initiative and referenda also exist at the cantonal and local levels, but procedures and content vary from one canton to another.

In this institutional context, equalization at the federal-cantonal level needs a constitutional amendment approved by double majority – majority of the cantons and the voters at the national level. In addition, it requires an implementation law which is subject to a referendum with the simple majority of voters (section 8.3 below).

8.2   OVERVIEW OF THE SWISS PUBLIC SECTOR

Quantitative measures of the Swiss public sector and social security are summarized in Tables 8.1 to 8.3. Table 8.1 presents the tax revenues of the three government levels (total I). The second part introduces the social security system including the other compulsory insurances sourced out to non-profit private companies (total II) or financial institutions (pension funds, total III). In order to allow for international comparison, the bottom part of the table gives the fiscal quotes of the three totals in percentage of GDP.

Table 8.2 details the revenue sources for three levels of government. Year 2016 is fairly representative of the last decade (Dafflon, 2015a). Transfer revenues received from other government levels are shown separately in order to measure financial autonomy (own revenues). Direct taxation is shared between the three tiers; in addition to their own direct taxes, the cantons receive 17 per cent of the federal direct tax collected at the cantonal level (Table 8.2: revenue sharing, 6 per cent of the total cantonal revenues). Furthermore, 13 per cent of the federal direct tax is allocated to revenue equalization. Value added tax (VAT), consumption and excise taxation are exclusively federal taxes. User charges are cantonal in the health and education sectors. User fees for environmental services (mandatory according to the federal legislation) are levied by communes. Own revenues represent 100 per cent in the federal budget, 70 per cent on average for the cantons and nearly 90 per cent for the communes. At the cantonal level, transfer revenues from other levels of government are: 6 per cent revenue sharing from federal taxes, 4 per cent from federal equalization, 13 per cent federal subsidies and specific grants-in-aid, and 7 per cent are contributions of communes for shared competencies; for the communes, less than 2 per cent

Table 8.1 *Tax revenues and compulsory social contributions on wages,
selected years, in per cent GDP*

Revenues in millions CHF	2000	2005	2010	2015	2016
Confederation	46 492	47 494	58 700	63 949	63 942
Cantons	28 869	34 030	39 917	44 365	45 595
Communes	20 226	21 089	24 564	27 555	28 439
total I	95 587	102 613	123 181	135 868	137 976
Social security* and other insurances** total II	49 541	56 639	66 541	78 082	79 909
Occupational pensions*** total III	29 499	35 721	46 336	54 316	54 525
GDP	*459 447*	*508 900*	*608 831*	*654 258*	*660 393*
Fiscal quote (in % of GDP) I	21	20	20	21	21
II	32	31	31	33	33
III	38	38	39	41	41

Notes:
* Only the employers' and employees' contributions levied on wages. Social security: old age, disability, unemployment, maternity, social and military services.
** Individual insurance premium in other compulsory insurances: illness, accident, family care.
*** Compulsory additional old age pension schemes. This represented 76 per cent of the total insurance finances in 2016 (176 736 millions CHF). Subsidies from the public sector (15 per cent) are not included. The remaining 9 per cent are the interests and dividends from the insurances' capital (reserves and compensation funds).

Sources: Federal Finance Administration (FFA), https//:www.efv.admin.ch > documentation > statistique financière > Données > tous les fichiers; updated 6 September 2018, access date 25 March 2019. For GDP: Federal State Secretariat for Economic Affairs (SECO), https//:www.seco.admin.ch > Thèmes > Situation économique > PIB estimations, access date 25 March 2019. Social insurances: CGAS14, https://www.bsv.admin.ch/bsv/fr/home/assurances-sociales/ueberblick/grsv/statistik.html, access date 25 March 2019.

of their revenues come from revenue sharing, 3 per cent from equalization at the cantonal level and 7 per cent from cantonal grants and subsidies.

The modest proportion of equalization in cantonal and communal resources can be explained by the long-term results of their public finance: almost no deficit since 2000 and low indebtedness in international comparison (less than 30 per cent GDP) (Dafflon, 2015a). Despite significant differences in inter-cantonal or intra-cantonal resource endowments, neither the cantons nor the communes can count on financial equalization for the long-term sustainability of their public finances. Above all, equalization reflects a political recognition of solidarity between and within subnational government tiers rather than bailing out non-performing subnational governments.

Table 8.3 summarizes the functional distribution of public expenditures

Table 8.2   Total revenues, 2016, three government levels

	Confederation	Cantons	Communes	Confederation	Cantons	Communes
	Million CHF			In % of total revenue		
Direct personal taxes	10 599	31 913	21 741	15.3	36.5	45.9
Direct corporate taxes	10 532	7 770	4 456	15.2	8.9	9.4
Other direct taxes	5 893	3 611	2 137	8.5	4.1	4.5
Consumption taxes, VAT	35 699	0	0	51.5	0	0
Other consumption taxes	1 218	2 300	104	1.8	2.6	0.2
Total I tax revenues (as in Table 8.1)	*63 942*	*45 595*	*28 439*	*92.2*	*52.2*	*60.0*
User charges	1 676	7 278	8 285	2.4	8.3	17.5
Patent, concession	601	1 637	358	0.9	1.9	0.8
Financial revenues, interest	1 324	2 827	3 170	1.9	3.2	6.7
Other revenues	603	1 200	245	0.9	1.4	0.5
Extraordinary revenues	1 221	2 606	1 383	1.8	3.0	2.9
Total II non-tax own revenues	*5 425*	*15 547*	*13 441*	*7.8*	*17.8*	*28.4*
Revenue sharing	0	5 066	759	0	5.8	1.6
Equalization	0	3 556	1 522	0	4.1	3.2
Federal transfers (vertical)	0	11 585	3 232	0	13.3	6.8
Contributions of communes	0	5 977	0	0	6.8	0
Total III transfer revenues	*0*	*26 183*	*5 512*	*0*	*30.0*	*11.6*
Total I + II + III	*69 367*	*87 324*	*47 391*	*100.0*	*100.0*	*100.0*

Source: FFA, www.efv.admin.ch > documentation > statistique financière > Rapport > tous les fichiers; updated 6 September 2018, access date 25 March 2019.

Table 8.3 Functional public expenditures, 2016, three government levels

Functions	Confederation	Cantons	Communes	Confederation	Cantons	Communes
Sub-functions		Million CHF			In % of total expenditures	
Administration	6079	4413	5051	9	5	11
Security, defence	5820	7897	3070	9	9	6
Education	6403	24411	12835	9	28	27
Compulsory education	*17*	*9476*	*12418*			
Second level education,	*768*	*5770*	*343*			
Tertiary education	*2640*	*7300*	*20*			
Research	*2970*	*1351*	*2*			
Other	*8*	*514*	*52*			
Culture, sports, leisure	518	1799	3380	1	2	7
Health	322	12665	2030	0	15	4
Hospital, homes for elderly	*0*	*10629*	*1214*			
Outpatient medical care	*0*	*726*	*515*			
R&D, other	*322*	*1'310*	*301*			
Social security, social aid	22694	18841	9109	34	22	19
Illness and accident	*2866*	*4554*	*585*			
Disability	*5460*	*4575*	*961*			
Old age and widowhood	*11808*	*2921*	*1458*			
Family and children	*165*	*1362*	*1449*			
Unemployment	*518*	*803*	*180*			
Social housing	*69*	*112*	*68*			
Social aid and refugees	*1804*	*4482*	*4381*			
Others	*4*	*32*	*27*			
Roads, traffic and telecom	9209	6123	4472	14	7	9

Table 8.3 (continued)

Functions	Confederation	Cantons	Communes	Confederation	Cantons	Communes
Sub-functions	Million CHF			In % of total expenditures		
Environment	1032	1483	4339	2	2	9
Economy	5504	4530	1546	8	5	3
Finance, taxation	9914	3921	1903	15	5	4
Tax administration	185	445	248			
Equalization	3246	1530	369			
Revenue sharing	4212	759	0			
Interest and cost of debt	1512	902	1211			
Others	759	285	75			
Total	67495	86083	47735	100	100	100

Source: FFA, https/-:www.efv.admin.ch > documentation > statistique financière > Rapport > tous les fichiers; updated 6 September 2018, access date 25 March 2019.

at different government levels; 2016 serves as the reference year. The military and civil defence are federal responsibilities; security and police forces are cantonal; neighbourhood policing and market policing are communal. Compulsory school education is a shared responsibility of the cantons and communes, but education programmes and teachers' training are harmonized through an inter-cantonal agreement (see note 3). The cantons finance tertiary education (universities). The Confederation finances the two federal polytechnic universities – in Lausanne and Zürich (92 per cent), the Swiss National Science Foundation (100 per cent) and subsidizes the cantonal universities (25 per cent). It also subsidizes student grants and mobility within European universities. Expenditures in culture, sport and leisure are communal responsibilities. Health is a cantonal responsibility. Homes for the elderly are partly subsidized by communes; sickness and disability insurances (not included in government expenditures – see Table 8.1) pay medical care; residents pay the accommodation from their pocket. Social security is federal responsibility, whereas social aid and assistance are shared between the cantons and their communes. Motorways, railway traffic and telecom are federal responsibilities; roads are cantonal or communal; urban traffic and public transportation are mainly inter-communal. Environmental policies provide an interesting case of shared responsibilities: the norms and policy objectives are set in federal laws; coordination and planning are left to the cantons; implementation, investments and current management are communal responsibilities. Environmental expenditures for solid waste collection and treatment, wastewater and water management are financed through local user charges. As for the government function 'finance and taxation', the majority of spending at the federal level is for the financial transfers to the cantons in revenue sharing and for equalization. Categorical incentive grants are accounted in the relevant functions, not under the finance heading.

Table 8.3 is informative about the links that could exist between the relative importance of the various functions and the indicators used in expenditure equalization to evaluate disparities in needs or costs. At the cantonal level, expenditures in education, social security and aid, and health are the three domains which require the most resources. In the case of expenditure equalization, three socio-demographic indicators only (poverty, old age and foreigners – Tables 8.5 and 8.8) refer to sub-functions in Table 8.3 (homes for the elderly, social aid and refugees). The other health and social security expenditures are not included: the reason is that their main financial sources come from contributors outside of the government sector. Government contributions (federal, cantonal and/or communal) take the form of specific (conditional) grants-in-aids that benefit individuals or institutions and not the cantons as such. Education also is left out of the equalization scheme between the Confederation and the cantons. The reason is that the cantons only are in charge of compulsory education, whereas cantonal tertiary education expenditures are subsidized by the Confederation outside of equalization. Thus, as explained below, the link between functional cantonal expenditures and the federal expenditure equalization scheme is rather diluted.

8.3 EQUALIZATION

8.3.1 The Historical Context

In 1959, the federal parliament introduced the first formula-based equalization system between the Confederation and the cantons. The cantons were ranked from 'rich' to 'poor' according to their 'fiscal capacity'. Over the years, the formulas combined several indicators of the cantons' tax capacity and of expenditure needs in various proportions (Dafflon, 1995: 66 and 70). The revenue equalization scheme contained the distribution of 13 per cent of the Federal Direct Tax (on personal income and business profit) according to the fiscal capacity and, as an additional indicator, the inverse of the cantons' fiscal effort (depending on the canton's tax bases – the tax rates needed to obtain the same per capita average tax revenue). Expenditure needs equalization was organized separately, using specific indicators for each category of functions (eventually 58 functions were partly 'equalized' in one way or another). Between 1959 and 1992, the equalization system was modified ten times with regards to both measurement variables and equalization formulas. Throughout the years, the system became technically complex, politically infeasible, incoherent and promoting wrong incentives, with poor equalizing performance (Frey et al., 1994; Dafflon and Della Santa, 1995; Federal Council, 2001).

The reform of the equalization system was a painful process. A new law was adopted in the federal parliament in October 2003, after ten years of contentious discussions (Dafflon, 2004; Federal Council, 2014). For several years, a group of experts, later a joint commission of cantonal representatives and the Confederation analysed various proposals and scenarios. The discussions focused not only on the objectives of equalization (how many fiscal disparities should be compensated), and the respective weights between revenue equalization and expenditure needs (which functions would be recognized and how needs would be measured), but also on the methodology (which variables would be the best indicators of disparities) and the ways of funding equalization (vertical-horizontal mix and the cost sharing between the Confederation and the cantons).

BOX 8.1   EQUALIZATION OF FINANCIAL RESOURCES AND
            BURDENS (ARTICLE 135 CST.)

1. The Confederation shall issue regulations on the equitable equalization of
   financial resources and burdens between the Confederation and the cantons
   as well as among the cantons.
2. The equalization of financial resources and burdens is intended in particular
   to:
   a. reduce the differences in financial capacity among the cantons;
   b. guarantee the cantons a minimum level of financial resources;
   c. compensate for excessive financial burdens on individual cantons due to
       geo-topographic or socio-demographic factors;
   d. encourage inter-cantonal cooperation on burden equalization;
   e. maintain the tax competitiveness of the cantons by national and interna-
       tional comparison.
3. The funds for the equalization of financial resources shall be provided by those
   cantons with a higher level of resources and by the Confederation. The payments made by those cantons with a higher level of resources shall amount to
   a minimum of two-thirds and a maximum of 80 per cent of the payments made
   by the Confederation.

Source: https://www.admin.ch/opc/en/classified-compilation/19995395/index.html.

The constitutional amendment on equalization (article 135 Cst.) and the 're-assignment of functions between the federal and cantonal tiers' were voted on in 2004 and accepted by 23 cantons,[4] and by 64 per cent of the voters. It came into effect on 1 January 2008 together with the federal law of 12 October 2003 on equalization and the reassignment of functions between the Confederation and the cantons, thereby fulfilling the constitutional amendment.[5]

The new system comprises of three components: (1) revenue equalization; (2) expenditure needs equalization – the latter divided in two equal parts, one taking into account socio-demographic, the other geo-topographic variables; and (3) a transition fund.

Box 8.1 presents article 135 of the Federal Constitution related to equalization. And based on the 2003 federal law, Figure 8.1 presents the actual architecture of the Swiss equalization policy at the federal-cantonal level.

8.3.2   Revenue Equalization

The constitutional objectives of revenue equalization are to: (1) reduce the differences in financial capacity among the cantons; and (2)

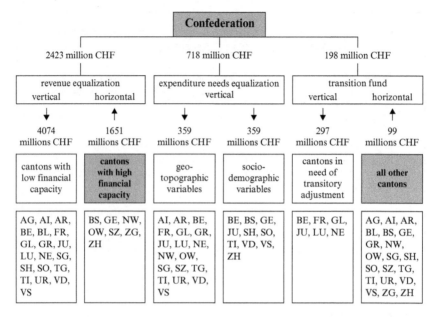

Note: AG: Aargau; AI: Appenzell Innerrhoden; AR: Appenzell Ausserrhoden; BE: Bern; BL: Basel-Landschaft; BS: Basel-Stadt; FR: Fribourg; GE: Genève; GL: Glarus; GR: Graubünden; JU: Jura; LU: Luzern; NE: Neuchâtel; NW: Nidwalden; OW: Obwalden; SG: Sankt-Gallen; SH: Schaffhausen; SO: Solothurn; SZ: Schwyz; TG: Thurgau; TI: Ticino; UR: Uri; VD: Vaud; VS: Valais; ZG: Zug; ZH: Zürich.

Source: Authors, adapted from FFA, https://www.efv.admin.ch/efv/fr/home/themen/finanz ausgleich/zahlen.html, access date 9 March 2019.

Figure 8.1   Fiscal equalization, Switzerland, 2018, million CHF

guarantee cantons a minimum level of financial resources. Article 6 of the 2003 implementation law fixed this minimum level at 85 per cent of the average per capita resource after revenue equalization. The result is expressed in the cantonal indices of financial capacities (average at 100 per cent).

Revenue equalization combines vertical and horizontal transfer payments. The federal contribution corresponds to approximately 13 per cent of the federal direct tax yield. This is in line with the spirit of the 1992 reform of the first equalization system.[6] During the 1992 reforms, the federal contribution is not provided for in the Constitution or the law. With the enactment of the 2008 equalization law, the federal parliament is mandated to decide the federal contribution to revenue equalization for four years. Within these four years, the total amount (contributions of the

Confederation and the cantons) is indexed to an average annual growth rate of direct taxation (article 5 of the law). For the 2018 reform, the contributions of the seven cantons with a 'resource potential' higher than the average correspond to 68 per cent of the federal allotment – that is just above the minimum threshold of two-thirds written in article 135 of the Federal Constitution.

The cantons' financial capacities or 'resource potential' are measured in the form of a representative tax system (RTS) based on four taxes: (1) personal income tax; (2) wealth tax; (3) corporate profit tax; and (4) profit tax on holding, domicile and mix companies.

Seven cantons with financial capacity higher than the national average contribute to the revenue equalization pool out of their general budget (that is, horizontal revenue equalization) in addition to the contribution of the Confederation (that is, vertical revenue equalization). Conversely, 19 cantons with financial capacity lower than average obtain benefits from the equalization fund. The distribution formula, calculated per capita, is strictly proportional. The outcomes of the 2018 reforms are summarized in Table 8.4. 'Cantonal contributions' correspond to horizontal revenue equalization, while the amount of vertical revenue equalization supported by the federal government is equal to the difference between the total contributions paid (4074 millions CHF) and the horizontal contributions (1651 millions CHF). The equalization performance is measured in terms of the differences in the cantonal indices of financial capacity before and after equalization. The required minimum threshold of 85 per cent has been respected for the fourth consecutive year in 2018, with a top 88.3 per cent reached in the cantons Uri, Valais and Jura.

8.3.3 Expenditure Needs Equalization

The constitutional objective of expenditure needs equalization is to compensate for excessive financial burdens on individual cantons resulting from geo-topographical or socio-demographic factors. *Ex ante*, three questions should be answered: (1) Which functions/tasks should be subject to equalization based on the definition of need (= minimum level of service, observed level including political preferences)? (2) What are the suitable determinants/explanatory variables? (3) Should 'low need' cantons participate in financing the equalization fund?

In the Swiss context, expenditure needs equalization is exclusively vertical (Figure 8.1).[7] The theoretical argument is that with horizontal equalization beneficiaries of services in low-costs-low-needs jurisdictions accept a tax-price supplement (that is, more expensive public services) in order to

Table 8.4   *Revenue equalization in the cantons (2018)*

Canton	Index of Financial Capacity Before and After Equalization			Beneficiary Canton in CHF		Cantonal Contributions in CHF	
	Before	After	Difference	Total	Per capita	Total	Per capita
Zürich	120.2	116.0	−4.2	0	0	525 847 071	367
Bern	75.2	88.9	13.7	1 201 650 040	1 196	0	0
Luzern	89.5	93.2	3.7	126 654 780	324	0	0
Uri	68.2	88.3	20.1	63 296 476	1 748	0	0
Schwyz	172.1	157.0	−15.1	0	0	199 037 438	1 310
Obwalden	102.4	101.9	−0.5	0	0	1 587 890	43
Nidwalden	159.7	147.2	−12.5	0	0	45 615 981	1 085
Glarus	71.2	88.5	17.3	60 261 578	1 502	0	0
Zug	244.1	214.0	−30.1	0	0	311 423 696	2 618
Fribourg	79.5	89.8	10.3	264 763 179	893	0	0
Solothurn	74.6	88.9	14.3	324 380 883	1 237	0	0
Basel-Stadt	149.7	139.3	−10.4	0	0	172 968 585	902
Basel-Landschaft	96.5	97.2	0.7	16 767 941	60	0	0
Schaffhausen	93.0	95.0	2.0	13 618 648	172	0	0
Appenzell Ausserrhoden	85.6	91.6	6.0	28 162 452	523	0	0
Appenzell Innerrhoden	85.2	91.5	6.3	8 577 481	542	0	0
Sankt Gallen	79.2	89.7	10.5	451 072 450	915	0	0
Graubünden	83.2	90.8	7.6	133 867 315	660	0	0
Aargau	85.3	91.5	6.2	342 773 344	538	0	0
Thurgau	79.0	89.7	10.7	241 513 997	927	0	0
Ticino	97.4	97.8	0.4	13 333 153	38	0	0
Vaud	99.6	99.7	0.1	1 442 779	2	0	0
Valais	66.8	88.3	21.5	620 152 410	1 864	0	0
Neuchâtel	94.3	95.7	1.4	22 680 399	128	0	0
Genève	146.1	136.5	−9.6	0	0	394 228 249	837
Jura	65.9	88.3	22.4	139 098 196	1 938	0	0
Total	100.0	100.0	0.0	4 074 067 501		1 650 708 910	

Source: Author, from FFA, https://www.efv.admin.ch/efv/fr/home/themen/finanzausgleich/zahlen.htm, access date 25 March 2019.

subsidize public services in high-costs-high-needs jurisdictions: this would distort the relative tax prices of subnational public services and result in allocative inefficiency and wrong incentives in deciding service levels.

The practical arguments pertain to uncertainty about the government functions to be included in the equalization basket as well as the absence of solid and verifiable statistical information about differences in costs/

needs of the selected functions (Federal Council, 2001). In order to circumvent these difficulties, the equalization programme is based on selected socio-demographic and topo-geographic determinants and explanatory variables which are deemed to express, respectively quantify, differences in cantonal needs. Table 8.5 summarizes this approach.

In Table 8.5, the weights in *italics*, which are situated in the last column relating to the needs categories, are a result of an intense bargaining between the Confederation and the cantons. First, the equalization funds attributed to geo-topographic and socio-demographic needs were partitioned in half (Figure 8.1) even though about 84 per cent of the population live in urban areas (geographically, the 'plateau suisse', which represents 41 per cent of the national territory, is distinct from the mountainous areas: Jura, Prealpes and Alpes). Second, the weights given to the geo-topographic variables were negotiated with the cantons before the federal vote in 2004 (Federal Council, 2001) after which they were written in the 2007 implementation decree. Third, the two-thirds/ one-third partition of the amount attributed to the socio-demographic and urban areas variables were also negotiated. Fourth and finally, the weights attributed to each determinant in parts (1) and (2) of the socio-demographic category in Table 8.5 were computed with the principal component analysis (PCA) technique. These weights are updated yearly. The expenditure needs equalization calculations for 2018 are presented in Table 8.6.

8.3.4 The Transition Fund

A transition fund was established in order to support financially weak cantons in transitioning from the old system to the new fiscal equalization system. In 2000, a financial simulation of the new revenue equalization estimated that eight cantons would suffer losses in revenue transfers. This was politically unacceptable and the affected cantons strongly protested. A new ad hoc fund was then invented so that the whole project would not be jeopardized (Dafflon, 2004).

The transitory fund is only of benefit to those cantons with a resource index lower than 100 with the introduction of the new revenue equalization scheme in 2008. If, subsequently, a canton's index of financial capacity increases to over 100, the canton will be pushed out of the fund and there is no return back. If a canton faces a decrease in its financial capacity and passes under the 100 mark, it will not get any payment either. So, the number of beneficiary cantons should decrease over time. The Confederation finances two-thirds of this compensation, and the remainder comes from the cantons (based on their population sizes). The initial

Table 8.5   System of expenditure needs equalization, 2018

Needs categories	Objective	Determinant	Explanatory variable	Weight*
Geo-topographic	Compensate for excessive financial burdens due to geo-topographical factors, mainly in the Alps and mountainous regions	Altitude	% of population living above 800 m. alt.	*0.330*
		Remoteness	% of productive land > 1080 m. alt.	*0.330*
		Smallness	Population density	*0.165*
			Population in commune with less than 200 residents	*0.165*
Socio-demographic	(1) Compensate for excessive financial burdens of individual cantons due to some characteristics of the resident population			For 2/3
		Poverty	% beneficiaries of social aid to population	0.55**
		Old age	% of aged > 80 to population	0.27**
		Foreigners (not including those from neighbouring countries)	% of foreigners of population	0.44**
	(2) Problems specific to agglomeration and urban areas			For 1/3
		Public security and order	Population size of the municipalities	0.47**
		Urban traffic, congestion costs,	Number of employments (equivalent full-time job places) and resident population in proportion to urban surface	0.49**
		Commuters, urban public transportation	Number of employments in proportion to resident population	0.34**
Transition fund	Facilitate the transition from the old (pre-2008) to the new (2008) system so that beneficiary cantons in the old system receive at least the same amount in the new system	Difference between the old and new system in its first year of introduction	Difference paid in proportion to available fund. If for one canton the difference reduces, the compensation is also reduced in proportion. The total available fund is further reduced by 5% a year from 2016 onwards	

Table 8.5 (continued)

Notes:
* Weights: fixed (arts 32 and 39).
** Calculation according to the principal component analysis (arts 35 and 37).

Source: Author, adapted from federal ordinance of 11 November 2007 on revenue equalization and the compensation of excessive financial burden of the cantons, https://www.admin.ch/opc/fr/classified-compilation/20071271/index.html, access date 14 April 2019.

Table 8.6 *Expenditure needs equalization in the cantons, 2018, in CHF*

	Geo-topographic		Socio-demographic		Urban areas	
	Index	Beneficiary	Index	Beneficiary	Index	Beneficiary
Zürich	32	0	0.17	15929418	6.250	65117655
Bern	125	27010038	0.20	12530321	1.620	0
Luzern	81	6087983	−0.48	0	1.480	0
Uri	274	11544271	−0.79	0	0.070	0
Schwyz	160	6725582	−1.03	0	0.440	0
Obwalden	204	6253820	−1.01	0	0.100	0
Nidwalden	97	1257137	−1.24	0	0.210	0
Glarus	151	5331790	−0.13	0	0.370	0
Zug	67	0	−0.27	0	1.520	0
Fribourg	133	8895845	−0.30	0	0.630	0
Solothurn	42	0	0.23	3886535	0.480	0
Basel-Stadt	12	0	2.74	33137831	11.550	18306193
Basel-Landschaft	32	0	−0.03	0	0.900	0
Schaffhausen	41	0	0.25	1250353	0.890	0
Appenzell Ausserrhoden	357	19206007	−0.66	0	0.150	0
Appenzell Innerrhoden	409	8261698	−1.04	0	0.000	0
Sankt Gallen	84	1878595	−0.46	0	1.130	0
Graubünden	451	136826831	−0.54	0	0.450	0
Aargau	34	0	−0.70	0	0.460	0
Thurgau	59	3885043	−0.93	0	0.420	0
Ticino	98	14241864	0.81	17978771	1.080	0
Vaud	91	67687	1.32	64414012	2.120	3636461
Valais	283	73343364	0.28	5935792	0.330	0
Neuchâtel	247	23361591	1.30	14563925	1.068	0
Genève	23	0	2.27	69387134	8.617	32584693
Jura	165	4755858	0.06	275911	0.102	0
Total	*100*	*358935004*		*239290003*		*119645001*

Source: Authors, from FFA, https://www.efv.admin.ch/efv/fr/home/themen/finanzausgleich/zahlen.htm, access date 14 April 2019.

amount fixed in 2008 was 430 million CHF, which was financed by the Confederation (287 million CHF) and the cantons (143 million CHF). It has been reduced by 5 per cent each year since 2016. In 2018, the contributions were reduced to 297 million CHF, indicated by Table 8.7.

Table 8.7   Transition fund, 2018, in CHF

	Cantonal contributions	Cantons beneficiary	Net benefit
Zürich	16 760 670	0	
Bern	13 077 544	44 314 461	31 236 917
Luzern	4 741 614	20 138 259	15 396 645
Uri	475 311	0	
Schwyz	1 754 716	0	
Obwalden	441 586	0	
Nidwalden	506 482	0	
Glarus	526 132	6 943 444	6 417 312
Zug	1 347 339	0	
Fribourg	3 255 796	116 688 025	113 432 229
Solothurn	3 330 464	0	
Basel-Stadt	2 642 180	0	
Bâle-Landschaft	3 529 277	0	
Schaffhausen	1 005 998	0	
Appenzell Ausserrhoden	732 973	0	
Appenzell Innerrhoden	200 891	0	
Sankt Gallen	6 156 013	0	
Graubünden	2 588 864	0	
Aargau	7 421 412	0	
Thurgau	3 122 485	0	
Tessin	4 214 666	0	
Vaud	8 624 064	0	
Valais	3 748 313	0	
Neuchâtel	2 287 622	92 507 817	90 220 195
Genève	5 604 492	0	
Jura	926 905	16 479 421	15 552 516
Total I	*99 023 809*	*297 071 427*	*272 255 814*
Confederation	198 047 618		
Total II	*297 071 427*		
Economies of the beneficiary cantons			24 815 613
Net contribution of the cantons	74 208 618		

Source: Author, from FFA, https://www.efv.admin.ch/efv/fr/home/themen/finanzausgleich/zahlen.htm, access date 14 April 2019.

8.4 PERFORMANCE ANALYSIS

According to the equalization law (article 18), the federal government must evaluate the performance of the equalization system and its effect on the reduction of disparities between the cantons every four years. The federal legislation describes, in detail, the objectives, items and instruments of this evaluation.[8] Three reports have been published for the periods of 2008–11, 2012–15 and 2016–19. The main conclusions of the third report (Federal Council, 2018a) are discussed below.

8.4.1 Revenue Equalization

Since 2014, the revenue equalization component has achieved better results than the targeted objective for each canton which aims to attain a tax potential that corresponds to the minimal threshold of 85 per cent of the national average after equalization (Federal Council, 2014: 9). Cantons contributing to the revenue equalization scheme soon claimed that the 85 per cent initial target should be respected and their contribution reduced in consequence. After lengthy and contentious debates at the federal level and between the cantons, the federal government proposed that, from 2022, the revenue equalization legal target be increased from 85 to 86.5 per cent. This is intended to fortify solidarity between the cantons[9] – which in fact disregards the claim of some contributing cantons maintaining the 85 per cent target. However, this new target will, de facto, lead to a reduction of the revenue equalization fund, because, in 2018, the lowest index of financial capacity was 88.3 per cent in three cantons (Jura, Uri and Valais – see Table 8.4). The reduction is estimated at 280 million CHF, which corresponds to 6.8 per cent of the 2018 endowment to the fund (Confederation and cantons).

8.4.2 The 2019 Reform[10]

The difference of 280 million CHF will not be returned to the cantons or saved by the Confederation. According to the federal government, half the amount should be used to increase the socio-demographic expenditure needs equalization (80 million CHF in 2021, 140 million each year thereafter). The other half should serve, for a transitory period of five years, to increase revenue equalization for the cantons with an index of financial capacity below 100 points.[11] After this period of time, this amount will serve to reduce the contributions of the cantons with a capacity index higher than 100. The Conference of the Cantons and the Council of States adopted this proposal in December 2018. The finance commission of the

National Council examined the proposal on 5 March, this year. It has adopted the changes in revenue equalization but did not accept that only the socio-demographic part of expenditure needs equalization will benefit from the increased dotation. It proposed – with a short majority of three votes – to maintain a strict parity between the two categories: both will be endowed with 40 million CHF in 2021 and 70 million CHF thereafter. This last proposal and the entire reform were accepted in the two Councils in the final vote held in 21 June 2019.

8.4.3 Expenditure Needs Equalization

For expenditure needs equalization, the performance evaluation is an elusive concept. The difficulties are multiple. Firstly, the formulation of the efficiency target '*compensate for excessive financial burdens*' written in the law is rather vague since neither the determinants nor the explanatory variables (see Table 8.5) express a causal relation to specific public functions and expenditure items. Questions relating to the functions considered, how one can estimate the burden and when this burden is considered excessive also remain unanswered. Secondly, several explanatory variables, such as 'altitude', 'remoteness' and 'surface of urban areas', do not register significant variations from one calculation to the next. Thirdly, the weights in the distribution formula are for some negotiated and fixed in the law and for others obtained through principal component analysis (PCA) – two parallel systems which can be questioned. And finally, since the functions in need of equalization are not specified and the transfers from and to the cantons are written in their general budget, it is impossible to assess the equalizing performance in functional terms. The before and after equalization positions of the cantons is simply measured in financial terms per capita (Federal Council, 2018b: 36–41).

8.4.4 Geo-Topographic Determinants

First, the proportion (one-half) of equalization payments attributed to the geo-topographic category is politically fixed and written in the law. Second, the explanatory variables (Table 8.5) are not dynamic in the short and medium term:[12] two 33 per cent weights are attributed to altitude – which does not change over time – so it has no further impact after being first introduced in the formula – and does not mirror the burden that topographic conditions and a dispersed population place on public expenditures (Frey, 2001). Third, smallness defined as 'communes with less than 200 inhabitants' is no longer adequate in view of the policies encouraging voluntary mergers of communes in many cantons (Dafflon, 2013).

The rigidity of the geo-topographic needs equalization is simply due to the fact that, beyond political decisions taken to address this equalization component, the statistical indicators which are suitable to evaluate the need differences are rare. The presently used indicators were accepted for want of better.

At the cantonal level, the amounts received under the heading of geo-topographic equalization fall in the general budget of the recipient cantons without being earmarked to any specific public function and expenditure. The strongest criticism, coming from cantonal political parties and lobby groups, is that the attribution of equal funds to geo-topographic and socio-demographic needs equalization is not acceptable owing to the territorial distribution of the population (15 per cent rural, 85 per cent urban): more should be given to the urban population. But a modification would be considered an affront to the mountain cantons and a serious lack of confederal solidarity. Political acceptance replaces the causality that economic logic requires between functional needs and the explanatory variables.

8.4.5 Socio-Demographic Determinants

The socio-demographic component of the expenditure equalization scheme would compensate for the 'excessive burden due to some characteristics of the population'. Yet, just as the geo-topographic component, neither the functions nor the delimitation of 'excessive burden' are explicitly defined in the law or the explicative reports. However, determinants and variables in Table 8.5 give some information about the arguments. The first part (two-thirds of the amount) relates to the concept of 'A-cities' (in German: *Arme, Alte, Ausländer, Arbeitlose*). It relates to categorical characteristics of the population in towns – poverty, old age, foreigners, unemployed – which require specific care and may result in additional public expenditures (Frey, 1996). The second part (one-third of the amount) addresses additional specific problems of city centres in urban agglomeration, such as public order and security, and traffic congestion. A comparison of the weights resulting from PCA (Table 8.3) with the proportions of the related functional expenditures in the cantons and the communes gives the figures shown in Table 8.8.

The results of the third performance evaluation were in general well received for both categories of expenditure needs equalization. There was no operational proposal for changing the determinants, the variables or the weights (Table 8.5). The only recurrent demand of the urban regions was to allocate more funds to the socio-economic category than the strict equality between the two categories (359 millions CHF each, Figure 8.1). But, this has been strongly rejected by the beneficiary mountainous

Table 8.8   Comparing CPA weights and PPE, 2016

Determinant	Component Principal Analysis (CPA) weight (as in Table 8.5, last column, but for 2016)	Weight in Proportion of Public Expenditures (PPE), 2016, cantons and communes
Poverty:	29	32
Disabled		*18*
Families and children		*10*
Unemployed		*4*
Old age	15	14
Foreigners (incl. refugees)	22	27
Public order and security	12	15
Public transport	22	12
Total	*100*	*100*

Source: Author, Table 8.5 and FFA, www.efv.admin.ch > documentation > statistique financière > Rapport > tous les fichiers; updated on 6 September 2018, access date 25 March 2019.

cantons and, also, by the finance commission of the National Council more recently (decision of 5 March 2019).[13]

8.5   CONCLUDING COMMENTS

This chapter demonstrates that a national equalization policy that juxtaposes revenue equalization and expenditure needs/costs equalization is feasible, though it faces numerous political and technical problems. With the discussions covered in the conceptual issues section of this volume, we can draw the following conclusions from the Swiss equalization system:

A first lesson emerges from this case study, which confirms the approach presented in Chapter 4 of this volume: some subnational government units dispose of financial resources above national average (per capita) when, at the same time, expenditure needs or costs are higher than the national average. Table 8.9 illustrates this ambivalent situation in the Swiss case. Aside from the transition fund to which all cantons contribute, one sees that six out of seven cantons contributing to revenue equalization benefit either from the geo-topographic equalization (Schwyz, Obwalden, Nidwalden) or from the socio-demographic equalization (Zürich, Basel-Stadt, Genève). Zug is the only canton which contributes to revenue equalization but does not obtain financial aid. Moreover, Zürich, Basel-Stadt and Genève also benefit from equalization reserved for urban areas.

Table 8.9   Cantonal benefit (B) or contribution (C) to equalization 2018

Canton	Revenue		Excessive burden			Transition fund	
			Topo-geographic	Socio-demographic	Urban areas		
	B	C	B	B	B	B	C
Zürich		C		B	B		C
Bern	B		B			B	C
Luzern	B		B			B	C
Uri	B		B				C
Schwyz		C	B				C
Obwalden		C	B				C
Nidwalden		C	B				C
Glarus	B		B			B	C
Zug		C					C
Fribourg	B					B	C
Solothurn	B			B			C
Basel-Stadt		C		B	B		C
Basel-Landschaft	B						C
Schaffhausen	B			B			C
Appenzell Ausserrhoden	B		B				C
Appenzell Innerrhoden	B		B				C
Sankt Gallen	B		B				C
Graubünden	B		B				C
Aargau	B						C
Thurgau	B		B				C
Tessin	B		B	B			C
Vaud	B		B	B	B		C
Valais	B		B	B			C
Neuchâtel	B		B	B		B	C
Genève		C		B	B		C
Jura	B		B	B		B	C

Source: Author, based on https://www.efv.admin.ch/efv/fr/home/themen/finanzausgleich/zahlen.html.

Revenue disparities are approximated with an adapted RTS which includes four items of the federal direct taxation standardized at the cantonal level. The inclusion of other cantonal direct taxes or revenues from natural resources – water concession in the Alps cantons – and from the cantons' participation in public enterprises – was again recently suggested and disregarded.[14]

The vertical-horizontal combination for revenue equalization reinforced the inter-cantonal solidarity since the federation is not the only contributor, but seven cantons with a financial capacity higher than the average also contribute. In the future, cantons with above-average-capacity will contribute exactly to two-thirds of the federal payment (Federal Council, 2018b).

The exclusively vertical funding of the 'excess burden' equalization corresponds to the economic logic that relative tax prices of cantonal functions should not be influenced through equalization (Dafflon, 2007).

In the equalization of 'excess burden', the geo-topographic indicators are not adequate since they are (1) static and (2) do not approximate specific functions, needs or costs in the mountain cantons (Frey, 2001). Because of the lack of better variables, decision makers choose to resort to political convenience. The socio-demographic variables are more plausibly related to cantonal functions, but miss important domains, such as expenditure disparities in compulsory education. Experiments in intra-cantonal equalization demonstrate that better targeted indicators are available (Dafflon and Mischler, 2007; Rühli et al., 2013; Dafflon, 2015b).

Historically, at almost all stages of the process, the weights and equalizing formulas have been fiercely debated since they directly influence the results. Rational choices prevailed in the weights given to the four taxes taken into account for revenue equalization (in proportion of each tax yield in the total). For the socio-demographic indicators (Table 8.5) and supposing one could link the explanatory variables to specific functional expenditures, according weights to the proportion of cantonal and communal functional public expenditures would likely give results different from those obtained with PCA. For example, the weight for foreigners is underestimated in PCA (22 per cent) compared to PPE (27 per cent), and inversely for public transportation in urban (PCA 22 per cent, PPE 12 per cent). In the absence of detailed calculation per canton, and the non-allocation of transfers to specific functional expenditures, it is difficult to assess whether these differences are really important and significant.

Finally, the total amount of equalization is explained from a historical perspective and traced to the change of the system in 2008. The objective at the time was not to increase the equalization fund, but to reform the scheme for more transparency and more efficiency. The fund allocated to equalization in the new system was the continuation of the existing situation. Yet, the growth rate of the future funds allocated to revenue equalization should correspond to the growth rate of the referred four federal direct taxes. As compared to revenue equalization, the funds earmarked to expenditure needs equalization have been continuously decreasing in relative terms, from 22 per cent to 18 per cent. But in both cases, the growth rate of the funds allocated to revenue equalization and to expenditure needs equalization do not essentially follow the present legal requirement (Table 8.A1). The future reform modifies this situation with a mechanism of automatic adjustment. For revenue equalization, the total funding must correspond to the objective of an 86.5 per cent financial capacity index in the poorest canton, with a federal contribution equal to 150 per cent of the contributions of the cantons with financial capacity indices higher than 100 points. The federal contribution to the expenditure needs equalization will correspond to the 2019 amount and will be adjusted yearly to the Swiss consumption price index (Federal Council, 2018a: 214–16).

In sum, the architecture of the Swiss fiscal equalization mirrors and answers all the core questions that are developed in Chapter 4 of this volume. However, in the absence of sufficient factors of causality (which explanatory variables for which functions, how to evaluate needs and costs that create 'excessive' burden), and where several schemes provide possible answers, the implemented solutions most frequently mirror political compromises. In such situations, the institutional architecture of Swiss federalism shows that the political answers are in the general interest of the cantons and are not exploited by cantonal politicians to gain local votes. The Conference of the Cantons must propose solutions that are acceptable for themselves and for the federal parliament. The process is severe enough to eliminate local egoism.

NOTES

*   Thanks to Alain Schönenberger, Paul Bernd Span, Serdar Yilmaz and two anonymous peer reviewers for their comments and suggestions on an earlier version of this chapter.

1. Communes are local government units, the lowest political tier. There were 3021 communes in 1990, 2899 in 2000 (-122), 2596 in 2010 (-303) and 2212 in 2019 (-384). The number of communes per canton varies between three in the cantons of Glarus, which has 40,000 inhabitants, and Basel-Stadt with 194,000 inhabitants, to 346 communes in the canton of Bern which has more than 1 million population. In several cantons, the merger of communes is a fundamental territorial reform that has accelerated since the early 2000s and will continue. See Dafflon (2013).

2. The cantonal resident population varies from 1.5 million in canton Zürich to 16,000 in Appenzell Innerrhoden. The average size of population per commune is 3669 inhabitants nationwide; it varies between 13,861 in Jura and 64,847 in Basel-Stadt as of 19 December 2018. Source: Federal Statistical Office, accessed 25 March 2019 at https://www.agvchapp.bfs.admin.ch/fr/state/query.

3. Regarding compulsory school education (from the age of 4 to 15) the cantons must agree (harmonize) the following issues: the school entry age, compulsory school attendance, duration and objectives of education levels, the transition from one level to another, recognition of qualifications, harmonization of school programmes, teachers' qualification. Where harmonization of school education is not achieved by horizontal coordination, the Confederation (i.e. central government) shall issue regulations to achieve such harmonization (art. 62 al. 4 Cst.). The cantons' answer to this constitutional rule on

harmonization was the 'concordat HarmoS', decided by the Conference of the Cantonal Ministers of Education on 14 June 2007 (accessed 25 March 2019 at http://www.edk. ch-> domaines d'activité -> HarmoS, only in French or German).

4. It was rejected by Nidwalden, Schwyz and Zug – three of the seven contributing cantons.

5. It is interesting to note that the federal parliament adopted on 3 October 2003 the law on fiscal equalization and the reassignment of functions between the Confederation and the cantons on equalization before the popular vote on the constitutional amendment (28 November 2004). The reason is that cantons and voters wanted to know the contours of the new equalization policy, which was to replace the one introduced in 1959. The 2003 federal law was subject to facultative referendum, which never took place. In 2004, the voter turnout for the constitutional amendment was 40 per cent.

6. The history of the Federal Direct Tax (FDT) sharing with the cantons can be summarized as follows. Since 1934, the cantons received a share of the FDT in compensation that the Confederation was allowed to tax income and profit in order to finance the national defence. In 1940, the cantonal share was fixed at 30 per cent of the federal tax yield for each canton according to the tax revenues collected in the canton. In 1959, with the introduction of the first equalization scheme, the cantons agreed that one-sixth of this share (5 per cent) be allocated to revenue equalization. It went up to 7.5 per cent in 1980 and 13 per cent from 1992 to 2007 (each canton still received 17 per cent of the FDT revenues collected within the canton).

7. We do not discuss here the pros and cons about whether expenditure needs/costs equalization should be vertical only. The theoretical debate is still on; however, the trend in theory and practice is to view vertical transfers as preferable for equalizing costs and needs; and to view horizontal 'Robin Hood' solidarity as unsuitable for this purpose (Lotz, 1997; Dafflon, 2007). Färber and Otter (2003) collected information on equalization systems at the local level in Austria, Flanders (Belgium), Denmark, France, Germany, Italy, Russia, Spain, Switzerland and the United Kingdom. Needs/costs equalization, if it exists, is nowhere horizontal.

8. Ordonnance sur la péréquation financière et la compensation des charges (OPFCC) du 7 novembre 2007.

9. Proposition of the Conference of the Cantons in Message concernant la modification de la loi fédérale sur la péréquation financière et la compensation des charges du 28 septembre 2018, accessed 25 March 2019 at https://www.admin.ch/opc/fr/federal-ga zette/2018/6607.pdf, pages 6616–17.

10. Federal Parliament, accessed 14 April 2019 at https://www.parlament.ch/fr/ratsbetrieb/ suche-curia-vista/geschaeft?AffairId=20180075.

11. The cantons with an index of financial capacity lower than 100 (national average) would receive 80 million in 2021, 200 million in 2022, 160 million in 2023, 120 million in 2024 and 80 million in 2025. The amount varies for years 2002 to 2024 in order to compensate for the reform of the business taxation (see note 9 above). The distribution will be made on the basis of the resident population of the canton and not according to the revenue equalization formula. As a result, the cantons with the lowest capacity indices will receive much less than they would with the formula.

12. In the 2016–19 Report (Federal Council, 2018a: 39 and 80 – our translation): 'This is not surprising when one knows that in the past years, the two determinants related to altitude needed not be up-dated . . . whereas the indicator of remoteness registered only minor changes . . . These indicators are structural and stable and will not vary in the near future'.

13. Federal Parliament, accessed 14 April 2019 at https://www.parlament.ch/fr/ratsbetrieb/ suche-curia-vista/geschaeft?AffairId=20180075.

14. Recommendation of the Finance commission of the National Council, 7 March 2019: 'large majority' for the non-inclusion of revenues from water concession; 10 votes for and 14 against taking into account the yields of cantonal participations in public enterprises, cantonal banks and similar institutions. Federal Parliament, accessed 14 April 2019 at https://www.parlament.ch/fr/ratsbetrieb/suche-curia-vista/geschaeft?AffairId=20180075.

REFERENCES

Ahmad, E., ed., 1997, *Financing Decentralized Expenditures: An International Comparison of Grants*, Edward Elgar Publishing, Cheltenham, UK and Northampton, MA, USA.

Boadway, R. and A. Shah, eds, 2007, *Intergovernmental Fiscal Transfers, Principles and Practice*, Public Sector Governance and Accountability Series, The World Bank, Washington, DC.

Conference of the Cantonal Ministers of Education, 2007, Harmos, http://www.edk.ch.

Dafflon, B., 2004, 'Federal-Cantonal Equalisation in Switzerland: An Overview of the Reform in Progress', *Public Finance and Management*, Symposium Fiscal Federalism, vol. 4 no. 4.

Dafflon, B., 2007, 'Fiscal Capacity Equalization in Horizontal Fiscal Equalization Programs', in Boadway and Shah, op. cit., pp. 361–99.

Dafflon, B., 2013, 'Voluntary Amalgamation of Local Governments: The Swiss Debate in the European Context', in Lago-Peñas and Martinez-Vazquez, op. cit., pp. 189–220.

Dafflon, B., 2015a, 'Swiss Fiscal Federalism: New Roads after the Reform of the Constitution', in Pola, op. cit., pp. 91–112.

Dafflon, B., 2015b, *Analyse de performance de la péréquation intercommunale dans le canton de Fribourg*, accessed at https://www.fr.ch/sommaire/perequation-financiere-intercommunale.

Dafflon, B. and M. Della Santa, 1995, *Fédéralisme et solidarité, Etude de la péréquation en Suisse*, PIFF, Institute of Federalism Fribourg.

Dafflon, B. and P. Mischler, 2007, *Réforme de la péréquation intercommunale dans le canton de Fribourg*, accessed at https://www.fr.ch/sommaire/perequation-financiere-intercommunale.

Färber, G. and N. Otter, eds, 2003, 'Reforms of Local Fiscal Equalisation in Europe', Speyerer Forschungsberichte, Nr. 232, Forschungsinstitut für Öffentliche Verwaltung, Deutsche Hochschule für Verwaltungswissenschaften, Speyer, Germany.

Federal Council, 2001, *Message 01.074 concernant la Réforme de la péréquation financière et de la répartition des tâches entre la Confédération et les cantons* (RPT), 14 November, Berne, accessed 25 March 2019 at https://www.admin.ch/opc/fr/federal-gazette/2002/2155.pdf.

Federal Council, 2014, *Rapport sur l'évaluation de l'efficacité 2012–2015 de la péréquation financière entre la Confédération et les cantons*, Berne, accessed 25 March 2019 at www.news.admin.ch > péréquation financière > Rapport.

Federal Council, 2018a, *Rapport sur l'évaluation de l'efficacité 2016–2019 de la péréquation financière entre la Confédération et les cantons*, Berne, accessed 25 March 2019 at https://www.efv.admin.ch/efv/fr/home/themen/finanzausgleich/wirksamkeitsberichte.html.

Federal Council, 2018b, *Message concernant la modification de la loi fédérale sur la péréquation financière et la compensation des charges du 28 septembre 2018*, accessed 25 March 2019 at https://www.admin.ch/opc/fr/federal-gazette/2018/6607.pdf.

Federal Finance Administration (FFA), 2017, 'Péréquation financière 2018 entre la Confédération et les cantons', Berne, June.

Frey, R.L., 1996, *Stadt: Lebens- und Wirtschaftsraum. Eine ökonomische Analyse*, Vdf, Hochschulverlag AG an der ETH Zürich.

Frey, R.L., 2001, 'Analyse de l'objectif et de l'efficacité de la nouvelle péréquation financière', Wirtschaftswissenschaftliches Zentrum WWZ der Universität Basel.

Frey, R.L., B. Dafflon, C. Jeanrenaud and A. Meier, 1994, *Le péréquation financière entre la Confédération et les cantons.* Expertise relative aux aides financières et indemnités de la Confédération en faveur des cantons, Berne, Administration fédérale des finances et Conférence des Directeurs cantonaux des finances.

Lago-Peñas, S. and J. Martinez-Vazquez, eds, 2013, *The Challenge of Local Government Size: Theoretical Perspectives, International Experience and Policy Reform*, Edward Elgar Publishing, Cheltenham, UK and Northampton, MA, USA.

Lotz, J.R., 1997, 'Denmark and Other Scandinavian Countries: Equalization and Grants', in Ahmad, op. cit., pp. 184–212.

Pola, G., ed., 2015, *Principles and Practices of Fiscal Autonomy, Experiences, Debates and Prospects*, Federalism Studies, Ashgate, Farnham UK and Burlington USA, and Éupolis Lombardia.

Rühli, L., M. Frey and R.L. Frey, 2013, *Irrgarten Finanzausgleich: Wege zu mehr Effizienz bei der interkommunalen Solidarität*, Avenir Suisse, Zürich.

APPENDIX

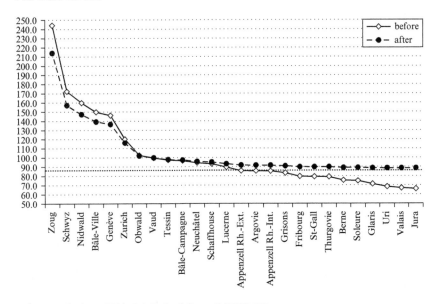

Sources: Authors, Table 8.4; Federal Council (2018: 71).

Figure 8A.1 Cantonal indices of financial capacity before and after revenue equalization, 2018

Table 8A.1 Evolution of equalization funds, 2008–2018, in 1000 CHF

Year	Revenue equalization						Expenditure needs equalization			
	Vertical	Horizontal	Total	Ratio H/V (%)	Growth rate 1 (%)		Payment	Ratio EN/R	Growth rate 2 (%)	
					op.	ref. FP			op.	ref. CPI
2008	1 798 569	1 258 998	3 057 567	70			**682 216**	22		
2009	1 861 854	1 315 027	3 176 881	71	3.9	3.5	702 000	22	2.9	−0.5
2010	1 961 872	1 406 130	3 368 002	72	6.0	5.3	694 980	21	−1.0	0.7
2011	2 100 592	1 532 643	3 633 235	73	7.9	7.2	704 710	19	1.4	0.2
2012	2 131 868	1 461 057	3 592 925	69	−1.1	−2.4	**737 624**	21		
2013	2 196 465	1 500 219	3 696 684	68	2.9	3.0	730 248	20	−1.0	−0.2
2014	2 220 010	1 507 952	3 727 962	68	0.8	1.1	725 866	19	−0.6	0.0
2015	2 273 025	1 552 285	3 825 310	68	2.6	2.4	725 866	19	0.0	−1.2
2016	2 300 683	1 752 308	4 052 991	76	6.0	5.5	**717 881**	18		
2017	2 350 133	1 598 592	3 948 725	68	−2.6	2.1	715 010	18	−0.4	0.5
2018	2 423 359	1 650 709	4 074 068	68	3.2	3.1	718 870	18	0.5	1.0

Notes:
Growth rate 1: op.: effective rate of growth of the total amount of revenue equalization/ref. FP: according to art. 6 of the 2003 federal law, the effective growth rate of the federal vertical amount corresponds to the rate of growth of the fiscal potential (FP) of the cantons mentioned in this column. The op. growth rate for the total amount is lower because the ratio horizontal/vertical equalization is decreasing. In the future, it will be fixed at 66 2/3 per cent.
Growth rate 2: according to art. 9 of the 2003 law, the amount of expenditure needs equalization is fixed by the federal parliament on the first year of each four-year period. The annual growth rates thereafter for the second, third and fourth years of the period correspond to the annual increase in the consumers' price index (CPI). From comparison between the column op. and ref. CPI, this is not quite respected in practice.

Source: Federal Council, 2014 and 2018a; price index, https://www.bfs.admin.ch/bfs/fr/home/statistiques/prix/indice-prix-consommation/resultats-ipc.assetdetail.762 6789.html, access date 14 April 2019.

9. Intergovernmental fiscal relations in Australia

Bob Searle

9.1 THE STRUCTURE OF GOVERNMENT IN AUSTRALIA

There are three tiers of government in Australia: the Commonwealth, the states[1] and about 550 local governments. The six states each have independent legal status and the Commonwealth could be seen as 'their child' as it was formed from six British colonies which became the states. The two territories exist as a result of Commonwealth legislation and the federal government limits their legislative capacity. Local government exists under state legislation and has no constitutional status. All states and the Northern Territory have local government, but the Australian Capital Territory operates without a local government structure. There are also parts of other states – South Australia and New South Wales in particular – where no local government exists. Like the states, local governments vary greatly in population, area and the extent of their urbanization.

The separation of powers between the Commonwealth and the states is determined by the Australian Constitution (Section 51) which leaves all unspecified functions to the states: they are responsible for all the major services to individuals: education, health, welfare, transport, police and so on. The distribution of responsibilities has only been changed twice since 1900 when the federation was established under an Act of the British Parliament:

- In 1946, to allow the Commonwealth to make social security payments to individuals; and
- In 1967, to allow it to make laws specific to indigenous Australians.

In addition to what is specified, however, Section 96 of the Constitution gives the Commonwealth the power to 'grant financial assistance to any state on such terms and conditions as the Parliament thinks fit'. This chapter will show the extent to which the Commonwealth has used Section 96 to widen its influence on public services.

9.2   VERTICAL FISCAL IMBALANCE IN AUSTRALIA

The distribution of expenditure responsibilities and revenue capacities results in a large vertical fiscal imbalance (VFI) with the states relying on the Commonwealth for a substantial proportion of their revenue. There is also some VFI that local government needs to be funded for: a much more important issue for rural localities than it is for urban councils.

There has never been a structured attempt to overcome the central/state VFI through a rationalization of mandates. Governments have agreed several times to permanently transfer responsibility for specific services to the Commonwealth, but these have not resulted in constitutional change. On the revenue side, there have also been adjustments (driven by legal decisions or agreements between governments) but these have generally resulted in the abolition of state taxes and an increase in VFI. The last major example of this was the July 2000 tax reforms under which the scrapping of a number of state taxes made room for the Commonwealth to introduce its Goods and Services Tax (GST). The result was to reduce states' tax collections without making any change to their responsibility for public expenditure: substantially increasing VFI. The biggest impact on VFI, however, remains the moving of income tax collections from the states to the Commonwealth during the 1940s to fund military expenditures, then never returning it to the states.

What VFI looks like in 2017–18 is shown in Figure 9.1. It shows that 43 per cent of state expenditure is funded through transfers from the Commonwealth. The local government sector also suffers from a VFI disadvantage, but that tier represents only about 5 per cent of total government activity, while the states are close to 33 per cent. Overall, local governments receive about half of their revenue from Commonwealth or state grants, with about a third of that being from the Commonwealth.

It also appears that there has never been a serious discussion at government level on the structure of the fiscal transfers that overcome the VFI. Individual states have frequently stated their preference for greater use of untied funding, but it has rarely resulted in any public discussion. The relationship between VFI, the funding mix and the maintenance of state fiscal autonomy has been largely ignored, but there is much room for reform in these areas. The size of the transfer and the pattern of tied and untied grants have evolved through political and budgetary processes rather than as a result of any structured approach to the issue. A truly cooperative

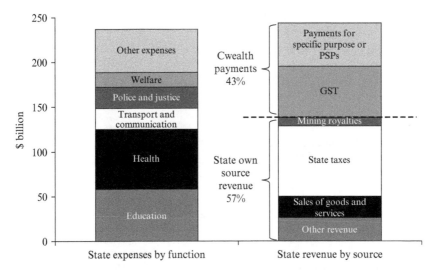

Source: Commonwealth Grants Commission, private correspondence.

Figure 9.1   Australia's vertical fiscal imbalance, 2017–18

federalism would give much more power to the states and the issues mentioned here would be resolved by both tiers of government and individual grants would be designed within agreed parameters. We will see later that there is capacity within inter-government agreements to undertake reform in these areas, but it has not been used.

9.3   OVERCOMING THE VERTICAL FISCAL IMBALANCE

Giving the states and local government sufficient funds to provide a reasonable standard of services is currently achieved through a mixture of tied and untied grants, as shown in Figure 9.2.

9.4   THE COMMONWEALTH'S TIED GRANTS SYSTEM

As shown, the Commonwealth classifies Specific Purpose Payments (SPPs) to the states into five groups. This typology does not seem to serve any real purpose and its removal may well improve transparency.

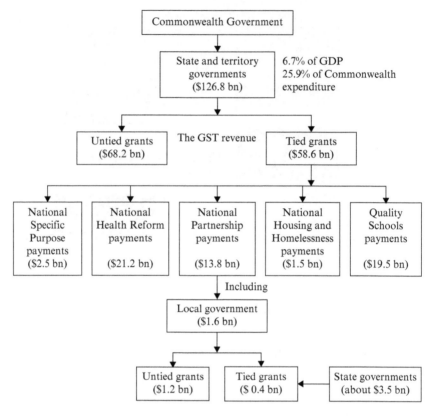

Sources: Commonwealth and State Budget Documents, 2018–19, author's analysis.

Figure 9.2   Size and structure of payments made to overcome VFI: 2018–19

National Specific Purpose Payments

There are only two National SPPs. The first is based on an agreement with the states and seeks to develop a vocational education and training system to improve service quality and greater transparency for students, employers and governments; and encourage greater efficiency. The pool of funds is varied each year by reference to a wage cost index and is distributed among the states based on their populations.

The second relates to the recently created National Disability Insurance Scheme (NDIS) under which the states have agreed to progressively hand responsibility for helping people with disabilities, and their carers, to the Commonwealth's National Disability Insurance Agency. This scheme is still being rolled out and, when it reaches full state coverage in 2019–20, the funding now flowing to the NDIS will become a Commonwealth budget-funded activity: another change to the distribution of mandates without change to the Constitution.

National Health Reform Payments

The National Health Reform Program seeks to improve health services and the efficiency of their provision. Until at least 2019–20, the funding will be linked to growth in public hospital activity and a national unit price for each activity (said to be the 'efficient' price) determined by the Independent Hospital Pricing Authority. The current agreement with the states is that the Commonwealth will fund 45 per cent of the 'efficient' growth in activity-based services, with growth in total Commonwealth funding capped at 6.5 per cent per year.[2]

National Housing and Homelessness Payments

The National Housing and Homelessness Agreement aims at improving access to affordable, safe and sustainable housing, including the prevention of homelessness. The Commonwealth funding is matched by the states and is increased annually by a wage cost index. In the past, Australia has had many 'matching' grant systems, but this has not led to efficiencies because states have seen each dollar spent as only costing their budget 50 cents.

National Partnership Payments

National Partnership payments to the states are the key vehicle used to facilitate Commonwealth-initiated reforms in the delivery of state services. To the extent possible, the Commonwealth aligns payments under National Partnerships with the achievement of milestones and makes the transfer of funds after the states have achieved the goals specified in relevant agreements. However, this does not place very stringent conditions on the states and the SPPs do not seem to create real incentives for states to change either service delivery or economic efficiency. As a result, there must be some doubt about the extent to which central government objectives are being met.

Numerically, these are the most common SPPs and are typically entered into for a fixed period. There were at least 85 National Partnership Programs funded in 2018–19, ranging from $3.7 bn for states' roads infrastructure to $200 000 for the development of a national fire danger rating and communication system.

An interesting aspect of these payments has been the increasing tendency by the federal government to fund small programmes that are for works which relate to a single geographic area. An example of this is a $10 m stadium to be funded in a provincial city, without any apparent assessment of how that city's need compares to other locations. Such commitments are most frequently made during election campaigns and illustrate the extent to which the Commonwealth is prepared to use Section 96 of the Constitution to extend its influence.

Quality Education Payments

The Quality Schools Program provides funding for all government and non-government schools. It covers both recurrent and capital funding and is aimed at influencing all aspects of school education. The growth rate of the Quality Education payments pool relies on agreements between the Commonwealth and the states.

Conclusions on SPPs to the States

SPPs are used only to influence service delivery: there is no attempt to use them to increase or change the pattern of state revenue. The proliferation of SPPs has been driven largely by a desire of federal governments to be involved in areas of state responsibility for assumed political benefits. This has greatly blurred governments' responsibilities in the eyes of the public and reform is needed to clarify mandates and reduce VFI to improve the link between revenue-raising powers and expenditure responsibilities. The conditions attached to SPPs do not often include efficiency objectives and are not sufficiently linked to the benchmarking Report on Government Services produced by the Productivity Commission and discussed elsewhere in this volume.

The categorization of SPPs is a hangover from a simplification attempted in 2009, under which there was to be only five SPPs, each distributed on an equal per capita (EPC) basis, plus a small number of national payments. This proposal, put forward by the Commonwealth and agreed to by the states, was not proceeded with because Commonwealth sectoral ministers and their departments would not relinquish their roles in the distribution of funds for sectoral functions. The proposal to distribute the SPPs as EPC grants was aimed, at least in part, at overcoming the duplication of needs assessments by the functional Commonwealth departments and the Commonwealth Grants Commission, an issue discussed in more detail later.

How the size of an individual SPP varies between years is determined either by agreement with the states, by reference to population, by reference to a cost inflator, by a mixture of these factors, or by budgetary considerations of the Commonwealth Government. For the major SPPs, growth factors are detailed in agreements, but for others, the basis of growth is very difficult to find. A rationalization of this element of intergovernmental fiscal relations would be beneficial.

The distribution of funding between the states also differs between SPPs and there has been no systematic attempt to make these more uniform. They are based either on written agreements with the recipients, acceptance of offers made by Commonwealth sectoral ministries, or even a 'historical basis' the reasoning for which is lost in time. Commonwealth departments managing the SPPs would probably all claim to use relative needs in the distribution, but there is no common Commonwealth position on how this concept should be understood. The largest of the SPPs, health and education, are very different in their structures and operating procedures, but there is public discussion of them and press coverage on both the size of the pool and the basis of funds distribution. Other SPPs get little if any public attention and insufficient detail of the arrangements is provided in annual budget documents. For these smaller grant programmes, the policy objective is often unclear.

In its 2018–19 Budget, the Commonwealth notes that SPPs now 'cover most areas of state and local government activity, including health, education, skills and workforce development, community services, housing, indigenous affairs, infrastructure and the environment'.[3] It is surprising that the steady reduction in states' autonomy has not been the subject of political discussion, and it seems that the Commonwealth's financial dominance is a very large influence on state reactions to their loss of autonomy: they cannot afford to create friction with the provider of funds. What the current arrangements do is create much confusion in the minds of the electorate and give both tiers of government capacity to blame the other when deficiencies in service standards are identified.

It is no wonder that the recent Productivity Commission report, discussed in the next chapter, recommended that the reform of federal financial relations includes development of a well-delineated division of responsibilities between the states and the Commonwealth. To this could be added the need to clarify national policy objectives, the creation of better links between SPPs and efficiency of service provision, and the need to make bases of distribution between the states more transparent and related to a philosophy under which intergovernmental fiscal relations is being managed.

9.5 COMMONWEALTH PAYMENTS FOR LOCAL GOVERNMENT

Local government has no constitutional status in Australia and is a construct of the states. State legislation determines both the expenditure mandates and own-source revenues of local government. Local government associations have called for both constitutional status and a clarification and widening of mandates, but nothing has been done in either area. The local government association in each state talks to its state government and, together, they talk as one to the federal government. But because mandates are a state issue and constitutional status is a national issue, there seems to be enough confusion of roles for the Commonwealth and state governments to make the prospect of real change unlikely. This is not a healthy position for local government to operate in and reform would appear beneficial.

Although about a third of local government's grant funding is received from the Commonwealth, there has been no discussion between the Commonwealth and the states, or local government associations, on the mix of tied and untied funding that make up these transfers. The limited mandates of local government, which is widely seen as being involved only in roads, rates and rubbish, might support the move to less SPPs and a greater use of untied funding.

Untied Funding

The untied Commonwealth grants to local government have existed for 45 years. They were initially based on principles of fiscal equalization and managed by the Commonwealth Grants Commission. After a very brief period, the basis of distribution was changed so as to introduce a minimum payment and all councils were thus assured of a grant. At the same time, the management of the distribution was given to State Grants Commissions which have since developed individual bases of distribution. These are said to be equity-based but now often show little influence of generally accepted equalization principles.

Local government untied funding is made up of two components – a general purpose component and a local roads component. Although based on local road needs, funding attributed to the later component is totally untied once the payments are received. The states' shares of the local roads component is based on shares that applied in 1991–92, at the time the funding became untied. The general purpose component is the largest and is distributed between the states on a per capita basis. The combined pool is increased annually by reference to population increases and changes in the consumer price index.

In reality, the Commonwealth appears to show little interest in these funds and probably sees the expense as being a political necessity that gives federal politicians a capacity to become more involved with their electorates on local issues. They were introduced at a time when there was discussion by governments on the future structure of government in Australia, but that discussion has long since ceased.

Tied Funding

There are only two SPPs that the Commonwealth classifies as being for local government: one for local roads and one for drought relief in rural areas. The local roads funding is for construction and maintenance projects and is split between the states on the same basis as the roads component of the untied funding discussed above. The distributions within states are determined by the State Grants Commissions and the decisions on projects to be funded are made by individual councils. Not all local councils receive funding from this source.

The funds for drought relief provide employment for people whose work opportunities have been affected by drought. Funding is provided to drought-declared areas and the distribution of funds is based on assessed need.

9.6   STATE PAYMENTS TO LOCAL GOVERNMENT

The states have always argued that they have no fiscal capacity to give large grants to local councils. Available data for 2014–15 indicates that the total state financial support to local government was about $3.4 bn, with nearly half of that being in Queensland. Nearly half of the total state assistance to local government in Australia is for local roads funding.

There is no detail available at the central level on how the states distribute their grant funds for local roads but it is probable that the relative needs determined by the State Grants Commissions are applied.

9.7   CONCLUSIONS ON VERTICAL FISCAL IMBALANCE AND TIED GRANTS

VFI is relatively high in Australia. Its impact on states' autonomy discourages them from thinking more widely about how tax efforts are linked to service standards; and confuses the public about how government mandates in their federation are distributed. It encourages inefficient governance by resulting in the central government becoming too-frequently involved in what should be state or local government decisions. It could be said to have changed the federal democracy designed in the Australian Constitution without this change having been agreed to by the electorate.

In terms of tied grants, it is difficult to see that the classification of these payments has any meaning and it is difficult to associate the conditions attached to them as benefitting efficiency. The systems for determining their size and distribution between states seem haphazard. There is much to be done in overcoming these issues.

9.8   UNTIED GRANTS, HORIZONTAL FISCAL EQUALIZATION AND THE COMMONWEALTH GRANTS COMMISSION

The Size of the Untied Grants Pool

When the principle of Horizontal Fiscal Equalization (HFE) of all six states was first applied in 1981, the pool of untied funds made available to achieve this objective was based on a pre-determined share of total personal income tax collections. It was very quickly changed to a share of total Commonwealth tax collections, then by a system under which the level of 'financial assistance grants was to be escalated annually in accordance with movements in prices and a real growth factor'.[4] The base for these calculations was the tax sharing pool of 1984–85, the movement in prices was to be the consumer price index and the growth factor was to be 2 per cent.

In 2000, the pool of untied funds became attached to the newly introduced GST. This still determines the size of the pool but it will change in a small way for the period 2019–20 to 2026–27 when the Commonwealth proposes to add between 1 and 1.5 per cent to the pool to overcome what it sees as inequalities in the current distribution. Under the agreement made when the GST was introduced,[5] the tax rate was set at 10 per cent and this can only be changed if a proposal has:

1. the unanimous support of the states and Territories;
2. the endorsement of the Commonwealth Government; and
3. the passage of relevant legislation by both Houses of the Commonwealth Parliament.

Change had been made deliberately difficult and, at that time, politicians from all governments considered that the GST had such growth potential that the rate of tax would probably never need changing. There was considerable discussion on the breadth of the tax base and it was agreed that it should not apply to foodstuff and essential services like education and health. Changes to the tax base were made subject to the same rigorous requirements as those applied to the tax rate.

Since 2000, there have been minor changes to the tax base but no change to the tax rate. Individual states, politicians and commentators have frequently argued for increases in the tax rate but there has never been any move to test whether all states, the federal government and the Commonwealth Parliament would support an increase.

The distribution of untied grants to the states is managed by the Commonwealth Grants Commission (CGC). The Commission does not have constitutional status but has existed since 1933. It was established to give stability to the processes through which the Commonwealth was providing untied funds to the states and as a result of a move by Western Australia to secede from the Australian Federation.

The Objective of Equalization

The principle of HFE was expounded for the first time when the CGC proposed, in its third report (1936), that:

> special grants are justified when a State, through financial stress from any cause, is unable efficiently to discharge its function . . . and should be determined by the amount of help found necessary to make it possible for that State, by reasonable effort, to function at a standard not appreciably below that of other States.[6]

The process would ensure the level of states' services were not 'appreciably' different. It would not ensure they could be the same.

This application of 'not appreciably different' remained in place until the 1980s when the CGC decided to avoid the judgement element involved in deciding what was appreciably different by incorporating all drivers of differences in fiscal capacity into its assessments. Judgement was still necessary in many of the assessments, but the overarching judgement of what appreciable meant had been avoided.

The states were complicit in this development. Their submissions to CGC inquiries had argued about the detail in the calculation of assessments rather than a judgement of an appreciable difference in overall capacities. They each argued for the assessment of influences that were beneficial to their position relative to others. They argued for more and more elements to the algorithm. Many of these were accepted and the Commission's 'black box' grew in complexity.

In its 1993 Review, the Commission formally revised its definition of equalization to replace the term 'appreciably different' with 'the same', thus aligning it with how HFE was being implemented. The Commonwealth accepted this change. The terms of reference for the following 1999 review told the Commission the funding distribution:

> Should enable each state to provide the average standard of State-type services, assuming it does so at an average level of operational efficiency and makes the average effort to raise revenue from its own sources.

It was this definition of HFE and its method of application that were implicitly accepted by all parties when they signed the Intergovernmental Agreement on the Reform of Commonwealth-State Financial Relations in 1999. It remained operational until 2010 but, by that time, suggestions were being made for a less comprehensive interpretation of equalization.

In 2010, the Commission accepted some of the suggestions for simplification and redefined the equalization objective as:

> State governments should receive funding . . . such that, after allowing for material factors affecting revenues and expenditures, each would have the fiscal capacity to provide services and the associated infrastructure at the same standard, if each made the same effort to raise revenue from its own sources and operated at the same level of efficiency.[7]

The Commission then reduced the number of elements in its algorithm by introducing a materiality test to their inclusion. This definition of HFE is still in use. It is said to still result in 'comprehensive' equalization in that all components of the states' budgets are considered, even if some of them are judged to no longer warrant a differential assessment, and immaterial differences in capacity are excluded.

Some states continued to argue that the change made in 2010 was not enough. As the revenue capacity of Western Australia grew with a boom in exports of iron ore, this pressure increased, and the Commonwealth initiated several inquiries into possible simplification to the HFE system. The difficulty confronted each time was that no funds other than GST collections were to be made available: gaining support for change from those states that would suffer reduced funding was impossible.

This position of the federal government remained unchanged until after the 2018 Productivity Commission Report into HFE[8] discussed in the next chapter. In July 2018, the Commonwealth proposed some changes to untied funding to the states. The major changes proposed, but not yet discussed or agreed to by the states, are that:

1. The funding for Western Australia in each of the eight years after 2018–19 will be subject to a floor but other states will be subject to the CGC's HFE principles, although none of those states will be worse off because of the change.
2. The Commonwealth will provide an extra $6.7 bn in untied grants over the eight years to achieve the 'no worse off' position.
3. After 2026–27, any funding needed to get Western Australia up to the minimum to which it is guaranteed will be at the expense of the other states.

The federal government described the change as reinforcing and protecting the 'fair go' system used to distribute the GST, and establishing a transition to a new HFE system over eight years. These claims, which are based on an assumed level of HFE funding to which Western Australia will be entitled in the long term, will create a system of one playing field for seven states and a different playing field for the fiscally strongest state: Western Australia. Only a week after the Commonwealth announced the proposed change, the press were speculating that the mining companies were entering their next boom and rapidly building new mines in Western Australia. It may be that the Western Australian relative need based on HFE principles will remain below the level now built into the Commonwealth's proposal.

The government's proposal also changes the dynamic of equalization in two other ways. If there is a new mining boom, more of the financial benefit of that boom will be kept by Western Australia and its capacity to reduce taxes, increase employee wages or improve services beyond the level of other states will be enhanced. It would be receiving GST funding beyond the level indicated by HFE at a time when its revenue capacity would be very high. Secondly, at present, any change in a state's relative share of SPPs changes its fiscal capacity and changes its share of GST, but the introduction of a GST floor means an increase in its relative share of SPPs would not reduce Western Australia's untied grant. That is, it would face no HFE consequences from the receipt of an abnormal increase in SPP funding.

The federal government has claimed to have 'protected the long-term integrity of the HFE system, ensured it is fit for purpose and can continue delivering on its objective'.[9] In fact, it has moved away from Australia's traditional HFE principles and proposed a two-tiered system of state service provision capacity. Western Australia will, if the proposals are accepted by the other states, be able to provide a better standard of services or lower tax rates than the other states, perhaps in perpetuity.

A two-tiered system of 'equalization' is not unknown in intergovernmental financial relations. Indonesia, for example, gives Aceh and West

Papua extra funding but makes it clear that this is to maintain national cohesion and because of the wealth those provinces contribute to the national economy. Similarly, it is not unknown for nations to leave some of the revenue derived from minerals in the province of origin, as in Canada for example, but this is usually accompanied by a statement giving this as the reason for the pattern of funds distribution.

One benefit in these developments is that the Commonwealth Government has, for the first time, decided what it wants to achieve through the HFE system, and what price it is prepared to pay to achieve that objective. For 85 years, it has let the CGC, often in consultation with the states, decide what HFE meant and how it was to be implemented. This led to grant recipients focusing on the numerical calculation of their positions rather than the wider question of the 'acceptable' degree of equalization. Particularly since 2000 when untied grants ceased to have any impact on its budget, the Commonwealth had shown relatively little interest in either the size of the GST pool or the way it was distributed. These were matters for the states.

Although the government's solution to Western Australia's complaints of inequalities in the GST distribution is different from that proposed by the Productivity Commission, that Commission is undoubtedly correct in having recommended that:

- the Commonwealth Government should set a revised objective of HFE;[10] and
- the Commonwealth Treasury should provide public input into the CGC's five-yearly review process.[11]

9.9   THE IMPLEMENTATION OF HFE

HFE in Australia is, at its most simple, shown to be:

$$G = E - R - O \qquad (9.1)$$

where:
G is a state's requirement for untied assistance;
E is the expenses it would incur if it provided average levels of services at average levels of efficiency;
R is the revenue it would raise if it applied average tax policies to its revenue bases; and
O is its revenue from SPPs that relate to functions in the assessment budget.

In arriving at its quantification of each of the E, R and O components, the CGC has made many decisions on how HFE was to be approached. We now discuss the changes since 2010 that could be said to have changed the concept of HFE.

The Breadth and Categorization of Assessments

In Australia, there has never been any serious thought given to whether or not HFE should be limited by excluding either side of states' budgets. The 1936 definition included both revenue capacity and service delivery in its formulation and that has continued to be accepted. The question remains, however, about how to define the revenue sources and services that are to be assessed.

After the late 1970s, the way the CGC defined the revenue sources and services it assessed changed as the quest for precision changed. The definition of individual services got more specific as the assessment detail increased. The number of separate services assessed in 1978 was 19, but this slowly increased to 41 before being reduced to 14 in 2010. On the revenue side, the 1978 assessments identified 16 different revenue sources. This number rose to 21 but was reduced to 7 in 2010.

The 2010 changes made the assessments more manageable and, possibly, more understandable. If the assessment category did not influence any state's grant by at least $100 per capita, it was subsumed elsewhere in the assessment budget or assessed separately but by the EPC method, thus ensuring it had no impact on the funding distribution.

On the question of revenue capacity, the issue of categorization has been most obvious in the area of mining where the geographic distribution of resources can result in an individual state dominating the average revenue effort if different minerals are each assessed separately. On the other hand, royalty rates and the measurement of revenue bases vary greatly between minerals, which creates difficulties for an overall assessment of states' revenue capacity from minerals. The categorization of mining revenue sources and the assessment of capacity in mining has been a perennial issue in Australia, as elsewhere. Over the years, several approaches have been taken but none has been found to be satisfactory in the long term. The recent Productivity Commission report concluded that there was no obvious approach that would mitigate the problem of policy non-neutrality that besets the mining assessment.

The Detail in the Assessments

The Australian system has also seen large shifts in the level of detail within the assessment of individual services. In this regard, the changes towards simplification in 2010 were dramatic in the level of detail to which assessments were made. The CGC decided that no disability, as they are called, would be assessed unless it redistributed at least $10 per capita for any one state.[12] Taking education as the example, the structure of the assessments and the disabilities assessed for each category in 1999 and 2010 are shown in Table 9.1.

In total, the 2010 simplifications were the cause of fairly large changes in the funds distribution.[13] In line with the amended definition of HFE, however, the results were considered to be an acceptable consequence of simplification and could be supported equally to those resulting from the previous more detailed procedures.

The Accuracy of Calculated Disability Factors

Before 2004, there was no consideration given of the level of confidence that might be attached to individual disability factors being applied to the assessment categories. In that year, the CGC decided that, for some assessments, it should discount the calculated factors because it had insufficient confidence in either the data being used or its relationship to differences in state expenditure needs in the future.

The Contemporaneity of HFE Assessment

HFE assessments in Australia are always based on data that is at least two years old. That is, the 2018–19 distribution is based on assessments of states' capacities for a period ending in 2016–17. This has been seen as inevitable because there are no financial data available for 2017–18 and the inclusion of a year based on estimated data has been avoided because of the uncertainty it would bring into the calculations.

A regular discussion point, however, has been the length of the assessment period and it has, over time, varied between three and five years. It has been three years since 2010. The argument for a five-year period is to give greater stability to the assessments, while the arguments for three years centre on making them more contemporaneous. However, whenever change is being considered, the states agree that HFE is achieved, over time, when the circumstances of each year are given equal weight over time.

Frequency of Updating the HFE Calculations

In 1981,[14] the CGC considered the frequency with which the basis of its assessments should be reviewed and whether or not the calculations should be updated between reviews. With the agreement of the states, it concluded

Table 9.1 The education assessments

1999 Assessments

	Socio-demographic composition	Urbanization	Administrative scale	Input costs	Dispersion	Service delivery scale	Isolation	Cross-border	National capital	Other
Education										
Pre-schools	*			*	*	*	*			
Government primary educ	*	*	*	*	*	*	*		*	
Non-government primary educ	*		*	*	*	*	*			*
Government secondary educ	*	*	*	*	*	*	*	*	*	*
Non-government secondary educ	*		*					*		*
Vocational education and training	*		*	*	*	*	*	*		
Higher educ										
Transport of rural school children	*				*					

2010 Assessments

	Indigenous status	Socio-economic Status	Age	Non-state sector	Wage costs	Regional costs	Service delivery scale	Cross-border
Schools education	*	*	*	*	*	*	*	
Post-secondary education	*	*	*	*	*	*		*

that there should be a five-yearly review of the methods used to determine states' HFE positions,[15] and the calculations should be updated annually between reviews to incorporate the latest available financial year and the most recent data on which to base disability factors. The update process supported the notion of equalization being achieved over time with each state's circumstances each year getting equal weighting over time.

Availability of data was not a consideration in whether updates would be possible. The Australian Bureau of Statistics (ABS) produces population, government finance data and a wide range of non-financial data on an annual basis. A decision taken very early was that the CGC should use data that was publicly available and derived from a central agency. The CGC should not be collecting data or evaluating the accuracy of data collected by reputable central agencies.

Coping with Changes to the Distributions

Undertaking five-yearly reviews of the states' HFE positions can lead to changes that are sufficiently large to be difficult for states to manage in their annual budgets. In these circumstances, the practice has been to phase in the changes to states' relativities over time. This has sometimes been proposed by the CGC but has, on other occasions, been the result of negotiations between states and the Commonwealth during their considerations of Commission recommendations. The transition period has usually been either three or five years, depending on the size of the required change in distribution.

Conclusions on Horizontal Fiscal Equalization Methodology

HFE has been in place in Australia since the late 1970s but the detail in the calculations has changed over time. It is only in 2018 that the Commonwealth Government seems to be taking an active role in specifying what the HFE objective is. This development is well overdue and must be beneficial to the Australian equalization system.

In terms of the calculation of states' relative funding needs, the CGC initially let the states drive the process. More recently, it has taken a more proactive role and has set limits to the impact of individual factors when deciding whether or not to include them in the calculations. Correctly, it has argued that neither process can be shown to give a better result than the other.

Many of the changes made over the last decade have been claimed to make the process simpler and more easily understood. No doubt it is a simpler calculation but whether it has improved understanding is not clear.

The general understanding of the HFE process still appears to be very limited but it could be that commentators simply like to emphasize the disgruntled politicians' position that 'it is too hard to understand'. The process can only benefit from the Commonwealth taking a more active role, as recommended in the recent Productivity Commission report.

9.10 THE INTERFACE BETWEEN TIED AND UNTIED GRANTS

As mentioned earlier, the Commonwealth attempted, in 2009, to get all SPPs distributed on an EPC basis. Inter alia, this was because the present arrangements result in sectoral departments determining a needs-based distribution of SPPs and then the CGC effectively doing it again when it assesses relative needs for state services. This arises because the CGC includes the services funded by the SPPs within its assessments, then reduces each state's need for untied funding by the value of the SPPs received to fund those services.

The CGC's process is consistent with the principle of HFE and is accepted as such by the state treasuries, but it does result in some conflict between HFE and other intergovernmental fiscal relations policies. It has been criticized at both the federal and state level: the claim being that agreed SPP distributions are overridden.

This principle of inclusion to treat SPPs was developed by the CGC in the 1970s, without federal government guidance. By accepting CGC findings since then, the government has implicitly accepted the Commission's position. On some occasions, the CGC has been given instructions not to use inclusion for specified payments and to keep those state receipts and the services they fund outside the assessments. Prior to the recent proposals on the level of HFE grants for Western Australia, the treatment of SPPs was the only aspect of HFE methodology on which the CGC had been given instruction.

9.11 INSTITUTIONAL ARRANGEMENTS FOR INTERGOVERNMENTAL FISCAL RELATIONS[16]

Council of Australian Governments

The Council of Australian Governments (COAG) is the peak intergovernmental forum in Australia. It is the key decision-making body with respect to monitoring and implementation of the framework for federal financial relations. COAG's roles include initiating, developing, endorsing and monitoring the implementation of policy reforms of national significance which require cooperative action by all governments. The Council is made up of the Prime Minister, the Premiers of the states and the Chief Ministers of the territories. It meets at least annually.

COAG Council on Federal Financial Relations

The Commonwealth Treasurer is the chair of this Standing Council of COAG which meets at least once each financial year. The treasurers of the states and territories are the other members. Within a framework determined by COAG, the Council considers matters relating to the Intergovernmental Agreement on Federal Financial Relations (IGAFFR). One of the Council's responsibilities is to consider ongoing reform of federal financial relations but it has not been active in this field.

The Commonwealth Grants Commission

The CGC was created by legislation in 1933. It is the key institution in the HFE process but has no constitutional basis. It is a permanent body comprised of between three and six members, including the chair. Members can be either full-time or part-time and are initially appointed for a five-year period, but appointments are renewable.

The process for selecting members of the Commission is not legislated but has traditionally involved the states. Membership of the Commission is a statutory position and the appointment is made by the Governor-General, not the minister to which the Commission reports or the Prime Minister.

9.12   THE INTERGOVERNMENTAL AGREEMENT ON FEDERAL FINANCIAL RELATIONS

The IGAFFR came into effect in January 2009 and was 'designed to be a living document, with detailed arrangements set out in schedules that can be updated as necessary, with the agreement of COAG'. It holds details of things the parties have agreed to and a series of general aspirational statements. It gives no idea of long-term intentions on the level of VFI, the degree of autonomy to be available to the states, or what is meant by HFE.

New policy proposals by the Commonwealth, like the recent GST redistribution in favour of Western Australia, are announced before they have been discussed with the states. If that proposal is accepted, the agreement will, presumably, be changed.

When first agreed to, the IGAFFR was given much publicity in the Commonwealth's annual Budget Papers, but now it is mentioned only in passing, or not at all.

In the 2016–17 Budget Paper No. 3, for example, we learnt that:

> At the COAG meeting in April 2016, the Commonwealth and states agreed to work together to develop options to share personal income tax revenue raised and collected by the Commonwealth in exchange for reducing Commonwealth payments for specific purposes.

This is a worthy aspiration, but there was no mention of the IGAFFR and we have had no information since on what progress, if any, has been made.

9.13 CONCLUSION

Intergovernmental Fiscal Relations in Australia are dominated by Commonwealth-State relations and these in turn are dominated by the size of the VFI. VFI in favour of the Commonwealth has been the greatest influence on what is done and how it is done, and the Commonwealth's movement into state (and local government) mandates has been enabled by Section 96 of the Constitution.

Federal financial arrangements, especially in relation to the major SPPs, are changed fairly frequently and the states therefore concentrate on the short-term impacts of Commonwealth proposals. The COAG arrangements are not working in a sufficiently broad way as to consider the big issues in intergovernmental fiscal relations.

It appears that Australia might be a long time away from having any real reform to its fiscal federalism. It is interesting to speculate, however, how different Australian government and society might be if there was a reassessment of mandates, revenue sources and levels of autonomy of the three tiers of government; an overall philosophy on the size of VFI; agreement on the mix of tied and untied grants used to overcome VFI; greater government interest in the meaning and application of HFE; how the pools of grant funding were changed annually; policy uniformity on the basis of tied grants distributions; and agreed links between the tied grant systems and the achievement of greater service delivery efficiencies.

NOTES

1. The term states covers the Australian Capital Territory and the Northern Territory unless otherwise indicated.

2. These mentions of efficiency seem to be a mechanism for cost limitation by the Commonwealth rather than a measure of the cost of activities performed at an average or optimum level of efficiency.
3. Australian Budget Paper No. 3, 2018–19, *Federal Financial Relations*, p. 11.
4. Commonwealth of Australia, Budget Paper No. 7, Payments to or for the States, the Northern Territory and Local Government Authorities, 1985–86, p. 15.
5. The Intergovernmental Agreement on the Reform of Commonwealth-State Financial Relations, 1999.
6. CGC *Third Report* 1936, p. 75.
7. CGC *Report on GST Revenue Sharing Relativities, 2010 Review, Main Report*, p. 34.
8. Productivity Commission Inquiry Report, *Horizontal Fiscal Equalisation*, Australian Government, 2018.
9. The Hon. Scott Morrison, Treasurer of the Commonwealth of Australia, Media Release, 5 July 2018.
10. In its interim response, the federal government has said this should be done in consultation with the states.
11. The interim response accepted this, 'where it would contribute additional value to the CGC'.
12. This limit was increased to $30 per capita in 2015.
13. The CGC did not quantify the impact of individual changes. In total, however, the changes redistributed over $725m, about 2 per cent of the pool.
14. CGC, *Report on State Tax Sharing Entitlements, 1981*.
15. The pattern of reviews coincides with the availability of new population data from the five-yearly census.
16. More information on COAG, its Council and sub-committee is obtainable from federalfinancialrelations.gov.au.

MAJOR REFERENCES

CGC (Commonwealth Grants Commission) (1936) *Third Report*, Melbourne.
CGC (1981) *Report on State Tax Sharing Entitlements, 1981*, Canberra.
CGC (2010) *Report on GST Revenue Sharing Relativities, 2010 Review, Main Report*, Canberra.
Commonwealth of Australia (1999) The Intergovernmental Agreement on the Reform of Commonwealth-State Financial Relations, 1999.
Commonwealth of Australia (2018) Budget Paper No. 3, 2018–19, *Federal Financial Relations*, Canberra: Australian Government.
Council of Australian Governments website: federalfinancialrelations.gov.au.
Morrison, Scott (2018) Media Release, 5 July 2018.
Productivity Commission (2018) *Horizontal Fiscal Equalisation*, Report No. 88, Canberra: Australian Government.

10. The economic impacts of horizontal fiscal equalization as practised in Australia

Jonathan Coppel

10.1 INTRODUCTION

Fiscal federal relations in Australia are unique in several respects. Australia has close to the highest level of vertical fiscal imbalance of any federated state, and its system of horizontal fiscal equalization (HFE) seeks to fully equalize state and territories' (hereafter states) *fiscal capacities* on both the revenue and expenditure sides of the budget. The latter also takes account of differences in the cost of supplying services.

This comprehensive approach to HFE, the institutional framework used to determine the distribution of funds and the processes to ensure accountability for how they are used are often portrayed by international commentators as the 'gold standard'. However, within Australia, HFE has repeatedly been a point of contention in federal state relations. Fiscally stronger states emphasize how the system may act as a disincentive to policy reform, or to develop particular industries or projects. Fiscally weaker states stress HFE's role in promoting fiscal equality across the Australian federation, especially given the inherent disadvantages some states face in raising revenue or delivering services.

These concerns reached a nadir as the mining boom, concentrated in Western Australia, elevated the extent of redistribution to an unprecedented high and saw Western Australia's share of the goods and services tax (GST) fall to a record low (Figure 10.1).[1] Never before has there been such a disparity in state relativities. It is against this backdrop that the Australian Productivity Commission was asked in May 2017 to undertake an inquiry into Australia's system of HFE.[2] This chapter examines how the current HFE system impacts on state budget management and whether it distorts public finance policy decisions. It also discusses the benchmarking arrangements in place to ensure accountability and transparency between levels of government.

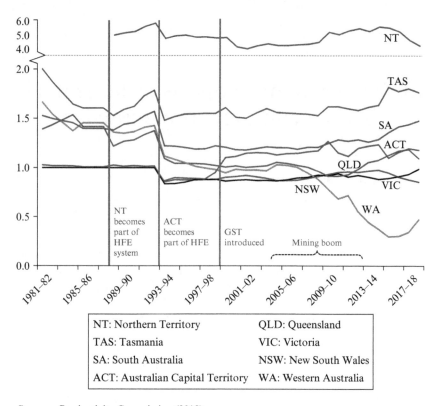

Source: Productivity Commission (2018).

Figure 10.1   The widening disparity in state per capita GST relativities

10.2   HOW DOES HFE WORK IN AUSTRALIA?

10.2.1   What Is HFE and Why Does It Exist?

Australia's federal financial relations landscape is characterized by a concentration of power at the Commonwealth level, comparatively lower taxing powers of the states (mainly consisting of payroll taxes, mining royalties, stamp duty and land tax) and a co-operative approach to federalism with widespread joint government involvement.

A consequence of this landscape is both *horizontal* and *vertical* fiscal imbalances. The latter refers to the fact that the Commonwealth government raises revenues in excess of its spending responsibilities, while state governments have insufficient revenue from their own sources to finance their spending responsibilities. Australia has among the highest vertical fiscal imbalance (VFI) in the world (Koutsogeorgopulou and Tuske, 2015), with close to half state revenues coming from the Commonwealth.[3]

In this context, the primary rationale for HFE is to seek the equal fiscal treatment of jurisdictions in the Australian federation, not interpersonal equity. It involves the transfer of funds from the Commonwealth to the states to offset differences in revenue-raising capacities and in the use and costs of providing services and infrastructure. Inevitably, this means there is a tension between HFE and the incentive for states to use their own tax bases (discussed in the next section).

This was a known risk in the earliest days of Australia's federation and nicely captured by Robert Garran, Australia's 'first public servant', using the following caricature:

> We thank you for the offer of the cow, but we can't milk, and so we answer now – we answer with a loud resounding chorus: please keep the cow and do the milking for us. (Garran, 1958, p.208)

10.2.2   The Practice of HFE in Australia[4]

The Commonwealth Grants Commission (CGC) recommends a distribution of GST revenue according to the following objective:

> State governments should receive funding from the pool of goods and services tax revenue such that, after allowing for material factors affecting revenues and expenditures, each would have the fiscal capacity to provide services and the associated infrastructure at the same standard, if each made the same effort to raise revenue from its own sources and operated at the same level of efficiency. (CGC, 2010, p.34)

This articulation of the HFE objective is noteworthy in several respects. First, it applies to both revenues and expenditures. Second, allowing for material factors affecting expenditures means taking into account differences in the cost of supplying services across jurisdictions, not just differences in their use. Third, the same fiscal standard implies equalizing to the fiscally strongest state. The primacy of the fiscal equality objective and equalization on both the expenditure and revenue side is unique to Australia.

Australia's institutional arrangements for determining the GST distribution are robust and independent. The CGC, an independent statutory agency, is charged with developing, applying and periodically revising the methodology used to calculate the distribution of the GST pool. The CGC was established in 1933 and greatly reduced the politicization of

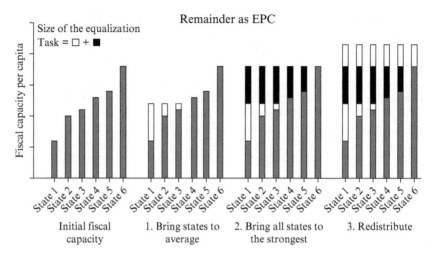

Source: Productivity Commission (2018).

Figure 10.2   Schema of the conceptual stages of the HFE process

Commonwealth state transfer decisions. It is well respected and trusted, and its processes are consultative and transparent.

The CGC's methodology is very complex and few people understand the method in detail. This gives scope for vested interests to mislead, and that in turn risks a loss of confidence in the system. Conceptually, however, the CGC's approach is straightforward and can be summarized in three steps (Figure 10.2):

1.   States with relatively low fiscal capacities are raised to the average (pre-GST) fiscal capacity of all states;
2.   all states are then raised to the capacity of the fiscally strongest state;
3.   any remaining revenue from the GST pool is distributed to all states on an equal per capita (EPC) basis.

After these equalization steps, all states are provided with the fiscal capacity to provide the national average level of services. Due to the VFI between the state and Commonwealth governments, even the fiscally strongest state requires an EPC component 'top up' (step three) to be able to provide the average level of services.

The size of the equalization task – that is, the share of the GST pool *not* distributed on a per capita basis to achieve equalization – peaked in 2016–17 at 12–13 per cent (Figure 10.3). The increase in the equalization

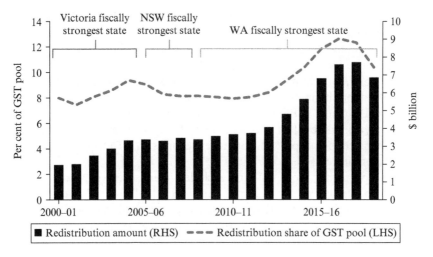

Source: Productivity Commission (2018).

Figure 10.3   Share of GST pool not distributed on a per capita basis

task reflects the increased disparity in the fiscal capacities of the states over the past two decades (as also revealed in the unprecedented dispersion in GST relativities).

Western Australia emerged as the fiscally strongest state about a decade ago, and is expected to remain so for some years to come. This reflects the mining boom and increased mineral production in the resource rich state. Typically, the fiscally strongest state has been less of an outlier and one of the two largest state economies, New South Wales (NSW) or Victoria. In contrast, the small state economies, such as South Australia and Tasmania, have consistently been assessed with a below average fiscal capacity.

The key factors affecting the redistribution of the GST are mining, remoteness and regional costs and indigenous status. Moreover, it is changes in these factors, rather than in the HFE methodology that mostly account for the shifts between states' fiscal capacities over time.

10.2.3   To What Extent Does HFE Achieve Fiscal Equalization?

In practice the CGC does not achieve perfect equalization. This is largely due to conceptual considerations and data limitations needed to apply the methodology. For example, not all activities are differentially assessed because they cannot be reliably measured or have an immaterial impact and are either discounted or assessed on an EPC basis. In 2016–17, nearly 40 per cent of revenues and about 20 per cent of expenditures were assessed on an EPC basis, or near EPC basis. Even still, Australia is recognized internationally as unique in almost completely eliminating disparities in fiscal capacity between states (OECD, 2013).

The Commonwealth is also a major provider of revenue to the states through other channels than the GST distribution. They include Specific Purpose Payments (SPPs) and National Partnership Payments (NPPs). These payments are taken into account by the CGC in state fiscal capacity assessments, either as part of state revenue, or as an offsetting reduction in state expenditure needs.

Some payments, however, are excluded from fiscal capacity assessments. The Treasurer, for example, can direct the CGC to 'quarantine' a Commonwealth payment that supports a project with national or cross-state benefits, such as national infrastructure. The Treasurer also has the power to target particular needs or shortfalls of individual states that may not be recognized in the CGC's analysis. For example, controversy about Western Australia's low relativity following the mining investment boom led to the state receiving quarantined funds for infrastructure.

Quarantined payments made to a state raise that state's 'effective relativity', enabling it to receive additional Commonwealth funds without the consequence of a reduction in its relativity as calculated by the CGC. The ability of the Commonwealth Treasurer to quarantine payments from HFE reduces transparency and accountability for the delivery of government services (discussed further in section 10.4) and adds an element of unpredictability to Australia's HFE system. In practice, only about 5 per cent of Commonwealth payments are quarantined by the Treasurer.[5]

The CGC also has the discretion to discount payments by up to 50 per cent from their fiscal capacity assessments. This is done in accordance with the principles of HFE and is usually reserved for when the CGC is not confident of the accuracy of their assessment.

Once all these payments are taken into account, the overall degree of fiscal disparity between the states narrows. Nonetheless, the heavy lifting with the redistribution is done by the GST distribution. Once it is factored in, the revenue disparities in most states fall to near negligible differences (Figure 10.4). The one exception is the Northern Territory, which raises close to the average own source revenue per capita, but after the GST distribution its revenue per capita is about 135 per cent higher than the average. This is because the Australian system also takes expenditure needs into account and the Northern Territory has both higher use and costs of government service delivery, due mostly to its remoteness and large indigenous population.

Revenue per capita relative to the average, per cent

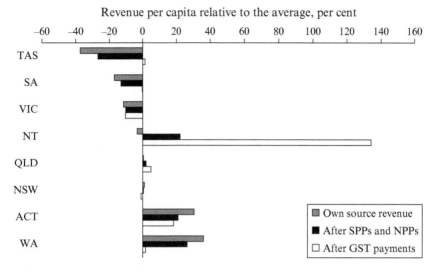

Source: Productivity Commission calculations.

Figure 10.4   The overall redistributive effects of Commonwealth transfers, 2015–16

10.3   THE ECONOMIC IMPACTS OF HFE

This section considers the economic impacts of Australia's system of HFE. Section 10.3.1 examines the disincentives facing states to initiate tax and expenditure reforms. Specific emphasis is given to mineral and energy resources, where the potential impacts of HFE have been highly contentious. Section 10.3.2 focuses on how HFE can alter how economic fluctuations bear on state budget cycles.

10.3.1   Disincentives to Undertake Public Finance Reforms

The CGC's methods for calculating GST shares to the states are intended to be policy neutral – that is, GST shares should reflect structural differences across states and should not be affected by an individual state's policy decisions, including the mixture of revenue sources that it chooses to use. But because average state policy is determined by what states collectively do, there is some tension with the principle of policy neutrality.

The tension between what states do and policy neutrality is inherent to *any* system of HFE, in that any increase in a state's fiscal capacity relative to others will see it receive less in equalization payments. There is also a debate between focusing solely on addressing the inherent advantages and disadvantages in the fiscal capacity of the states and allowing some fiscal reward for effort, risk taking and policy reform (fairness). In practice, these tensions and hence concerns about incentives for inefficient policy choices are more evident on the revenue side, with some large potential effects in relation to major state tax reform and the taxation of minerals and energy.

State tax reform
By virtue of how the GST distribution formula works, state tax policy reform can lead to a change in that state's share of the GST through:

- the average-rate ('Robin Hood') effect – a higher tax rate increases the national weighted-average rate, which can either reduce GST payments (for states with a relatively large share of the tax base) or increase GST payments (for states with a relatively low share); and
- the elasticity effect – a higher tax rate leads to a reduction in the state's own tax base, due to lower demand or the movement of resources to other states. The state's GST payments increase as it is assessed as having lower revenue-raising capacity.

The direction and size of these effects is not straightforward and depends on where the state sits relative to the average. In general, where a state changes its tax rate, the subsequent effect on the GST distribution will be small. It will be larger for the larger states, as they have a bigger impact on the national average tax rate. In the event of a state increasing one tax rate and reducing another (for example, to make a reform revenue neutral), there would be two average-rate effects to take into account.

A general measure of the effect of changes to revenue-raising effort on GST payments can be calculated by examining the change in GST payments due to raising an extra $100 in revenue by a tax rate increase in any state. Table 10.1 presents this measure for selected revenue assessments. For most tax categories the estimates are less than 5 cents per dollar change in own source revenue, and the median effect is close to 1 cent. The main exception is iron ore royalties (discussed below), for which Western Australia (WA) has a very large share of the revenue base. A $100 increase in WA iron ore royalties raised by a higher royalty rate in WA would result in an $87.9 decline in its GST distribution. Other states would benefit, especially the large population states of NSW and Victoria (Table 10.1).

In contrast, policy changes that affect the tax base can have a significant effect on the GST distribution. This is because changes to the base mean changes to assessed revenue-raising capacity (vis-à-vis other states). For example, if a state like Victoria (with 25 per cent of Australia's

Table 10.1   Average-rate effects per $100 revenue increase, 2016–17

Revenue category	NSW	VIC	QLD	WA	SA	TAS	ACT	NT
Insurance tax	−2.6	1.9	0.7	0.3	−0.5	0.4	0.1	−0.1
Land tax on income-producing property	−7.5	−3.7	5.6	−0.2	3.5	1.2	0.8	0.3
Iron ore royalties	32.0	25.6	20.0	−87.9	6.1	1.5	1.7	1.0
Taxes on heavy vehicles	5.3	0.8	−1.3	−5.2	−0.2	−0.3	1.3	−0.3
Payroll tax	−2.9	1.3	2.1	−3.1	1.9	0.8	−0.1	−0.2
Stamp duty on property	−10.4	−1.5	1.5	5.3	3.4	1.0	0.0	0.6

Note: * Figures indicate the change in each state's GST payments, in dollars, for a $100 increase in revenue raised by a tax-rate increase in any state (the amount by which that state's tax rate needs to increase to raise the $100 in revenue will depend on the state), assuming no change in the size of tax bases.

Source: Productivity Commission (2018).

population), expanded its tax base and therefore increased tax revenue by $100, it would see $75 ($100 less its population share) of the additional revenue redistributed to other states.

Taken together, there is little doubt that state tax reform disincentives exist in principle. Whether such effects actually influence policy decisions is harder to discern; decisions not to pursue reforms are impossible to directly observe. Not surprisingly, there is widespread disagreement on the occurrence and magnitude of disincentive effects and conclusive evidence is scarce. Against this background and to illustrate how tax reforms can influence a state's GST payment, the Commission considered several stylized reform 'cameos'.[6]

The cameos rest upon simple assumptions and share a number of limitations. They assume that a state can fully offset its revenue or balance its spending in the same year the reform is implemented. The analysis does not consider the transition path for reform or any indirect effects that might occur as a result of the policy change. Nor does it factor in any long-term impact of the policy change in the state or how other states may respond. Furthermore, the impact of the reform on a state tax base (the elasticity effect) is by assumption only. Notwithstanding these simplifying assumptions, the cameos remain useful for illustrative purposes.

The first cameo involves a state halving its average rate of stamp duty on property and replacing the lost revenue with a new broad-based tax on all residential land. While the direct impact is revenue neutral, the net effect is a reduction in GST payments for any state that undertakes this reform unilaterally. This is because the reforming state would be assessed as having a stronger capacity to raise revenue from stamp duty because of the growth in its assessed tax base, even though the reform would mean that it actually now raises less revenue. Moreover, the land tax reform would also cause the larger states to lose GST payments as they are assessed to have a stronger capacity to raise revenue from land taxes.

The impacts on the GST distribution are much smaller in the case where all states pursue the tax switch reform in parallel, as the national average stamp duty rate would also fall by half (bringing down assessed revenue in all states). Because no state would be a big outlier from average policy after multilateral reform, some states would see a modest gain in GST payments, whereas others would experience a reduction (depending on where each state stands in relation to the average for each tax base). Hence, there can be a distinct first-mover disadvantage among states intent on pursuing tax policy reform.

A second cameo illustrates what would happen if a state abolished its insurance taxes. Every state would lose GST revenue from unilateral reform of this kind because their tax base has increased (due to increased demand for insurance) and because they are still assessed as having the capacity to raise revenue through insurance taxes. However, the GST impacts are small due to the small size of the insurance tax base (just over $5 billion nationally in 2016–17). If all states were to multilaterally abolish their insurance taxes the effect would be the same as if insurance taxes were removed from the HFE methodology.

In summary, most state tax reforms would likely have limited impacts on the GST distribution. However, despite the CGC's aspiration and endeavour, Australia's HFE system is not policy neutral. There are circumstances where the effects of tax policy reform on the share of GST revenue flowing to each state can be material – such as for a state undertaking large scale tax reform – and act as a significant disincentive for states to implement efficient tax policy. These incentives are exacerbated where the state is a first mover on reform or where there is uncertainty about how significant tax changes will be assessed by the CGC.

Mineral and energy resources
The potential for HFE to distort state policy is particularly striking for some mineral and energy resources, as their extraction is very unevenly distributed across states. For example, over 98 per cent of Australia's iron ore production is in WA. In such extreme situations, WA's policy *is* average state policy – and thus the mining assessment is not policy neutral because that state's own choices directly influence the level of GST payments it

receives. If WA raised royalties on iron ore, it would lose close to 90 per cent of the additional revenues to other states.

Due to these outsized effects, some have argued that states have an incentive to under-tax mineral rents or extract rents through other means. For example, states could require mining companies to provide infrastructure and services directly to remote communities in exchange for paying lower royalties (Ergas and Pincus, 2011, p.8; Pincus, 2011, p.17), or could set low royalty rates and use other charges to extract rents from mining companies (such as freight charges). Academics have suggested that HFE is likely to be one of many factors driving the under-taxation of mineral rents by Australian states (Petchey, 2018, p.18).

Efficiency of service delivery
The potential for HFE to distort tax policy is much lower on the expenditure side than it is on the revenue side. In principle, incentive effects could arise because when the CGC assesses state expenditure needs, it considers the *cost* of providing a service and the levels of service *use*.

In practice, however, where a state reduces or increases its average costs for service delivery, it has very little impact on the GST distribution. An additional dollar of expenditure in any state will move the national average by less than 1 cent (analogous to the average-rate effect). As such, the current HFE system is unlikely to materially distort state incentives to provide public services cost-effectively.

However, where a state addresses its structural disadvantage and therefore affects the use of its services and infrastructure, its GST share would move in line with the structural change, meaning the state would only receive its population share of the fiscal benefits (analogous to the tax base effect). This could create disincentives for states to address their structural disadvantages, particularly if they would incur high costs to do so. To give one example, the Productivity Commission has previously found that the equalization of spending on natural disaster recovery, but not of disaster mitigation expenses, biases states' incentives to efficiently manage natural disaster risks (Productivity Commission, 2014, p.33).

More generally, there are long-running concerns that HFE leads to grant dependency in the smaller states and a failure to pursue economic development. Again, these in-principle incentive effects are hard to substantiate with direct evidence.

10.3.2 How Does HFE Affect State Budget Management?

GST payments provide most states with a substantial share of their overall revenue, ranging from 25 per cent in WA to nearly 70 per cent in the Northern Territory in 2017–18. Hence, the HFE distribution has considerable scope to influence states' budget outcomes and management. This section, therefore, focuses on how features of Australia's HFE system affect states' ability to manage their budgets.

HFE can amplify state budget cycles

Two features of Australia's HFE system act to limit the timeliness of GST payments, potentially amplifying budget fluctuations at the state level. First, relativities are averaged over three years (the assessment period). Second, there is a two-year lag between the assessment period and the year in which relativities apply (the application year), which is the result of delays in data availability. This means that equalization payments for the 2018–19 financial year are determined by states' circumstances in the financial years 2014–15 to 2016–17.

In turn, non-contemporaneity can flow through to a 'mismatch' between states' economic circumstances and GST payments in two ways. First, when a state is experiencing a structural shift (so that its fiscal capacity is growing – or declining – more rapidly than the change in the GST pool) and second when a state is experiencing a sudden change in its fiscal capacity (for example, an idiosyncratic shock).[7]

In these circumstances a state's actual GST payments can differ substantially from their contemporaneous GST requirements – the payments they would receive if relativities reflected their circumstances in the application year. With GST payments failing to respond to particularly rapid changes in fiscal capacity, the GST distribution can be pro-cyclical for individual states – potentially amplifying the size and impact of economic fluctuations. In practice, the value of the mismatch has generally been small relative to the states' GST payments overall. WA's recent experience with the mining boom-induced shift in its fiscal capacity being a rare, but notable exception.

From a policy perspective, the most appropriate response to a lack of contemporaneity lies with the states themselves; offsetting cyclical influences on state budgets is not the primary objective of HFE. States borrow and save to manage gaps between their GST payments and actual payments, as they already do for other sources of budget volatility. Moreover, states are generally able to forecast the direction of changes in their GST relativities. Indeed, some states argue that applying a three-year moving average to relativity calculations, plus a two-year data lag, promotes stability of GST payments and provides states with more certainty when planning their budgets.

Volatility in equalization payments and budget planning
The counterpart to contemporaneity of equalization payments is volatility. As outlined above, greater contemporaneity of payments tends to be accompanied by their greater volatility. Volatility, in turn, can contribute to uncertainty in budgetary planning processes.

Other important influences of the HFE system on revenue volatility and predictability include:

- *the size of the total GST pool* – Australia's national GST collection determines the total amount of funding to be distributed to states. Growth in the GST pool has ranged from 14 per cent in 2002–03 down to −3 per cent in 2008–09. In many years, changes in the size of the pool have contributed more to changes in most states' GST payments than changes to populations and relativities combined.
- *revisions to data and the CGC's methodology* – because the data used by the CGC are often revised following initial release, annual relativities for an assessment year can vary materially across updates, particularly given adjustments to states' population shares. These effects can be compounded by changes in the CGC's methodology, which is reviewed every five years.
- *judgements regarding the exclusion of Commonwealth payments* – both the Commonwealth Treasurer and the CGC have the ability to determine whether specific Commonwealth payments are excluded from the calculation of states' relativities. These determinations are unpredictable and can have significant impacts on state budgets, particularly for smaller states (Brumby et al., 2012, p.70).

GST payments are relatively stable compared to other sources of state government revenue. Over the past 16 years, the relative variation in GST payments to the states from one year to the next has been smaller than for other major sources of revenue (Figure 10.5). Moreover, in some cases GST payments appear to partially offset fluctuations in other revenue streams, dampening the volatility of overall state revenues.

10.4   UNTIED GRANTS, ACCOUNTABILITY AND BENCHMARKING

Ultimately, states are accountable to their electorates for how they use HFE funds, not to the Commonwealth government. This is the basis for why the distribution of GST funds from the Commonwealth to the states is not tied, and for the more general move away from strict controls over how

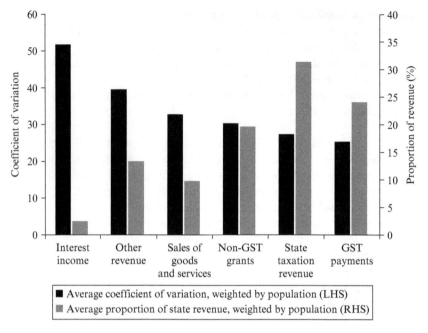

Notes:
[a] The coefficient of variation is a measure of dispersion, showing the degree to which values are spread above and below the mean, relative to the size of the mean itself. It takes into account both positive and negative changes and is calculated by dividing the standard deviation by the mean.
[b] Royalty income is included in 'other revenue'. 'State taxation revenue' includes stamp/transfer duty, land tax, insurance tax and vehicle licensing charges. 'Current grants and subsidies' presented in the ABS Government Finance Statistics have been disaggregated into 'Non-GST grants' and 'GST payments'.

Source: Productivity Commission (2018).

Figure 10.5   Year-on-year volatility of state revenue sources,[a, b] 2000–01 to 2015–16

federal transfers to the states are deployed. But to be effective it requires a clear delineation of roles and responsibilities and finding a way to instil accountability.

   In this regard, Australia has never considered in a serious and detailed manner the division of roles and responsibilities between the Commonwealth and state governments, but it has been at the forefront of experimentation with benchmarking as a tool to improve accountability and service delivery in federal systems of government.

   There are two broad approaches to intergovernmental benchmarking.

BOX 10.1   EXPERIENCE WITH INTERGOVERNMENTAL
BENCHMARKING IN AUSTRALIA

In 1991 Heads of Government requested the Industry Commission (the predecessor of the Productivity Commission) to benchmark Government Trading Enterprises (GTEs) in the electricity, gas, water, transport and communication sectors. The resulting series of reports, known as the 'Red Books', stimulated substantial debates and reforms, including the privatization of many GTEs.

Following the success of the 'Red Books' Australian Governments recognized the potential to apply a similar performance reporting regime to government-provided services. This led to the creation in 1993 of the Report on Government Services, also known as RoGS, or as the 'Blue Book'. RoGS is a leading example of benchmarking in federal systems of government.

Its distinguishing feature is its collegial approach, with the Commonwealth government playing a facilitative role, rather than a directive or coercive one. RoGS governance arrangements also ensure buy-in through a genuine 'Whole of government' approach. It is guided by a Steering Committee, comprising senior representatives from central agencies from all governments who determine the performance monitoring framework and oversee publication of the report.

It is the combination of top-down authority exercised by a Steering Committee with bottom-up expertise contributed by line agencies which sets RoGS apart from most other national reporting exercises. The Productivity Commission chairs the Steering Committee and serves as an independent secretariat, compiling the data, producing the report and ensuring a neutral assessment. The scope is comprehensive, capturing some $250 billion in recurrent expenditures by governments, equivalent to about two-thirds of the total.

The first is a top-down method where the federal government uses benchmarking, much as a large business enterprise with its operating units. The second approach is a bottom-up method. It is more collegiate and intended as a learning-oriented governance arrangement. Both approaches are far from straightforward to implement. On the continuum between the two approaches to intergovernmental benchmarking Australia lies more firmly towards the bottom-up method.[8] The Productivity Commission has played a key role in intergovernmental benchmarking for more than 25 years, making it an interesting case study (Box 10.1). It is in effect an annual report card on governments' performance across an array of politically sensitive services. This makes it a key accountability tool, as it receives extensive media coverage, academics use the indicators in policy research and the community sector draws on it for their advocacy.

But benchmarking is one instrument among others of accountability within Australia's system of federal state relations. While it plays a useful role, accountability for how governments fulfil their roles and responsibilities will inevitably remain blurred, given the high level of VFI in Australia.

10.5 SUMMING-UP

The Productivity Commission's overall assessment found that Australia's HFE system is functioning reasonably well in regard to:

- *a high degree of fiscal equality:* Australia is the only OECD country that seeks to fully eliminate disparities in fiscal capacity for both revenue and expenditure between subnational governments. It enables all states to provide the average national level of services and mostly adjusts for material structural disadvantages that are out of states' control. The principle of fiscal equalization is strongly supported;
- *an independent process:* the CGC, as an expert agency independent from governments, is well placed to conduct the HFE distribution process. It has well-established processes that involve consultation and regular methodology reviews. This helps to remove some of the political melee around the distribution of GST; and
- *stability for state budgets:* HFE results in reasonably stable GST payments and a level of predictability for most states regarding budget outcomes.

However, there are deficiencies in a number of areas, which have become particularly conspicuous recently. These include:

- *the system is not policy neutral:* while most state tax reforms and changes in state service delivery policies would have limited impacts on the GST distribution, there are circumstances where distortions are particularly pronounced for major tax reform exercises. These disincentives are exacerbated where the state is a first mover on reform or where there is uncertainty about how significant tax changes will be assessed by the CGC. There is also a large potential for HFE to discourage efficient taxation and extraction of some mineral and energy resources. States that increase mineral production or royalty rates will lose much of the additional revenue to equalization due to the dominance of select minerals in particular states.
- *too little weight is afforded to the importance of fairly rewarding effort:* because the system does not systematically provide for states to retain a reasonable share of the fiscal dividends of their policy

efforts without them being 'equalized away' through lower GST payments.

- *lack of transparency and accountability:* the HFE system is fiendishly complex. While this may not be a problem in itself, it can give scope for vested interests to feed misinformation and undermine accountability for decisions and public confidence in the system.

The Commission's final report proposed a package of changes to improve the HFE system and to bolster trust and community confidence in the system. They covered the need for:

- a revised and clearer articulation of the objective of HFE to allow the system to provide a better balance between fiscal equality and efficiency;
- improved governance arrangements to enhance transparency and accountability through more robust decision-making frameworks and stronger communication;
- improving the way fiscal capacities are assessed through 'in system' changes (for example, higher materiality thresholds) to correct for some of the equity and efficiency problems with the HFE system;
- a different equalization standard that recognizes reward for policy effort to unlock additional equity and efficiency benefits; and
- broader reforms to federal financial relations, recognizing that there is only so much an improved HFE system can deliver in isolation.

For an in-depth discussion of the rationale for, and assessment of these changes, readers should refer to the Commission's final report.

NOTES

1. A state's tax share relativity is the ratio of a state's per capita GST allocation to the national average per capita GST distributed for a given year.
2. This chapter draws on the Australian Productivity Commission's final report *Horizontal Fiscal Equalization*, which can be downloaded from: https://www.pc.gov.au/inquiries/completed/horizontal-fiscal-equalisation/report. The CGC also conducts an in-depth Methodology Review every five years. The next review is underway and will be released in 2020.
3. VFI refers to the situation where the Commonwealth raises more revenue than it requires for its own direct expenditure responsibilities, whereas states raise less revenue than they require for their expenditure responsibilities.
4. For a more detailed exposition of Federal State Financial arrangements in Australia and how HFE is implemented in Australia see Chapter 9 in this volume.
5. For a more detailed discussion of quarantined payments, see Appendix B of the Productivity Commission's final report on Horizontal Fiscal Equalization.

6.	For a detailed and fuller discussion on the cameo analysis, including the caveats and assumptions used, readers are referred to the Productivity Commission's final report (PC, 2018, Appendix C).
7.	Equalization will nevertheless respond over the longer term to structural change in states' fiscal capacities. In contrast, no state can escape the fiscal consequences of a collective downturn in the economy's fiscal position; HFE would not be able to offset all states' declines in their other revenues (non-GST).
8.	For a more detailed exposition on the rationale and approaches to benchmarking in federations, see PC and Forum of Federations (2012).

REFERENCES

Brumby, J., Carter, B. and Greiner, N. (2012). *GST Distribution Review*, Final Report, Australian Government, Canberra.
CGC (Commonwealth Grants Commission) (2010). *Volume 1: Main Report*, Report on GST Revenue Sharing Relativities: 2010 Review, Canberra.
Ergas, H. and Pincus, J. (2011). 'Reflections on fiscal equalisation in Australia: Submission to the GST Distribution Review', Issues Paper, Canberra.
Garran, R. (1958). *Prosper the Commonwealth*, Angus and Robertson, Sydney.
Koutsogeorgopulou, V. and Tuske, A. (2015). *Federal-State Relations in Australia*, OECD Working Paper, No. 1198, Paris.
OECD (Organisation for Economic Co-operation and Development) (2013). *Fiscal Federalism 2014: Making Decentralisation Work*, Paris.
PC (2018). *Horizontal Fiscal Equalisation*, Report no. 88, Canberra.
PC and Forum of Federations (2012). *Benchmarking in Federal Systems*, Roundtable proceedings, Melbourne, 19–20 December 2010, eds A. Fenna and F. Knüpling, Canberra.
Petchey, J.D. (2018). 'Inter-regional transfers and the induced under-taxation of economic rents', *Regional Studies*, **52** (2), 1–11.
Pincus, J. (2011). 'Examining horizontal fiscal equalisation in Australia', Research Paper No. 2011-25, University of Adelaide School of Economics, Adelaide.
Productivity Commission (PC) (2014). *Natural Disaster Funding Arrangements*, Report no. 74, Canberra.

PART III

Intergovernmental Transfers in Evolving
Federations

11. Intergovernmental fiscal transfers and performance grants in Brazil

Deborah L. Wetzel and Lorena Viñuela

11.1 INTRODUCTION

Brazil is one of the world's largest federal countries. It has a population of about 209 million and is highly urbanized with some 85.4 per cent of the population living in urban areas. Its gross domestic product (GDP) per capita in 2017 was US$10,720.[1] It is a country of great size, resources and diversity – from the relatively wealthy Southeast, to the agricultural heartland of the Centre-West, to the less developed North and Northeast, and the sparsely populated North-West Amazon. The size and complexity of the country have led to diverse approaches to intergovernmental finance over the decades.

Since the Constitution of 1988, the Brazilian government has operated in a highly decentralized way. Brazil has 26 states plus the Federal District of Brasilia, which serves as the capital, and over 5,500 municipalities. The 1988 Constitution establishes municipalities as full federation members with the same autonomy and sovereignty as the states. With this status, municipalities are not subordinated to the states or any other jurisdictions such as metropolitan areas. This has important implications for the system of transfers as both shared taxes and transfers may move directly from the federal level to states or municipalities, or from the state level to the municipal governments. In other words, not all transfers to municipalities pass through state governments.

This chapter provides an overview of Brazil's system of intergovernmental transfers and three cases of performance-based transfers. The first is the Bolsa Família programme that provides grants directly to beneficiaries and to both states and municipalities for administering one of the largest social protection programmes. The other two include the performance-based transfers from the Ceará and Rio de Janeiro states to municipalities in the education and water and health sectors respectively. In the case of Ceará, the state has adopted a conditional revenue-sharing mechanism to allocate the proceeds of the state value added tax (VAT) to municipalities that meet performance targets in basic education and water. Rio de Janeiro has similarly implemented transfers to municipal hospitals that seek to encourage better service provision and improve economies of scale and inter-municipal cooperation.

Brazil's variety of experiences with different types of transfers at the subnational level provide interesting lessons and ideas for other countries. The approaches used suggest a mechanism to align subnational actions with goals. They also help strengthen accountability and a focus on outcomes that could be relevant for other federal systems.

11.2   EVOLUTION AND SPECIAL FEATURES OF BRAZIL'S FEDERAL SYSTEM

Over the decades, Brazil has undergone several cycles of centralization and decentralization. The choice of a federal design can be traced to the need to mitigate centrifugal forces and threats to territorial integrity that have been present since colonial times. Alternating civil and military governments changed the distribution of authority across levels of government but states have always played a strong role, being initially responsible for the provision of all basic services and collecting their own revenues. State-based politics and elites continue to be influential in determining intergovernmental policies.

Democratization after the last military dictatorship led to the introduction of a high degree of decentralization. The 1988 Constitution made the 27 states, including the Federal District, and 5,560 municipalities[2] equal members of the Union with relative financial independence and significant service delivery responsibilities. The devolution process also led to a marked 'municipalization'. The devolution of resources and responsibilities to subnational governments was less the result of a clear decentralization plan but instead was driven by political pressure and a strong reaction to the military regime. The assignment of revenues was not accompanied by a clear distribution of the responsibilities for public service provision across levels of government or matching of needs with revenue sources (Rezende 1995).

Fiscal decentralization was most extensive in the 1990s with the full implementation of revenue and expenditure assignment changes introduced by the new Constitution. By 1995, states and municipalities accounted for 45 per cent of public expenditure and 42 per cent of revenue. This implied a 30 per cent increase from the level observed a decade before.

Until the early 2000s, the fiscal behaviour and indebtedness of state and municipal governments in Brazil were a major source of macroeconomic instability in Brazil. Expansionary fiscal policies and a lack of effective controls on indebtedness resulted in subnational debt crises and bailouts in 1989, 1993 and 1997. In 1997, the Federal Government assumed the debts of 25 of the 27 states that were unable to service their debt – an amount equivalent to about 13 per cent of GDP. About 90 per cent of the states' debt was restructured, so as to be paid off in 30 years at a favourable interest rate while a small part was forgiven.

As part of the last bailout agreement, the Federal Government simultaneously negotiated several structural adjustment and reform measures with the states. These measures included privatization, restrictions on incurring new debt, limits on spending and targets on fiscal performance. Conditions were included in annual Programmes of Fiscal Adjustment (PAFs). In 2000, the controls on subnational fiscal performance were further strengthened by the adoption of the Fiscal Responsibility Law (Lei de Responsabilidade Fiscal or LRF). The LRF institutionalized fiscal discipline at all levels of government, incorporating hard budget constraints into a single unified framework. It explicitly prohibited debt refinancing operations between different levels of government making future bailouts more difficult but failed to include a subnational bankruptcy provision. Since this agreement, subnational spending as a share of total spending stabilized at about 35 per cent.

Despite the success of the LRF in curbing the growth of subnational debt, moral hazard issues still remain in the system, as evidenced by the buildup of debt by some states in more recent years and the destabilizing impact of the recession that began in 2014. There is a group of states with large and burdensome debts to the Federal Government, mostly states from the more developed South and Southeast regions, although the majority have relatively low levels of debt.

In addition to the usual complexities of designing and implementing the technical aspects of the intergovernmental system, the Brazilian political system adds to the challenges of striking and sustaining credible commitments on fiscal discipline and government policies. Brazil's electoral institutions and party financing favour the representation and inclusion of a variety of political and regional interests. The open-list proportional representation system, combined with large districts (each state is one district), allows political parties with relatively few national votes to gain seats in the national legislature. Parties specialize in specific regions or states and make alliances to compete strategically in local elections. In some cases, electoral alliances at the subnational level differ from the national ones. Party financing rules disproportionately benefit small parties.

The nature of elections and representation in a context of comparatively strong federalism generates a high number of veto players in the policymaking process. The open-list electoral system erodes party discipline, while the state-based organization of political competition makes gathering support for reforms that limit subnational autonomy or affect state interests quite difficult. At the same time, decentralization has increased the opportunities for subnational party leaders to control patronage resources independently from national leaders and offered more opportunities for smaller parties. The extensive responsibilities of subnational governments in many areas create partially autonomous arenas for policy action. The multiplicity of entry points increases the success chances of special interests and reduces incentives for countrywide collective action and comprehensive policy reform.

Fragmentation across levels of government and parties makes it difficult for decision makers to put national interests above regional, local or even particular interests. For members of Congress, the focus is on building support and raising money for future campaigns. Such efforts lead policy-makers to concentrate on very local interests and ensure that allocations benefit campaign contributors (Alston and Mueller 2006; Samuels 2002). Over time, earmarking of expenditures has been built into the system to respond to these pressures; however, this complicates the implementation of policies at all levels. Moreover, coherent national policies require all levels of government to cooperate in their implementation given the decentralization of responsibilities and resources.

Unbalanced political representation, combined with the widely different economic interests of states, complicate economic and political reform, especially around matters related to fiscal federalism. Small states have significant influence and their support is needed to pass reforms. Brazil has one of the highest levels of malapportionment, or divergent ratios of voters to representatives, in the world. The current rules overrepresent the sparsely populated and less developed North and underrepresent populous and affluent states in the Southeast.[3] These divergent rates of representation make small states attractive coalition partners and often translate into distortions in the distribution of transfers, especially in the cases where small states are not also poor.

Governors have a powerful influence in the Senate, more so than in most federations around the world; they also have a strong sway over representatives of the Lower House. Through their ability to allocate resources and posts, state governors have considerable power to determine the future of deputies, who are expected to support the incumbent governor and the state (Abrucio 1994; Hagopian 1996; Samuels and Abrucio 2000; Samuels 2003). As a result, state-level factors, in particular the control of public jobs and campaign financing, drive congressional elections. Rather than seek re-election, many legislators aspire to positions in their state or municipal governments. Decentralization has increased the attractiveness of subnational posts. Because of the importance of governors in determining the future of representatives, presidents need to negotiate regularly with them. All of these factors limit the design and effective implementation of any improvements to the system of intergovernmental finance in Brazil.

11.3   INTERGOVERNMENTAL FISCAL RELATIONS

In recent years, Brazil's tax revenue as a share of GDP has ranged between 32 and 36 per cent of GDP. However, the distribution of revenue across the three levels of government reflects a complex set of assigned and shared taxes. The bulk of taxes – about 70 per cent – are levied at the federal level. However, the states also raise one-quarter of taxes at their level. Municipalities raise only 6 per cent of total taxes (Figure 11.1).

Taxes assigned to the federal level include personal income (IRPF), which at about 6 per cent of GDP is the second largest source of revenue; corporate profits tax (IRPJ); industrial products tax (IPI), tax on financial operations (IDF), tax on fuels (CIDE), rural property tax (ITR), tax on imports (II) and the payroll tax to fund social security (see Figure 11.2).

Brazilian states have more tax autonomy than their counterparts in other federations. The states' primary source of revenue comes from the

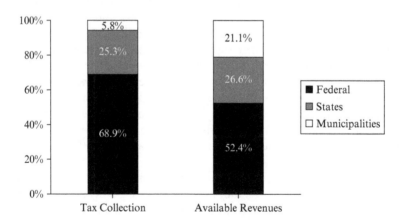

Note: The figure for the Federal Government includes social contributions.

Source: Secretária do Tesouro Nacional.

Figure 11.1   Tax collection versus tax revenue sharing by levels of government, 2012

VAT (Imposto sobre Circulação de Mercadorias e Serviços – ICMS), representing the largest revenue source in the country at about 7–10 per cent of GDP. States are also assigned the personal property tax (IPVA) and taxes on donations and inheritances (ITCMD). A distinctive feature of the Brazilian system is that the states also have obligations to share taxes with the municipalities – 25 per cent of the ICMS and IPVA taxes. The ICMS is shared under a rule in which three-quarters is based on derivation and one-quarter can be defined by the state. The IPVA is shared among municipalities based on the number of registered vehicles.

Municipalities are assigned taxes on consumption of services (ISS), the property tax (IPTU) and the tax on property transfer (ITBI). Figure 11.2 also indicates which taxes are shared with lower levels of government, for

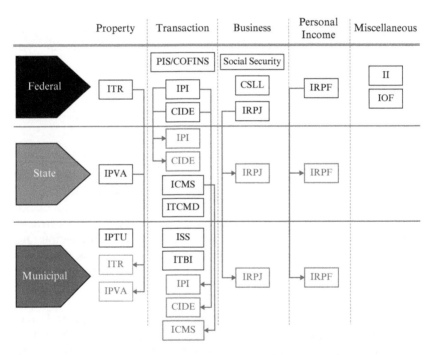

Note: Vertical lines represent sharing of taxes between different levels of government. Social Integration Program or Programa de Integração Social (PIS), Personal Contribution to Social Security or Personal Contribuição Social para o Financiamento da Seguridade Social (COFINS), Social Tax on Net Profits or Contribuição Social sobre o Lucro Líquido (CSLL), and Imposto sobre Operações de Crédito (IOF).

Source: Araujo and Barroso (2014).

Figure 11.2   Brazil's tax assignment across levels of government

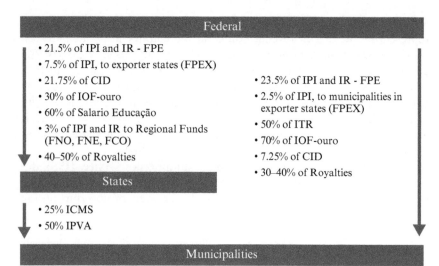

Note: See paragraphs 18–20 for definition of acronyms.

Source: Blanco et al. (2007); Araujo and Barroso (2014); Secretária do Tesouro Nacional.

Figure 11.3   Revenue shared by tax (percentage)

example, the Federal Government automatically shares the rural property tax with the state level and the states automatically share 25 per cent of the ICMS with municipalities. These shares are set out in Figure 11.3.

Revenues from royalties also need to be considered in the system of tax sharing and transfers. Two taxes are levied on oil production – a royalty rate that varies between 5 and 10 per cent and a special participation rate up to 40 per cent charges on net production value. In most cases, producing states are entitled to 26.25 per cent of the royalties and 40 per cent of the special funds. Non-producing states receive collectively only 1.75 per cent of the royalties collected.

This system has created additional gaps between producing and non-producing states. The primary beneficiary of oil revenue has been Rio de Janeiro. While subsoil natural resources belong to the Union, the legislation dating to the 1980s granted states and municipalities about 60 per cent of royalty revenue. In 1997, the Petroleum Act kept the essential features of the decentralized oil revenue-sharing structure favourable to the few offshore states. A new law passed in 2012, expected to generate major redistribution of resources away from producers and help finance education and health mandates, has not yet become effective because of the opposition of the producing states and municipalities.

The assignment of ICMS to the states has led to a complex system that has lent itself to a harmful competition through exemptions to attract investors – the so-called 'fiscal wars'. The efficiency of tax administration at the state and municipal level remains generally low, whereas compliance costs to taxpayers continue to be very significant.

On the expenditure side, assignments and responsibilities are much more blurred, especially in certain areas, such as health and education, where each level of government has some responsibilities. In recent years, overall general government expenditure as a share of GDP has hovered around 38 per cent in Brazil. About 53 per cent of current spending is by states and municipalities, and they also account for about 68 per cent of personnel expenditure.

States and municipalities are responsible for the provision of services, including education, health, sanitation and security (see Figures 11.4 and 11.5). They also play a considerable role in the implementation and financing of programmes that complement federal social protection programmes.

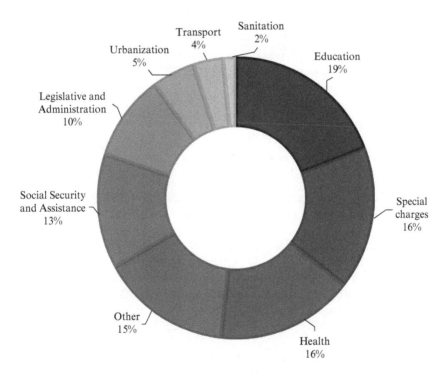

Source: OECD (2017).

Figure 11.4   State expenditure by function (percentage)

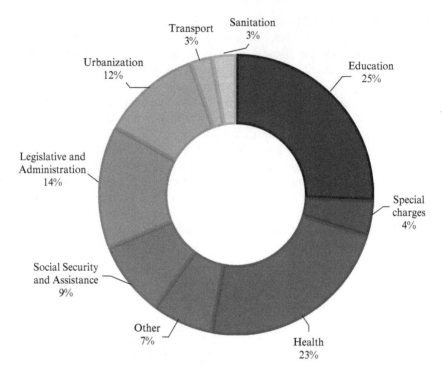

Source: OECD (2017).

Figure 11.5   Municipal expenditure by function (percentage)

States allocate approximately 35 per cent of their expenditure to education and health, while these sectors represent close to half of the municipal outlays.

Capital expenditure is highly decentralized in Brazil. States and municipalities execute approximately 40 per cent of total public investment. If state-owned enterprises are excluded, they represent approximately 76 per cent of total public investment (Mendes and Viñuela 2017). While state and municipal governments play an important role in public investment, they face challenges in effectively managing capital projects and meeting infrastructure gaps.

The evolution of the Brazilian federal framework has translated into sizable vertical imbalances. While the 1988 Constitution devolved functions and increased transfers from the federal level to states and municipalities and from states to municipalities, it did not fully match expenditure responsibilities and revenues.

Over time, the Federal Government reduced the percentages of taxes automatically shared and shifted more to revenues that were pooled and shared based on a formula. The Social Emergency Fund (Fundo Social de Emergencia or FSE) created in 1993 removed 20 per cent of taxes automatically shared. The FSE was later transformed into the Fiscal Stabilization Fund (Fundo de Estabilização Fiscal or FEF) designed to address short-term fiscal crises during the 1990s. The share of automatic, non-earmarked transfers, of which the majority is contributed by the Fund of State Participation (Fundo de Participação Estadual or FPE), fell substantially during the 2000s. Incremental changes reinforced the clawback over resources, while discretionary transfers multiplied.

Approximately a third of subnational expenditure is financed through transfers, yet there is a wide variation across states in the level of dependence on transfers. About half of the states finance between 50 and 80 per cent of their expenditure from transfers. There is a strong distinction between paying and receiving states and small states receive substantial transfers per capita (Rodden 2015).

Disparities in the ability to deliver services are significant at both state and municipal levels. Through the transfer system, the Federal Government takes most of the responsibility for equalization. The revenue-sharing mechanisms noted above are highly procyclical and only partially address regional disparities. There are two key transfer mechanisms with horizontal equalization objectives, namely – the Fund for State Participation (FPE) and the Fund of Participation for Municipalities (FPM) (Table 11.1). The FPE is funded with revenue from the federal income tax and the tax on industrialized products (21.5 per cent of the total from each). The FPM is funded with 24.5 per cent of the same taxes. These transfers are distributed through a simple formula based on per capita income and population criterion.

The FPE and FPM have some equalizing effects because they collect taxes from regions with higher fiscal capacity and distribute a part of the funds to the less developed regions. But the distribution is based on population and income per capita rather than a more precise specification of the amount of resources required to meet similar service delivery across all governments at the same level. Moreover, the population and income per capita indicators are outdated further limiting equalization. During this time, the Centre-West has grown much faster than the Northeast and can no longer be considered poor. Also, while the redistribution is still progressive, the thinly populated states of Acre, Amapá, Roraima and Tocantins receive more than twice the per capita FPE transfers compared to the Northeast states with a lower human development index (HDI).

*Table 11.1	Intergovernmental transfers by type, 2006–16*

Government Levels		TOTAL	Federal to States	Federal to Municipalities	States to Municipalities
Type	Transfer	Percentage of GDP			
Unconditional — Equalization	FPE	1.2	1.2		
	FPM	1.3		1.3	
Origin Based Devolutionary	ICMS	1.7			1.7
	IPVA	0.2			0.2
	ITR	0.001		0.001	
	IPI – FPEX	0.1	0.1		
	ICMS – Exp Compen.	0.1	0.1		
	Royalties	0.5	0.3	0.2	
Earmarked — Matching	FUNDEF/ FUNDEB (Education)	1.3	0.3	0.4	0.6
	SUS (Health)	1.0	0.4	0.6	
Non-matching	Voluntary Grants	0.4	0.2	0.2	
	CIDE (Transport)	0.1	0.1	0.0	
Other — Regional Dev. Funds	FNO/FNE/FCO	0.2			
Total		8.2	2.7	2.8	2.5

Notes:	FUNDEF/FUNDEB: National Fund for the Development of Education; SUS: Sistema Único de Saúde.

Source:	Updated from Blanco et al. (2008); calculations based on Secretária do Tesouro Nacional data.

The FPM distribution rules are more equalizing for capital cities than for small municipalities. State capitals receive 10 per cent of the FPM resources, while non-capital municipalities receive 86.4 per cent. The remaining 3.6 per cent is distributed among the most populous municipalities. The allocation to state capitals is determined using population and per capita income. However, the allocation to non-capital municipalities is determined exclusively on the basis of population. A minimum allocation is given according to population ranges. The minimum allocation strongly favours small municipalities regardless of their per capita income, which weakens equalization objectives and encourages municipalities to split.

The FPM benefits very small municipalities. Per capita FPM transfers to municipalities with fewer than 5,000 inhabitants are five times greater than those to municipalities with more than 50,000 inhabitants.

The system also includes regional development funds that seek to reduce economic disparities. The 1988 Constitution established that 3 per cent of the income and product taxes would finance three regional development funds for the development of Centre-West, Northeast and North (Fundo do Financiamento do Centro Oeste or FCO, Fundo do Financiamento do Nordeste or FNE and Fundo de Financiamento do Norte or FNO). However, there is limited evidence that these funds have been effective in achieving their goals.

Earmarked transfers have become increasingly important over the last two decades. Most of them are matching grants for the health and education sectors, such as the National Health System (SUS) and National Fund for the Development of Education (FUNDEF/FUNDEB) and are distributed according to the number of beneficiaries to ensure a minimal level of spending (Table 11.1). These funds are financed by the Federal Government, states and municipalities. Non-matching grants account for 0.5 per cent of GDP, comprising mainly voluntary grants that are executed through agreements between the Federal Government and states and municipalities. In general, these agreements are part of federal pro-grammes delegated to lower levels of government, while CIDE is directed to road transportation sector investments.

The FUNDEF/FUNDEB[4] programme provides matching transfers to subsidize education expenditures by lower levels of government. The Federal Government defines regional minimum levels of expenditures per student, which vary according to region, grade and location (urban/ rural). State governments and municipalities contribute 20 per cent of their current revenues to a common pool, which is then distributed according to the number of students in the respective state and municipality and the minimum level of expenditures specified by the Federal Government. If the resources of the pool are not enough to cover the minimum expenditure per student, the Federal Government makes up the difference. While the federal contributions can be considered equalizing, the minimum level of expenditures specified by the Federal Government is quite low and regional disparities in expenditure per capita still persist. The more developed South and Southeast regions have a considerably higher level of education expenditure per student than the other regions given the much larger size of their tax base.

The national health system (Unified Health System or SUS) has promoted convergence in health per capita expenditures and better coverage of basic care. SUS is also managed and executed by all three levels of government.

In general, municipalities are responsible for basic health: prevention, ambulatory procedures and low-complexity hospital procedures. States and large municipalities carry out more complex hospital treatments. The Federal Government is responsible for defining the health policy and the coordination and regulation of the SUS. It also provides direct payments to private health services providers and executes certain activities directly. States and municipalities are required to contribute to the system with 15 per cent and 12 per cent of their current revenues, respectively. The Federal Government supplements these to reach a minimum level of expenditure.[5] While SUS promotes regional equalization, the quality of the services and access to secondary and complex services continue to vary substantially and are still strongly correlated with economic development.

Overall, municipal governments seem to be the main beneficiaries of the system of intergovernmental transfers. Transfers from the federal and state governments to municipalities are equivalent to 5.3 per cent of GDP. The right panel of Figure 11.1 shows that the system provides municipalities with a share of resources (21.1 per cent) that far exceeds what they collect in taxes (5.8 per cent).

An unintended effect of the transfer system was the multiplication of municipalities. Between 1988 and 2007, the number of municipalities in Brazil increased from 4,491 to 5,560. The majority of these have a population below 150,000 people. This increase has been attributed largely to the incentives created by the rules governing the distribution of FPM unconditional transfers. As municipalities received a generous minimum per municipality, if a municipality split into two, it increased the total transfer received by the former municipality. The rules governing the distribution of the ICMS and royalties also contributed to the proliferation of municipalities. If economic activity is generally concentrated in a district of the municipality, there were strong incentives for this district to break away and form its own municipality, thereby increasing its revenues per capita at the expense of the rest of the former municipality.

11.4 EXPERIMENTING WITH PERFORMANCE GRANTS AT THE FEDERAL LEVEL: BOLSA FAMÍLIA

In addition to the traditional systems of shared taxes, conditional and unconditional transfers, Brazil has experimented with other types of performance-based grants. Along with Mexico, Brazil was one of the early experimenters with conditional cash transfers directly to citizens. The conditional cash transfer approach in Brazil proved to be highly effective.

The Bolsa Família Programme (BFP) has been implemented by the Federal Government since 2003 with the goal of combatting hunger, food insecurity and poverty, as well as supporting access to key services for the poor. About a quarter of the Brazilian population is enrolled in the programme with 99.7 per cent of municipalities participating. Bolsa Família targets the poor and extreme poor.

The Ministry for Social Development (MDS) is responsible for the programme, defines the eligibility criteria and authorizes payments to families in return for meeting specific criteria. The programme focuses on families as beneficiaries (those with monthly per capita incomes lower than R$154.00) and provides variable benefits according to the family composition prioritizing children and adolescents. Programme requirements include mandatory school attendance (85 per cent of the time for children 6–15 years old and 75 per cent for those 16–17 years old), mandatory immunization for children aged 7 and under, regular medical check-ups for mothers and children and mandatory prenatal and postnatal care for pregnant and new mothers.

Beneficiaries are entered in a unified registry (Cadastro Único) and the programme makes direct payments to beneficiaries through a bank card. These two innovations proved to be quite important to the success of the programme. The unified registry was implemented in an inclusive way with the government undertaking extensive outreach campaigns, as opposed to more traditional approaches in which beneficiaries must seek out a government official. This created a positive dynamic in which the poor – often excluded – saw the BFP as making them a part of society. The direct payments from central government to beneficiaries through a bank card removed the passing of resources through several hands before it arrived at the intended beneficiaries, so it helped to keep the system transparent and clean.

The management responsibilities of the programme are shared among states and municipalities and the Federal Government offers financial incentives to comply with minimum service standards. MDS enters into formal joint management agreements (Termos de Adesão) with each municipality. These agreements follow a standard 'template' and serve two key functions in establishing the overall framework for decentralized implementation: (1) they clarify roles and responsibilities for the implementation of the programme; and (2) they establish minimum institutional standards for the programme's operation at the municipal level. Specifically, the agreements require that municipalities maintain a local coordinator (local point-of-contact), register potential beneficiaries in the Cadastro Único, monitor and consolidate information on compliance with health and education conditionalities, and operate social control councils (SCCs). These agreements also specify that municipalities agree to prioritize BFP beneficiaries for other complementary services (literacy, professional training, and income-generation programmes), as part of the BFP's role to 'horizontally integrate' social policy.

BFP has had a significant impact on poverty reduction – lifting over 20 million people (about 10 per cent of the population) out of poverty between 2003 and 2014 – and improving health and education outcomes of the children and adolescents that benefit from the programme. With a budget equivalent to 0.5 per cent of the GDP, it helped reduce the infant mortality rate caused by undernourishment by more than 50 per cent and increased the pass rate of students in secondary education from 75.7 to 79.7 per cent (Campello and Neri 2013). Moreover, it played an important role in promoting the dignity and autonomy of the poor. It also served as an example of an effective conditional cash transfer programme that has been a model for other countries around the world.

11.5   STATES' PERFORMANCE GRANTS AND SUBNATIONAL INNOVATION

As noted above, states have discretion over the formula they use to allocate a quarter of the state VAT that they transfer to municipalities. This is a non-trivial amount given that the 1988 Constitution increased the share allocated from states to municipalities to 25 per cent of the state ICMS. Several states have experimented since with introducing performance criteria. Some states have more recently changed their laws to condition the distribution of the quarter of the state ICMS on performance indicators as an incentive for better governance. The Federal Government is also considering introducing performance criteria in the conditional transfers that finance the adoption of full-time secondary education (*escolas de tempo integral*).

Ceará

One successful case of the introduction of performance measures in the allocation of grants is from the Northeast state of Ceará that has supported significant progress in improving access to and quality of municipal services. Since the late 1980s, successive governments have reformed Ceará's public administration and invested heavily in social programmes. These efforts have been reflected in economic growth, balanced public finances, sustainable levels of indebtedness and significant improvements in social welfare. Access to education and health services has improved markedly over the past two decades, and there has also been significant progress in the quality of service provision.

Building on earlier reforms, Ceará introduced numerous results-based elements in the state management in the 2000s, including the adoption of a strategic plan. The 2003 Strategic Plan sought to improve fiscal space and modernize the state's management practices, and focused on four programmes: Working Ceará (Ceará Empreendedor); Ceará for a Better Life (Ceará Vida Melhor); Integrated Ceará (Ceará Integração); and Ceará at the Service of Citizenry (Ceará a Serviço do Cidadão). A system of detailed indicators was developed to facilitate monitoring and programme evaluation and a Committee for Results-based Management and Fiscal Administration (Comitê de Gestão por Resultados e Gestão Fiscal) was established to oversee the implementation of the state's results management model. The introduction in 2007 of an integrated Priority Actions and Projects Monitoring system (Monitoramento de Ações e Projetos Prioritários) strengthened the capacity of the state to monitor strategic programmes.

Results criteria for allocating the ICMS share was introduced in 2007 in line with the new strategy and results-based management model. Since 1996, the state had used a formula to distribute a quarter of the shared ICMS to close municipalities' financing gaps in the education sector in the following manner: (1) 5 per cent according to the ratio between the municipality's and the state's population; (2) 12.5 per cent by the relationship between the sum of municipal expenditure on the maintenance and development of education and the municipal revenue from taxes and constitutional federal and state transfers; and (3) 7.5 per cent equally distributed among all municipalities. The additional resources did not, however, result in improvements in key indicators of the quality of spending such as reductions in school evasion, improved grades in standardized tests and reductions in age-grade distortion. The state then revised the formula to distribute resources according to measures of the improvements achieved in the quality of education, health and environmental services. The discretionary portion is distributed as a weighted average of indicators of performance in the areas of education (72 per cent), health (20 per cent) and environment (8 per cent). In education, for example, the formula rewards municipalities that improve enrolment, reduce repetition rates and improve learning outcomes.

While there were many contributing factors, this approach had a positive impact on student proficiency in the municipal education system and in learning outcomes in the standardized Portuguese and mathematics tests. Evaluations (Brandão 2014; Petterini and Irffi 2013) show statistically significant positive results on enrolment and learning outcomes (Portuguese and mathematics). The poorer municipalities in the state, which had previously performed worse than the rest, also observed improvements and began to converge with the state average. Importantly, there has been no significant change in the magnitude of municipal expenditures – so the approach is generating better results with similar resources.

Rio de Janeiro

Under the Brazilian health system, states are primarily responsible for providing tertiary (hospital-level) healthcare but not all healthcare facilities are run by states. Basic primary healthcare is the responsibility of municipal governments. There are also hospitals owned by municipalities and philanthropic organizations. To address dismal results in the health sector, the State of Rio de Janeiro introduced performance grants in the late 2000s to complement other transfers to municipalities. Interventions were guided by a new policy and strategic plan and involved the establishment of monitoring of results and the training and recruitment of new staff.

Only hospitals located in municipalities with fewer than 110,000 residents were eligible. Rural municipalities without hospitals were also eligible to receive grants, provided they referred patients to hospitals located in other municipalities that belong to the programme.[6]

The Programme of Assistance to Hospitals of the Interior (Programa de Apoio aos Hospitais do Interior Municipal – PAHI) grant consisted of two parts: (1) a fixed component that was scaled according to the size and characteristics of the hospital; and (2) a variable component based on performance benchmarks. The state also implemented a monitoring system (Sistema de Gestão de Metas e Indicadores de Saude or SIGMIS).

The conditional part of the grant included several performance targets related to hospital management and the provision of services to patients from other municipalities. Improvements in the hygiene standards and disease management in municipal hospitals, as well as an increase in the number of patients that had access to hospitals in nearby municipalities and the number of intensive care beds available, were seen to be achieved through the PAHI programme.

The Programme for Rural Hospitals provided results-based transfers to municipalities to incentivize a greater quality of service delivery and incentivize service provision across municipality boundaries to increase economies of scale. The programme started as a pilot and was quickly adopted by all municipalities.

11.6   CONCLUSIONS AND LESSONS

Brazil's large and complex structure of government, combined with a highly fragmented political system, has generated an intricate system of tax sharing and fiscal transfers. Revenue assignments provide a significant amount of automatic tax sharing built into the system, but discretionary transfers are increasingly important. Expenditure responsibilities, as in many countries, are overlapping. This structure has led – even after automatic sharing of taxes – to vertical gaps among levels of government and to differences in government provision of services to citizens across governments in the country.

A rather unique feature of the system is the sovereignty of both states and municipalities, which in turn has led to dual systems of equalization transfers – with equalization transfers going from the federal level to states (FPE), as well as from the federal level to municipalities (FPM). However, the failure to update the key population indicators in the equalization formula suggests that equalization lags behind the demographic and economic changes that have occurred since the early 1990s. Royalties and specific targeted transfers to regions have become mechanisms that complement the equalization system for both financial and political purposes. Targeted conditional grants are added in to ensure sufficient state and local spending on key priorities such as education and health. The complexity of the system, combined with the fragmented political system, is such that making incremental improvements becomes quite difficult – whether it is to alter the tax sharing regime or to adjust the design of transfers themselves. When all is added up, resources shift to municipalities, but equalization is less effective across municipalities.

Despite the difficulty in making improvements to the transfer system overall, the states have been innovative in applying results-based mechanisms to the transfers they have some control over. The system in Ceará demonstrates a case where tying the distribution of resources to the achievement of key goals created the incentives that improved performance for all localities, especially in education. In Rio, a system of incentive-based transfers aimed to improve the allocation of resources in the health sector and to support more effective use of both larger and rural hospitals.

The complexity of the system of transfers also likely played a role in the development of Brazil's best-known system of transfers – Bolsa Família – the conditional cash transfer system in which the Federal Government streamlined implementation by providing benefits directly to citizens, drawing on technology to create a single registry for all participants and drawing municipalities in to re-enforce accountability in the system. For the equivalent of 0.5 per cent of GDP per year the programme achieved very significant results and served as a model worldwide.

For all its complexities, the system of transfers in Brazil has been resilient in the face of major internal and external shocks and has allowed one of the world's largest federations to continue to adapt and adjust.

NOTES

1. World Bank, World Development Indicators. Available at: https://databank.worldbank.org/source/world-development-indicators, accessed in April 2019.
2. Of the 5,560 Brazilian municipalities, only 12 have more than 1 million inhabitants, 1,300 have fewer than 5,000 inhabitants, 2,700 have between 5,000 and 20,000 inhabitants, 1,300 have between 20,000 and 150,000 inhabitants and 132 have between 150,000 and 1 million.
3. In 1977, a reform introduced by the then military regime increased the number of seats in the Lower House for the poorer and more sparsely populated states of the North and Northeast. This precedent later influenced the design of the 1988 Constitution, which introduced an even bigger shift in regional representation. A minimum of 8 and a maximum of 77 representatives to the Lower House favours states with smaller populations. As a result, the North controls 15 per cent of seats with 8 per cent of the population, while the Southeast has 43 per cent of the population but only a third of seats. A representative of the more developed states needs 16 times the votes to be elected than a less developed one (Samuels 2003).
4. Fund for Primary School Maintenance and Development and Teacher Training (Fundo de Manutenção e Desenvolvimento do Ensino Fundamental e Valorização do Magistério – FUNDEF) was created in 1996 and covered primary education (grades one to eight). In 2006, the Fund for Maintenance and Development of Basic Education and Teacher Training (Fundo de Manutenção e Desenvolvimento do Ensino Básico e Valorização do Magistério – FUNDEB) replaced FUNDEF and extended its coverage to also include day care, pre-school, secondary school and adult youth education.
5. The Constitutional Amendment No. 29 of 2000 defined the minimum level of health expenditures to be financed by the Federal Government. It set the minimum expenditure level for 2001 and specified that it be adjusted annually by the growth rate of nominal GDP.
6. This rule removes a potentially perverse incentive for small municipalities to create their own hospitals.

REFERENCES

Abrucio, Fernando Luiz (1994). 'Os barões da federação'. *Lua Nova* 33: 165–83.
Alston, Lee J. and Bernardo Mueller (2006). 'Pork for Policy: Executive and Legislative Exchange in Brazil'. *Journal of Law Economics and Organization* **22** (1): 87–114.
Alston, Lee J., Marcus A. Melo, Bernardo Mueller and Carlos Pereira (2006). *Political Institutions, Policymaking Processes and Policy Outcomes in Brazil*. Washington, DC: Inter-American Development Bank (IDB).
Ames, Barry (2009). *The Deadlock of Democracy in Brazil*. Ann Arbor: University of Michigan Press.
Araujo, Jorge Thompson and Rafael Chelles Barroso (2014). 'Another attempt to reform Brazil's intergovernmental financing arrangements: preliminary results

and future prospects.' *Economic Premise*, no. 147. Washington, DC: World Bank Group. https://hubs.worldbank.org/docs/ImageBank/Pages/DocProfile.aspx?nod eid=19678481

Blanco, Fernando, Rogério Miranda, Anderson Silva, William Baghdassarian, Marco Bonomo, Carlos Eugenio da Costa and José Guilherme Reis (2007). *Topics in Federalism*. Washington, DC: World Bank.

Brandão, Julia (2014). *O rateio de ICMS por desempenho de municípios no Ceará e seu impacto em indicadores do sistema de avaliação da educação*. Rio de Janeiro: Fundação Getúlio Vargas.

Campello, Tereza and M.C. Neri (2013). 'Programa Bolsa Família: uma década de inclusão e cidadania'. Brasília: IPEA.

Hagopian, Frances (1996). *Traditional Politics and Regime Change in Brazil*. Cambridge: Cambridge University Press.

Melo, Marcus A. and Carlos Pereira (2015). 'The Political Economy of Public Investment'. Background paper for the Brazil Systematic Country Diagnostic. Brasilia: World Bank.

Mendes, Marcos José, and Lorena Viñuela (2017). 'Institutional and Governance Challenges in Public Investment Management'. Background paper. Washington, DC: World Bank.

OECD (2017). Brazil Regional Profile. Available at: https://www.oecd.org/regional/regional-policy/profile-Brazil.pdf, Accessed March, 2019.

Petterini, Francisco Carlo, and Guilherme Diniz Irffi (2013). 'Evaluating the Impact of a Change in the ICMS Tax Law in the State of Ceará in Municipal Education and Health Indicators'. *Economia* **14** (3–4): 171–84.

Rezende, Fernando (1995). 'Federalismo Fiscal no Brasil'. *Revista de Economia Política* **15** (3): 5–17.

Rodden, Jonathan (2015). 'The Political Economy of Reform in the Brazilian Federation'. Background paper for the World Bank Systematic Country Diagnostic. Washington, DC: World Bank.

Samuels, David (2002). 'Pork Barreling is Not Credit-Claiming or Advertising: Campaign Finance and the Sources of the Personal Vote in Brazil'. *The Journal of Politics* **64** (3): 845–63.

Samuels, David (2003). *Ambition, Federalism, and Legislative Politics in Brazil*. Cambridge: Cambridge University Press.

Samuels, David and Fernando L. Abrucio (2000). 'Federalism and Democratic Transition: The "New" Politics of the Governors in Brazil'. *Publius* **30** (2): 43–62.

Secretária do Tesouro Nacional (2019). 'Boletim de Finanças dos Entes Subnacionais'. Brasília.

World Bank (2008). 'Brazil: Topics in Fiscal Federalism'. Report. Washington, DC: World Bank.

12. Intergovernmental fiscal transfer system in Argentina: historical evolution, current performance and reform options to promote efficiency, equity and transparency

Marco Larizza and Julian Folgar

12.1 STRUCTURAL AND INSTITUTIONAL FEATURES OF THE ARGENTINE FEDERATION[1]

Argentina is a very unequal federation, with areas as rich as developed nations, and provinces as poor as low middle-income countries. Heterogeneity across provinces in terms of income is very large. The poorest province, Formosa, has a gross domestic product (GDP) per capita 7.4 times smaller than the richest oil producing province of Santa Cruz in the Patagonia region (World Bank 2018a). In addition, Argentina is one of the most decentralized countries in the world, with a growing share of spending responsibilities transferred to the provinces. The combination of subnational inequality and highly decentralized spending define a structural feature of Argentina's federation, in stark contrast with the historical experience of OECD countries (see Figure 12.1). As the following sections will demonstrate, the institutional arrangements and the need to provide homogeneous services across heterogeneous provinces generate perverse expenditure and revenue collection incentives, resulting in substantial fiscal challenges.

Argentina is a federal country comprising 23 provinces and the autonomous federal capital City of Buenos Aires (Ciudad Autónoma de Buenos Aires, CABA for its Spanish acronym).[2] According to the 1853 Constitution, each province has its own constitution, generating different institutional designs and administrative structures. The Argentinian federation grants a substantial degree of policymaking authority to the provinces, but responsibilities are not always clearly defined. The federal government has exclusive responsibility for defence, foreign affairs, immigration and

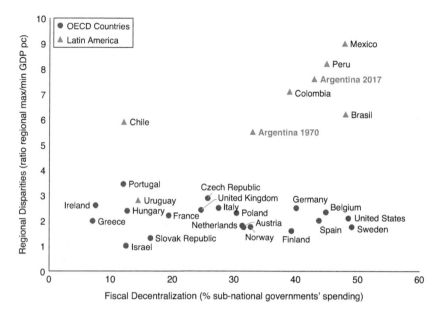

Note: The two data points for Argentina illustrate how the structural features of the country's federal system have become more pronounced over time. This is the combined effect of policy interventions decentralizing responsibilities to provinces and constitutional reforms creating new provinces, which in turn increased territorial disparities.

Sources: Authors' own elaboration using data from Ministry of Treasury (Argentina), OECD database and Cetrángolo and Goldschmit (2012).

Figure 12.1   *Argentina's federal system combines large regional inequalities with highly decentralized expenditure patterns*

international trade, currency and banking regulations. Provinces have exclusive competences in the organization and delivery of local (municipal) public services, while sharing responsibilities with national authorities for social services such as education and health.[3] However, the institutional and regulatory framework is not always clear in articulating the constitutional principle of concurrent responsibilities shared by the federal and the provincial governments. Provinces are in charge of executing national public policies (such as social plans/welfare programmes), for which the national government maintains significant regulatory powers. Moreover, according to the constitution's residual power clause, provinces reserve all powers not explicitly delegated to the federal government and are responsible for defining municipalities' powers within their territories.

In terms of revenues, a majority of them are collected at the national level. To help fund subnational expenditures, a portion of national revenues is redistributed back to provinces through an 'automatic' revenue sharing scheme ('Coparticipación Federal de Impuestos' – CFI for its Spanish acronym), and by discretionary transfers. As of 2018, overall transfers from the federal government to subnational administrations reached 8.7 per cent of GDP, of which 70 per cent (6.2 per cent of GDP) comes from the CFI. The remaining 30 per cent comprises a sub-set of other 'automatic' transfers regulated by Special Laws (18 per cent of total transfers; 1.6 per cent of GDP) and 'non-automatic' budgetary transfers (12 per cent of total transfers; 1 per cent of GDP) (Figure 12.2). In practice, all 'automatic' transfers (CFI plus Special Laws) are referred as the 'Co-participation System'.[4] As Figure 12.2 illustrates, intergovernmental transfers expanded significantly since the early 2000s, growing from an average of 5 per cent of GDP during the 1980s and the 1990s to about 9 per cent of GDP in 2017. This was the combined effect of increasing relevance of non-automatic transfers to provinces (financing both recurrent and capital spending) and the increase in overall tax burden experienced during the 2000s.

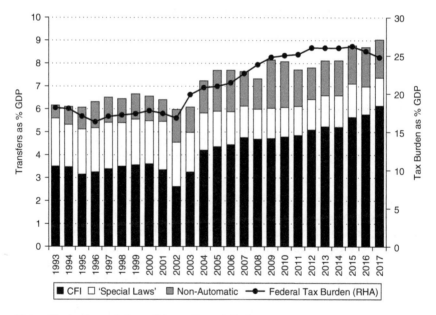

Note: Tax burden excludes social security contributions.

Source: Authors' own elaboration based on data from the Ministry of Treasury.

Figure 12.2   Evolution of intergovernmental transfers and tax burden over time, as percentage of GDP, 1983–2017

12.2 HISTORY AND EVOLUTION OF ARGENTINA'S INTERGOVERNMENTAL TRANSFER SYSTEM

The distribution of tax authority in Argentina has been subject to multiple policy interventions over time, which account for the current configuration of the intergovernmental transfer system. The 1853 Constitution assigned the federal government exclusive authority over trade taxes (import and export), while provinces kept exclusive authority on taxes on production and consumption of specific goods. Trade duties, which represented the lion's share of federal government revenues (close to 60 per cent),[5] were strongly affected by the world economic crisis following the 1929 Great Depression, forcing the central administration to expand its sources of financing by reforming existing excise taxes and incorporating new taxes collected by the federal branch and shared with the provinces.[6] In 1935, the federal revenue sharing CFI agreement was introduced, establishing the obligation for the federal government to transfer to the provinces a percentage of the total tax collection, compensating the provinces for their decision to delegate tax revenue authority over crucial taxes to the federal government. It was not until 1973, during the Lanusse military dictatorship,[7] that a federal law (Law 20.221) was adopted to regulate the CFI system. This new scheme set secondary distribution shares with dynamic and egalitarian criteria. According to the law, the CFI was supposed to be regulated and shares decided on a yearly basis for a period of transition. However, by the end of the transition period, and amidst the strong macro-fiscal crisis, central and provincial authorities were unable to reach an agreement on a new legal framework for the revenue sharing system. This led to a 3-year period (1985–87) with bilateral and unilateral arrangements for providing transfer resources to the provinces through ad hoc arrangements. In 1988, following an election, a new regime was negotiated with the federal and provincial governments under Law 23.548; this regime is still in place today.[8]

The CFI history suggests that changes in the intergovernmental transfer system have traditionally been driven by exogenous factors, including the need to address macro-fiscal and financial crises originating at the federal level. More specifically, most of the changes introduced in the co-participation scheme (CFI) over the past 30 years have been designed with the primary objective of covering the growing fiscal costs generated by other policy reforms, including reforming the National Pension System (see Box 12.1), rather than being driven by the objective of improving the provision of public goods and services across the country.

The distribution of administrative functions has also been subject to multiple policy interventions over time, producing a highly decentralized

BOX 12.1   POLICY REFORMS IN THE NATIONAL PENSION
SYSTEM AND THEIR IMPACT ON
INTERGOVERNMENTAL FISCAL TRANSFERS

The National Pension System (NPS) has been at the centre of the federalism discussions in Argentina during the past 30 years. Argentina established a contributory social security scheme, within which the public pay-as-you-go NPS was the key pillar. The NPS covered most private sector employees, as well as federal government civil servants. Since the early 1980s, the system started to run deficits in a context of significant macroeconomic instability (ILO 2011).

A major reform to the NPS was passed during the 1990s, which generated significant fiscal costs for the federal government. The policy reform was centred around the creation of an individual voluntary private insurance pillar in the system. Thus, while the public sector would continue to finance current pensioners, it would stop receiving part of the contributions from active workers that decided to contribute to an individual capitalization account, managed by private insurance companies. Shifting from a unique pay-as-you-go public scheme to a mixed one was expected to have large fiscal costs during the transition period (Cetrángolo and Grushka 2004).

The need to cover the financial costs of the pension reform led to policy changes in the intergovernmental transfer system, reducing transfers to the provinces. As a first step, in 1992 the federal government applied a special deduction of 11 and 20 per cent to value added and income taxes, respectively, to finance the NPS.[9] Later, provinces and federal government agreed to impose a 15 per cent deduction to the common pool of funds to be shared between levels of government ('*masa coparticipable*'), to finance the NPS.[10] One year later, to partially compensate the fiscal costs for the provinces, the federal government agreed to absorb the provincial pension systems (for provincial public servants) of those jurisdictions that voluntarily decided to transfer them. Almost half of the provinces – 11 out of 24 – signed the agreement to transfer their pensions system to the federal government (Apella 2014).

In 2008, Argentina eliminated the private pillar of the NPS going back to a unique pay-as-you-go public scheme. After this (re-)nationalization of the pension system, provinces took legal actions against the federal government to stop special deductions from the shared federal taxes to finance the NPS. By 2010, the provinces' share of those special deductions intended to finance the NPS (11 per cent of value added tax (VAT), 20 per cent of income tax, 15 per cent of cumulative funds to be shared), reached close to 2 per cent of GDP per year, on average. In October 2015 the Supreme Court ruled in favour of three provinces (setting a precedent), ordering the federal government to stop deducting the 15 per cent of the shared funds (*masa coparticipable*). At the end of her mandate, former President Cristina Kirchner issued a decree expanding the Supreme Court ruling to all 24 provinces, for a significant fiscal cost to the upcoming federal administration. The decree was rescinded by President Macri in early 2016, reaching an agreement with the provinces to gradually eliminate – over a 5-year period – the special deductions.[11]

system with large vertical fiscal gaps. During the 1940s–70s, both democratic and military governments tended to centralize administrative responsibilities. However, starting from the late 1970s Argentina experienced a strong decentralization of responsibilities from the federal government to the provinces in social sectors such as education and health, without the corresponding devolution of revenue sources, to stabilize the federal budget in the context of a significant fiscal crisis (Cetrángolo and Gatto 2002).[12] Since these decentralization reforms were motivated by macro-fiscal considerations and emergency needs rather than by a strategic vision on the devolution of administrative responsibilities to subnational governments, they ended up with sub-optimal outcomes which impacted the provision of basic public services (Becerra et al. 2003; Steinberg et al. 2011).

Following these decentralization efforts, provinces have become responsible for a growing share of total spending over the past 50 years. However, their revenue patterns have not substantially changed. In 2016, for example, provinces collected only a small fraction of the revenues, up to about 20 per cent of the overall tax burden (including municipal revenues). In 2017, federal transfers from a common pool of national taxes, on average, accounted for 46 per cent of total provincial revenues, reaching close to 60 per cent – if non-automatic transfers are included. There is also a large variation in the degree of fiscal dependency across provinces. There are areas such as the City of Buenos Aires, which finances over 75 per cent of its budget with own taxes, while less developed provinces (such as Formosa, la Rioja, Catamarca, Corrientes, Santiago del Estero, Jujuy and Chaco) receive between 80 and 90 per cent of their total revenue from federal transfers (Figure 12.3).

Local taxes on average only cover a small share of the provincial budgets. Provinces have the power to set their own tax rates,[13] and concentrate their tax collection effort in sales tax (Ingresos Brutos), a cascade tax with strong distortive properties, which represents on average more than 72 per cent of own provincial tax revenue.[14] In Santa Cruz, Misiones and Neuquen, sales tax represents close to 90 per cent of provincial tax collection, while in Entre Rios and La Pampa it is around 60 per cent. To a lesser extent, provinces also rely on property tax, automobile tax and stamp duties. The most important federal taxes (VAT, income tax, trade taxes, and so on) are collected at the central level.

Provincial budgets are dominated by recurrent expenditures for basic public services, leaving a small fiscal space for capital investments/infrastructure spending. As Figure 12.4 shows, subnational governments are mostly in charge of the provision of basic education, health, security and urban services, while the federal government spends mainly on

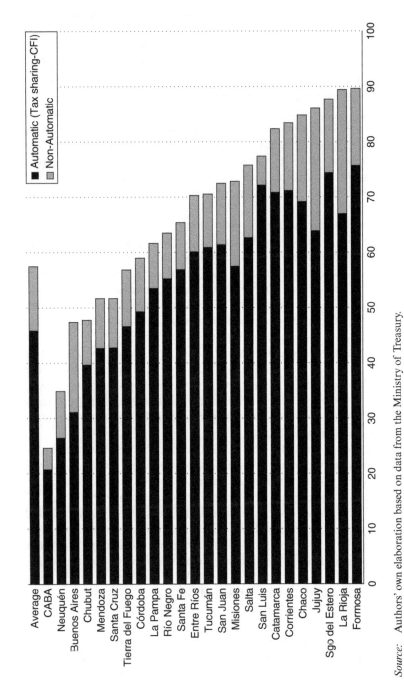

Legend:
- Automatic (Tax sharing-CFI)
- Non-Automatic

Source: Authors' own elaboration based on data from the Ministry of Treasury.

Figure 12.3   Federal transfers as percentage of total revenues, by province, 2017

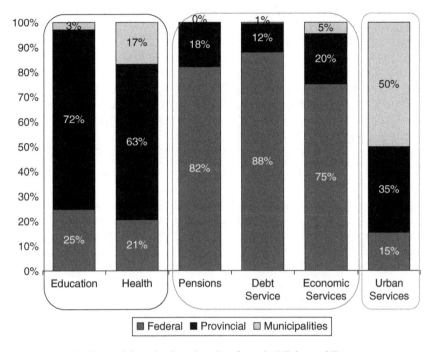

Source: Authors' own elaboration based on data from the Ministry of Treasury.

Figure 12.4 Spending functions by level of government

pensions and healthcare for the elderly, debt services and, to a lesser extent, on public universities. On average, provinces spend 50 per cent of their budgets to cover the public sector wage bill. Moreover, when added transfers to municipalities (automatic, and mainly used to pay municipal wages), transfers to private educational institutions (subsidy to teachers' salaries) and pension benefits, more than 75 per cent of provincial budgets are accounted for by wage expenditure and/or social benefits. Similarly, when sorting public expenditure by its functions, education, public administration, security and health services are responsible on average for more than 70 per cent of provincial budgets.

While on average capital expenditure allocations are low, comparison across provinces reveals interesting differences. Buenos Aires City, Santiago del Estero, San Luis, Cordoba and San Juan spend more than 20 per cent of their budgetary resources on capital expenditure. Whereas, half of the 24 provinces do not get to spend more than 8 per cent. Moreover, if those spending are measured in per capita terms, differences spike, reflecting a serious divergence in social equity. For instance, San Luis, the province that spends the most in public investment per capita, devotes nine times more than the Province of Buenos Aires.

12.3   HOW POLITICS INFLUENCE POLICIES: UNDERSTANDING THE POLITICAL ECONOMY OF FISCAL FEDERALISM IN ARGENTINA

The 'rules of the political game' play an important role in accounting for the observed features of the Argentine fiscal federalism, and its historical evolution over time. Argentina's tax allocation and spending authorities and its system of intergovernmental transfers do not correspond to equity or efficiency economic criteria, and often provide perverse incentives and obstacles for sound economic policies (Tommasi et al. 2001; Spiller and Tommasi 2008). From a political economy perspective, some of these features of Argentina's fiscal federalism can be better understood as the outcome of the 'rules of the political game'. Indeed, the policy decisions to centralize or decentralize revenues and functions were not the result of planned policy decisions grounded in equity and efficiency considerations, rather an outcome of macro-fiscal crisis at the federal level (as discussed above), as well as a by-product of the power relationship between national politicians and provincial governors (Eaton and Dickovick 2004; González 2013).

The history and evolution of co-participation law illustrates this point. After the revenue sharing rule was introduced in 1935, powerful military and civilian governments between the 1930s and 1950s were able to modify the provisions of the law to reduce provincial shares and further centralize functions and revenues (Pírez 1986). This changed in the early 1960s, when governors mobilized and took advantage of weak presidencies to push for larger transfers to provinces. A centralizing tendency emerged again under the military rule starting in 1966, when governors and mayors became military appointees and their weakened status facilitated the military junta's efforts to substantially cut federal transfers and further centralize revenue and tax authority. It was only towards the end of the Lanusse military rule (1973) that resources were decentralized again. Interestingly, this reform was driven by the military's effort to limit the power of the new democratically elected president – as they were expecting Peronist to win – and strengthen the role of conservative provinces in the interior (González 2013: 11–13). These revenue decentralizing trends were again reversed after the 1976 military coup, when the new military junta

(1976–83) reduced transfers to provincial governments while decentralizing spending responsibilities in health and education services, as a way to deal with its large fiscal deficit at the federal level (reaching more than 10 per cent of GDP in 1976).

Several features of the 'rules of the political game' in Argentina do not facilitate intergovernmental cooperation and tend to generate fiscal policies that are economically inefficient. These features include – among others – the dominant role of the president and governors in intergovernmental relations and the related bargaining process that take place between these actors, the lack of incentives among national legislators, and the ability of the presidents to alter agreements through unilateral actions (Tommasi et al. 2001: 183; Scartascini and Tommasi 2013). The stark economic inequalities among provinces and the structural features of Argentina's federal system (vertical imbalance) imply that most provinces are highly dependent on the national government to finance their expenditures. In turn, presidents need to secure votes in the Congress to implement economic policies. As a result, the policymaking process can be in large part characterized as 'deals' or 'exchanges' between president and governors (Spiller and Tommasi 2003, 2008), whereby governors grant political support in exchange for policies benefitting their constituencies. The governors' political support is provided through the *electoral* channel (by mobilizing votes during presidential elections); and the *legislative* channel (by securing votes from provincial legislators for the president's policy agenda and projects in the House and the Senate). The dominance of governors as key political actors in national politics and their ability to control the careers of individual legislators allow them to secure short-term benefits at the expense of long-term national interests, undermining the role of the Congress as an institution.[15] As Tommasi et al. (2001: 195) put it, 'intergovernmental relations have predominantly been much more informal . . .'. Many changes to the CFI scheme have taken place either in the president's quarters or in ad hoc meetings between the president and the governors.

Less developed and underpopulated 'peripheral' provinces have traditionally been the low hanging fruit in the construction of the ruling coalitions between presidents and governors. While non-metropolitan, 'peripheral' provinces only account for about 30 per cent of the national population, their political representation in the bicameral Congress far exceeds their population, granting them a central role in the institutional power structure and the coalition dynamics of the country's major political parties. According to a comparative study, Argentina's Senate ranked highest in terms of territorial over-representation.[16] This over-representation also extends to the lower chamber of the Congress, the Chamber of

Deputies, where peripheral provinces, with 30 per cent of the population, hold 52 per cent of the seats.[17] Therefore non-metropolitan/peripheral provinces have considerable political influence over national policymaking, influencing the distribution of economic resources across provinces. This in turn has contributed to create a fiscal transfer system that tends to favour economically marginal but vote-rich provinces to ensure the political survival of the national ruling coalition.[18] A statistical analysis of the electoral dynamics of market reform in Argentina between 1989 and 1995 illustrates this point, showing how the economic costs of structural reforms were concentrated primarily on 'metropolitan' provinces, while public spending and patronage continued in economically marginal but politically over-represented peripheral provinces, to ensure support for the governing party (Gibson and Calvo 2000).

The aggregate result of this historical process and political economy dynamics is a vertical fiscal imbalance between federal and subnational governments, which stands out as a distinctive feature of Argentina's fiscal federal system (see Figure 12.5).[19] While other federal countries like Brazil, Colombia and Mexico also show high levels of expenditures decentralization, what makes Argentina an outlier is the high degree of vertical fiscal imbalance, which is largely financed through the CFI and, to a lesser extent, with non-automatic intergovernmental transfers (Tommasi et al. 2001).

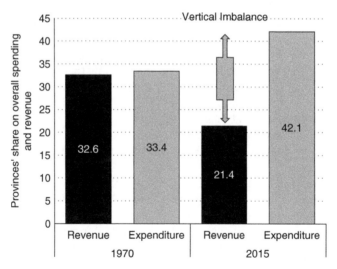

Source: Authors' own elaboration based on data from the Ministry of Treasury.

*Figure 12.5   Vertical imbalance: provincial share of overall revenue
collection and public spending (1970–2015)*

This is in part explained by the fact that the allocation of tax authority and administrative functions/spending responsibilities – and the intergovernmental transfer system underpinning both – do not correspond to any economic criteria; nor does it reflect efficiency considerations. It is instead largely driven by historical legacies, fiscal emergencies at the federal level and the complex power relationships between the president and governors across provinces. Moreover, both the composition and the magnitude of the federal transfers has increased over time (see Figure 12.3), contributing to what observers define as 'federal fiscal labyrinth' (Tommasi et al. 2001) or 'hybrid federation' (González 2015a). Such complex networks of fiscal federal relationships in Argentina create perverse incentives and multiple obstacles to sound economic policies. The rest of the chapter will analyse the effect of the intergovernmental fiscal transfer system in terms of horizontal and vertical imbalances.

12.4 CURRENT INTERGOVERNMENTAL FISCAL TRANSFER SYSTEM IN ARGENTINA: AN EMPIRICAL ANALYSIS[20]

The following sections of this chapter aim to empirically assess the extent to which the Argentine transfer system effectively addresses the vertical objective of income return (correcting vertical imbalances) as well as the horizontal redistribution of income (correcting horizontal imbalances). As illustrated in the previous section, the Argentine case concentrates the bulk of its transfer system around the revenue sharing agreement (CFI plus Special Laws), with the implication that two separate objectives usually associated with intergovernmental fiscal transfer systems – namely, closing the vertical fiscal gap (revenue sharing) and reducing the horizontal fiscal gap – are mixed in the same instrument. In addition, given the substantial lack of transparency in the management of resources at the provincial level, it appears difficult to assess clearly to what extent some of the transfers that are considered conditional are in fact obliging the recipient governments to use the resources in a binding manner.

How Does the Argentine Transfer System Address the Vertical Imbalances by Appropriate Parameters?

The existence of a transfer mechanism that manages to 'return' part of the revenues to a given locality becomes essential to continue generating the right incentives to mobilize revenues among subnational governments. To assess the degree to which income is returned through the transfer system,

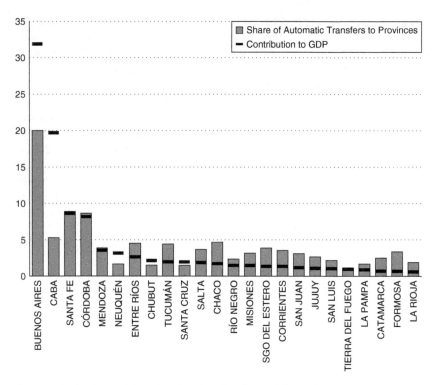

Source: Authors' own elaborations based on data from Ministry of Treasury.

Figure 12.6   Contribution to GDP and percentage share of federal taxes transfers, by province 2018

it is useful to compare it with the contribution of each province to the aggregate income generation process. Using the latest available information of the geographic Provincial GDP (2004), the analysis can provide a good proxy variable of the territorial tax base on which the collection of federal taxes falls. As Figure 12.6 illustrates, taken together the four jurisdictions that contribute the most to the national GDP are also the ones that receive the largest contribution from the total revenues transferred: Province of Buenos Aires (PBA), City of Buenos Aires (Ciudad Autonoma de Buenos Aires – CABA), Santa Fe and Cordoba. However, a closer look shows substantial variation among provinces. Specifically, the difference between what the PBA and the CABA 'contribute' and what they 'receive' implies that provinces with a low contribution to the GDP receive more than what they contribute. Since 2017, following the

BOX 12.2   RECENT DEVELOPMENTS: THE 2017 FISCAL PACTS AND FISCAL RESPONSIBILITY LAW

After reaching agreements with governors from 22 provinces (excluding San Luis and La Pampa), in December 2017 the Congress passed a new Fiscal Pact (Law 27.429) to improve efficiency in subnational public finances and equity in intergovernmental transfers.[21] The agreement addresses part of the long-lasting fiscal disputes between different levels of government in Argentina. Among the most relevant topics of the agreement are the following:

a) Increasing transfers to PBA: a partial redesign of the revenue transfer system to compensate for the historical erosion of the Province of Buenos Aires, where 56 per cent of the urban poor live;

b) Resolution of lawsuits against the federal government: the provinces will reach an agreement with the federal government on their legal disputes and refrain from initiating new legal actions regarding the tax sharing system (CFI). The federal government issued a 10-year bond with an AR$5bn interest payment in 2018 and AR$12bn from 2019 onwards, distributed within all the provinces who signed this agreement.

c) Gradual reduction of provincial distortive taxes: the provinces agreed to gradually reduce distortive taxes by 1.5 percentage points of GDP (turnover tax and stamp duties –Ingresos Brutos y Sellos) in 5 years. To compensate for the revenue shortfall an increase of progressive real estate tax is expected. In this context, a newly established Federal Agency of Property Valuation will be in charge of assessing market values on properties across the country. As a result, the Fiscal Pact points to a gradual shift of Argentina's (subnational) tax structure from a very distortive, procyclical and regressive composition towards a more efficient, stable and progressive taxation.

d) Addendum to the Fiscal Pact (decentralization of spending in energy subsidies to the provinces; increase in the base of shared taxes): in the context of the International Monetary Fund (IMF) programme and the 2019 budget discussions, the federal government agreed to decentralize some spending responsibilities to provinces in order to meet 2019 fiscal targets. Congress passed an addendum to the Fiscal Pact incorporating the commitment of the provinces to be in charge of water, electricity and transport subsidies. To partially offset this expansion, the government also expanded the base of some shared taxes (e.g. VAT, income tax, wealth tax) that will bring additional financing to the provinces.

Together with the Fiscal Pact, 22 provinces and the federal government agreed on changes in the Fiscal Responsibility Law (FRL; Law 27.428), by putting in place new fiscal rules. Containing the real growth of current spending and public employment are at the core of these changes. Accordingly, recurrent primary spending is set to increase below average inflation. Similarly, the annual change in public employment cannot exceed demographic growth. Moreover, interest payments cannot represent more than 15 per cent of recurrent net revenues (excluding automatic transfers to municipalities). These fiscal rules are expected to create more space to run countercyclical fiscal policy and/or increase public investment in infrastructure. In addition, the FRL also incorporates institutional requirements regarding transparency, accountability and forward fiscal planning, among others.

Sources:　Law 27.429/2017 and Law 27.428/2017.

reforms under the Fiscal Pacts (see Box 12.2), the share of resources that each province receives from the common pool changed. Specifically, the share that PBA receives is now higher (from 18 to 20 per cent), reducing its vertical gap, while the rest of the provinces now receive a marginally smaller share of the total.

How Does the Argentine Transfer System Address the Horizontal Imbalances by Appropriate Parameters?

Looking at the equalization effects of the transfer system, interesting patterns emerge. Ordering jurisdictions by their level of poverty (percentage households with NBI (necesidades basicas insatisfechas – unmet basic needs)) to capture social needs, a simple regression analysis shows that the relationship with the transfers per capita received by each province is very weak (Figures 12.7 to 12.10). In fact, provinces with very different percentages of population share (such as Formosa and La Pampa) receive similar levels of per capita transfers. Moreover, breaking down the different pillars of transfers, data suggest that the set of automatic transfers by Special Laws (18 per cent of the total) are those that present a greater redistributive bias. On the other hand, the CFI regime itself (70 per cent of the total) is the pillar with the least redistributive impact. Likewise, ordering jurisdictions by their level of wealth (GDP per capita) shows that even smaller impact is observed.[22]

In 2018, there were jurisdictions such as the PBA, whose transfers are considerably below what their level of wealth would indicate, or Santa Cruz which, being one of the provinces with the highest level of wealth per inhabitant, receive transfers per capita similar to provinces such as Formosa or La Rioja, among the poorest ones. This deficiency of the transfer system becomes especially relevant given the high territorial heterogeneity existing in the country, indicating the urgency to introduce reforms to the current scheme to achieve greater redistributive power.

12.5 CONCLUSIONS: PRINCIPLES AND GUIDELINES TO REFORM THE INTERGOVERNMENTAL TRANSFER SYSTEM

As the analysis in this chapter has illustrated, in Argentina the transfer system in general – and the CFI in particular – mix revenue sharing elements with equalization transfer elements since the secondary distribution of funds is not based on purely 'income return' criteria, but on the basis of formulas that include at least some criteria of need for expenditure and/or funding capacity. Moreover, the distribution of resources from the revenue sharing mechanisms (CFI) is made according to fixed coefficients politically negotiated more than three decades ago. Consequently, given that the transfer system in Argentina targets the objectives of devolution and redistribution with the same instrument – namely, the CFI regime and its Special Laws – in practice these effects play in the opposite direction making the regime end up having weak or non-existent net 'income return' and redistributive effects. Finally, although Argentina has in practice a pillar of non-automatic budgetary transfers, which could typically fulfil the role of a pillar of conditional transfers to achieve specific sectoral objectives, in practice the system fails to achieve this objective, as non-automatic transfers have been traditionally used as a tool of political bargaining and elite co-optation. A good transfer system is the one that has a separate instrument for each objective to be pursued and a financing system that is transparent and simple (Martinez-Vazquez and Searle 2007; Martinez-Vazquez and Sepulveda 2011).

The complexity and lack of transparency of the transfer system in Argentina raises the need for a comprehensive reform to simplify its design and align it with international best practices to better achieve three fundamental objectives: closing the vertical gap, closing the horizontal gaps and promoting sectoral objectives. The study of the Argentine case also highlights the priority need to provide the system with a greater redistributive bias than the current one, given the high levels of territorial heterogeneity that exist across provinces. The political environment and the specific economic and social circumstances faced by the country will in large part determine the scope and ambition of a reform path. While a structural reform trajectory seems infeasible in the short run, it is important to highlight a few aspects that any reform effort should take into account, in light of historical experiences of other countries and emerging international best practices (Schroeder and Smoke 2003), as well as taking into consideration the specific challenges that Argentina faces given the current macro-fiscal context:

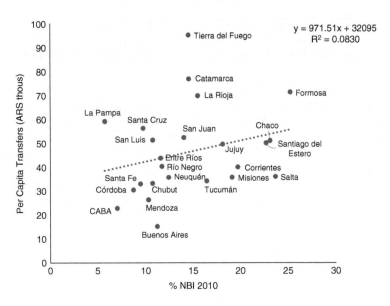

Source: Ministry of Treasury and INDEC.

Figure 12.7   Overall transfers and poverty –2018

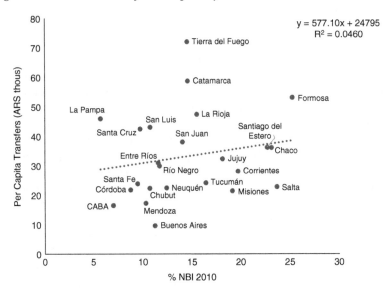

Source: Ministry of Treasury and INDEC.

Figure 12.8   CFI transfers and poverty – 2018

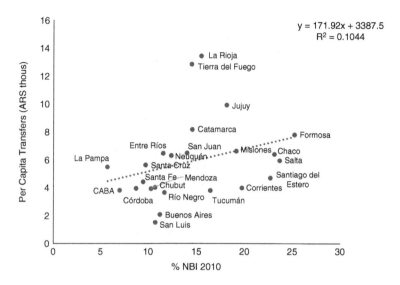

Source: Ministry of Treasury and INDEC.

Figure 12.9   Non-automatic transfers and poverty – 2018

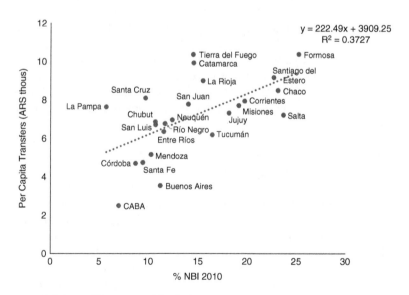

Source: Ministry of Treasury and INDEC.

Figure 12.10   Special laws' transfers and poverty – 2018

1. Rethinking the size of the funds to be distributed, that is, the degree to which the transfers are expected to close the aggregate vertical imbalance, with a focus on improving efficiency and equity in the provision of basic services, while defining a pension system that is fiscally sustainable in the long run. As discussed in the chapter, the provinces received only partial financing compensation to cover decentralized spending responsibilities, leading to poor outcomes, more budget rigidity and crowding out of provincial public investment in infrastructure, given the narrow fiscal space. Given such deficiencies in the design of decentralized spending responsibilities in public health and basic, primary and secondary public education, Argentina needs to rethink its aggregate approach towards the provision of these services. A comprehensive discussion on the way Argentina wants to ensure its basic service delivery, ideally pointing to close horizontal gaps, needs to be a top priority while discussing any reform to the fiscal federalism. Furthermore, if the long-run sustainability of the NPS is not defined (which may include structural reform discussions), the door is open to future conflicts between levels of government to fight for additional resources to postpone reforms. Both discussions will largely determine the size of the vertical imbalance that the intergovernmental transfer system will aim to close.

2. Providing the system with a priority redistributive bias to correct the deep territorial inequalities in Argentina. An ideal federal scheme should aim to promote fiscal autonomy of all subnational members of the federation. However, the difference in income levels across provinces in Argentina is higher than many other federal countries, making it very difficult to provide similar levels of public services across provinces without assistance from central government. A redistributive bias in the fiscal transfer system would therefore take into account the differences in fiscal capacity and spending needs across provinces, helping to achieve a more equitable system where citizens can have access to similar standards of public services, regardless of the provinces where they reside.

3. Improving the transparency and reducing the complexity of the system, adopting a 'one objective/one instrument' approach, in line with international best practice. Argentina's intergovernmental transfer scheme stands out by being an extremely complex system, commonly referred to as a labyrinth. And despite having different pillars of transfers (CFI, Special Laws and Non-automatic Transfers), the truth is that neither of them follows a specific mandate, resulting in very poor outcomes. Accordingly, reducing its complexity by unifying the different transfers as much as possible will help improve the way the system works, making it more transparent and coherent. In addition,

a simpler system will most likely help policymakers to think of better reforms, since the implementation process should be simpler, too. Furthermore, in order to achieve the most common goals of sharing revenue collection ('income return' pillar), closing horizontal gaps (a redistributive pillar) and financing pre-determined sectoral objectives, the system would benefit from applying a specific instrument for each proposed objective.

4. Strengthening fiscal rules by promoting cooperative behaviour across levels of government and providing incentives to provinces to adopt (and comply with) federal regulations. As indicated above, the need to provide homogeneous services across heterogeneous provinces generates perverse expenditure and revenue collection incentives, resulting in substantial fiscal challenges. Historically, the policy instruments and processes used to negotiate these distributional tensions between the national and provincial governments – including public transfers, pensions, subsidies and taxation – have proven harmful to the nation as a whole. Moreover, in many cases, the decision-making and implementation is decentralized to a variety of regulatory agencies, without appropriate coordination mechanisms, leading to increased fragmentation. There is therefore an urgent need to make federalism work in Argentina by promoting a more cooperative behaviour in which national, state and local governments cooperate to solve common problems. While the institutional architecture that defines the nature of fiscal federalism in Argentina is hard to change in the short term, the Fiscal Pact recently signed on December 2017 by the federal government and by 22 out of 24 provinces is an important contribution to this goal, suggesting there are opportunities to introduce incremental improvements. Fiscal rules could be further strengthened by rolling out federal guidelines on public financial management, to better monitor expenditures and promote more efficient allocation of resources. In this context, incentives could be provided for the provinces in the form of results-based grant schemes and conditional transfers that reward efficiency in public spending, prudent fiscal management as well as compliance with federal guidelines, policy regulations and jointly agreed reform priorities.

NOTES

1. This section is based on World Bank (2018a), which provides further elaboration of the macro-fiscal challenges connected with the unequal structure of the Argentinian federation.

2. When the constitution was signed in 1853, the Argentinian federation comprised 14 provinces. During subsequent administrative reforms in the 1950s and the 1990s, new provinces were created, including Santa Cruz, Chubut, Formosa, Neuquen, Rio Negro, Misiones, Chaco, La Pampa, CABA and Tierra del Fuego (Cetrángolo and Jiménez 2003).
3. The 'shared' responsibilities are not explicitly defined in the Constitution nor in subsequent regulations. They are a result of informal arrangements which may also vary across provinces.
4. 'Automatic' refers to tax revenues which are centrally collected by Administracion Federal de Ingresos Publicos (AFIP) and transferred back to the provinces, according to the percentage share as defined either in the CFI or through Special Laws. As such, they are not part of the federal budget. 'Non-automatic' refers to budgetary transfers and includes both discretionary transfers and programme-based and sectoral transfers.
5. See Porto (2003).
6. The Congress passed three laws: unification of excise taxes (12.139); sales tax (12.143) and extension of a profit tax (12.147).
7. The dictatorship in power from 1966 to 1973, the so-called 'Argentine Revolution', had three military presidents: Ongania (1966–70), Levingston (1970–71) and Lanusse (1971–73).
8. For a review of the historical stages of the Coparticipacion in Argentina, see Cetrángolo (2003), Porto (2003).
9. See Decree 879/92 and Law 23.966 for the income tax and VAT deductions, respectively.
10. See Law 24.130, also known as 'Pacto Fiscal 1'.
11. See 'Acuerdo Nacion-Provincias para el Nuevo Federalismo': accessed 24 October 2019 at https://www.argentina.gob.ar/interior/subsecretaria-de-relaciones-con-provincias/acue rdo-nacion-provincias.
12. The first decentralization process started in 1978. Laws 21.809 and 21.810 transferred initial and primary public education, while Law 21.883 transferred 65 national hospitals to the provinces. Later, in 1991, Law 24.061 continued to delegate federal responsibilities to the provinces for hospitals and education institutions. For further details, see Cetrángolo and Gatto (2002).
13. Most recently (December 2017), the Fiscal Pact included the commitment for the participating provinces (22 out of 24) to set homogenous sales tax (Ingresos Brutos) rates – by economic sectors – as well as gradually reduce (over a 5-year period) rates for primary activities, following a precise schedule included in the Fiscal Responsibility Law.
14. This calculation does not include royalties.
15. Due to the closed-list proportional electoral system, governors control the candidate selection process and the nominations for congressional elections, to the point that political careers of individual politicians are often structured and decided at the provincial level. Consequently, 'president need to negotiate not only electoral but also legislative support with governors' (González and Mamone 2015: 55). Moreover, given that local party bosses have the incentives to remove individual legislators from high-visibility positions, individual politicians have little incentives to build a long career in Congress, invest in policymaking capabilities and acquire specific expertise (Jones et al. 2004; Jones and Hwang 2005).
16. For example, with a population of 12.6 million, Buenos Aires province is granted three senators, the same number received by Tierra del Fuego, with a population of 59,000. Thus, one vote in Tierra del Fuego is worth 214 votes in Buenos Aires.
17. Argentina has a bicameral Congress composed of the Senate (where each one of the 24 provinces has three senators) and the Chamber of Deputies, where each province has a number of deputies proportional to its population, with a maximum of five deputies for each province.
18. From the perspective of the president, it is in the peripheral provinces where votes can be obtained at the lowest price possible. From the perspective of the governor, the flow

of income from the national government helps to secure resources to sustain the provision of jobs in the provincial bureaucracy and social welfare programmes. Moreover, investing in less developed provinces is more attractive for presidents because governors from these provinces tend to be weaker political challengers than governors from more developed districts (González 2015a: 2).

19. See Tommasi et al. (2001) for a comparison of Argentine fiscal federalism to other federations.
20. The analysis and data presented in this section draws upon the World Bank (2018b).
21. Dated 21 December 2017, published in the Official Gazette No.33782 of 2 January 2018. The two provinces that did not sign the agreement do not have to comply with its commitments under the Fiscal Pact and the Fiscal Responsibility Law, but will not receive its benefits either (authorization to issue debt, worst credit rating, and so on).
22. Multivariate regression tables are available from the authors upon request.

REFERENCES

Apella, I. 2014. 'La relación Nación-Provincias en el financiamiento del sistema previsional argentino', in R. Rofman (ed.), *La protección social en Argentina. El rol de las provincias.* Buenos Aires, Banco Mundial, pp. 15–52.

Becerra, Marcelo, Sergio Espana and Ariel Fiszbein. 2003. 'Enfoques sobre la Eficiencia del Gasto en Educación Básica en la Argentina'. World Bank working paper 6/03. Washington, DC: World Bank.

Cetrángolo, Oscar and Francisco Gatto. 2002. 'Descentralización fiscal en argentina: restricciones impuestas por un proceso mal orientado', ILPES.

Cetrángolo, Oscar and Ariela Goldschmit. 2012. 'Descentralización de los servicios públicos, cohesión territorial y afianzamiento de las democracias en América Latina', in A. Barcena and K. Acel (eds), 'La política fiscal para el afianzamiento de las democracias en América Latina. Reflexiones a partir de una serie de estudios de caso', CEPAL, Santiago del Chile: United Nations Development Program.

Cetrángolo, O. and C. Grushka. 2004. 'Sistema previsional argentino: crisis, reforma y crisis de la reforma', *Serie financiamiento del desarrollo* No. 151, CEPAL, Santiago de Chile.

Cetrángolo, Oscar and Juan Pablo Jiménez. 2003. 'Las relaciones entre niveles de gobierno en Argentina', Revista de la CEPAL 84.

Eaton, Kent and J.T. Dickovick. 2004. 'The politics of re-centralization in Argentina and Brazil', *Latin American Research Review* **39**(1), 90–122.

Gennaioli, N., R. La Porta, F.L. De Silanes and A. Shleifer. 2014. 'Growth in regions', *Journal of Economic growth* **19**(3), 259–309.

Gibson, E.L. and E. Calvo. 2000. 'Federalism and low-maintenance constituencies: territorial dimensions of economic reform in Argentina', *Studies in Comparative International Development* **35**(3), 32–55.

González, Lucas. 2013. 'Tensions between centralization and decentralization in the Argentine federation', in John Kincaid, John Loughlin and Wilfried Swenden (eds), *Routledge Handbook on Federalism and Regionalism.* London: Routledge, pp. 471–80.

González, Lucas and I. Mamone. 2015. 'Distributive politics in developing federal democracies: compensating governors for their territorial support', *Latin American Politics and Society* **57**(3), 50–76.

ILO. 2011. 'Encrucijadas en la seguridad social argentina: reformas, cobertura y desafíos para el sistema de pensiones' / Fabio Bertranou (et al.). 1ra. ed. Buenos Aires: CEPAL y Oficina Internacional del Trabajo, 2012.

Jones, M.P. and W. Hwang. 2005. 'Provincial party bosses: keystone of the Argentine Congress', in S. Levitsky and M.V. Murillo (eds), *Argentine Democracy: The Politics of Institutional Weakness*. University Park, PA: The Pennsylvania State University Press, pp. 115–38.

Jones, M., S. Saiegh, P. Spiller and M. Tommasi. 2007. 'Congress, Political Careers and the Provincial Connection', in P. Spiller and M. Tommasi (eds), *The Institutional Foundations of Public Policy in Argentina*. Cambridge: Cambridge University Press, pp. 53–88.

Ley 27.428. 2017. HONORABLE CONGRESO DE LA NACION ARGENTINA 21-dic-2017, REGIMEN FEDERAL DE RESPONSABILIDAD FISCAL Y BUENAS PRACTICAS DE GOBIERNO, Publicada en el Boletín Oficial del 02-ene-2018 Número: 33782 Página: 25.

Ley 27.429. 2017. HONORABLE CONGRESO DE LA NACION ARGENTINA, 21-dic-2017, CONSENSO FISCAL, Publicada en el Boletín Oficial del 02-ene-2018 Número: 33782 Página: 24.

Martinez-Vazquez, Jorge and Bob Searle (eds). 2007. *Fiscal Equalization: Challenges in the Design of Intergovernmental Transfers*. New York: Springer.

Martinez-Vazquez, Jorge and Cristian Sepulveda. 2011. 'Intergovernmental transfers in Latin America: a policy reform perspective'. Working Paper Series, International Studies Program, Andrew Young School of Policy Studies, Georgia State University.

Pírez, Pedro. (1986). 'La Coparticipación y Descentralización del Estado Nacional', *Revista Mexicana de Sociología* **48**(4), 175–224.

Porto, A. 2003. 'Etapas de la Coparticipación Federal de Impuestos', Documento de Federalismo Fiscal N°2, Buenos Aires, Universidad Nacional de La Plata, Facultad de Ciencias Económicas, Departamento de Economía.

Scartascini, C., E. Stein and M. Tommasi. 2013. 'Political institutions, intertemporal cooperation, and the quality of public policies', *Journal of Applied Economics* **16**(1): 1–32.

Schroeder, Larry and Paul Smoke. 2003. 'Intergovernmental fiscal transfers: concepts, international practice, and policy issues', in P. Smoke and Y.H. Kim (eds), *Intergovernmental Fiscal Transfers in Asia: Current Practice and Challenges for the Future*. Manila: Asian Development Bank.

Spiller, P. and M. Tommasi. 2003. 'The institutional foundations of public policy: transactions approach with application to Argentina', *Journal of Law, Economics, and Organization* **19** (2), 281–306.

Spiller, P. and M. Tommasi. 2008. 'Political institutions, policymaking processes, and policy outcomes in Argentina', in E. Stein, M. Tommasi, P. Spiller and C. Scartascini (eds), *Policymaking in Latin America: How Politics Shapes Policies*, Harvard University David Rockefeller Center for Latin American Studies. Washington, DC: Inter-American Development Bank, pp. 69–110.

Steinberg, Cora, Oscar Cetrángolo and Francisco Gatto. (2011). 'Desigualdades territoriales en Argentina. Insumos para el planeamiento estratégico del sector educativo', Santiago de Chile: Cepal.

Tommasi, M., S. Saiegh and P. Sanguinetti. 2001. 'Fiscal federalism in Argentina: policies, politics, and institutional reform [with comments]', *Economia* **1**(2), 157–212.

World Bank. 2018a. *Argentina Systematic Country Diagnostic.* Washington, DC: World Bank.

World Bank. 2018b. 'Diagnóstico y Opciones de Reforma del Sistema de Coparticipación Federal de Impuestos en Argentina'. Unpublished draft report. Washington, DC: World Bank.

13. Evolving role of the Finance Commissions in India in the last 25 years*

Farah Zahir

13.1 INTRODUCTION

India has emerged in the twenty-first century as the largest democratic federal polity and a global economic power inhabited by over a billion people spread over 29 states and 7 Union territories (UTs). Below the states in urban areas there are 96 municipal corporations, 1494 municipalities and 2092 small municipalities. There are 247,033 rural local bodies or Panchayats,[1] of which 515 are at the district level, 5930 at the block level and 240,588 at the village level. The devolution of power to the third tier is, however, uneven among states and their participation in public service delivery is marginal. India is a vast and diverse country, with its states differing in size, socio-economic conditions and basic characteristics. In 2015/16, among the major states, the per capita National State Domestic Product (NSDP) was the highest in Haryana at INR 162,034 (excluding a small state, Goa, with NSDP per capita of INR 334,576) and the lowest was in Bihar at INR 30,213. Interstate disparities are quite high in India and they have increased over time. The per capita revenues vary with per capita incomes due to variations in taxable capacity and effort among different states. Per capita transfers are higher in states with lower per capita incomes, however, the intergovernmental transfer system is unable to fully offset the revenue disabilities of the poorer states and more advanced and well-off states spend significantly higher per capita expenditures compared to the poorer states.

Genesis of Key Institutional Arrangements

Historically, India adopted a federal Constitution with strong unitary features and progressed from a two-tiered federal structure to a three-tiered structure in 1992. The 73rd and 74th Constitutional Amendments provided constitutional sanctity to the rural and urban local bodies as the third sphere of local self-governance in India. The centre-state relationships in the pre-1992 period rested on principles largely defined under the colonial rule of centralized governance. As a result, there was a strong bias towards a unitary framework in the Constitution. Under the Indian Constitution, many high-yielding taxes (productive taxes) are assigned to the centre due to reasons provided in the Union List that the centre is responsible for macroeconomic stabilization and redistribution. These include the corporate and personal income taxes, customs duties, and certain excise taxes (excluding those on alcoholic liquors, opium and other narcotics). State governments are authorized to impose a limited Value Added Tax (VAT) (and now Goods and Services Tax (GST)) as well as a small tax on agricultural income. Local governments' taxing powers are largely confined to taxes on property.

The core arrangements with regard to the sharing of resources and responsibilities are built into the Indian Constitution itself. The Constitution defines the exclusive powers of the centre[2] in the Union List; exclusive powers of the states are specified in the state list (including public order, police, public health, agriculture and others); and those falling under the joint jurisdiction of both levels are placed in the concurrent list (with the Union vested with overriding powers in subject matters). This stands in sharp contrast to Canada, where the federal fiscal relationships have evolved through a non-constitutional process, except for the equalization transfers, which have a constitutional status. Most arrangements derive from a series of negotiations between the two tiers of government. Also, in countries like the United States (US) and Canada, states have access to all broad tax bases including Sales Tax, while in Australia the constitution postulates central government exclusive powers to impose customs and excise duties and the judiciary have interpreted this to include Sales Tax too.

The key institutional arrangement that guides the sharing of resources between the various levels of government in India is entrusted to the Finance Commission (FC). In addition, resource transfers also take place through the Planning Commission[3] and other central ministries. Other institutions of importance in India are the National Development Council and the Inter-State council. These institutions are comparable with the Premiers' or First Ministers' Conference in Canada. In Australia, the determination of the vertical share of resources to be transferred to the states is not in the hands of the Commonwealth Grants Commission. It gets determined automatically by the amount of revenues collected under the GST supplemented by the special purpose grants that are in the hands of the Commonwealth government. In India, the FC determines a large part of the transfers in the form of tax devolution under a global sharing arrangement (the divisible pool) and grants, requiring it to determine a significant part of the volume of the vertical transfers. The FC transfers are supplemented by the Planning Commission[4] grants and other discretionary grants determined by the central government. The FC award remains valid for a five-year period.

Core Mandate and Recent Developments

Since 1951, there have been *14* such Finance Commissions in India, the Fifteenth Finance Commission (15th FC) was constituted in November 2017. The terms of reference (TOR)[5] of the 15th FC is to make the recommendations for the following:

- the distribution between the Union and the States of the net proceeds of taxes which are to be, or may be, divided between them under Chapter I, Part XII of the Constitution and the allocation between the states of the respective shares of such proceeds;
- the principles which should govern the grants-in-aid of the revenues of the states out of the Consolidated Fund of India and the sums to be paid to the states by way of grants-in-aid of their revenues under Article 275 of the Constitution for purposes other than those specified in the provisos to clause (1) of that Article; and
- the measures needed to augment the Consolidated Fund of a State to supplement the resources of the Panchayats and municipalities in the state on the basis of the recommendations made by the FC of the State.

Over the years the core mandate of the Commission has remained unchanged, though it has been given the additional responsibility of examining various issues depending on the challenges faced by Indian public finances from time to time. For instance, the Twelfth Finance Commission (TwFC or 12th FC) evaluated the fiscal position of states and offered relief to those that enacted their Fiscal Responsibility and Budget Management (FRBM) laws. The Thirteenth (13th) and the Fourteenth (14th) FC assessed the impact of GST on the economy. The 13th FC also incentivized states to increase forest cover by providing additional grants. In this milieu, even the Fifteenth Finance Commission has been given some additional responsibilities such as to: (i) review the impact of the 14th FC recommendations on the fiscal position of the centre; (ii) review the debt level of the centre and states, and recommend a roadmap; (iii) study the impact of GST on the economy; and (iv) recommend performance-based incentives for states based on their efforts to control population, promote ease of doing business, and control expenditure on populist measures, among others.

It needs to be noted that the importance of FCs in India not only lies in shaping and recalibrating the Indian federalism from time to time but also in keeping the country together with continuity even in the midst of the worst macroeconomic crisis of 1991. The story of Indian federalism is one of gradualism, resilience and change with continuity. In this context, the various FCs have played an important role of serving as a glue in balancing the intergovernmental relationships and fiscal transfers in a multilevel government system for ensuring provision of public services to over a billion people. As Bagchi (2003) had noted 'one cardinal reality that should never be lost sight of is that federalism is the only possible form of government for a polyglot country like India'.

This chapter traces the history of the FCs in India over the last two and a half decades in shaping the intergovernmental transfer system in India. The India case presents an interesting transition from a market preserving federalism towards laboratory federalism in the light of the recommendations made by the 14th FC. The chapter is organized as: (i) market preserving federalism, economic reforms and the evolving role of the FCs; (ii) the horizontal and vertical imbalances in the last 25 years; and (iii) laboratory federalism and the 14th FC – a circumstantial aberration or permanent change.

13.2 MARKET PRESERVING FEDERALISM, ECONOMIC REFORMS AND EVOLVING ROLE OF FINANCE COMMISSIONS

In 1991, India experienced a balance-of-payments crisis which pushed it to the verge of default on its external debt. The crisis followed an acceleration in growth to 6 per cent in the second half of the 1980s; but fiscal deficits bordering on 10 per cent of GDP during this period fed into growing current account deficits. Fiscal deficits were financed in the main by a combination of financial repression and external borrowing, with relatively limited monetization to keep inflation low. As a result of the 'twin deficits', public and external debt grew while reserves fell (Pinto and Zahir, 2004a, 2004b, 2007). The year 1991 is regarded as a 'watershed' for the Indian economy as the macroeconomic stabilization and structural adjustment initiated in this year constituted a fundamental break from the past. The Indian government signalled a systemic shift to a more open economy with greater reliance upon market forces, a larger role for the private sector including foreign investment, and a restructuring of the role of government (Ahluwalia, 2002a).

Under this new policy regime, economic growth combined with economic efficiency became the objective function of the government. However, the most persuasive objective of earlier decades emphasizing poverty reduction was subsumed in the pursuit of growth on the grounds that economic growth was both necessary and sufficient for improving the living standards of the poor. With the change in the objective function of the government, the 10th FC was asked (in addition to its core mandate) by the Government of India to reflect upon issues of better fiscal management and efficient use of resources by the government sector and public enterprises. The 10th FC was set up at a time when the Indian economy was opening up and there was a push as well as demand for greater federalism in the country. Chelliah et al. (1992) had pointed out that the 10th FC should be cognizant of the very changed economic and political context while performing its task. The reason being the restructuring of the Indian economy has brought radical changes in economic policies and the reform programme so far initiated is backed by consensus of the political parties and the citizens of India.

The 10th FC which was set up in 1992 made recommendations for the period 1995–2000. This was the period which was marked by a significant deterioration in the public finances of Indian states. Fiscal transfers in federations as well as in India play several roles, such as closing vertical imbalances, achieving redistribution goals, and insuring states or UTs against macroeconomic shocks (IMF, 2017). The insurance function is of two types – insurance against common shocks (may hit all states and UTs simultaneously) and insurance against idiosyncratic macroeconomic shocks (affect individual state/UT). Disentangling the redistribution, stabilization, and risk sharing roles of fiscal transfers is complicated in India as centre-state fiscal transfers are believed to affect all roles simultaneously. The 10th FC thus had to carry out its remit in a particularly difficult fiscal situation, more as a part of a policy trilemma of shocks- stabilization-redistribution.

In the light of the changes in the economic policy which aimed at liberalization, questions were raised whether the vertical imbalance had increased or decreased. This debate was in the context that the shift to a market driven economy altered the functions of both the central and state government, while the constitutionally mandated functions remained the same, the emphasis on various subject matters changed. It implied that the state governments now enjoyed powers that, in the spirit of the Constitution, they were meant to enjoy which earlier the central government in its endeavour to implement centralized planning had prevented.

The environment within which the states in India operated had undergone two phases of significant change: first, over the 1970s and 1980s with the growth of regional political parties; and second, after 1991 with the central government's liberalization of the trade and investment regime. These developments had allowed as well as required of the states a larger role in determining their development paths and in attracting private investment (Wes, 2007).

The growth experience of the 1990s showed that developed Indian states with broad industrial bases and developed market institutions and infrastructure had performed much better than those without them. However, it was necessary to be mindful and not penalize those states that performed more efficiently in the delivery of services or raised more revenues relative to their tax bases. As a result, the situation demanded that the intergovernmental transfer system ought to respond to the shifts in economic policymaking. Post economic reforms, it became important for FCs in India to establish a fine balance between equity and efficiency, a system where fiscal disadvantage is taken care of, but fiscal imprudence is effectively discouraged (Rangarajan, 2006). The fundamental change in economic policy required both the central and the state governments to face global competition and the market forces together in a coordinated manner in the spirit of cooperative federalism.

The period following the economic reforms in India can be regarded as a phase of 'market preserving federalism'. The '*ex ante*' policy framework post 1991 was embedded in gradualism and careful articulation of economic objectives, implying a clear definition of the goal and a deliberate choice of extending the time taken to reach it, in order to ease the pain of transition. The goals were often indicated only as a broad direction, with the precise end point and the pace of transition left unstated to minimize opposition – and possibly also to allow room to retreat if necessary. This reduced politically divisive controversy, and enabled a consensus of sorts to evolve, but it also meant that the consensus at each point represented a compromise, with many interested groups joining only because they believed that reforms would not go 'too far' (Ahluwalia, 2002a). The result was a process of change, the emergence of an *ex post* policy framework, that was not so much gradualist but fitful and opportunistic. In a nutshell, the phase of market preserving federalism in India made the task of the subsequent FCs more challenging. Despite the challenges, the contribution of later Commissions in rebalancing the centre-state relationships in the context of liberalization of the Indian economy was significant as explained in the following sections of the chapter.

13.3 VERTICAL AND HORIZONTAL IMBALANCES IN THE LAST 25 YEARS

According to Rangarajan and Srivastava (2011), in reviewing the *inter se* distribution of the aggregate share of central tax revenues, the approach of the FCs can be summarized in terms of three distinct phases. The three phases are:

(i)   *Phase I:* First (1952–57) to the Seventh (1979–84) FCs relied on distribution criteria which was distinct for income tax and union excise duties, income tax sharing was mandatory while there was in-sharing of union excise duty at the discretion of the centre;

(ii) *Phase II:* Eighth (1984–89) to the Tenth (1995–2000) FCs before the implementation of the alternative scheme of devolution of central taxes. Two noticeable changes during this phase were a move towards unifying the formulae for the *inter se* distribution of both income and union excise duties and secondly a portion of the union excise duties was kept aside for distribution according to 'assessed deficits';

(iii) *Phase III:* Eleventh (2000–05) FC onwards, and a phase of full convergence. This led to replacing four distinct sets of shares: (i) portions of income tax and union excise duties subject to common criteria; (ii) a portion of devolution against assessed deficits; (iii) additional excise duties in lieu of sales tax on cotton, sugar and tobacco; (iv) the grants in lieu of tax on railway passenger fares, by only *one set of shares* under the global sharing agreement.

From the 11th to the most recent 14th FC, the overriding criteria under the global sharing agreement was based on four factors: (i) vertical transfers; (ii) equity; (iii) incentives for efficiency; (iv) cost disadvantages. Another salient feature of the full convergence phase was that the 11th, 12th and 13th FCs were headed by economists with experience in policymaking and the 14th was chaired by an administrator and a distinguished economist. These appointments reflected the political consensus in favour of economic reforms and acceptability of the growing importance of partnership between the centre and the states on economic development.

Measuring Vertical Imbalances

In India, the relationship of revenues relative to expenditure responsibilities can be measured in terms of the four ratios as shown in Table 13.1. P1 shows the pre-transfer excess or deficiency state wise and P2 shows the

Table 13.1   Measuring vertical imbalances in India (percentage)

Years	P1	P2	C1	C2
Tenth FC: States in Crisis, Severe Resource Constraints				
1995–96	50.4	19.5	36.9	42.1
1996–97	54.4	20.4	34.7	39.6
1997–98	54.7	21.3	35.7	41.8
1998–99	57.5	30.3	40.4	45.1
1999–2000	58.4	31.3	37.4	41.7
Twelfth FC: Fiscal Consolidation both at the Centre and States				
2005–06	52.1	16.8	29.9	33.6
2006–07	49.8	12.9	23.2	26.6
2007–08	51.4	11.4	22.9	26.3
2008–09	54.4	16.3	38.6	45.0
2009–10	54.9	20.4	44.1	51.2
Memo:				
1990–91	57.9	22.8	40.9	52.4
Eleventh FC: Significant Fiscal Correction at the State Level				
2000–01	57.0	27.7	38.4	43.7
2001–02	57.2	27.2	41.8	46.9
2002–03	55.5	27.2	36.8	41.6
2003–04	56.5	28.1	26.4	30.0
2004–05	54.9	22.6	24.3	27.6
Thirteenth FC: Constrained Fiscal Space for Inclusive Growth				
2010–11	51.6	14.5	34.0	39.2
2011–12	50.2	13.7	41.6	48.3
2012–13	46.9	13.7	37.3	42.8
2013–14	48.2	15.6	34.5	39.5
2014–15	51.9	16.9	33.6	42.1
Memo:				
2015–16 (RE)	56.7	20.2	33.2	40.4

Notes:
P1 is defined as states' expenditure minus own revenues divided by states expenditure.
P2 is defined as ratio of states' expenditure minus own revenues plus central transfers divided by states' expenditure.
C1 is defined as centre's expenditure inclusive of transfers minus centre's gross revenue receipts divided by centre's expenditure inclusive of transfers.
C2 is defined as centre's expenditure net of transfers minus centre's revenue net of transfers divided by centre's expenditure net of transfers.
Expenditures are net of recoveries. Central expenditure and revenues net of transfers are derived by deducting grants as tax devolution is already deducted in expenditure and revenue data.
RE refers to Revised Estimates.

Source: Indian Public Finance Statistics, 2016/17 and previous issues, Ministry of Finance, Government of India (GoI).

post-transfer uncovered gaps necessitating borrowing. The P1 ratio indicates that over the last 25 years, on average more than half of the states' expenditure remains uncovered from the states' own revenues. However, there have been changes in the Indian tax system with the introduction of consumption-based VAT in 2005 replacing the Sales Tax and recently the introduction of destination-based GST in 2017.[6]

The P1 ratio indicates that the state expenditures in India are far larger than states' own revenues. Also, states play a larger role in spending and they bear more expenditure responsibilities as noted elsewhere in the chapter. The P2 ratio indicates that after transfers there is still an uncovered gap, although there is significant 'correction' of the vertical fiscal gap. In 1990/91, the year of the macroeconomic crisis, while P1 was 58 per cent (i.e. states' own revenues financed only 58 per cent of the states' expenditure), the P2 ratio at 23 per cent showed significant correction compared to the P1 ratio, indicating post-central government transfers, the vertical fiscal gap was reduced substantially but it did not disappear. Despite considerable correction, the uncovered expenditures of the states need to be met as indicated by the positive sign, necessitating borrowings. Similarly, over various FCs (Table 13.1), the P2 ratios showed significant correction in the vertical fiscal gap compared to P1 ratios, albeit amidst different macroeconomic conditions. The post-transfer imbalances increased sharply after 1997/98 given the deteriorating fiscal situation at the state level. During the 12th and 13th FC period a sharper correction is seen in the P2 ratios owing to higher growth, buoyant revenues, better fiscal management in terms of adherence to FRBM Act, 2003 at the state level.

The C1 ratio indicates that the central government is not in surplus even prior to transfers. In comparison, the C2 ratio indicates the centre's own expenditures exceed its revenues (excluding transfers) by a large margin. The positive sign of the C2 ratio shows that in the case of India, the centre's 'fiscal space' for development (productive) spending shrinks further after it makes transfers to the states and the centre has to resort to borrowings for meeting its own expenditure commitments.

Balancing Fiscal Policy in Full Convergence Phase

The adoption of the 80th Amendment Act, 2000 brought all central taxes and duties (except those referred to in Articles 268 and 269, and the surcharges and cesses) in the divisible pool to be shared between centre and the states. The 11th FC fixed the share of states in the net proceeds of all central taxes at 28 per cent for each of the five years starting from 2000/01 until 2004/05. It further recommended that 1.5 per cent of all shareable union taxes and duties be allocated to the states separately, thus totalling

29.5 per cent of the net proceeds of all union taxes and duties. The recommendations of the 11th and the 12th FCs covered the periods 2000–05 and 2005–10 respectively. In light of the economic reforms pursued since 1991, the TOR of the two Commissions were expanded. They were additionally asked to review the state of the finances of the centre and states and suggest ways and means by which the government, collectively and separately, may bring about a restructuring of the public finances so as to restore budgetary balance and maintain macroeconomic stability.

Ravishankar et al. (2008) highlighted that the fiscal improvement during 2000–06 was a result of three underlying factors, namely: (i) fiscal correction efforts by the majority of states due to the 11th FC; (ii) a rise in the share of central resources, especially to the poorer states, resulting from the awards of the 11th and 12th FCs; and (iii) the acceleration of economic growth in India since 2003/04. The fiscal deficit of all states taken together declined from 4.7 per cent of GDP in 1999/00 to 3.2 per cent in 2005/06. States' deficit on current account (revenue deficit) for the same period declined from 2.7 per cent of GDP to 0.5 per cent of GDP. A close examination of the state specific performance revealed that poorer and fiscally more dependent states had, in general, achieved stronger fiscal correction than the high-income states. However, fiscal performance by Indian states during 2000–06 had to be seen in the context of the historical backdrop of the 1990s, a decade characterized by serious deterioration in the fiscal position of all states that culminated in a fiscal crisis towards the end of the 1990s.

Many states approached the 12th FC to increase the state's share of central taxes in the divisible pool from 29.5 per cent to at least 33 per cent. The need for ramping up infrastructure spending was severely felt by the states for ensuring access as well as improving provision of services to a large and growing population base. In a more globalized and competitive environment, the importance of good infrastructure could not be ignored. Several studies analysing India's growth prospects identify infrastructure as among the most important constraints to future rapid growth (Ahluwalia, 1998; Krueger and Chinoy, 2002; World Bank, 2006). Thus, the TORs of the 12th FC were framed in a manner so that the Commission could provide a way forward in finding a solution to the infrastructure gap story.

The 12th FC did not accede to the request of the states and instead argued that grants provided a more effective mechanism for meeting the equalization objective and increased the states' share in central taxes by only one percentage point to 30.5 per cent compared to the 11th FC. However, the 12th FC made some path-breaking recommendations in terms of strengthening the macroeconomic framework of the country requesting the states to enact Fiscal Responsibility Legislations (FRLs), which should, at a minimum, provide for: (i) eliminating current deficit by 2008/09; (ii) reducing fiscal deficit to 3 per cent of GSDP (Gross State Domestic Product) or its equivalent, defined as the ratio of interest payments to revenue receipts; (iii) bringing out annual reduction targets of revenue and fiscal deficits; (iv) bringing out an annual statement giving prospects for the state economy and related fiscal strategy; (iv) bringing out special statements along with the budget giving in detail the number of employees in government, public sector, and aided institutions and related salaries; and (v) enacting the fiscal responsibility legislation, a necessary precondition for availing debt relief.

In a nutshell, it can be concluded that the 12th FC did not reject in totality the plea of the states for meeting their serious resource constraints but used the FRLs to create the necessary fiscal space for capital spending by recommending the states to reach a 'zero' revenue deficit (current account deficit). Linking debt relief to states to the enactment of FRLs/FRBM similar to that of central government proved an excellent strategy of restructuring the states' public finances.

It needs to be noted that it was not possible to bridge the huge infrastructure gap by vertical transfers alone. The overall strategy of increasing infrastructure spending required complementary reforms, the enabling environment for which was remarkably crafted in the 12th FC recommendations. The task required both coordination and burden sharing between the centre and states in terms of reducing their fiscal deficits and debt more so, at the state level. Burden sharing is a two-way traffic, if states agreed to reduce their debt burden, the centre had to step in to write off some of the costly debt or replace the costly debt of the pre-1991 era with low cost debt. The 12th FC responded to the states' call for burden sharing and agreed to provide debt relief through a combination of debt write-off and debt restructuring. In fact, it encouraged the states to access the market for future borrowings so that they rely less on the resource transfers from the centre. In overall terms, the 12th FC recommended a less risky alternative path for India by addressing the weaknesses in public finances and the infrastructure gap simultaneously through an overhaul of public finances rather than recommending a debt financed increase in infrastructure spending given the vulnerability posed by the high debt-GDP ratio (as depicted in Figure 13.1a–b).

The 13th FC was constituted against the backdrop of strong fiscal correction and consolidation by most of the state governments. The major recommendations of the 13th FC were: (i) the share of states in the net proceeds of the shareable central taxes to be 32 per cent, 1.5 percentage points higher than the recommendation of the 12th FC; (ii) the revenue deficit to be progressively reduced and eliminated, followed by revenue

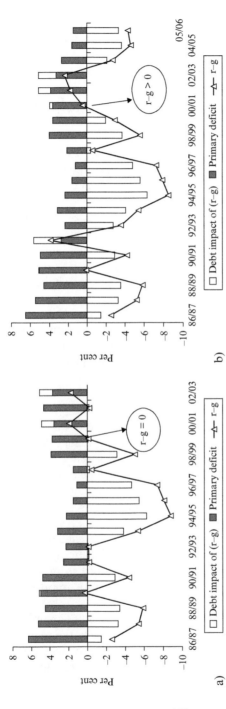

Note: The debt dynamics at the central government level deteriorated after the mid-1990s. After 1997/98, primary deficits reversed course and started rising, while real interest rates converged to and then exceeded growth rates between 2000/01 and 2002/03. This then changed with the pick-up in the growth after 2003/04. All this was possible through conscious policy and careful calibration of economic policy from time to time. The role of the FCs in stabilizing the policies every five years through its additional mandates has been crucial.

Sources: a) Pinto and Zahir (2004a) for Figure 13.1a; b) Pinto et al. (2006) for Figure 13.1b. Data collected from Handbook of Statistics, Reserve Bank of India, various budget documents, Ministry of Finance (GoI), author's estimates.

Figure 13.1 Debt dynamics

surplus by 2013/14; (iii) the fiscal deficit to be reduced to 3 per cent of the GDP by 2014/15; (iv) a target of 68 per cent of GDP for the combined debt of the centre and states; (v) FRBM Act, 2003 to be amended to appropriately reflect the nature of shocks which shall require targets relaxation; (vi) both centre and states should conclude a 'Grand Bargain' to implement the model GST; (vii) urged to reduce the number of Centrally Sponsored Schemes (CSS); and (viii) states to address the problem of losses in the power sector in a time-bound manner.

Chakraborty (2010), however, pointed out that the 13th FC's recommendation to increase the vertical share of tax devolution to states will help, but its horizontal distribution formula leaves much to be desired. The reason being: (i) its design is such that two of the four key indicators are in conflict[7] with each other; (ii) the Commission's revised road map for fiscal consolidation at the centre and the states, which recommends state specific, year-wise, fiscal adjustment paths, not only limits the fiscal manoeuvrability of states but also impinges on their fiscal autonomy. He further concluded that the 13th FC has taken a narrow technocratic view which emphasizes deficit fundamentalism.

In overall terms, the FCs in the full convergence phase played a crucial role in balancing the centre-state relationship through a combination of durable and meaningful reforms aimed at providing a strategic road map that responded to the macroeconomic challenges faced by the centre and state governments from time to time.

Horizontal Devolution (Sharing) Criteria

For ensuring horizontal equity various FCs used different criteria with relative weights, in particular, the horizontal criteria were simplified after the 10th FC. The 11th and 12th FCs were more inclined towards using a unified formula for horizontal devolution. For determining the criteria and the relative weights two basic principles of equity and fiscal efficiency were emphasized by both Commissions. Equity implied, as a result of revenue sharing, the resource deficiencies across the states are evened out. The 11th FC was of the opinion that continuing with resource deficiency can create perverse incentives or it can manifest a vested interest in maintaining a status quo. It thus emphasized including a criterion for rewarding fiscal efficiency.

Population has been a stable variable Commission after Commission for determining the share of states in tax devolution – only the weights have changed from time to time (Table 13.2). Area as a criterion was introduced by the 10th FC and it served more as a proxy for cost of providing services. For instance, states with large area and low population density had to incur

Table 13.2   *Criteria and relative weights for determining* inter se *share of states (Phase III) (percentage)*

Parameter	Finance Commissions				
	Tenth (1995–2000, Alternative Scheme of Devolution)	Eleventh (2000–05)	Twelfth (2005–10)	Thirteenth (2010–15)	Fourteenth (2015–20)
Population 1971	20.0	10.0	25.0	25.0	17.5
Adjusted Area	5.0	7.5	10.0	10.0	15.0
Income Distance/ Fiscal Capacity Distance[a]	60.0	62.5	50.0	47.5	50.0
Fiscal Discipline		7.5	7.5	17.5	
Tax Effort	10.0	5.0	7.5		
Index of Infrastructure	5.0	7.5			
Demographic Change 2011 Population					10.0
Forest Area					7.5
Total	100	100	100	100	100
Memo:					
States' Share in Divisible Pool of Central Taxes as Recommended by FC	Income Tax: 77.5; Union Excise: 47.5[b] (All Commodities)	29.5[c]	30.5	32.0	42.0

Notes:

[a] While computing the distance-based shares the 9th and the 10th FCs followed the practice of measuring the distance of the per capita income of state from that of the highest per capita income state. The 11th FC, however, changed this from a single high-income state to an average of three high-income states (Punjab, Goa and Maharashtra) as a benchmark from which distances were to be measured. The 12th more or less conformed to the 11th FC practice. The 13th FC changed the estimation criteria (measured fiscal capacity in terms of per capita taxable capacity), whereas the 14th FC reverted to the earlier method of measuring fiscal capacity as the distance of actual per capita income of a state from the state with the highest per capita income.

[b] Includes revenue deficit grants of 7.5 per cent.

[c] Of this, 1.5 per cent is on account of additional excise duties in lieu of sales tax on sugar, textiles and tobacco.

Source: Report of the Finance Commission (10th–14th), Ministry of Finance, Government of India.

heavy expenditure for providing basic administrative infrastructure. This stands in sharp contrast to a state with an area of similar size but a high density of population where costs of providing services are much lower.

The weights have varied from 5 per cent in the 10th FC to 15 per cent in the 14th FC. Infrastructure played an important role in unbundling the constraints to growth during the 10th, 11th and 12th FCs. However, the 12th FC dropped the infrastructure index from the horizontal formula on the grounds that it was *correlated* with the income distance criteria. In order to evolve a suitable structure of incentives in fiscal transfers, the 10th FC introduced 'tax effort' as a criterion for sharing the tax proceeds with the states. The 11th FC went further and added 'fiscal discipline' as a criterion. Tax effort together with fiscal discipline was given a weight of 12.5 per cent in the 11th FC which increased to 15 per cent by the 12th FC. The 13th FC was of the view that there was a strong case to incentivize states to follow fiscal prudence, particularly in the context of the need to return to the path of fiscal correction. Accordingly, it assigned a weight of 17.5 per cent to fiscal discipline.

The 14th FC went further ahead and dropped both fiscal discipline and tax effort criteria from the horizontal distribution formula. The 14th FC introduced two new variables instead: (i) 2011 population; and (ii) forest cover. The 2011 population criteria were aimed to capture the demographic changes since 1971, both in terms of migration and age structure. The Commission introduced forest cover since its TORs mandated the need to balance management of the ecology and environment. The weightage of area was enhanced to 15 per cent compared to 10 per cent in the 13th FC and that of income distance increased to 50 per cent from 47.5 per cent in the 13th FC.

While all states stand to gain in absolute terms due to greater devolution by the 14th FC (as noted in the next section), the sharing pattern among states had been affected by the change in the horizontal formula.[8] The 14th FC transfers had a more favourable impact on the states which were relatively less developed having low per capita income such as Madhya Pradesh, Odisha, Uttar Pradesh, Bihar, Chattisgarh, Jharkhand and West Bengal. In all these states, the benefits of 14th FC transfers were in the range of 3–5 per cent of state income and the ratio of benefits to states' own tax revenues was also high, hence substantial increase in the spending capacities of these states (Economic Survey, Government of India, 2014/15).

Grants-in-Aid

While the distribution of tax proceeds between the centre and states have dominated the popular debates and discussions around the FCs in India, the 'Grants-in-Aid' as a component of FCs has its own importance and relevance. The size of the grants has varied from 7.7 per cent of total transfers under the 7th FC to 26.1 per cent of total transfers under the 6th FC. In the full convergence phase, where the global sharing agreement became increasingly important as a source of vertical devolution, the share of grants in total transfers has been declining and in the 13th FC it declined to 18 per cent of total transfers. However, the Grants-in-Aid provided by various FCs included grants for meeting revenue deficit, disaster relief, local bodies, sector specific schemes and state specific schemes. The revenue deficit (current deficit) grants were provided to those states which were projected to have a post-devolution non-plan revenue deficit in any year. The 14th FC departed significantly from earlier FCs as it did not recommend any grants for sector-specific and state-specific schemes. The reason behind such a move was that these grants were not based on any formula or any uniform principle and have thus been quite ad hoc in nature. Also, it led to duplication of funding in many such schemes.

13.4   LABORATORY FEDERALISM, 14TH FC: AN ABERRATION OR A PERMANENT CHANGE?

India's federal structure is witnessing a paradigm shift in the relationship between the centre, states and local bodies. There are several reasons for this shift:

- The recent experimentation by the 14th FC of choosing a 'big bang' approach, compared to a 'gradualist' approach of the previous FCs, of transferring huge sums of money (untied formula-based transfers) to the states and local bodies has led to a perception that states' fiscal autonomy is substantially strengthened.
- The number of CSS was brought down to 28 from 67 and the CSS were restructured, and their funding pattern changed.
- The 'operative' word used in the 14th FC report was a 'trust-based approach' in the spirit of strengthening cooperative federalism.
- The establishment of the GST council which has emerged as the most significant body in fiscal federalism since independence.
- Abolition of the Planning Commission in 2014, an extra-constitutional body that has been a source of important plan funding for states since 1950. With this also came the dismantling of the National Development Council (NDC) which had been the guiding force for the Planning Commission and served as an important interlocutor between the states and the centre.

- Discontinuation of the Plan and Non-Plan distinction while reporting expenditures in the budgets from 2017/18.
- Establishment of a NITI (National Institution for Transforming India) Aayog in 2015 replacing the erstwhile Planning Commission. NITI has no mandate to control resources, it is a technical and advisory body whose aim is to evaluate government programmes and strategies for resource allocation. The NDC has been replaced by a Governing Council that has the Prime Minister as the chairperson, a vice chairperson, full-time members of NITI Aayog, chief ministers of all states and so on.

The impact of some of the changes will unfold over time and it would be premature to draw any conclusions in haste. However, what one can convincingly examine is the impact of the changes due to the 14th FC as the data for at least the first four years of the award are now available at the aggregate level.

Laboratory Federalism

The 14th FC points to an interesting period in Indian federalism which one may call 'laboratory federalism'. It is a phase of experimentation in India because some of the traditional and deeply entrenched institutions which have been the fulcrum of economic policy for several decades have either been dismantled or restructured. Federalism at work would now be based on the results of the experimentation and the 'technical progress' in public policy. The 14th FC can be viewed as one of the vehicles for bringing desired changes in public policy in a somewhat loose sense. The changes in policy were necessary given the abysmally low level of service provision for the citizens in India due to state and local governments' limited implementation capacity and their high dependency on central government's tied transfers. The schematic transfers in the form of CSS have left little room for states and local governments to design and implement projects that reflect local preferences.

The experience elsewhere in the world on schematic tied transfers is somewhat similar and there has been in India lately a greater push towards untied transfers, more in the form of block grants. This is reminiscent of the stance that the US contemplated in the 1990s. In the mid-90s, the US took a decision for shifting primary responsibility for poor relief back to the states. The federal government replaced long-standing federal entitlement programmes, which came both with detailed rules and generous matching grants to the states, by a system of block grants with few strings attached.[9] The states had broad scope to determine both the form and levels of assistance under their programmes to assist poor households. The new welfare legislation was signed into law in 1996 in an attempt to better understand the failure of federal welfare programmes in the US and to use states as 'laboratories' to try to find out what sort of programmes would work. In a similar vein, after exactly 20 years, the 14th FC provided a basis where both states and local governments could serve as 'laboratories' for understanding what programmes would work that can address issues of poor service delivery. In fact, the 14th FC has met a long-standing demand from the states for greater devolution and greater flexibility in the design of vertical programmes (CSS), while leaving appropriate fiscal space for the centre.

The attempt to use states as 'laboratories' had both political and economic reasons in India. In the last two decades there has been a general trend towards coalition governments with a number of states and local representatives now participating in politics at the centre. In addition, the 73rd and the 74th Constitutional Amendments in 1992 had incentivized grass-roots level politicians to rise above the petty politics of local and state level and occupy a space at the centre.

14th FC and Budget Outcomes

The 14th FC made several bold recommendations that gave greater autonomy to the states and local governments in delivering services. Major recommendations included: (i) an unprecedented increase in states' share of central taxes from 32 per cent of the central divisible pool (during the 13th FC) to 42 per cent; and (ii) a threefold increase in the total grants to local bodies for improving basic services during the period 2015–20, total grants to local bodies was fixed at INR 2874.4 billion (US$ 46 bn), including INR 871.4 billion (US$ 14 bn) for urban local bodies and INR 2002.9 billion (US$ 32 bn) for rural local bodies. This 10-percentage-point jump in tax devolution of the sharable central tax (divisible pool) over the 13th FC is the largest increase in the history of Indian fiscal federalism. The earlier Commissions had recommended changes in tax shares in the range of about 1–2 per cent: 29.5 per cent in the 11th FC and 30.5 per cent in the 12th FC (Table 13.2). The increased tax devolution has been partly compensated by a reduction in the CSS (Table 13.3). The increase for urban local bodies over the 13th FC is *fourfold*, while for the rural local bodies more than three times the 13th FC award (see details in Babu et al., 2018).

The 14th FC concluded that rather than continuing with a fragmented approach of passing money to the states through multiple channels, it would be more effective to devolve money by increasing states' share in central taxes in the spirit of cooperative federalism. The demand for cooperative federalism has been echoed several times by various FCs, but due to the dominance of the Planning Commission in economic policy and proliferation of CSS with centripetal biases, the recourse to cooperative federalism remained largely weak.

However, recently Rao (2017) has explained that increasing devolution from 32 per cent to 42 per cent is not as generous as it looks. In order to cover the requirements under both Plan and Non-Plan accounts, 5.5 per cent of the divisible pool was required. In addition, the 14th FC eschewed discretionary sectoral grants of 1.5 per cent of the divisible pool previously. Thus, the legitimate comparison should be between 39 per cent and 42 per cent. The increase from 32 per cent or 39 per cent (implicitly) to 42 per cent in the share of central taxes for the states was justified on two grounds: (i) bringing a compositional shift from grants to tax devolution; the shift would not result in any additional burden on the centre and it would also meet a long pending demand of states for more unconditional transfers; (ii) keeping the level of aggregate transfers to states to around 49 per cent of the gross revenues, in line with previous trends.

The 14th FC, however, did create an impression that the fiscal space available to the states had significantly increased and the award was a game changer. A closer examination of the 2015/16 budget does endorse the compositional shift with a 1-percentage-point rise in tax devolution offset by a less than commensurate decline in plan grants. According to the central budget 2015/16, the aggregate central transfers to states as a share of GDP increased from 5.4 per cent in 2014/15 to 6.0 per cent in 2015/16. The tax devolution had increased from 2.7 per cent in 2014/15 to 3.7 per cent of GDP in 2015/16. Part of the increase was offset by a decline in the plan grants from 2.1 per cent of GDP in 2014/15 to 1.5 per cent of GDP in 2015/16. The share of non-plan grants to states had increased from 0.6 per cent in 2014/15 to 0.8 per cent of GDP in 2015/16. Further, it needs to be noted that the 10-percentage-point increase (or 3-percentage-point increase as per Rao, 2017) in the share of central taxes to states subsumed part of normal plan assistance, special plan assistance, special central assistance and sector specific grants. It is important to appreciate that the substantial tax devolution increase had factored in a number of variables on the plan side which the government decided to either discontinue or replace by untied transfers. The transition from tied to untied transfers thus was a well thought out strategic shift in expenditure policy which the 14th FC facilitated.

An Aberration or Permanent Change

The question now arises is whether this experimentation is seen in India more as a permanent change or as a circumstantial aberration. Since

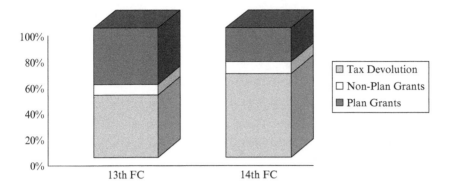

Source: Central Government Budget Documents (various issues), Ministry of Finance, GoI.

Figure 13.2   *Changes in transfer of resources from centre to states between 13th and 14th FCs*

2019/20 is the terminal year of the 14th FC, a review of the entire period (2015/16 to 2019/20) may help to provide some answers. A comparison with the 13th FC indicates clear trends towards untied transfers (Figure 13.2). While there was a 1-percentage-point increase on average in tax devolution to GDP under the 14th FC period, there was a 0.9-percentage-point decline in plan grants to GDP, a 0.1-percentage-point increase in non-plan grants to GDP during the same period. As a result, the total transfers as a percentage of GDP increased by 0.1 percentage points compared to the 13th FC period. The major change is that the share of FC transfers has substantially gone up during the 14th FC period (74 per cent) compared to the 13th FC period (56 per cent).

Tied transfers (includes CSS and others) are now only a quarter of the total transfers compared to 44 per cent during the 13th FC period (Table 13.3). The changes so far indicated will in the medium term bring a qualitative change in spending both at the centre and states. While the centre would find its fiscal space less constraining since a large part of the transfers to the states will be linked to the divisible pool which is formula driven, it will render greater predictability and transparency in resource transfers. Chelliah et al. (1992) had remarked that a time would come when transfers would impart greater autonomy to states through the FC and the Planning Commission would only lay down broad contours of development policy. Two decades later, the 14th FC did find itself recommending and assessing the entire revenue account of the centre for transfer of resources.

However, there is some dissatisfaction among the states over plan transfers which have been discontinued, in particular, the formula driven

Table 13.3   Transfer of resources from centre to states (percentage GDP)

	Thirteenth FC	Fourteenth FC[a]
Tax Devolution	2.9	3.9
Plan Grants[b]	2.7	1.6[c]
Non-plan Grants	0.5	0.6
Total Transfers	6.0	6.1
Memo:		
Finance Commission Transfers as % of Total Transfers	55.9	74.1
Tied Transfers (specific purpose) as % age of Total Transfers	44.1	25.9

Notes:
[a] The Budget 2015/16 had delinked eight centrally sponsored schemes from central support. The 14th FC had identified 30 centrally sponsored schemes to be delinked from central support but all have not yet been delinked considering the national priorities and legal obligations. Until 2014, specific purpose grants did not pass through the states' budget, instead the money was directly transferred from the central government budget to the accounts of the societies or the implementing agencies.
[b] Refers to normal central assistance (NCA) and discretionary grants (CSS and others) provided by the Planning Commission until it was discontinued in 2014. NCA remained a predominant channel of central plan assistance to states, however, over time with proliferation of CSS there has been a significant reduction in the formula-based NCA (from 34.6 per cent in 10th Plan to 9.6 per cent in 2014/15 as a share of total central assistance). Part of NCA and other grants are now subsumed in tax devolution from the 14th FC onwards.
[c] The sharing pattern of the CSS has undergone a change and is now 60:40 compared to 80:20, with states' contribution being increased to 40 per cent with the objective of imparting greater responsibility and accountability to the states both in design and implementation.

Source: Central Government Budget, Ministry of Finance (GoI), various volumes, author's estimation.

normal central assistance. In addition, states have started demanding that the cesses and surcharges which are now a rising proportion of the gross tax revenues of the centre should also be shared with them. The relative stability in the share of tax devolution to gross tax revenues of the centre is primarily because of the levy of cesses and surcharges which are currently outside the divisible pool. The surcharges together with the various cesses increased from 5.8 per cent of gross tax revenues in 1990/91 to 14.6 per cent in 2017/18 (Revised Estimate (RE)). This has resulted in neutralizing the effect of the increase in tax devolution recommended by various FCs for the centre. The centre in turn has been pre-empting a part of the tax revenues due to increasing recourse to this stream of income. It was believed that roll-out of GST would subsume some of these cesses and surcharges, but the central government introduced some new cesses to make up for the cesses subsumed under GST.

A comparison of the 2015/16 budget fiscal outcomes with the recent 2019/20 budget indicate fiscal consolidation at the centre has paused (Figure 13.3a–b). The central government has recalibrated the FRBM targets to reach a fiscal deficit of 3 per cent of GDP in 2021/22 instead of 2017/18 as envisaged at the time of the budget 2015/16. In addition, the resolve of the centre to make the effective revenue deficit (which excludes grants for capital creation) zero by 2017/18 has been stretched to 2021/22. A pause in fiscal consolidation and relaxation in targets to adjust for the transitional impact of GST in the interim make the task of the 15th FC difficult as it would need to emphasize adherence to FRBM targets and fiscal consolidation in order to restore the confidence in the Indian economy. The 15th FC will have to recast the fiscal consolidation path through tough fiscal discipline rules (based on fiscal deficit and debt targets), particularly for the central government. Furthermore, it should also review rational ways of handling significant non-tax revenues from natural resources on the surface (such as water), underground (such as coal) and in space (such as spectrum).

Reddy and Reddy (2019) note that the TOR of 15th FC seem to not just reverse some of the recommendations of the previous Commission but give greater discretion than ever before to the Union (centre) government. The outcomes of this are unclear. There are several reasons which the authors have cited: (i) there has been some politicization of the TOR since the FC has been asked to use 2011 population instead of 1971 population figures in their estimation of the horizontal distribution; (ii) discontinuation of the revenue deficit grant has constitutional ramifications; (iii) the central government is granting access to borrowings to states with discretionary conditionalities despite rules governing the fiscal deficits. The concern is that the vertical and horizontal distribution that was so far confined to revenues and expenditures is now being extended to public debt; (iv) the one-nation-one-tax through GST is associated with erosion of fiscal autonomy of states because the Sales Tax/VAT which is being transformed into GST was the only broad-based tax with the states; (vi) a growing sense among states that cooperative and competitive federalism is being replaced with coercive federalism since many a time central government officials are deployed for village outreach programmes to evaluate the working of the schemes funded by the centre.

In this context, the 14th FC recommendations may appear to be circumstantial or an accidental aberration. This, however, is not true. In the history of Indian fiscal federalism, the 14th FC became the first Commission which brought a structural change in the configuration of

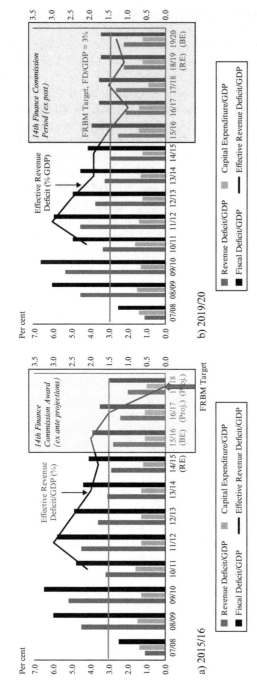

Notes: The FRBM Act was amended twice, 2012 and 2015, to take into account the change in macroeconomic circumstances in the country. The Act was amended for the third time in 2018 based on the recommendations of the FRBM Committee which submitted its report in January 2017. Following the implementation of the GST in 2017, the fiscal deficit to GDP target in 2017/18 was recalibrated to 3.5 per cent in order to accommodate the transitional impact of GST on the economy. The Budget 2019/20 is a Vote on Account and not a full budget of the government due to election. Revenue Deficit refers to current deficit and effective revenue deficit excludes grants for capital creation from the current deficit. BE refers to Budget Estimate.

Source: Budget 2019/20, 2015/16 and some previous issues, Ministry of Finance, GoI.

Figure 13.3   Trends in key deficit indicators and FRBM targets as per central government budget, 2015/16 and 2019/20

intergovernmental transfers to states by considering the entire revenue (current) account and subsuming plan transfers in tax devolution. This new arrangement is permanent and is less likely to be reversed by future Commissions.

13.5   CONCLUSION

In sum, this chapter traces the history of the FCs in India over the last 25 years in shaping the intergovernmental transfer system in India. The India case presents an interesting transition from a market preserving federalism towards laboratory federalism in the light of the recommendations made by the 14th FC. The Indian federal structure is in search of a narrative, in which the third tier can play an important role along with the states (second tier) in strengthening objective and accountable subnational governments (states and local governments together). In policy terms, the biggest reform undertaken in the 2015/16 central government budget was the acceptance of the bold recommendations of the 14th FC by the government. The recommendations of the 14th FC reiterated building a trust-based approach between the centre and the subnational governments going forward. There was a conscious move to gradually shift public expenditure policy decisively and firmly to the jurisdiction of the state governments. This, along with the ongoing trend in decentralization of fiscal policy, including the taxation policy through the implementation of the GST, have altered the design of fiscal federalism in India.

NOTES

*   The author is grateful for comments from Dr D.K. Srivastav (Advisory Council Member, Fifteenth Finance Commission of India), Professor Roy Bahl (Regents Professor Emeritus and Dean Emeritus, Georgia State University, USA) and Serdar Yilmaz (Lead Public Sector Specialist, Governance Global Practice, The World Bank, Washington DC, USA).
1.   They are also called Panchayat Raj Institutions (PRIs); the third tier in India is divided into urban and rural local bodies. The rural local bodies are multi-tiered comprising of district, block and village, while urban local bodies are single tiered.
2.   According to the Constitution, India is referred to as a union of states and union territories. In the chapter, Union is interchangeably used and refers to federal or central government.
3.   A policy think tank of the Government of India (GoI), NITI Aayog (National Institution for Transforming India Aayog), has replaced the Planning Commission in 2015 which will provide strategic and technical advice to the centre and state governments.
4.   While the FC role was confined to the examination of the non-plan revenue account of the states' budget, the Planning Commission assessed the overall requirements (in terms of transfers to states) on the plan side until 2014 until it was discontinued.

5. Order made by the President, Government of India, 27 November 2017.
6. In India, economic reforms have led to the deepening of federalism in terms of expenditure decentralization which demanded at the same time decentralization of revenue raising powers at the subnational level. However, implementing VAT, to make India a single integrated market, led to revenue losses for the states in the interim and reduced their autonomy indicating greater centralization. The implementation of GST in 2017 marks a departure from more centralizing behaviour of the federal government in India towards a trust-based approach with its subnational governments. The rates for GST are decided by a GST council which comprises the Union finance minister and the finance ministers of all the states. The objective of the GST council is to have one uniform tax rate for goods and services across the country.
7. The existence of a fiscal capacity distance and an index of fiscal discipline in the same formula contradict the objective of achieving horizontal equity. The reason being that while fiscal capacity distance tries to enhance the fiscal capacity of states, the index of fiscal discipline tries to limit their expenditure in relation to their own revenue.
8. In a nutshell, the net impact on the states has been positive and some of the negative effects of a change in formula have been offset by the large positive effect of the change in divisible pool.
9. For details, refer to Wallace E. Oates, 'An Essay on Fiscal Federalism' in *Readings in Public Finance*, edited by Bagchi (2005).

REFERENCES

Ahluwalia, Montek S. (1998). 'Infrastructure Development in India's Reforms' in *India Economic Reforms and Development: Essays for Manmohan Singh*, edited by Manmohan Singh, Isher Ahluwalia and I.M.D. Little, Oxford University Press, New Delhi, India, pp. 92–121.

Ahluwalia, Montek S. (2002a). 'Economic Reforms in India since 1991: Has Gradualism Worked?' *Journal of Economic Perspectives*, **16** (3), pp. 67–88.

Ahluwalia, Montek S. (2002b). 'India's Vulnerability to External Crisis: An Assessment' in *Macroeconomics and Monetary Policy: Issues for a Reforming Economy – Essays in Honor of C. Rangarajan*, edited by Montek Ahluwalia, S.S. Tarapore and Y.V. Reddy, Oxford University Press, New Delhi, India.

Babu, M. Devendra, Farah Zahir, Rajesh Khanna and Prakash M. Philip (2018). 'Two Decades of Fiscal Decentralization Reforms in Karnataka: Opportunities, Issues and Challenges' Working Paper No. 416, Institute for Social and Economic Change, Bengaluru, India.

Bagchi, A. (2003). 'Fifty Years of Fiscal Federalism in India: An Appraisal' Working Paper No. 2 NIPFP, New Delhi.

Bagchi, A. (2005). *Readings in Public Finance*, edited, Oxford University Press, New Delhi, India.

Bahl, Roy and Richard M. Bird (2018). *Fiscal Decentralization and Local Finance in Developing Countries: Development from Below*, Edward Elgar Publishing, Cheltenham, UK and Northampton, MA, USA.

Chakraborty, Pinaki (2010). 'Deficit Fundamentalism vs Fiscal Federalism: Implications of 13th Finance Commission's Recommendations' *Economic and Political Weekly*, 27 November 2010: 56–63

Chelliah, Raja J. (2000). 'Fiscal Federalism in India: Contemporary Challenges' in *Issues before the Eleventh Finance Commission*, edited by D.K. Srivastava, National Institute of Public Finance and Policy, New Delhi.

Chelliah, Raja J., M. Govinda Rao and Tapas Kumar Sen (1992). 'Issues before Tenth Finance Commission' *Economic and Political Weekly* (EPW), **27** (47), 2539–50.

Government of India (GoI) (1995). *Report of the Tenth Finance Commission*, Ministry of Finance, New Delhi, India.

Government of India (GoI) (2000). *Report of the Eleventh Finance Commission*, Ministry of Finance, New Delhi, India.

Government of India (GoI) (2004). *Report of the Twelfth Finance Commission*, Ministry of Finance, New Delhi, India.

Government of India (GoI) (2009). *Report of the Thirteenth Finance Commission*, Ministry of Finance, New Delhi, India.

Government of India (GoI) (2015). *Report of the Fourteenth Finance Commission*, Ministry of Finance, New Delhi, India.

Government of India (2014/15). *Economic Survey*, Ministry of Finance, New Delhi, India.

IMF (2017). 'Strengthening Indian Center State Fiscal Frameworks' IMF Country Report No.17/55, *India: Selected Issues*, International Monetary Fund (IMF), Washington DC, pp. 19–25.

Krueger, Anne O., and Sajjid Chinoy (2002). 'The Indian Economy in Global Context' in *Economic Policy Reforms and the Indian Economy*, edited by Anne O. Krueger, The University of Chicago Press, Chicago, IL.

Oates, Wallace E. (1999). 'An Essay on Fiscal Federalism' in *Readings in Public Finance*, edited by Amaresh Bagchi, Oxford University Press, New Delhi, India, pp. 1120–49.

Pinto, Brian, and Farah Zahir (2004a). 'India: Why Fiscal Adjustment Now' Policy Research Working Paper WPS 3230, Washington, DC: World Bank.

Pinto, Brian, and Farah Zahir (2004b). 'Why Fiscal Adjustment Now' *Economic and Political Weekly*, 6 March: 1039–48.

Pinto, Brian, Farah Zahir and Gaobo Pang (2006). 'From Rising Debt to Rising Growth in India: Microeconomic Dominance?' in *India: Inclusive Growth and Service Delivery – Building on India's Success*, Development Policy Review, The World Bank, Washington, DC, pp. 103–19.

Pinto, Brian, Farah Zahir and Gaobo Pang (2007). 'Fiscal Policy for Growth in India' in *Job Creation and Poverty Reduction in India: Towards Rapid and Sustained Growth*, edited by Sadiq Ahmed, SAGE Publications India Pvt. Ltd, New Delhi, India, pp. 85–131.

Rangarajan, C. (2006). 'Fiscal Federalism: Some Current Concerns' in *India in a Globalizing World: Some Aspects of Macroeconomy, Agriculture and Poverty*, edited by R. Radhakrishna, S.K. Rao, S. Mahendra Dev and K. Subbarao, Academic Foundation with Centre for Economic and Social Studies, Hyderabad, India, pp. 115–23.

Rangarajan, C., and D.K. Srivastava (2011). *Federalism and Fiscal Transfers in India*, Oxford University Press, New Delhi, India.

Rao, Govinda M. (2017). '15th Finance Commission: To Realize the Goals under New India 2022, Here is What Center Must Remember', *Financial Express*, 5 December.

Ravishankar, V.J., Farah Zahir and Neha Kaul (2008). 'Indian States' Fiscal Correction: An Unfinished Agenda' *Economic and Political Weekly*, 20 September: 57–62.

Reddy, Y.V., and G.R. Reddy (2019). *Indian Fiscal Federalism*, Oxford University Press, New Delhi, India.

Wes, Marina (2007). 'India's State Finances' in *Job Creation and Poverty Reduction in India: Towards Rapid and Sustained Growth*, edited by Sadiq Ahmed, SAGE Publications India Pvt. Ltd, New Delhi, India, pp. 132–4.

World Bank (2006). 'India: Inclusive Growth and Service Delivery – Building on India's Success', Development Policy Review, The World Bank, Washington, DC.

Zahir, Mohammad (1972). *Public Expenditure and Income Distribution in India*, Associated Publishing House, New Delhi, India.

14. Emerging trends in fiscal transfer systems in selected federations: implications for India*

Jorge Martinez-Vazquez

14.1 BACKGROUND AND MOTIVATION

Despite the significant policy reforms in recent years, the challenges facing India's decentralized system of finance run wide and deep.[1] There is still a significant vertical imbalance between the Union government and the states. Currently, states have most of the responsibility for providing social services while the Union government has the monopoly on most broad-based taxes other than goods and services tax (GST). Second, transfers continue to mix the objectives of tax devolution and equalization. Thus, it is not clear for the Union government what is really being achieved, which is accompanied by considerable unhappiness and frustration among other stakeholders. Third, considerable economic and fiscal disparities across the states remain; the disparity in spending per capita was almost tenfold in 2015. The ineffectiveness of the transfer system is at least partially to blame. And fourth, even though there has been significant simplification of Central Sponsored Schemes (CSS), the effectiveness and efficiency of those transfers still appear to be woefully lacking.

With that background, the 15th Finance Commission (FC) was constituted in November 2017 and scheduled to deliver its recommendations by October 2019. Its terms of references (TOR) are in many ways conventional, but there is a significant departure (see details in Chapter 13). The FC is mandated to use population data from 2011 in its recommendations, instead of the population figures from the 1971 census used by all previous FCs. This will imply significant shifts of resources from states in the south, which experienced moderate population growth to northern poorer states which have experienced faster rates of population growth over the past four decades.

The chapter explores possible options for the reform of India's transfer system. To do that, the chapter takes a cross-country view of the international experience with the design and implementation of transfer systems, especially drawing from the experiences of large federations.

14.2 EMERGING INTERNATIONAL TRENDS IN TRANSFER DESIGN RELEVANT TO INDIA

Issue 1: As opposed to further expanding transfers, India's considerable vertical imbalance between the Union and state governments should be first tackled by providing state governments with increased revenue autonomy.

India's intergovernmental finance system shows a high level of vertical imbalance. Using data for 2014–15, Rao (2017) shows that states collect in taxes around 8 per cent in gross domestic product (GDP) but they spend over 18 per cent of GDP.

Increased revenue autonomy can be achieved by devolving additional new taxes to the states, or by inducing states to make better use of their tax sources by enhancing administrative capacity and removing negative incentives to tax effort. Low levels of tax revenue autonomy or transfer dependency lowers accountability and reduces expenditure efficiency and fiscal responsibility. These are all key issues for the long-term dynamic performance of fiscal federalism in India.

The introduction of the new GST in 2017 represents a significant step forward. The new GST rate of 12 per cent is equally split between the Centre and the states and applied to a common base – final consumption.[2] However, from the viewpoints of visibility (accountability) and revenue sufficiency, the introduction of the GST has contributed much less. The new GST revenues for the states substitute for other taxes that states were using, which being much more distortionary, one may claim, were as visible to taxpayers if not more so. Being eminently a shared tax with the Union government, it is arguable that many taxpayers will not identify the GST as a state tax.

However, increasing states' tax autonomy will not be easy. A distinctive feature of India's fiscal federalism is adherence to the principle of separation of tax bases. In addition, the residual powers to tax lie with the Union government. Fundamentally, the states' inability to tax non-agricultural income has hindered access to broad-based and more buoyant taxes, other than the GST. Also, some taxes in the state list, such as the property tax or the professions tax, remain largely unexploited.

Internationally, a number of federal countries allow the concurrent use of bases, at least for some levies, prominently, taxes on income. Concurrent tax bases would appear to have more advantages than disadvantages.

When properly coordinated, concurrent use of the same base helps simplify administration and reduce compliance costs. Canada, the US and many European countries have concurrent powers to levy income taxes at the federal and subnational levels.[3]

The time may be ripe for allowing the states to tax personal income. An optimal way to do this is through a state piggyback tax, using the same base as the Union's but with a state selected flat rate between minimum and maximum federal legislated rates. Tax proceeds would accrue to the states on a derivation basis. Another area where states' revenue autonomy can be enhanced, and with the double dividend of reducing negative externalities, is with the wider extension of special excise taxes on alcoholic beverages, tobacco products, transportation fuels and vehicle use.

The problem can be also addressed by improving the administration of the property tax, a tax that has consistently underperformed in India. Much remains to be done to modernize fiscal cadastres by implementing fair and efficient valuation methods, and carrying out fair and transparent administration procedures, including efficient appeals. There is also room for the introduction and expansion of betterment levies and implementing land value capture levies.

Issue 2: India could follow the international trend of fixing in the law the sharing rate for the divisible pool in order to bring more stability and predictability, and more importantly, to harden the states' budget constraint.

After the rise in the sharing rate of the divisible pool to 42 per cent by the 14th FC there have been calls to fix the sharing rate in the law (or even the Constitution) and scale down the work of the FCs only to the distribution of funds among the states.[4]

There are certainly examples of countries in the international practice that fix the size of the divisible pool in the law. For example, Australia exclusively assigns to the pool of equalization transfers 100 per cent of the collected value added tax (VAT) revenues. Other countries that use a defined sharing rate of the revenue pool include Canada, Germany, Switzerland, Russia and most of the Nordic European countries. There are two main types of arguments in favour of this policy: the increased stability and predictability of state revenues, and the elimination of an implicit soft budget constraint for the states – they can fight for higher revenue shares and do lower own tax effort. This would appear to have been an overlooked important issue in the system. Probably the second argument is the most meaningful in India's context.[5] There are, on the other hand, arguments for the need of central flexibility in determining the pool of funds, such as macroeconomic fiscal stabilization policies. Over time, the type of argument has lost strength, as central governments have been increasingly seen as the ablest to absorb cyclical risks.

A closer look at the incentives argument may be warranted. The states' share in the divisible pool, fixed for 5 years by each FC, is a common lobbying target, with the states regularly asking for increases and historically getting them. This is easier for the states, but not more efficient, than increasing their own tax effort – and thus they become more accountable to their constituencies. The components and trappings of a soft budget constraint (increases in expenditures are met with subsequent additional transfers) are all in place.

Different FCs have argued the need for discretion in setting the devolution share to reflect the expenditure needs of the Union and state governments. However, they have done a rudimentary, at best, job in measuring expenditure needs. On the states' side, incentives have been clearly set to underestimate their tax revenue potential and overstate their needs. The reality has been a bargaining game played for decades. The result is a historical pattern of consistent increases in tax devolution shares[6] overwhelming evidence that increased transfers have reduced states' tax revenue collection efforts.[7] Finally, questions of incentives have weighed heavily in the past reform of the tax devolution system in India with the 80th constitutional amendment. The 10th FC redefined the composition of the divisible pool of funds in 1996, following the Chelliah Committee recommendations in 1991, to remove the then-existing perverse incentives for the Union to neglect the collection of sharable taxes.[8]

Issue 3: Tax devolution and redistribution are two very different objectives of transfer pursued in many countries using separate instruments. India could follow this international trend in the implementation of its tax sharing with state governments.

The conventional financing systems of subnational governments around the world include, beyond own tax revenues, revenue sharing on a derivation basis to pursue devolution objectives and help close vertical fiscal imbalances, an equalization grant to reduce horizontal fiscal imbalances, and conditional grants to reinforce national sectoral objectives and address externalities.

India, as most Latin American countries including large federations like Argentina and Brazil, uses a single instrument to pursue devolution and redistribution objectives. The result is that in the end it is not clear what is being achieved in any particular dimension or objective.

The objective of redistribution pursued via an equalization grant is pretty obvious: to equalize access to basic services throughout the national territory regardless of where citizens live. The objective of devolution may be less well understood. Most OECD (Organisation for Economic Co-operation and Development) countries – including Australia, Canada and Germany – and many developing countries, implement some form of revenue sharing on a derivation basis to provide incentives to develop the state economies and some sense of national cohesion.

Revenue sharing following devolution objectives clearly benefits the most economically dynamic regions of the country. That is also true for India. Often the southern, relatively richer, states in India express feelings that their contributions are not being recognized and that, overall, they are being penalized for trying harder to grow their economies. Revenue sharing on a derivation basis would address those concerns. The larger inequality or horizontal fiscal imbalances so created can be offset via a stronger equalization grant, recognizing revenue sharing funds as part of the fiscal capacity of the states. All this will imply splitting the divisible pool into revenue sharing and equalization components. The FC would have to decide on what level of equalization is feasible vis-à-vis straight devolution.[9] The corporate income tax is generally a bad choice – income tends to be exaggerated at the location of headquarters. The personal income tax and the VAT are the largest most commonly shared taxes.

Issue 4: India's equalization system could transition from its obsolete multivariable weighted index methodology, and follow the international trend using a formula based on the 'fiscal gap' methodology with the explicit estimation of expenditure needs and fiscal capacity across the states.

Fiscal disparities among Indian states are extremely large by international standards. The disparity between Goa and Uttar Pradesh in spending per capita was almost tenfold in 2015. These fiscal disparities are partly explained by smaller – but still large – economic disparities: in 2015, the state of Haryana had per capita income five times that of Bihar (Rao 2017).[10]

Given the size of the fiscal disparities it may not be possible to sufficiently close them. However, one may also ask whether those large disparities are partly associated with the defective weighted index methodology used for many decades.

Can a reformed methodology be effective in further reducing existing fiscal gaps? Increasing the equalization impact can be achieved by increasing the pool of funds that goes into equalization, a political issue already touched upon above, or by improving the distribution formula, a possibility further discussed in this section.

India's Current Equalization Methodology Is Flawed

At the risk of simplifying, a synopsis of how the current tax devolution formula is as follows.[11] First, the multiple criteria formula involving several criteria like population, land area, and so on – is applied to the divisible (sharable) pool of funds – which last was 42 per cent, with which a transfer amount is obtained for each state in the base year. Then, the FC projects the normed amounts of 'expenditure need' and 'fiscal capacity' for each state for the next 5 years, which involve a number of economic assumptions. The transfer amount obtained applying the multiple criteria formula is then used to close the gap between the projected 'expenditure need' and 'fiscal capacity' for each state for each of the 5 years with the amount remaining fixed in nominal terms over the entire period. The 'normative' principles used by the FC to project 'expenditure need' and 'fiscal capacity' are complex and vary significantly with each FC.[12] Once the work of the FC is done, there are no adjustments over the next 5 years. As a result, often states are unhappy because projected revenue and expenditure flows are grossly different from reality (Bhaskar 2018).

The current weighted index formula uses four variables, three of which can be interpreted as measuring expenditure needs: population, land area and forest area. The fourth, the distance of a state from the highest per capita income state, can be interpreted as approximating fiscal capacity.

The different FCs have changed the devolution weighted index formula.[13] The most prominent trend has been a reduction of the weight given to proxies for expenditure needs, especially population – and increases in the weight given to the proxy for fiscal capacity. The formula adopted by the 14th FC gave a 50 per cent weight to the deviation from the highest per capita income, 27.5 per cent weight to population, 15 per cent weight to the area, and 7.5 per cent weight to the forest area.

One fundamental problem with the weighted index approach is that the criteria selected are more or less arbitrary and that their weights are also in large measure arbitrary. From that perspective states have made continuous efforts to change the criteria and their weights. For example, as reported by the 14th FC, some states pushed for the inclusion of the Human Development Index (HDI), others for the inclusion of poverty measures or an index of social and economic backwardness, the lack of infrastructure and communication facilities, or the cost of living. From the perspective of equalization, many of these other suggested criteria could be as well justified, if not more so than the criterion introduced by the 14th FC related to 'forest cover'.[14] The implication is that a more comprehensive methodology is needed to address the complex nature of the states' expenditure needs.

Another obvious problem relates to the fact that the FC makes projections for 5 years and those estimates are never updated. Very few countries adopt this approach, which would appear to be related to the old practice of the 5-year plans; one exception is Vietnam. This practice has been defended as imparting stability; transfers will keep coming no matter what. A different approach would allow a new 'permanent secretariat' of the FC to make updates every year. This would bring India's practices more in accord with international practices.

One long-recognized limitation of the distribution formula has been the use of outdated population figures (from 1971). Fortunately, this issue has been addressed in the TOR for the 15th FC, which mandate the use of the 2015 Census population. However, the long-lasting use of the 1971 Census population has likely introduced distortions and inequities in the system that will take time to correct. The reason for using the 1971 population was to discourage states from following lax population control policies. Since population increases have been much more moderate in the south, states there are now complaining about being penalized. Nevertheless, it is incontrovertible that no meaningful equalization policy can be established based on population figures that are more than four decades old.

A more fundamental problem is that the current equalization methodology does not account well for many differences in expenditure needs. For example, Rao (2017) indicates that poorer states have a disproportionate number of poor people requiring anti-poverty programmes, and a much higher share of children under age 14, requiring higher outlays in education and healthcare. Other demographic factors can add to expenditure needs, such as a relatively higher presence of the elderly.[15] There are other types of state features that may impact expenditure needs. For example, Rajaraman (2017) points to the environmental cost damages in the states with mining activities.

In addition, the current methodology does a largely inadequate job in measuring differences in fiscal capacity across the states. Obviously, low-income states may have lower fiscal capacity. But fiscal capacity can be more accurately measured by using methodologies that deal explicitly with the size of tax bases or that can include proxies that can measure tax revenue potential. For example, the states' share of the GST – as will be argued below – can be used to directly measure the largest component of states' fiscal capacity.

International Trends and State of the Art across Countries in the Design of Equalization Grants

The state of the art in the design of equalization transfers in the international practice is the fiscal gap approach, defined as the difference between separate estimates of expenditure needs and fiscal capacity of the states. An increasing number of countries have adopted this methodology. Among developed OECD countries we find Australia, Canada for the Northern Territories, Italy, Japan, Korea, United Kingdom and in many US states; among countries in transition, China, Latvia, Russia, Ukraine and Vietnam; and among developing countries, Indonesia, Peru and Uganda. Actual implementation differs in its complexity. In Australia the fiscal gap formula is administered by an autonomous commission, and revenue capacity and expenditure needs are meticulously calculated every year for a long list of revenues and expenditure areas. However, in Canada equalization for the provinces (as opposed to the territories) is only on the basis of fiscal capacity per capita. Germany, Poland and Spain use yet another variation of the methodology by equalizing fiscal capacity per adjusted population reflecting differences in expenditure needs.

Different methodologies are available to compute expenditure needs and fiscal capacity across subnational government, as there are also different ways to apply their difference – the fiscal gap – to implementing the actual distribution of the available equalization funds among subnational governments.[16] Estimates of tax capacity quantify the potential revenues that can be obtained from the tax bases assigned to the subnational government, when they exercise an average (or maximum) level of collection effort. This avoids using actual revenues and therefore perverse incentives to lower actual collections. The actual measurement of fiscal capacity also includes actual revenue sharing and possibly other unconditional transfers. For these latter sources actual quantities can be used since central governments, not subnational governments, control their amounts.

Significantly, the recent reforms of the GST would simplify the measurements of states' tax capacity (Rajaraman 2017). The GST tax base is uniform across states and it is nationally administered by the GST Network.[17] Therefore, actual revenue collections should be very close to potential tax revenues. Thus, the largest component of states' tax capacity is already measured. The task then would remain to estimate the potential revenues for the rest of state taxes.[18]

Regarding expenditure needs, the task would be to quantify the funding necessary to cover all state expenditure responsibilities at a common standard level of service provision.[19] Typically, the estimation of expenditure needs excludes those arising from capital expenditure needs. The latter are more complex, lumpy and discontinuous, and generally they are better addressed separately via capital grants.

Once expenditure needs and fiscal capacity have been estimated, the pool of funds can be distributed among those jurisdictions – for which expenditure needs exceed fiscal capacity, proportionally to the fiscal gap or in several alternative manners.

One final issue is the standard of equalization, fundamentally constrained by the pool of available resources. The standard used by the 14th FC was to ensure that in the final year of the period, every state reached at least 80 per cent of the all-state average projected per capita revenue expenditure. If a fiscal gap approach were adopted, the equalization pool of funds would need to be calibrated to allow that result.

Issue 5: If a fiscal gap methodology is not adopted, India could consider refining the index formula approach to better capture needs and capacity. An additional possibility would be just to explicitly estimate the fiscal capacity (tax revenue potential) of the states and introduce the 'ratio of fiscal capacity to adjusted population' methodology – to implement equalization grants.[20]

Refining the Current Weighted Index

Even though the current weighted index approach used in India could be improved, it must be clear that these improvements would only help ameliorate a substandard methodology, in which the choice of variables to be included in the weighted index formula are still rather arbitrary, as are the relative weights attached to each one of those variables.

First, for fiscal capacity there are alternatives to the criterion of 'deviations from the highest per capita income'. One used in countries like Brazil and Argentina, which also use a weighted index formula, is the inverse of the state per capita income. On the set of criteria approximating expenditure need, the case for using forest ground cover as a proxy for expenditure need is weak – and highly unusual in the international practice. This objective would be better pursued with a conditional performance-based grant. The most critical aspect would be to approximate some expenditure needs that now go unmeasured, such as those due to the different composition of the population (more young people in need of education and more elderly in need of assistance), the incidence of poverty, the presence of unsatisfied basic needs (water, sanitation, and so on), and regional differences in the costs of service provision due to mountainous terrain or remoteness.

Adopting a Fiscal Capacity per Adjusted Population Approach for Equalization

Within the fiscal gap methodology, there are some countries which only equalize differences in fiscal capacity per capita and ignore potential differences in expenditure needs, as for example is the case of Canada. On the other hand, there are a number of countries that go a step beyond and use a fiscal capacity per adjusted (for expenditure needs) population approach, as in the cases of Germany, Poland and Spain. This methodology requires the estimation of fiscal capacity for which the different approaches discussed under the previous issue could be utilized and, second, the estimation of expenditure needs, but in a simplified way. The basic intuition is that the adjusted population in a state will exceed its actual population when its expenditure needs are above the average expenditure needs of all the states, while the adjusted population would be smaller when the state's expenditure needs are below the average. Those simplified expenditure needs may be measured via a weighted index, as discussed above. The adjusted population for each state can be obtained by multiplying the value of the weighted index for the state by the total population of the states – that is, the national population. The ratio of adjusted population to actual population in the state denotes whether fiscal capacity per adjusted population will go up or down and therefore whether the state will be eligible for more or less equalization funds.[21]

Issue 6: India should follow the international trend towards further consolidation of specific grants into block grants. However, there is no absolute dominance of block grants; specific purpose grants (with ex ante *conditionality or* ex post *performance-oriented conditionality) may be what are needed depending on the objectives of the Union government.*

Over the past several decades there has been an international trend towards the simplification of transfer systems in order to provide subnational governments with more autonomy in the use of transferred funds. In fact, this general trend can be decomposed into sub-trends both working in the same direction of providing greater subnational authority: first an increase in the share of unconditional grants over conditional grants, and second, within conditional grants, an increase in general purpose block grants with a decrease in specific purpose conditional grants. For several decades before, the experience of many countries had been to see their transfer systems grow into a jungle-like mix of specific purpose grants, many of them too small, costly to administer and often times overlapping in targeted roles with contradictory objectives.

Beyond seeking greater autonomy for subnational governments, other reasons the general trend is avoiding include high administration and monitoring costs and not taking over subnational competencies.

Departing from a similar scenario of a multiplicity of earmarked specific grants, India has experienced in recent years a drastic simplification of federal government specific grant schemes. As previously noted, the 14th FC increased the states' share in the divisible pool of Union tax revenues to the highest level on record of 42 per cent, with general purpose unconditional transfers representing over two-thirds of the total transfers. In addition, there has been a considerable reduction in the number of specific purpose grants, including the CSS from 147 in 2012 to 66 in 2013 (Rao 2017). Further simplification took place in 2014, when a committee of chief ministers of the states appointed by the Union government eliminated the pass-through transfers and reduced the CSS to 28.

But, there is still room for further simplification. There are still 73 Union transfers – 28 CSS plus 45 other Union schemes – competing for funds. With total funding representing less than 2 per cent of GDP, it is hard to see how so many transfers can have a significant impact on final public service outcomes, and especially of services that are the exclusive responsibility of the states. Many of the CSS are still seen as a backdoor for the intervention and micromanagement of states' exclusive responsibilities, overburdening state administrations and diluting their priorities (Mathur and Safdar 2018).[22] A smaller number of Union CSS and other grants should concentrate on service areas that present significant interstate externalities and on service areas that can be considered highly meritorious (Rao 2017).

The international experience offers a rich body of practice that can inform further reforms of the conditional grant system in India.[23]

One of the essences of conditional transfers is that more often than not they become a source of conflict between central and subnational governments because of the different priorities given to particular expenditures. The resolution of that conflict often entails the use of conditional matching grants – as is the case with most CSS in India – which allows central governments to impose their priorities while subnational governments are free to exercise their own budget decisions. Conditional grants – whether block or specific – typically are best implemented (when feasible) on a 'capitation basis' (i.e., per student and per inhabitant), with this basis appropriately modified for costs or needs differences.[24] Using fewer conditions and making those transfers block grants generally has the added advantage of allowing subnational authorities to exercise budgetary autonomy in terms of setting some spending priorities and selecting the most efficient method of service delivery. However, this is not to say that block grants are always a superior instrument compared to specific purpose grants. In fact, there are legitimate central government objectives that can be significantly better pursued by means of specific purpose grants – for example, the vaccination of children to eradicate encephalitis – than by block grants.

In recent years, many countries have transitioned from long lists of earmarked grants to simplify much shorter portfolios of conditional block grants.[25] However, this transition has not been permanent, and in many cases it experienced reversals. One of the reasons for the reversal to specific purpose grants from block grants is associated with the political economy of grant making, in what Borge (2009) calls the 'blame game' between the central and subnational governments in Norway. The former were blamed for providing insufficient funding, while the latter were blamed for the wrong spending priorities and low tax effort. This led central authorities to revert to using specific grants instead of block grants. It has been also the case that the introduction of block grants has been accompanied by an increase in regulations by the central governments.[26] What we have learned is that there are both advantages and disadvantages to using both types of conditional grants, and there is no intrinsic superiority of one type of grant over the other in all relevant dimensions. Administrative capacity at the subnational level, degree of institutional fiscal autonomy and the extent of horizontal accountability can differ considerably across countries. Significant deficiencies in those areas may call for more reliance on specific grants.

Even though specific grants tend to be costlier to administer, less respectful of subnational autonomy, less predictable budget-wise, and more subject to rent seeking and clientelism threats, they may work better where the central government has incomplete information on costs and expenditure need differences. They can also contribute to intergovernmental cooperation and be more conducive to developing more horizontal accountability given the higher visibility of the expenditure-revenue link, and be less prone to soft budget problems and lack of effective cost containment (Smart and Bird 2009; Lotz 2009; Kim 2009b).

Issue 7: India should follow the international practice of using distinctive separate capital grants in support of states' needs to build public capital infrastructure. Because of their 'lumpiness' and non-recurrent nature, the needs for capital infrastructure cannot be adequately taken into account in the recurrent equalization transfer.

The most recent advances in public budget management call for the integration of all expenditure categories in the same budget – that is, not to have a separate capital budget – so that all budget priorities can be compared, and overall efficient decisions can be made on the allocation of scarce fiscal resources. However, when it comes to supporting subnational governments with their capital expenditure needs, it is generally necessary to count on separate instruments. In particular, the international practice is not to mix capital expenditure need support with the equalization transfers – which only consider expenditure needs arising for recurrent obligations and fiscal capacity from recurrent funding. Capital infrastructure investment needs are characterized by their lumpiness and discontinuous nature, features that are very different from those of recurrent expenditure needs. In addition, from the financing potential side, in the case of capital infrastructure it is generally necessary to consider the role that credit and borrowing can play. However, access to credit cannot be easily incorporated in the computation of the fiscal capacity measures typically incorporated in equalization grant formulas.

In India, the 14th FC, following the demise of the Planning Commission in 2014, made the decision to incorporate capital expenditure needs considerations in the general devolution sharing formula. Before that, there had been distinctive and separate capital grants – although with many problematic features – implemented by the Planning Commission, which de facto relegated the role of the FC to only considering the non-plan (or recurrent) expenditure needs of the states (Rao 2017). Going forward, there will be a need to review the options for using separate capital transfer instruments. Should the FC introduce a separate devolution formula for capital transfers that can take into account capital infrastructure needs and borrowing ability of the states? Or, given the temporary nature of the FC, should the responsibility fall on the Union government? Actually, both options are possible and non-exclusive.

The international practice with capital transfers is highly varied (Martinez-Vazquez 2000). In terms of objectives, capital transfers are generally designed to assist subnational governments with financing constraints for lumpy capital, ameliorate significantly different infrastructure endowments across those units, pursue and support central government specific sectoral objectives, and possibly to address externalities across subnational governments. Two major policy biases need to be openly addressed in the design of capital grants: the belief that capital expenditures are always more efficient than recurrent expenditures, and the lack of maintenance of existing subnational government infrastructure. In the latter regard, matching grant arrangements are generally used to help subnational governments to take ownership of capital infrastructure projects.[27]

In terms of design, capital grants vary by the degree of flexibility in the use of the funds. They can either be specific project-based grants, closely monitored by line ministries, and categorical or block grants, which can be designed with strong equalization features and which give much more discretion to subnational governments.

For their allocation, capital grants can be ad hoc, use pre-established formulas, or require competition processes with defined application procedures. No single approach is best in all cases.

Institutionally there has been a significant trend to remove the implementation of capital grants from ministries of planning to integrate them with the rest of the budget process in ministries of finance. This has been an imperative result from the need to coordinate all aspects of budgeting. Despite that trend, countries often retain the vehicle of a PIP (Public Investment Program) but integrated into a medium-term expenditure framework (MTEF) or multi-year budget that covers the entire budget.

Finally, as in the case of most other transfers, incentives matter in the design of capital grants. One of the overriding concerns is to achieve 'additionality' or 'maintenance-of-effort' by subnational governments, usually through matching requirements. In addition, capital grants should not be a substitute for using surplus funds and prudent borrowing policies under the 'golden rule' (borrowed funds can only be used for capital investment).

Issue 8: India could follow the international trend towards further use of performance-based grants and increased accountability of programmes/ schemes.

Performance-based grants have been suggested by some experts and increasingly used in some countries as an alternative to specific earmarked and block conditional grants. In India, the approach was recently suggested by the Ministry of Finance during the consultations of the 14th FC with stakeholders.

In general, 'performance-based grant systems' (PBGS) incentivize improvements in service delivery by linking performance to access, level and discretion in the use of funds.[28] The basic idea is to move away from *ex ante* controls intrinsic to most conditional grants (be specific or block grants) to a system based on performance incentives coupled with *ex post* monitoring and assessments.

PBGS have been used in OECD countries (Australia, Canada, Italy, the UK and the US) and also in some developing countries (Uganda, Philippines, Tanzania, Kenya, Bangladesh and Indonesia). The most delicate design area in PBGS lies in the specification of the performance measures. Socio-economic eligibility criteria is critical to ensure that richer subnational governments – and therefore a priori already better performing – do not capture all the available transfer funds. Performance measures should include only indicators that are under subnational government control and should be employed only for activities that are completely decentralized. This explains that the focus of most PBGS has been on institutional process (such as budgeting or reporting) and on intermediate output indicators, which can be accepted as being controlled by subnational government actions.[29]

Issue 9: India could follow international practice of increasing the effectiveness of conditional transfers by carrying out an in-depth evaluation of the most important CSS.

In some circumstances, conditional grants achieve all they were designed to achieve. In other circumstances, they achieve very little (if anything). But, how do we know? There is wide agreement among experts that all transfer programmes should be subjected to rigorous evaluations.[30] An increasing number of countries have put that into practice. For example, in Australia, the evaluations of transfer programmes, but also of all other federal government spending programmes, have been carried out periodically since the budget management reforms of the 1980s. In the United States, routine evaluations of federal programmes are carried by the Government Accountability Office (GAO). The most important transfer programme in the European Union, the Structural Fund, has been evaluated routinely since the mid-1990s. Some countries, like Sweden, go back many decades with routine evaluations of transfers and other central government spending programmes.

In India, there has been little or no evaluation of CSS. Here it is important to remark that evaluation is quite different from monitoring, since the latter does indeed take place. In the case of monitoring the concern is with compliance with overall conditionalities, schedules, uses of inputs, and meeting financial requirements. In contrast, the nature of evaluation is to focus on comparing the intended objectives and the actual impact on the targeted clientele and whether the desired changes can be observed.

Typically, performing a good evaluation is not an easy task since it is complex to isolate the impact of the transfers from other confounding factors that may also have a bearing on the observed outputs and outcomes. Essentially, the questions to ask are: what would have been the outcome or outputs in the absence of the transfer? Are the observed outcomes cost-effective given the size of the transfers?

Some recent assessments of a few CSS give a powerful hint of the benefits that could be achieved from careful routine evaluation of existing transfer programmes, the CSS in India. The National Health Mission (NHM) is a specific transfer[31] – the largest in India – to the states to provide wide access to health services. Rao's (2017) analysis of this programme finds it wanting in several critical aspects, including lacking a clarity of purpose, a defective distribution formula, and suffering from serious operational issues. In the same vein, Berman et al. (2017) report that the NHM has largely failed to achieve greater equity/convergence between states or an increase in health spending.

The Universal Elementary Education Program or Sarva Shksha Abhiyan (SSA) is a matching grant to the states with the goal of ensuring access to elementary education in the whole country.[32]

The programme is actually implemented through 42 different interventions (access, retention, gender, some tuition reimbursement to private schools, infrastructure and so on). Rao (2017) identifies a long list of issues with this transfer including poor identification of minimum standards, a focus on physical inputs, or lack of equalization of expenditure per pupil with untrained teachers, absenteeism and lack of learning materials in poorer states.

Finally, the Mahatma Gandhi National Rural Employment Guarantee (MGNREGA) is a conditional transfer for income support by providing 100 days of guaranteed employment each year for an adult member of every household that enrols in the programme and operates in all Indian states since 2008. The essence of the programme is to mitigate rural poverty. But as Rao (2017) points out, the states with higher concentrations of poverty do not receive higher transfers: transfer disbursements as recently as 2014–15 were highly negatively correlated with the states' rural poverty ratio.

In India, currently, there is no institutionalized form of evaluation and no formal evaluation policy for schemes and projects. And yet an August 2016 ministerial order mandated appraisal of all schemes (both new and ongoing) and independent evaluation of all schemes for onboarding to the next funding cycle. Going forward, the international practice offers several lessons: the need for a general policy that regulates the evaluation activity and sets standards, the preservation of transparency and independence in the evaluation process, and the existence of a formal evaluation agenda. The new Development Monitoring and Evaluation Office (DMEO) in NITI Aayog could perhaps be expanded to become the main focal point for the evaluation function of all transfers in India, including all CSS.

14.3   CONCLUSION

From a broad reflection on international experience and the specific Indian political and institutional context, the following policy messages emerge from the chapter: (i) address vertical imbalance through increased revenue sources; (ii) define a medium-term period in the law for the divisible pool for greater predictability in states' finances and harden states' budget constraint; (iii) separate transfer instruments to distinguish between devolution and redistribution objectives in the implementation of tax sharing with state governments; (iv) transition from the obsolete multivariable weighted index methodology to a distribution formula based on the '*fiscal gap'* methodology. If the fiscal gap methodology is not adopted, the country could refine the index formula approach to better capture fiscal needs and capacity; (v) further consolidate conditional grants to reduce fragmentation and move towards block grants; (vi) use distinct capital grants or transfers to support states' public capital infrastructure needs; (vii) expand use of performance-based grants and increase accountability of programmes/schemes; (viii) carry out an in-depth evaluation of the most important CSS in order to increase the effectiveness of conditional transfers.

NOTES

*   I am grateful to Pedro Arizti, Aurelien Kruse and Farah Zahir for comments, and to Krishanu Karmakar and Indira Rajaraman for useful insights.

1.   See Rao (2017) and Forum of Free Enterprise (2018).
2.   The 6 per cent Central GST is further devolved to states as part of their overall share of 42 per cent of central tax revenues in the divisible pool. In addition, there is a further 5-year guarantee of a top-up by the Union government to ensure state revenues increase by 14 per cent.
3.   A potential problem with concurrent tax bases is the presence of vertical externalities.
4.   See, for example, Sivagnanam and Naganathan (2000). Of course, this is a totally different issue from what the actual sharing rate should be.
5.   Rajaraman (2017) concludes that there has been stability and predictability of Union transfers over a long period of time. In the international practice, predictability is increased by using a 1- or 2-year lag for defining the pool of funds.
6.   This has been offset at times by decreases in other Union transfers, as with the 14th FC (Rajaraman 2017). See details in Chapter 13.
7.   Chelliah (1981), Rao (1981), and Sivagnanam and Naganathan (2000).
8.   As noted in Chapter 13, currently, the divisible pool still excludes cess and surcharges because those funds are already committed to specific expenditure needs of the Union government. States have continued to complain about that since cess revenues have practically doubled in the last 15 years, representing now close to 15 per cent of all Union revenues.
9.   See, for example, Rangarajan and Srivastava (2018) and Rao (2017).
10. As presented by Rao (2017), in 2014–15, an increase of 1 per cent in the state per capita income represented an increase of 0.65 per cent in total expenditures per capita.
11. The Finance Commission makes other transfers including the 'revenue deficit grants', grants to local bodies, grants for disaster management, sector-specific grants and state-specific grants. Despite its rather misleading name – making it sound like a gap filling grant between actual expenditure and revenues – the most relevant to equalization is the revenue deficit grant, which is a top-up transfer redistribution for states that show significant differences between estimated (normed) expenditure and revenue projections.
12. There is also an element of bargaining since the FC solicits from the states their projected revenues and expenditure needs.
13. Other variables used by former Finance Commissions reflected population composition, infrastructure, tax effort and fiscal discipline (Rao 2017).
14. We also need to add that the 14th FC in so doing was reacting to its TOR which require addressing environmental concerns in the devolution formula.
15. This may impact higher income states. For example, Kerala would appear to have higher health expenditure needs due to its ageing population.

16. See Martinez-Vazquez and Boex (2006).
17. Only the responsibility for audit is split between centre and the states, and states may not vigorously pursue audit because they have ensured their revenue will increase at least 14 per cent year on year for the next 5 years.
18. The list of other taxes includes state excise duties, stamp duty and registration fee, motor vehicle tax, goods and passenger tax and other minor taxes. There are in addition own non-tax revenues that should also be accounted for.
19. See Martinez-Vazquez and Boex (2006) for the different methodologies that can be used.
20. Although the methodology of 'fiscal capacity to adjusted population' would certainly be new to India, a similar approach was used by the 14th FC to adjust states' expenditure projections for their fiscal capacity.
21. Note that in Germany, Poland and Spain, the states with ratios above the average are forced to contribute, in a progressive manner, depending on how far they are above the average, to the pool of equalization funds distributed to the poorer units.
22. Some of the reasons states have been against the extensive use of CSS should have an easier fix. Many CSS are actually introduced quite far in the budget year creating distortions and uncertainties in budget execution. Clearly, improvements in federal budgeting actual procedures are needed.
23. Internationally, there is some terminology confusion regarding block grants because different countries use the same terminology for quite different types of grants. See Bahl (2009).
24. In particular, using existing capacity as the basis of the grants should be avoided so not to penalize jurisdictions with less adequate physical facilities.
25. However, the strength of this trend may be easily exaggerated. A survey of Sweden, United Kingdom, Italy and the United States finds that that there is almost no common feature or pattern in the choice between general block grants and earmarked specific grants (Kim 2009b). See also Blom-Hansen (2009), Hermansson (2009) and Blöchliger and Vammalle (2009).
26. See, for example, Blom-Hansen (2009) for the case of Denmark and Brosio and Piperno (2009) for Italy.
27. Matching arrangements may require adjustments for the fiscal capacity of subnational governments.
28. See, for example, Steffensen (2010) for a description of PBGS.
29. There can be political economy factors associated with the application of PBGS (Shah 2009).
30. For further discussion on PBGS, see, for example, Blomquist (2003) and Ezemanari et al. (1999).
31. Contributing 60 per cent in the case of general category states and 90 per cent in the case of special category states.
32. The matching rate is 60 per cent for general category states and 90 per cent for the special category states.

REFERENCES

Aiyar, Yamini and Avani Kapurb. 2018. 'The centralization vs decentralization tug of war and the emerging narrative of fiscal federalism for social policy in India', *Regional and Federal Studies*. https://doi.org/10.1080/13597566.2018.1511978.
Bahl, Roy. 2009. 'Conditional vs. unconditional grants: The case of developing countries' in *General Grants versus Earmarked Grants Theory and Practice: The Copenhagen Workshop 2009*. Junghun Kim, Jørgen Lotz and Niels Jørgen Mau (editors). Albertslund: Korea Institute of Public Finance and Danish Ministry of Interior and Health, pp. 126–48.

Berman, Peter, Manjiri Bhawalkar and Rajesh Jha. 2017. 'Government financing of health care in India since 2005: What was achieved, what was not, and why?' A Report of the Resource Tracking and Management Project Harvard T.H. Chan School of Public Health, Boston, MA.

Bhaskar, V. 2018. 'Challenges before the Fifteenth Finance Commission', *Economic and Political Weekly*, 10 March.

Blöchliger, Hansjörg and Camila Vammalle. 2009. 'Intergovernmental grants in OECD countries: Trends and some policy issues' in *General Grants versus Earmarked Grants Theory and Practice: The Copenhagen Workshop 2009*. Junghun Kim, Jørgen Lotz and Niels Jørgen Mau (editors). Albertslund: Korea Institute of Public Finance and Danish Ministry of Interior and Health, pp. 167–90.

Blom-Hansen, Jens. 2009. 'The fiscal federalism theory of grants: Some reflections from political science' in *General Grants versus Earmarked Grants Theory and Practice: The Copenhagen Workshop 2009*. Junghun Kim, Jørgen Lotz and Niels Jørgen Mau (editors). Albertslund: Korea Institute of Public Finance and Danish Ministry of Interior and Health, pp. 107–25.

Blomquist, John. 2003. 'Impact evaluation of social programs: A policy perspective'. Revised draft. September.

Borge, Lars-Erik and Grete Lilleschulstad. 2009. 'General grants and earmarked grants in Norway' in *General Grants versus Earmarked Grants Theory and Practice: The Copenhagen Workshop 2009*. Junghun Kim, Jørgen Lotz and Niels Jørgen Mau (editors). Albertslund: Korea Institute of Public Finance and Danish Ministry of Interior and Health, pp. 191–217.

Brosio, Giorgio and Stefano Piperno. 2009. 'Conditional intergovernmental transfers in Italy after the constitutional reform of 2001' in *General Grants versus Earmarked Grants Theory and Practice: The Copenhagen Workshop 2009*. Junghun Kim, Jørgen Lotz and Niels Jørgen Mau (editors). Albertslund: Korea Institute of Public Finance and Danish Ministry of Interior and Health, pp. 218 38.

Chelliah, R.J. 1981. *Trends and Issues in Indian Federal Finance*. New Delhi: Allied Publishers.

Ezemanari, Kene, A. Rudqvist, K. Subbarao. 1999. 'Impact evaluation: A note on concepts and methods'. Mimeo, Poverty Reduction and Economic Management Network. World Bank (January).

Forum of Free Enterprise. 2018. '15th Finance Commission', Newsletter (with contributions by Indira Rajaraman; Abhay Pethe; and C. Rangarajan and D.K. Srivastava), Delhi.

Fourteenth Finance Commission Report. Ministry of Finance. 2015. *Report of the Fourteenth Finance Commission*. New Delhi: Government of India.

Garg, S., A. Goyal and R. Pal. 2014. 'Why tax effort falls short of capacity in Indian states: A stochastic frontier approach'. IGIDR Working Paper WP-2014-032. IGIDR, Mumbai.

Hermansson, Andreas. 2009. 'Specific and general grants in Sweden: What has happened after the grant reform in the 1990s?' in *General Grants versus Earmarked Grants Theory and Practice: The Copenhagen Workshop 2009*. Junghun Kim, Jørgen Lotz and Niels Jørgen Mau (editors). Albertslund: Korea Institute of Public Finance and Danish Ministry of Interior and Health, pp. 239–62.

Jha, R., M.S. Mohanty, S. Chatterjee and P. Chitkara. 1999. 'Tax efficiency in selected Indian states', *Empirical Economics*, **24** (4), 641–54.

Kim, Junghun. 2009a. 'Introduction' in *General Grants versus Earmarked Grants Theory and Practice: The Copenhagen Workshop 2009*. Junghun Kim, Jørgen

Lotz and Niels Jørgen Mau (editors). Albertslund: Korea Institute of Public Finance and Danish Ministry of Interior and Health, pp. 13–39.

Kim, Junghun. 2009b. 'General grants vs. earmarked grants: Does practice meet theory?' in *General Grants versus Earmarked Grants Theory and Practice: The Copenhagen Workshop 2009*. Junghun Kim, Jørgen Lotz and Niels Jørgen Mau (editors). Albertslund: Korea Institute of Public Finance and Danish Ministry of Interior and Health, pp. 149–66.

Lotz, Jorgen. 2009. 'Member states' practices for the funding of new competences of local authorities'. Unpublished manuscript. European Committee on Local and Regional Democracy, Council of Europe.

Martinez-Vazquez, Jorge. 2000, 'An introduction to international practices and best principles in the design of capital transfers'. Mimeo. Georgia State University, Atlanta.

Martinez-Vazquez, Jorge and Jamie Boex. 2006. 'Designing intergovernmental equalization transfers with imperfect data: Concepts, practices, and lessons' in *The Challenges in the Design of Fiscal Equalization and Intergovernmental Transfers*. Jorge Martinez-Vazquez and Robert Searle (editors). New York: Springer Verlag, pp. 291–344.

Mathur, Om Prakash and Midhat Fatima Safdar. 2018. 'Reforming vertical programmes: The case of India'. Mimeo: Centre for Urban Studies, Institute of Social Sciences New Delhi (June).

Mukherjee, S. 2017. 'Changing tax capacity and tax effort of Indian states in the era of high economic growth: 2001–2014'. NIPFP Working Paper No. 196. NIPFP, New Delhi.

Rajaraman, Indira. 2017. 'Continuity and change in Indian fiscal federalism', *India Review*, **16** (1), 66–84. DOI: 10.1080/14736489.2017.1279927.

Rao, H. 1981. *Centre-State Financial Relations*. New Delhi: Allied Publishers.

Rao, M. Govinda. 2017. 'The effect of intergovernmental transfers on public services in India'. NIPFP Working Paper No. 218. NIPFP, New Delhi.

Shah, Anwar. 2009. 'Autonomy with accountability: The case for performance oriented grants' in *General Grants versus Earmarked Grants Theory and Practice: The Copenhagen Workshop 2009*. Junghun Kim, Jørgen Lotz and Niels Jørgen Mau (editors). Albertslund: Korea Institute of Public Finance and Danish Ministry of Interior and Health, pp. 74–106.

Sivagnanam, K.J. and M. Naganathan. (2000). 'Federal Transfers and Tax Efforts of the States of India', *Indian Economic Journal*, **47** (4), 101–10.

Smart, Michael and Richard Bird. 2009. 'Earmarked grants and accountability in government' in *General Grants versus Earmarked Grants Theory and Practice: The Copenhagen Workshop 2009*. Junghun Kim, Jørgen Lotz and Niels Jørgen Mau (editors). Albertslund: Korea Institute of Public Finance and Danish Ministry of Interior and Health, pp. 40–73.

Steffensen, Jesper. 2010. 'Performance-based grant systems: concept and international experience'. Mimeo. United Nations Capital Development Fund, New York.

PART IV

Intergovernmental Transfers in Unitary
Federations

15. Intergovernmental fiscal transfers in Kenya: the evolution of revenue sharing under new devolution in a quasi-federal system

Jamie Boex and Paul Smoke

15.1 INTRODUCTION

Kenya has a long and diverse history of local governance, both traditional forms used by its varied ethnic groups and the British structures set up during the colonial period.[1] The formal local government system was originally designed to serve the interests of British settlers, but the jurisdictions were relatively autonomous and well resourced. The basic system was maintained when Kenya gained independence in 1963. Deconcentrated administration that reported to the national government was also set up during the colonial period and played an important role in managing national policies and resources.

From early independence negotiations, there were debates about how to organize the public sector in the ethnically fragmented country. Some groups – particularly ethnic minorities who feared domination and marginalization – desired a federal ('Majimbo' in Swahili) state rooted in (ethnically identified) regions. Others – led by the largest ethnic group – promoted a centralized unitary system framed as better serving nation building. A fleeting victory for Majimboism at independence led to the creation of a federal system in the 1963 constitution, but it was soon displaced by centralist forces who took power in the first national election. Kenya became a unitary state under the 1969 constitutional reform.

Post-independence local governments were gradually weakened under the banner of promoting 'national unity', while the deconcentrated system of provincial and district administration increasingly played a larger role in managing public functions. Kenyan local governments, however, continued to be governed by elected councils with devolved (if limited) responsibility for local revenues and services, with only very limited intergovernmental fiscal transfers being provided for decades after independence. When the economy began to experience challenges at a number of points in the 1980s and 1990s and concerns about inequities intensified, broad dissatisfaction with all levels of government gradually emerged. This resurfaced some of the governance controversies and ethnic rivalries of the independence period, and severe violence broke out during the 2007 elections. Attempts to deal with the aftermath of this violence and its underlying causes generated momentum to rethink national governance. After a few years of debates and public consultations, a new constitution was adopted by popular referendum in 2010. One of its major provisions was a fundamental restructuring of the intergovernmental system, with significant devolution to a single tier of subnational government at the county level that essentially replaced the previous variety of subnational entities.

This chapter describes and assesses the intergovernmental transfer system adopted under the 2010 constitution. The next section provides a brief history of subnational government and intergovernmental fiscal relations prior to 2010 to help explain the motivations behind the new system and the context in which it is being built. The third section outlines the new county government system prescribed in the 2010 constitution and offers a sense of its implementation to date, both accomplishments and challenges. The fourth section explains the main unconditional transfer – the equitable sharing of national revenues – and reviews its history, what is known about its effects, its positive features and potentially desirable reforms. This is followed by a review of the legal basis and role of conditional transfers, their use to date and ideas about improving them. We conclude by offering suggestions for priority reforms and a brief assessment of political economy realities that may provide opportunities for and impose constraints on further reform.

15.2   A BRIEF HISTORY OF INTERGOVERNMENTAL FISCAL RELATIONS IN KENYA

Kenya's intergovernmental system prior to the new constitution was a problematic mix of entities, levels and systems with poorly defined and/ or poorly respected roles and responsibilities.[2] A provincial/district system that reported to the Office of the President (de-concentration) existed in parallel with the semi-independent system of elected local governments (devolution) under the oversight of the Ministry of Local Government (MOLG). In this dual system, the deconcentrated provincial/district system was the main mechanism for public service delivery, while the role of local governments was narrower in scope, focusing primarily on the management of local affairs.

The set of subnational jurisdictions was relatively stable for years, with 112 single-tier elected local (municipal, town, urban and county) councils and a deconcentrated administration that consisted of 8 provinces and 39 districts (geographically identical to the 39 county councils) in 1990. Later in the 1990s, a large number of new districts and local governments – many of them non-viable as service providers – were created (through uncoordinated mechanisms that led to different numbers of districts and county councils) to meet political objectives without systematic analysis or the adoption of measures to ensure that they could deliver on their responsibilities.

Immediately prior to the current system adopted in 2010, there were 175 single-tier elected local councils, including 67 county councils; 62 town councils; 43 municipal councils; and 3 city councils. Despite their legal empowerment and long history, many local governments inadequately responded to the needs and priorities of a growing and more educated citizenry. Central government officials typically attributed weak performance to local government incapacity and corruption but seemed incapable or disinclined to turn the situation around. Local government officials often claimed they were impeded by undue central regulation and interference, usurpation of their roles by provincial/district administration and limited funding. Citizens, of course, bore the consequences of this intergovernmental stalemate, but challenging political realities hindered their ability to generate meaningful change.

Despite recommendations by a national commission and an official sessional paper calling for local governments to be strengthened soon after independence, centralizing political dynamics in the 1970s and 1980s contributed to hastening their decline. The power consolidation that began after Kenya's independence was intensified by a public sector restructuring initiated in response to a 1982 coup attempt.[3] Over time, deteriorating local public services – although substantially a function of national policies and outright neglect – bolstered the central government's portrayal of local governments as problematic entities requiring central control instead of key developmental actors meriting financial and technical support. Many citizens must have questioned the benefits of voting in local government elections and paying local taxes given what they received in return.

The Post-Independence Intergovernmental System and Its Challenges

The relative fiscal importance of local governments before the 2010 devolution reforms was modest, generally accounting for less than 6 per cent of total public expenditures and less than 5 per cent of total public revenues (deconcentrated provincial and district administrations were incorporated under the national budget). Local governments had (primarily permissive rather than mandatory) legal authority for a number of public services, including local roads, water schemes, sanitation services, and pre-primary education, among others. They also provided other services important for local economic development, such as markets, slaughter houses, livestock auction yards and bus parks. The original colonial-era municipalities had enhanced functions, including health services, which were elsewhere managed by the deconcentrated administration. Exact functions in practice depended on a mix of national decisions, local capacity and resources, and rural versus urban location, among other factors, and delivery of some devolved functions, such as roads and water, was later reorganized in ways that bypassed or limited the local government role.

On the revenue side, Kenyan local governments relied heavily on property rates, and from the late 1980s the local authority service charge (LASC), a complex and unpopular own source revenue (the only new local revenue source created after independence) that was later abolished. Local governments also had access to various local fees, licences and a range of other mostly modest revenues that varied in importance across highly diverse jurisdictions.

Also consequential for local government fiscal performance was the development planning and financial management system. Kenya had a bifurcated system of subnational planning and budgeting that reflected the dichotomy between the deconcentrated provincial-district system and the semi-autonomous elected local authority system.[4] Territorial spatial land-use plans were produced on an ad hoc basis by the central government. At all levels, there was only a weak linkage of development plans to the annual budgeting process (the national budget for provinces and districts, and the local budgets for local government councils) and local accountability.

Evolving Realities and Local Government Reforms

Although there had been previous efforts to strengthen local governments, changing global and domestic conditions in the 1990s opened opportunities for stronger reform. These efforts were largely pursued under the broad-based Kenya Local Government Reform Program (KLGRP) supported by multiple donors over a long period.[5] KLGRP's most notable achievements were with intergovernmental fiscal reforms, which started in the late 1990s with steps to harmonize problematic central and local revenues.[6] In 2000, the productive but administratively difficult and politically unpopular LASC was replaced by the Local Authority Transfer Fund (LATF), the first transfer created since Kenya largely abolished transfers during post-colonial recentralization.[7] Despite these fiscal reforms to strengthen local governments, the problematic planning system outlined above received scant attention.

The pre-2010-constitutional reforms were particularly deficient with respect to citizen engagement in an environment where basic governance was clearly at the core of government performance problems. Participatory mechanisms were weak, and civil society's ability to drive more meaningful participation from below was hampered by central regulation and political apathy. Some promising improvements were adopted, but their use was uneven and results poorly documented.[8]

Further complicating the public service delivery challenges created by the provincial-district and local government systems, the Kenyan Parliament created a Constituency Development Fund (CDF) in 2003 to fight poverty by providing allocations to parliamentarians to serve their electoral districts.[9] The CDF further confused the accountability channels open to Kenyan citizens. In national budgets around the time the new constitution was passed, an increasing proportion of resources for other programmes was also being allocated on a constituency basis.[10]

Summary of the Post-Independence Evolution of Local Administration and Local Government

Since independence, there have been many efforts targeted at improving local government fiscal and service-delivery performance in Kenya. Some were genuine, while others were likely cosmetic or largely undertaken to secure donor funding. Underlying institutional complexities and political dynamics, however, did not favour successful and sustainable local government empowerment. A core challenge was the deliberate weakening of the local government system and the assumption of responsibility for delivering major public services by an increasingly unresponsive and politicized central government. The post-2007 election violence generated new and urgent interest in redressing historical inequities and more genuine local governance, but through a systemic restructuring of the public sector rather than in ways that tried to fix existing local institutions. Accordingly, the 2010 constitution included provisions for a devolution that differs considerably from the previous local government system.

15.3 DEVOLUTION AND THE 2010 CONSTITUTION: INSTITUTIONAL STRUCTURES, FUNCTIONS, OWN SOURCE REVENUES AND INTERGOVERNMENTAL TRANSFERS

Compared to the previous centralized system, Kenya's 2010 constitution introduced far-reaching changes to the way that government operates and relates to its citizens, with the goal to make the public sector more fair, efficient, transparent and accountable.[11] The previous system was a hybrid between a presidential and a parliamentary system (with cabinet positions filled by Members of Parliament), while the new system is presidential, creating some space between the legislature and the executive (the national departments of which were seen as having dominated parliamentary decisions). The intergovernmental system was also dramatically restructured. Whereas under the previous system the central government provided many public services, the 2010 constitution established 47 county governments to play a lead role in service delivery.

These new county governments replaced the disjointed system of deconcentrated and devolved jurisdictions that had dominated for decades, including both the provincial and district administration and the independent urban and other local government authorities that had existed since the colonial period. Although this dramatic consolidation of subnational government and administration dealt with many of the planning, budgeting, financing and service-delivery fragmentation challenges outlined above, a number of concerns about this organization structure were also highlighted during debates on the new constitution.

Kenya's path towards a devolved public sector with a single subnational tier was informed by a combination of governance objectives (e.g. local self-governance and popular participation in the exercise of the powers of the state) as well as developmental objectives (e.g. service delivery and social and economic development). Underlying these objectives, however, was a deep-seated mistrust of an unresponsive central government (and its deconcentrated agents) detached from local needs/priorities and a broadly shared perception that historical inequities in government attention to some regions urgently needed to be redressed. The depth of these sentiments created an opportunity to push for a more independent and well-resourced system of local government than the one that had existed since independence. These forces and inclinations in some ways resurrected the concerns of the federalist factions that were prominent during the independence negotiations.

The structure of the new county governments mirrors that of the national level, with full separation of the executive and legislature in a presidential system. County governors are directly elected by simple county majority and are expected to nominate a cabinet from outside the county assembly. The county assemblies are comprised predominantly of representatives from single member constituencies, with some additional members representing women and marginalized groups selected from party lists. There are strong provisions in the constitution to ensure an important role for civic engagement.

The devolved governance framework was effectively operationalized by the election of county governors and county assemblies in March 2013. Since then, county governments have been working to take on the important political, administration and fiscal powers assigned to them in the constitution and have started providing essential public services. As the government level closest to the people, the introduction of county governments has fundamentally reshaped the public sector and the relationship between people and the public sector in Kenya.

Assignment of Functional Responsibilities

Similar to many other federal and quasi-federal constitutions, Kenya's constitution (in the Fourth Schedule) provides for the distribution of functions and powers between national and the county governments. The following functions and powers are assigned to the county governments:

a.   Agriculture;
b.   County health services (including county health facilities, as well as functions such as cemeteries and solid waste management);
c.   Control of air pollution, noise pollution, other public nuisances and outdoor advertising;
d.   Cultural activities, public entertainment and public amenities;
e.   County transport, including county roads;
f.   Animal control and welfare;
g.   Trade development and regulation;
h.   County planning and development;
i.   Pre-primary education, village polytechnics, homecraft centres and childcare facilities;
j.   Implementation of specific national government policies on natural resources and environmental conservation;
k.   County public works and services (including water and sanitation services);
l.   Fire-fighting services and disaster management;
m.   Control of drugs and pornography;
n.   Ensuring and coordinating the participation of communities in governance at the local level.

Although the Public Financial Management Act (PFM Act 2012) requires counties to follow prudent financial management practices and requires them to spend at least 30 per cent of their budget on development expenditures, county governments are otherwise free to plan and budget their resources across different functional responsibilities in accordance with county priorities.

The constitution (in Article 186(2)) recognizes the existence of concurrent functions and specifies that national legislation prevails in areas of concurrent jurisdiction when there is a conflict between national and county legislation (Article 191). However, unlike in some countries, the constitution does not enumerate the specific powers and functions that are concurrent or how the funding or delivery of concurrent functions ought to differ from exclusive county functions.

Upon the first round of county elections in March 2013, county governors moved quickly to establish control over administration in their respective counties, including all aspects of service delivery within their mandated functions (facilities, staff and funding).[12] Although some national ministries have successfully retained resources for activities that *de jure* fall under county responsibility, governors – individually, and collectively through the Council of Governors – have advocated consistently to assume their legal powers. The challenges involved in forming a consolidated county government have been considerable since new counties absorbed functions, assets, resources and staff from multiple former jurisdictions within their boundaries. These represented a mix of deconcentrated and devolved entities, which, as explained above, used different systems, further complicating the transition process.

For the most recent completed financial year (FY 2017/18), total county government expenditures amounted to KShs. 303.8 billion, comprising KShs. 236.9 billion for recurrent expenditure and KShs. 66.9 billion for development expenditure (OCOB 2018a: xv).[13] County expenditures, however, reflect only approximately 12 per cent of total government spending (OCOB 2018b: x).

Own Source Revenues

By design, Kenya's devolution involves a large disparity between the aggregate county expenditure responsibilities and own source revenue assignment. While substantial public sector functions are assigned to counties, they are, under Article 209(3) of the constitution, only assigned revenue authority over property rates, entertainment taxes, and any other tax authorized by an Act of Parliament.[14] These are essentially the sources assigned to the local level under the previous local government system, suggesting that increasing the independent revenue powers of the new county governments was not an initial priority. Greater revenue autonomy would have empowered county governments further (and arguably stimulated county revenue mobilization efforts). Addressing historical geographic and ethnic inequities, however, was a driving force behind the new constitution, and there may have been concerns that greater revenue decentralization could have made equalization more difficult to achieve.

During the most recent financial year (FY 2017/18), the aggregate revenue raised by county governments amounted to KShs. 32.5 billion. Given the size of other county funding sources (including intergovernmental fiscal transfers), own source revenues only account for slightly more than 8 per cent of total county revenues (OCOB 2018a: xv).

Structure of Intergovernmental Fiscal Transfer System

The third pillar of any fiscal decentralization reform or any system of intergovernmental finance is the provision of intergovernmental fiscal transfers, the main focus of this volume. As in other countries, transfers are needed to fill the gap between the extensive expenditure responsibilities of county governments in Kenya and the limited own revenue sources assigned to them.

Guided by the constitution (Article 202), the backbone of Kenya's intergovernmental fiscal transfer system is formed by a large, unconditional grant scheme – known as equitable sharing. The constitution (Article 218) further lays out the process through which the 'Division on Revenue' (both between government levels and among county governments) is determined annually. As discussed in greater detail below, the equitable sharing of national revenue accounts for close to 92 per cent of transfers to counties, while conditional grants account for slightly more than 8 per cent.[15]

Although the constitution places a lower bound on the size of the vertical sharing of sharable national revenues (at 15 per cent of national revenues), it does not require this channel to dominate total transfers.[16] In operationalizing the constitution, however, a vigorous debate on how to share resources eventually resulted in a decision that the cost of devolved public services – such as health services, agriculture extension services, and so on – should be funded as part of the equitable revenue sharing mechanism rather than through conditional (sectoral) grants (CRA 2012).

Intergovernmental Fiscal Arrangements

The Kenya Commission on Revenue Allocation (CRA) is constitutionally mandated to make recommendations concerning the equitable sharing of revenue raised by the national government between national and county governments and among counties. Parliament, however, has the final word in determining the vertical sharing and horizontal allocation formula. In turn, detailed intergovernmental transfer allocations (for equitable sharing, as well as for conditional grants) are determined by the CRA and National Treasury as part of the annual Division of Revenue Act (DORA), which precedes the preparation of the national budget.[17] In this sense, there are close parallels between the Kenyan transfer system and the South African intergovernmental fiscal transfer system (discussed further in Chapter 16 of this volume).

The constitution also established the Office of the Controller of Budget (OCOB) in order to oversee and report on implementation of budgets of both the national and county governments. Among its other responsibilities, the OCOB approves the transfer of funds from the national Consolidated Fund to the various County Revenue Funds (CRFs) in line with the DORA, ensuring the regular and timely disbursement of funds by the National Treasury. The OCOB further prepares quarterly budget implementation review reports at the national as well as county levels, thereby providing improved transparency and accountability of public sector finances vis-à-vis the prior centralized system.

Summary of Current Situation

Five years into the devolution process under the new quasi-federal constitution, Kenya's path towards devolution has largely been an initial 'political' success: county governments were established, they prepare annual plans and budgets, control their own public servants and operate service-delivery facilities. The central dominance over political power has been reduced, and a more politically competitive political system was introduced. Power and resources are generally perceived to be more equitably distributed across Kenya under the new system, both geographically as well as across the country's main ethnic groups. Public support for the new devolved system appears to be strong, as county governors and assemblies – being closer to the people – are widely perceived to have legitimate power and authority (e.g. IPSOS 2016). The extent to which devolution has led to more accountable governance and improved service delivery, however, is far less self-evident and much less well broadly documented.[18] As such, perhaps the most important challenge facing the intergovernmental fiscal transfer system in Kenya is the need to ensure that fiscal devolution achieves improved service-delivery outcomes and responsiveness to citizens.

15.4 EQUITABLE SHARING OF NATIONAL REVENUES[19]

As noted above, the equitable share of national revenue provided to county governments is their most important source of revenue. The constitution is clear about the general basis of this transfer, but with the exception of the minimum threshold of 15 per cent, considerable scope is given to the central government – through the CRA, Parliament and National Treasury – for determining the vertical and horizontal allocation of national funds.

Constitutional and Legal Context of Equitable Sharing of Revenues

Article 202 of the Kenyan constitution states that revenue raised nationally should be shared equitably among the national and county governments. Article 203 indicates that the equitable (vertical and horizontal) distribution of these revenues shall take account of the following factors:

a. The national interest;
b. Any provision that must be made in respect of the public debt and other national obligations;
c. The needs of the national government determined by objective criteria;
d. The need to ensure that county governments are able to perform functions allocated to them;
e. The fiscal capacity and efficiency of county governments;
f. Developmental and other needs of counties;
g. Economic disparities within and among counties and the need to remedy them;
h. The need for affirmative action in respect of disadvantaged areas and groups;
i. The need for economic optimization of each county and to provide incentives for each county to optimize its capacity to raise revenue;
j. The desirability of stable and predictable allocations of revenue; and
k. The need for flexibility to respond to emergencies/temporary needs using objective criteria.

The Vertical Allocation of the Equitable Share

In line with the constitutional guidance that the distribution of resources should take into account 'the need to ensure that county governments are able to perform the functions allocated to them', the CRA has traditionally drawn a strong link between the expenditure needs of county governments

Table 15.1   Financing of county government functions (in KShs. million)

Devolved Functions	Actual 2016/17	Actual 2017/18	Recommend 2018/19
Health Services	76,677	89,131	95,846
Planning and Development	57,661	54,694	58,815
Agriculture, Livestock and Fisheries	21,881	26,452	28,445
Culture, Public Entertainment and Public Amenities	3,351	3,272	3,519
Youth Affairs and Sports	4,848	6,481	8,969
Trade, Cooperative Development and Regulation	4,855	6,096	6,555
Roads and Transport	44,256	49,596	59,677
Lands, Housing and Public Works	6,316	6,754	7,263
Water, Natural Resources and Environmental Cons.	7,937	8,119	8,731
Pre-Primary Education	2,605	4,241	4,560
Subtotal devolved functions	*230,387*	*254,836*	*282,380*
New County Structures	49,913	47,164	54,783
Total equitable share	*280,300*	*302,000*	*337,163*

Source: CRA (2017: Table 7).

(based on their constitutional mandates) and the vertical distribution of nationally collected resources.

The Commission's recommended vertical allocation of nationally raised revenue to the county level for FY 2012/13 (the first full year of devolution) included (a) the estimated cost of county administration; (b) National Treasury's estimate of the cost of current devolved functions; and (c) a contingency allocation of 10 per cent (CRA 2012: 18). The recommended vertical allocation of resources regarding the counties' collective equitable share in subsequent years has continued to be based on the estimated cost of county-level administration and service provision (Table 15.1).

The Horizontal Allocation of the Equitable Share

In line with its constitutional and legal mandate, the CRA has prepared over the last six financial years two bases that have guided the sharing of revenues among the 47 county governments from 2013 forward. A summary of these two horizontal allocation formulas is provided in Table 15.2. Although there are slight differences between the formulas that were applied, the variations in the horizontal distribution were quite minor.

Table 15.2   The horizontal allocation of the counties' equitable share: first and second basis

Parameter	First Basis % Weights FY 2013/14–2015/16	Second Basis % Weights FY 2016/17–2018/19
Population	45	45
Equal Share	25	26
Poverty	20	18
Land Area	8	8
Fiscal Effort	2	2
Development Factor*		1

Note: * The county development factor is based on access to economic infrastructure, including road access, and the per cent of households with access to electricity and improved water sources.

Source: CRA (2017: Table 10).

The rationale behind the mix of factors included in the allocation formulas or horizontal 'bases' for equitable sharing was transparently documented by the CRA (CRA 2012; 2014). In contrast to the vertical allocation of the counties' equitable share, the horizontal allocation is only (very) loosely driven by the functions and expenditure responsibilities assigned to the county level. Although the formula provides a small window (2 per cent) to stimulate revenue performance, it does not include any measures of county budget performance or service-delivery performance. In fact, the horizontal allocation formula almost completely loses the link between the allocation of funds and the functional responsibilities of counties.

Although there was considerable discussion of the importance of this link and debate about if and how to incorporate it, the data required to operationalize a more 'functional' allocation formula did not exist. In addition, there were further challenges created by the fact that the new counties were an amalgamation of a set of subnational jurisdictions that were managed under the different planning and budgeting systems outlined earlier.

The relative simplicity of the first and second bases was not necessarily merely a technical matter. As Kenya began to implement the 2010 constitution, there were serious concerns raised by some who sought to ensure a more federal-like public sector structure (hailing back to the period of Majimboism in the 1963 constitution) that a more detailed, functionally linked allocation formula could serve as a pretext for the national government to continue the top-down micromanagement and control entrenched in the system since independence. Instead of a technically precise formula, their priority was to protect counties from central capture, as well as to ensure that historical injustices were redressed by shifting public finances away from regions (and ethnic groups) that had been advantaged since British times, in favour of areas/groups that had been historically disadvantaged.

The current (so-called 'second basis') allocation formula does not result in the same – or *equal* – per capita allocations to all counties. This is consistent with the constitutional (policy) objective of achieving an *equitable* (rather than equal) per capita allocation across counties. Some counties are expected to have greater needs (per resident) and therefore should receive a greater per capita allocation, while other counties are expected to have lower needs (or greater revenue capacity) and therefore should receive a smaller per capita allocation.

During the first five years of devolution in Kenya, an important consideration driving the horizontal allocation was the historical disadvantage of some areas as noted above. Accordingly, the horizontal allocation formula distributes considerably greater resources to these undeveloped and less (densely) populated counties due to the effects of the 'equal share', land area, and poverty factors. Whereas the 2017/18 distribution of the equitable share resulted in an average per capita allocation of KShs. 10,199, county allocations range from KShs. 34,973 per capita (Lamu County) to KShs. 5,033 per capita (Nairobi City County).

Assessment of the Equitable Share

An assessment of the role of Kenya's equitable share ought to note a number of positive features as well as some areas of concern. On the positive side, equitable sharing has provided county governments with a meaningful level of unconditional financial resources that has allowed county governments to establish themselves as a significant sphere of governance and service delivery in the public sector. By and large, the institutional mechanisms surrounding equitable sharing have ensured that these funds are distributed in an objective, formula-based, predictable, equitable (as defined by the government) and transparent manner.

The constitution has placed the stewardship of the equitable sharing under the CRA, which analyses county-level expenditure needs and spending patterns and annually recommends vertical sharing arrangements – as well as develops periodic recommendations on the revision of the horizontal allocation formula – in order to ensure the efficient and equitable distribution of national revenues.

The main areas of concern and possible reform with respect to the equitable sharing mechanism include:

a. Given its importance in county finances, the vertical allocation of the equitable share does not appear adequate to fund county functional mandates. While the equitable share (as highlighted in Table 15.1) might be more or less sufficient to finance the recurrent costs of service delivery, these resources are inadequate to simultaneously fund recurrent costs and to fill the infrastructure gap in previously disadvantaged (and even other) county governments.
b. The horizontal allocation formula only provides a weak link between the distribution of revenues among counties (finances) and the pattern of expenditure needs (based on county functions).
c. While the horizontal allocation formula aims to be redistributive to historically disadvantaged counties, it may underfund the productive areas of the country and send resources to counties that do not have the capacity to effectively absorb them. It is unclear whether the current allocation formula strikes an adequate balance between redistribution and growth.
d. While the CRA provides recommendations on the vertical and horizontal allocation of resources (thus providing a space for evidence-based advice), the ultimate decision on equitable sharing – by Parliament – seems to be made on basic political considerations.

A final concern with equitable sharing concerns the balance between unconditional and conditional grants. Given the relative weaknesses of many county institutions and intergovernmental relations, the current approach may be considered excessively unconditional. The provision of a large unconditional grant achieved its initial political objectives, but without strong vertical, horizontal and downward accountability mechanisms, the largely unconditional grant scheme may be ineffective at promoting improved county service delivery.

15.5   CONDITIONAL TRANSFERS

Although conditional transfers were provided for in the constitution, the initial focus in implementing the new system was almost exclusively on the unconditional equitable sharing of revenue. This was in large part due to the political dynamics that motivated Kenya's transition to a more decentralized state as outlined above – reducing central state power and addressing historical inequities. As counties' sustainable political relevance seems increasingly assured and some concerns have been raised with their failure to allocate enough resources to certain key services, more attention has recently been given to conditional transfers, with both some positive steps and some areas of concern evident.

Constitutional, Legal and Policy Context of Conditional Grants

Article 202(20) allows county governments to be given additional allocations (beyond the 15 per cent minimum) from the national government's share of revenue, either conditionally or unconditionally. The broad responsibility of the CRA to make recommendations to Parliament on matters concerning the financing of county governments includes conditional grants.

As such, in its first recommendations to Parliament in 2012, the CRA dealt not only with the distribution of equitable share, but also with the role of conditional grants (CRA 2012). Despite effectively deciding to fund all county mandates from the unconditional equitable share, in formulating the design of the Kenyan transfer system, the CRA (2012: 39–40) acknowledged five broad economic arguments for conditional grants, including:

a. To ensure common minimum standards across subnational governments and enable poorer areas to provide an acceptable level of service for the attainment of national equity objectives.
b. To compensate for interjurisdictional spillovers, where one county provides a service that people from other counties can benefit from. If those who benefit do not contribute to the cost of providing it, counties may under-provide and focus benefits only on their constituents.
c. To create macroeconomic stability in depressed regions.
d. To influence local priorities in areas of high national interest but low local priority and provide flexibility of national government in carrying out targeted functions.
e. To address special issues, such as, gender, age and disability.

In 2016, the National Treasury issued guidelines for managing intergovernmental fiscal transfers. These guidelines define conditional transfers as those with the primary objective of providing incentives for county governments to carry out specific programmes or activities or to support a particular sector central to specific national policy objectives. They also broadly specify a range of conditions which may be imposed, including one or a combination of the following:

a. Input-based conditions, which must specify the type of expenditure that can be financed. These may be capital expenditures, operating expenditures or both.

b.   Output-based conditions, which require the attainment of certain
results in service delivery.
c.   Grant matching requirements, which may incorporate a provision
that requires county governments to finance a specified percentage of
expenditures using their own resources.

The Evolution of Conditional Grants in Practice

A range of different conditional grants is currently being provided by
the national government to county governments. The conditional grants
contained in the County Allocation of Revenue Act, 2017 are summarized
in Table 15.3.

In the absence of a well-defined policy framework and detailed criteria
(beyond the relevant 2016 guidelines) it appears that conditional transfers
in Kenya have emerged in a more or less ad hoc manner from sectoral and/
or political requests, rather than based on any strategy or technical acumen.
In fact, many of the current conditional grants are simply a carry-forward

Table 15.3   Conditional grant allocations, FY 2017/18

	KSh. Billion	% of Total
National Government Conditional Grants		
Leasing of Medical Equipment	4.5	10.3
Level 5 Hospitals	4.2	9.6
Road Maintenance Fuel Levy Fund	11.1	25.3
Compensation for User Fee Foregone	0.9	2.1
Development of Youth Polytechnics	2.0	4.6
Construction of County HQs	0.6	1.4
Development Partner Grants		
World Bank Supplemental Financing of County Health Facilities,	0.9	2.1
World Bank Kenya Devolution Support Programme	2.2	5.0
World Bank Transforming Health System for Universal Care	2.8	6.4
World Bank National Agricultural and Rural Inclusive Growth	1.1	2.5
DANIDA Universal Healthcare Grants	0.8	1.8
European Union (EU) Grants	1.0	2.3
KSDP 'Level 2' Grants	4.0	9.1
Other Loans and Grants	7.8	17.8
Total Conditional Grant Allocations	*43.9*	*100.0*

Source: OCOB (2018a).

of sectoral programmes initiated prior to the new constitution, or specific earmarked programmes funded by donors.

Although the 2016 guidelines provide some context for the adoption of new conditional grants, they were not an attempt to reform the existing system, or to impose binding policy constraints on new sectoral/conditional grants. As such, the adoption of conditional grants may remain idiosyncratic and risks becoming supply driven and highly fragmented. The CRA recognizes that a more systematic approach would optimize the benefits from such grants (CRA 2017: 10).

Assessment of Conditional Grants

There has been little attempt to document the effects of conditional grants in Kenya, including any impact that they have had on service delivery and infrastructure development. In order to properly assess the effectiveness of the system, it is important to answer a more fundamental question: what are conditional grants supposed to fund vis-à-vis activities from the equitable share and own source revenues? This question cannot be meaningfully answered without clearer guidance on the functions (and/or level of services) counties are expected to fund from their equitable share. After all, most constitutional mandates of county governments are actually concurrent responsibilities, so counties would be expected to spend a considerable share of their unconditional resources on concurrent service functions, even if the central government does not provide conditional grants.

That being said, it should be noted that many – if not all – current conditional grants are targeted at county-level functions for which the national government has a legitimate interest in ensuring adequate service provision. The current list, however, seems somewhat arbitrary, raising concerns as to whether the conditional grant system achieves (or even has) intended policy objectives. At present, it seems that conditional transfers may be used excessively in some sectors and not enough in others: for instance, the health sector relies extensively on conditional grants to encourage better health services, while other key sectors, such as agriculture or water and sanitation, do not use them.

Another expressed concern is the legitimacy of using conditional grants at all. County governors have argued that functions that fall within their mandate should be funded through unconditional equitable sharing, rather than through conditional grants. Given that many of the powers and functions assigned to county government are concurrent in nature, however, the national government does have a valid policy interest in targeted funding towards specific sectors and functions. Indeed, a cursory review of the conditions imposed by the different conditional grant schemes generally appear to be appropriate in balancing the policy objectives of the national government, on one hand, and the ability of county governments to effectively perform their constitutionally mandated functions, on the other hand.

At same time, county governments have reason to be concerned about the increasing number of conditional grants being introduced within the various sectors. The excessive fragmentation of such grants within the same sector (e.g. health) results not only in decreased spending discretion on the part of county officials, but also increases their administration and compliance costs. In order to prevent unnecessary fragmentation, it would be prudent for the CRA, in collaboration with sectoral stakeholders in each key sector – including health, agriculture, water, urban development and (pre-primary and vocational) education – to develop conditional grant position papers that help to ensure coordination, integration and rationalization of the conditional grant schemes within each sector.

15.6   PROSPECTS FOR THE FUTURE

Five years into the devolution process under the 2010 constitution, there is a sense that Kenya's path towards devolution has in some ways been a 'political' success. The basic elements of the county government systems have been defined and are being implemented. The focal element of this chapter, the intergovernmental fiscal transfer system, is firmly in place, providing a reasonably sound framework for intergovernmental funding and ensuring a degree of vertical balance in the division of power and resources between the national government and county governments.

The extent to which devolution has led to improved service-delivery and governance outcomes, however, is far less self-evident. An important challenge in converting fiscal devolution into improved outcomes is to ensure the development and use of an appropriate intergovernmental fiscal framework. The CRA – together with other stakeholders – is seeking to address this challenge in a number of ways:

a.   Better linking finances to functions and improving the horizontal distribution of equitable sharing resources;
b.   Continuing to address the vertical fiscal imbalance;
c.   Strengthening the conditional grant system;
d.   Ensuring adequate financing of urban development; and
e.   Revisiting the role of own source revenues and borrowing.

In addition, there is a need to strengthen the broader intergovernmental institutional framework and provide for mechanisms for regional or inter-jurisdictional cooperation. Each of these key issues is briefly discussed in turn.

Better Linking Finances to Functions and Improving the Horizontal Distribution of Equitable Sharing

At the time writing this chapter, the Commission of Revenue Allocation is preparing for a 'Third Basis' for equitable sharing, which is supposed to cover the five-year period from FY 2019/20–FY 2023/24 (CRA 2018). The Commission has identified the lack of a conceptual foundation of the horizontal allocation under the first and second bases as one of the most significant weakness of the horizontal distribution of financial resources.

To address this problem, the CRA is developing proposals to create a stronger link between the horizontal distribution of the equitable share and the main policy objectives for which these resources are provided to the county level, including county service delivery; the promotion of balanced development; the encouragement of county revenue collection; and the promotion of fiscal prudence at the county level. This may lead Kenya's equitable sharing formula to evolve in a similar direction to South Africa's provincial equitable shares formula, which divides the funding pool (for indicative purposes) into a number of functional components.

Stopping short of shifting the grant system to a stronger reliance on conditional grants, a more 'functional' approach to equitable revenue sharing would provide an opportunity for the national government to have a discussion with county governments on one of the main financing challenges at the county level: counties do not appear to plan or prioritize their spending in a results-based manner. For instance, county leaders may prefer to allocate greater resources for highly visible infrastructure projects, such as roads, rather than fund the recurrent cost associated with pro-poor county services, such as health services or agricultural extension services. Similarly, in the health sector, there is a concern that while the equitable share and conditional grants may reach the counties, funding often does not reach the facility level where services are delivered. Unless county services start improving gradually over the coming years, the popular support for devolution noted above is likely to falter.

Addressing the Vertical Fiscal Imbalance

Ensuring that the Third Basis adheres to the mantra that 'finance should follow function' also highlights an emerging vertical fiscal imbalance – if the equitable share resources were divided among the various functional mandates assigned to the county level as part of the allocation formula, it would become increasingly clear that the current vertical share allocated to the county level is not adequate to fund the services the counties are expected to provide.

Although determining the vertical fiscal balance is ultimately a national political decision, the CRA is positioning itself to make an evidence-based argument that there is need to increase the share of nationally raised revenues that is transferred to the county level, particularly if this increase can be linked more effectively to expected improvements in county services.

Strengthening the Conditional Grant System

As already noted above, if the CRA opts to move the Third Basis of equitable sharing in the direction of a function-based allocation formula, it would be appropriate for relevant stakeholders – the CRA and the relevant sectoral ministries – to determine an affordable, realistic level of public services that each county should be able to attain with the equitable share resources provided to it. Beyond helping guide the vertical allocation of resources between the national and county levels, this analysis would also provide an important point of departure for determining which services could be productively funded from conditional grants.

Although Kenya started with a largely unconditional transfer system, it may be appropriate to use conditional transfers more significantly and strategically, including more use of performance-based transfers, which development partners are already experimenting with. A number of countries, such as Indonesia, South Africa and Uganda, moved towards greater conditionality over time. This approach, however, can have both positive and negative effects, so it is important to conduct the analyses necessary to use conditional transfers constructively if they are to be a more important fiscal instrument in Kenya.

Establishing Urban Bodies and Ensuring Adequate Urban Finances

One of the 'victims' of the 2010 constitution was at the local government level, as urban local governments – which had existed since before independence and some of which played a valuable role in local governance and service delivery – were abolished in favour of the new county governments. Prior to 2017, few counties had moved to establish urban boards provided for in the legal framework, and local political economy pressures kept many governors from encouraging urban development (Boex et al.

2017). This is a potentially significant consideration because urbanization is high in Kenya and is seen as the foundation for economic growth. Under the pre-2010 system, independent urban governments kept the revenues they generated. Now that these revenues go to the county governments, there are concerns that, at least in some counties, revenues collected in the urban areas that could be providing valuable urban services and promoting urban development will instead be used to buy rural votes. More evidence is needed on this front.

With this concern in mind, the Kenya Urban Support Program (KUSP) is supporting implementation of the National Urban Development Policy (NUDP). The main component of KUSP is a performance-based urban development grant (in the amount of US$300 million) to municipal areas – through their respective county governments – in counties that have legally established municipal bodies and appointed municipal boards in line with the Urban Areas and Cities Act. If the value of such an initiative can be proven, there may be renewed interest in reinvigorating urban government.

Revisiting the Role of Own Source Revenues and Borrowing

In addition to the strengthening of the intergovernmental transfer system, the role of own source revenues and borrowing should not be ignored. As noted earlier, the county government own source revenues are largely the revenues that were assigned to the pre-2010 local governments. That was not an impressive set of sources to begin with, and there was clearly substantial under-collection in many areas. Despite claims and evidence that there is considerable untapped own source revenue potential in many local jurisdictions (as under the former system), use of own source revenue has for the most part not been a focal policy of county governments to date. Given that own source revenue can be critical not only for financing local service delivery, but also for enhancing the efficiency and accountability with which county resources are spent, this is clearly a priority area for considering future reforms and incentives.

Thus far, there has not been much attention to county government borrowing, a potentially critical component of subnational finance in a rapidly urbanizing country with substantial infrastructure gaps. County governments are obligated to spend a share of equitable sharing resources on development, but that is not likely to be sufficient to meet the needs. Local governments under the previous system used to borrow for infrastructure development, largely through the now defunct Local Government Loans Authority. Under the present system, there has been no significant movement on the borrowing front. Country governments are allowed to borrow under the 2010 constitution, but they need central government permission and guarantees, a provision that can create problematic behaviour. Working on how to offer county governments options to secure and responsibly manage development finance in the future is an essential consideration in developing the evolving intergovernmental fiscal system.

Strengthening the Intergovernmental Institutional Framework and Mechanisms for Regional or Interjurisdictional Cooperation

It is important to re-emphasize that the intergovernmental fiscal system is only part of the formula that makes up a successful devolved system. As Kenya moves down the path of greater devolution in the context of the quasi-federal 2010 constitution, the effectiveness of intergovernmental relations is also a key concern. Attention will have to be paid to ensuring that an institutional framework is in place to ensure adequate intergovernmental coordination, at national level (among national-level stakeholders), vertically (between national and sectoral stakeholders), as well as at county level (between different counties and groups of counties that may benefit from interjurisdictional or regional cooperation that used to be managed by the former deconcentrated provincial administration). Such changes take time to design and implement, and measures will be required to ensure that policies are informed from experience and that successful reforms can be mainstreamed, sustained and improved as needed.

15.7   CONCLUDING THOUGHTS

Kenya has experienced disagreements about how to structure its intergovernmental system since independence negotiations. The persistent lack of consensus on this front and the ethnic and political power issues in which it is grounded (and which unleashed the post-2007 election violence) shaped the path to the 2010 constitution as well as recent actions and ongoing debates over public sector reform. However, uncertainty remains about how the nascent devolution will unfold.

One point, however, is certain – the reformists, who clearly wanted to leave behind the disappointing performance of the unduly centralized pre-2010 government system, have prevailed. The devolution enshrined in the 2010 constitution bypasses the provincial administration (long associated with an elite, rent-seeking, top-down system) and the marginalization of the previous local governments (popularly perceived as unaccountable and ineffective). Few countries have swept away a fragmented set of public sector institutions in the way that Kenya has, and the devolution of powers and functions to the new county entities has been substantial and dramatic. Mistakes have been made by most accounts, but Kenya's devolution has been bold and transformative.

The intergovernmental transfer system, which is substantial and primarily unconditional, has been a cornerstone of the devolution. This chapter has outlined key positive features and major challenges of the transfer system, as well as some of the ongoing debates and possible options for improving the system and other interrelated elements of fiscal decentralization. More work needs to be done on the technical side and is already in process. At the same time, the political economy dynamics that have shaped Kenya's history as an independent country are not going to go away. They will continue to evolve and influence the debates over the nature, mix and allocation of equitable revenue sharing.

NOTES

1. See Hicks (1961), Mueller (1984), Smoke (1993, 1994, 2003, 2008), Steffensen et al. (2004), Branch and Cheeseman (2006), Government of Kenya Task Force on Devolved Government (2011), Smoke and Whimp (2011) and World Bank (2012) for details on the evolution of Kenya's public sector and local government system.
2. This section is largely drawn from background readings provided in the previous note.
3. The most important intergovernmental policy on this front was District Focus for Rural Development (DFRD), which significantly strengthened the deconcentrated provincial and district administration under the Office of the President and further undermined the relationship between local governments and their constituents.
4. See Cohen and Peterson (1999), Republic of Kenya (2005) and Romeo and Smoke (2016).
5. See Smoke (2003) and Steffensen et al. (2004) for a summary of evolving conditions and Kenyan reforms in the late 1990s and early 2000s and the KLGRP.
6. Devas and Kelly (2001) provide details on business licensing harmonization reform.
7. Local Authority Transfer Fund Law, Government of Kenya, Law No. 8 of 1998.
8. For discussions of civil society in Kenya, see Orvis (2003), Nyamu-Musembi and Musyoki (2004), World Bank (2012) and Munene and Thakhathi (2017).
9. Constituency Development Fund Act, Government of Kenya Law No. 10 of 2003.
10. For example, a percentage of funding for rural roads earmarked through the Road Maintenance Levy Fund was allocated by constituency. Funding under an economic stimulus package responding to the 2008 global economic crisis was also allocated by constituency.
11. See Kramon and Posner (2011), Barkan (2016), Cornell and D'Arcy (2016).
12. See, for example, Cheeseman (2016).
13. The exchange rate currently fluctuates around KShs. 100 per US dollar.
14. Schedule 4 of the constitution also assigns county governments the responsibility for trade development and regulation, which has been interpreted as providing a constitutional basis for Single Business Permit collection to transition from local authorities to county governments (World Bank 2012: 76).
15. Kenya's constitution also introduced an Equalization Fund to provide basic services to marginalized areas. This Fund receives 0.5 per cent of all national revenue. However, rather than being transferred to marginalized county governments, the constitution determines that spending from this Fund is directed by the national government (with the option to disburse resources in the form of conditional grants).

16.	The lower bound was a compromise between those who did not want to specify any minimum and those who wanted to have a much higher minimum. The positive effect of this lower bound is to ensure that national government would be unable to hollow out the constitutional mandate of county governments by underfunding them to the point that they would no longer be a meaningful political and institutional actor.

17.	In dividing responsibilities between the CRA, National Treasury and the Senate, the process seeks to ensure that the national government honours its constitutional obligations with regard to the vertical sharing of revenues.

18.	See, for example, Khaunya et al. (2015), Cornell and D'Arcy (2016), D'Arcy and Cornell (2016), Cannon and Ali (2018).

19.	This analysis of Kenyan transfers in this chapter draws on Boex and Smoke (2018a and 2018b).

REFERENCES

Barkan, J. (2016), 'Devolution and the New Politics of Development in Kenya', *African Studies Review*, **59** (3): 155–67.

Boex, J., A. Muwonge and M. Winter (2017), *Strengthening Urban Institutions, Urban Finances and Urban Development in Kenya*, Washington/Nairobi: The World Bank.

Boex, J. and P. Smoke (2018a), 'An Analysis of the Basis for Equitable Sharing of Revenues among County Governments in Kenya', discussion paper prepared for the Commission on Revenue Allocation, August 2018.

Boex, J. and P. Smoke (2018b), 'Conditional versus Unconditional Grants: Theory, International Experiences and Lessons for Kenya', discussion paper prepared for the Commission on Revenue Allocation, October 2018.

Branch, D. and N. Cheeseman (2006), 'The Politics of Control in Kenya: Understanding the Bureaucratic-executive State, 1952–78', *Review of African Political Economy*, **33** (1): 11–31.

Cannon, B. and J. Ali (2018), 'Devolution in Kenya Four Years On: A Review of Implementation and Effects in Mandera County', *African Conflict and Peacebuilding Review*, **8** (1): 1–28.

Cheeseman, N. (2016), 'Decentralization in Kenya: The Governance of Governors', *Journal of Modern African Studies*, **54** (1): 1–35.

Cohen, J. and S. Peterson (1999), *Administrative Decentralization in Developing Countries*, Boulder, CO: Lynne Reinner.

Commission on Revenue Allocation (CRA) (2012), 'Recommendations on Sharing of Revenue Raised Nationally between the National and County Governments for the Fiscal Year 2012/2013 and among County Governments for the Fiscal Years 2012/13 – 2014/15'. 8 August 2012.

Commission on Revenue Allocation (CRA) (2017), 'Recommendation on the Basis for Equitable Sharing of Revenue between National and County Governments for the Financial Year 2018/2019'. 18 December 2017.

Commission on Revenue Allocation (CRA) (2018), 'The Third Basis for Sharing Revenue among County Governments', Consultation Draft.

Cornell, A. and M. D'Arcy (2016), *Devolution, Democracy and Development in Kenya*, Visby: Swedish International Center for Local Democracy.

D'Arcy, M. and A. Cornell (2016), 'Devolution and Corruption in Kenya: Everyone's Turn to Eat?', *African Affairs*, **115** (459): 246–73.

Devas, N. and R. Kelly (2001), 'Regulation or Revenues: Analysis of Local Business Licenses, with a Case Study of the Single Business Permit in Kenya', *Public Administration and Development*, **21** (5): 381–91.

Government of Kenya (2005), *Guidelines for the Preparation, Implementation and Monitoring of Local Authority Service Delivery Action Plans*, Nairobi: MOLG.

Government of Kenya (2011), *Final Report of the Task Force on Devolved Government*, Nairobi: Office of the Deputy Prime Minister and Ministry of Local Government.

Hicks, U. (1961), *Development from Below: Local Government and Finance in Developing Countries of the Commonwealth*, Oxford: Oxford University Press.

IPSOS (2016), 'SPEC Barometer: 1st Quarter Survey'. Mimeo. 6 September 2016.

Khaunya, M., B. Wawire and V. Chepng'eno (2015), 'Devolved Governance in Kenya: Is it a False Start in Democratic Decentralization for Development?', *International Journal of Economics, Finance and Management*, **4** (1): 27–37.

Kramon, E. and D. Posner (2011), 'Kenya's New Constitution', *Journal of Democracy*, **22** (1): 89–103.

Mueller, S. (1984), 'Government and Opposition in Kenya, 1966–9', *The Journal of Modern African Studies*, **22** (3): 399–427.

Munene, J. and D. Thakhathi (2017), 'An Analysis of Capacities of Civil Society Organizations Involved in the Promotion of Community Participation in Governance in Kenya', *Journal of Public Affairs*, 2017:17:e1668.

Nyamu-Musembi, C. and S. Musyoki (2004), 'Kenya Civil Society: Perspectives on Rights-Based Approaches to Development and Participation'. IDS Working Paper No. 236. Brighton: Institute of Development Studies, University of Sussex.

Office of the Controller of Budget (OCOB) (2018a), 'Annual County Governments Budget Implementation Review Report for FY 2017/18'. September 2018.

Office of the Controller of Budget (OCOB) (2018b), 'National Government Budget Implementation Review Report for FY 2017/18'. September 2018.

Orvis, S. (2003), 'Kenyan Civil Society: Bridging the Rural-Urban Divide', *Journal of Modern African Studies*, **41** (2): 247–68.

Romeo, L. and P. Smoke (2016), 'The Political Economy of Local Infrastructure Planning in Developing Countries', in Jonas Frank and Jorge Martinez-Vazquez (eds), *Decentralization and Infrastructure in the Global Economy: From Gaps to Solutions*, Oxford: Routledge, Chapter 13.

Smoke, P. (1993), 'Local Government Fiscal Reform in Developing Countries: Lessons from Kenya', *World Development*, **21** (6): 901–23.

Smoke, P. (1994), *Local Government Finance in Developing Countries: The Case of Kenya*, Oxford and Nairobi: Oxford University Press.

Smoke, P. (2003), 'Erosion and Reform from the Center in Kenya', in J. Wunsch and D. Olowu (eds), *Local Governance in Africa: The Challenge of Decentralization*, Boulder, CO: Lynne Reinner, pp. 212–35.

Smoke, P. (2008), 'The Evolution of Subnational Development Planning under Decentralization Reforms in Kenya and Uganda', in V. Beard, F. Miraftab and C. Silver (eds), *Planning and Decentralization: Contested Spaces for Public Action in the Global South*, Oxon: Routledge, pp. 89–105.

Smoke, P. and K. Whimp (2011), 'The Evolution of Fiscal Decentralization under Kenya's New Constitution: Opportunities and Challenges', *National Tax Association Proceedings*, pp. 109–15.

Steffensen, J., H. Naitore and P. Tidemand (2004), *A Comparative Analysis of*

Decentralization in Kenya, Tanzania and Uganda, Report by Nordic Consulting Group for the World Bank. Oslo: Nordic Consulting Group.

World Bank (2012), *Devolution without Disruption: Pathways to a Successful New Kenya*, Nairobi: Australian AID/World Bank.

16. Reforming vertical programmes: the case of South African local government

David Savage

1. INTRODUCTION

Many intergovernmental fiscal systems, particularly in developing countries, experience the mutually reinforcing pressures to horizontally fragment funding schemes and vertically centralize expenditure authority. These pressures are often underpinned by demands to rapidly address urgent development priorities, particularly to provide basic services, often in an environment of weak public sector capacity.

This chapter reviews the trajectory of intergovernmental fiscal reforms in South Africa from 1994 to the present, with a particular focus on local government. It characterizes the main periods of reform in South Africa, identifies cross-cutting debates and issues, and draws out key lessons from the South African experience for other countries.

The South African experience provides a useful comparator for other countries, due both to relatively limited time since its introduction and subsequent periods of reform, as well as the relative coherence of efforts to reform the overall system of public financial management. Importantly, the South African system represents a relatively more mature and coherent fiscal framework for the local government tier.

The South African case is, however, like most other countries, deeply influenced by the context in which reforms have been introduced and the effectiveness with which they have been designed and implemented. In both its brevity and nature, this review does not seek to provide a comprehensive description or analysis of the South African experience, but rather to highlight key priorities, concerns and issues that informed and continue to shape the ongoing evolution of the intergovernmental fiscal system in South Africa.

Comparative analysis of this nature is a useful exercise to the extent that it reveals similarities and contrasts between contexts, facilitating domestic policy dialogue. It allows policymakers to build on the wisdom and errors of other approaches, rather than providing standardized solutions. The key questions this chapter seeks to contribute to include: (a) how have other countries shifted from specific-purpose grants to unconditional transfers?; (b) how have transfer systems been designed to align subnational spending with national policy priorities while accommodating locally defined preferences?; and (c) what arrangements are in place to address fiduciary, value for money and accountability concerns?

2. BACKGROUND

a) Country Context

No two countries are alike, and South Africa differs from others in many respects. South Africa has a population of 55.7 million people (2016), with Gauteng (the largest province) having a population of 13.4 million in 2016. The South African population is young and urbanizing, with an economy that is not growing fast enough to keep pace with the demands of demographic and economic change. South Africa is, however, a significantly urbanized country with a relatively slow urbanization rate in comparison to many other developing countries.

b) Intergovernmental Functional Assignments

South Africa is a unitary state with federal characteristics. The Constitution establishes three interdependent and interrelated 'spheres' of government at national, provincial and local levels, which are intended to work together in a cooperative manner. This arrangement provides for functional assignments between spheres, but also a significant degree of concurrency in functions. In general, the nine provincial governments are assigned health, education and social welfare functions, while local governments are assigned basic local service delivery functions such as water services, electricity distribution, roads and transport and refuse removal. Importantly, local government is also assigned spatial planning functions.

In general, therefore, provincial governments perform labour intensive functions that are largely funded through transfers from nationally collected taxes, while local governments focus on capital-intensive functions that can – at least in part – be funded through user charges or property taxation. The relatively greater discretion this provides to local government has led the South African intergovernmental framework to be characterized as an 'hour-glass federalism', with national and local governments having considerably greater powers and autonomy than provincial governments,

However, the South African Constitution also provides for significant concurrency in functions. These are particularly important in relation to:

- The management of the urban built environment, where provinces and municipalities are both involved in public housing and transport services;
- The provision of bulk services, where national government entities and municipalities are both involved in aspects of energy generation and water resource management (such as dams); and
- The performance of some social services, where provinces and municipalities both deliver primary healthcare and early childhood development services.

In some instances, a reassessment of concurrency has led to a reassignment of functions. This has been the case in social protection services, where grants are now administered through a single national agency, and in spatial planning, which has been assigned via a judicial process to the local sphere. However, despite a constitutional commitment to the principle of subsidiarity, and extensive regulation of the process of functional and fiscal transfers, these shifts have tended to be the exception rather than the norm. Concurrency thus remains a key point of friction in the system of intergovernmental relations. This is typically managed through an elaborate and extensive system of coordination at both political and administrative levels.

c) The Intergovernmental Fiscal Framework

The South African intergovernmental fiscal framework attempts to resolve these frictions through a regulated system of revenue assignments and transfers. The Constitution assigns revenue powers to local governments for property taxes and user charges, as well as providing for long-term borrowing by municipalities to fund infrastructure investment. Similar powers are not granted to provinces, which are largely dependent on transfers from national government. The Constitution guarantees both subnational spheres an 'equitable share of nationally raised revenues' to address the mismatch between revenue and expenditure assignments. Significantly, however, the Constitution:

- Prevents functional reassignments from occurring without concomitant resources;

- Does not require national government to compensate for a lack of own revenue effort by subnational governments; and
- Allows for the direct transfer of national resources to local governments, rather than via provinces.

For local governments, who have significant own revenue authority, the fiscal framework is then regulated by both overarching legislations governing the assignment local revenue sources (the Municipal Fiscal Powers and Functions Act, the Municipal Property Rates Act, and the Municipal Systems Act) and borrowing powers (the Municipal Financial Management Act). Special attention is given to the regulation of the borrowing powers of municipalities, given their largely capital-intensive functions. Municipalities are only permitted to borrow for beyond a financial year in order to fund infrastructure investment (capital expenditure) programmes, and their borrowing operations may not be guaranteed by other spheres of government. The exercise of these powers is subject to procedural regulation that requires extensive public disclosure.

Transfers to subnational government
Transfers to both spheres of subnational government are also regulated through the annual national budget process. This is managed on a three-year rolling cycle (the Medium-Term Expenditure Framework, or MTEF), that enables parliamentary appropriations through both an annual national Appropriations Act, and an annual Division of Revenue Act (DoRA). Given the constitutional status of both provinces and local government, the DoRA establishes the vertical division of revenue between spheres of government and regulates the individual programmes that transfer nationally raised revenues to subnational spheres as well as between provincial and local governments. The schedules to the DoRA also provide for three-year, rolling allocations from individual transfer programmes to individual receiving governments. Funding for individual conditional transfer programmes is appropriated to the transferring national departments in the national Appropriations Act.

The equitable share of nationally raised revenue   The primary transfer to subnational government is the unconditional, constitutional entitlement known as the 'equitable share'. This is distributed to provinces and municipalities through the Provincial Equitable Share (PES) and the Local Government Equitable Share (LGES), both of which are formula-based allocations that are distributed without conditions.

The PES accounts for 81.5 per cent of transfers to provinces and allocation is through a weighted formula based on six variables (with indicators and weights provided in brackets): basic share (share of population, 16 per cent), education (school-aged population and enrolment, 48 per cent), health (population without medical aid, health risk, and hospital and clinic use, 27 per cent) poverty (share of poverty, 3 per cent), economic activity (share of regional gross domestic product, 1 per cent) and institutional (equal allocations to each province, 5 per cent).

The LGES is allocated through a formula to enable all municipalities to provide basic services to poor households and assist those municipalities with limited own resources to afford basic administrative and governance capacity and perform core municipal functions. It is designed around a threshold measuring the affordability of basic services to households that provides R293 per month for a package of free basic services to those households with an income of less than two old age public pensions per month. This variable is complemented by institutional and community services components to the formula that are targeted to poorer municipalities for the costs of administration and community services respectively.

The formulae for both of these transfers have been fairly stable and are published annually as part of the national budget documentation (see Figure 16.1 for provincial and local government transfers for 2019/20). They are updated annually with cost data to account for price increases and estimates of household growth A new LGES formula was introduced in 2013/14 following extensive consultation and is being phased in over five years. This has a more redistributive structure than the previous formula, while the phasing in provisions provide for a stable transition.

South Africa's tax base is highly concentrated in urban areas. The system of intergovernmental transfers is thus extensively distributive towards more rural provinces and municipalities. For example, allocations per household to rural municipalities are more than twice as much as those to metropolitan municipalities.

Conditional grants   The DoRA requires that any transfer of resources between spheres of government happens in terms of the Act. It allows conditional transfers for both operating and capital expenditures. It also regulates non-cash (or in-kind) transfers in the case of assets that are created on behalf of another sphere of government, or functions that are performed on their behalf. The Act distinguishes between grants that are specific-purpose transfers and those which provide supplementary allocations to the budgets of receiving authorities. It also requires that all grant programmes publish a clear framework of rules for their allocation and use, including their measurable objectives, conditions, disbursement schedules, reporting requirements, records of past performance and criteria for allocation.

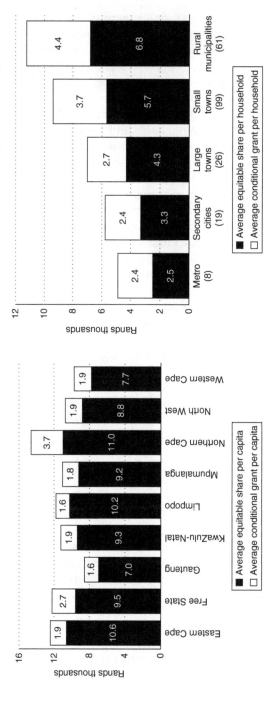

Source: National Treasury (2019).

Figure 16.1 Provincial and local government transfers (2019/20)

Although not mandatory, the majority of these programmes allocate their resources through formulae, which vary depending on the grant purpose.

The division of revenue process   The process leading to the annual division of revenue between spheres of government is procedurally elaborate. It is initiated with recommendations from Parliament, those of the constitutionally independent Financial and Fiscal Commission, and a 'mandate paper' from the executive on developmental and fiscal priorities. An extensive set of technical meetings between the National Treasury, national sector departments, functional groupings of departments and intergovernmental technical committees results in technical budget proposals being forwarded to a legislated political process of consultation. This includes the Budget Council, consisting of the Minister of Finance and his or her provincial counterparts, and the Budget Forum, consisting of the Budget Council and representatives of local government. The recommendations of these fora are forwarded to the Ministers Committee on the Budget and then to an extended cabinet meeting, including Premiers of all nine provinces.

This process produces a Medium-Term Budget Policy Statement in October of each year that is subject to parliamentary hearings and recommendations, adjustment and subsequently the tabling of the Medium-Term Expenditure Framework (or main budget, including the Division of Revenue Bill) in February of each year. It is important to note that the division of revenue appropriations do not include own revenue raised by subnational governments, which are significant for the local government sphere. If these are included, local government accounts for about a quarter of the total revenues raised by the three spheres of government.

Data underpinning allocations   In terms of the Statistics Act, only officially published data may be used for the calculation of any allocations made through the DoRA. This data is updated in decadal census, interspersed with various other statistical surveys that vary in their utility for allocative purposes. Concerns remain on the accuracy of census data, and on the utility of inter-census data for allocative purposes at the subnational (and particularly local) level. Various techniques have also been assessed in efforts to improve the accuracy and relevance of measurement, for example reviewing the relative accuracy of reported household income versus imputed household expenditures as the basis for poverty measurement. Notwithstanding these concerns – and the ongoing extensive debates in the statistical community – the quality and coverage of data has generally improved.

In introducing this information into the intergovernmental resource allocation process, Government has sought to balance the competing needs for objectivity and impartiality with that of fiscal stability. Put simply, those subnational entities that stand to benefit from changes in underlying data have an interest in the rapid adoption of changes (without necessarily always having the expenditure programmes in place), while those that lose out will often have existing expenditure commitments to wind down. The approach adopted has been to introduce a stabilization factor into the formulae that is activated during a period of change. This typically provides a 'glide path' to entities with declining allocations that will guarantee them a percentage of their former allocation on a sliding scale

Monitoring transfers and the intergovernmental fiscal framework   An extensive system of in-year and annual monitoring has been developed to assist with the oversight of the intergovernmental fiscal framework and individual transfer programmes. All provinces and municipalities are required to report monthly and quarterly on their revenues and expenditures, and quarterly on non-financial performance. These reports are submitted to both the relevant sector department and the National Treasury, which in turn submits quarterly reports to Parliament. Annual reports and financial statements are also prepared and audited by the Auditor General. Unspent or misspent conditional grant funds do not automatically roll over to the next financial year and can be recovered against future equitable share transfers.

3.   CONSTRUCTING THE LOCAL GOVERNMENT FISCAL FRAMEWORK

Although little detailed data existed at the time, it was generally understood that, at the dawn of democracy in 1994, South Africa faced massive, racially based backlogs in access to basic services (see Figure 16.2 for the historical evolution of the percentage of households with access to basic services). This crisis was deepened by both a deep recession that weakened public finances, as well as the racially based distribution of available resources. Public policy priorities in this period were focussed predominantly on efforts to universalize access to basic services across the country, while simultaneously restructuring service delivery arrangements – particularly at subnational level. Thus, basic services investment programmes were driven centrally by national sector departments (for water, electricity, and so on), while deep institutional reforms were introduced in local government in particular. This legislatively driven local government

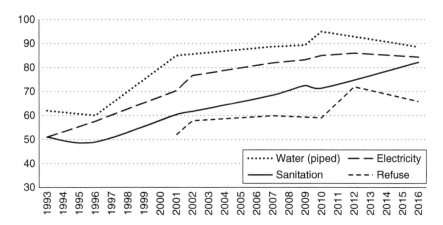

Source: Statistics South Africa (2017) and own calculations.

Figure 16.2   Percentage of households with access to basic levels of service (1993–2016)

reform programme resulted in the establishment of large, wall-to-wall municipalities (the Municipal Demarcation Act), the establishment of standardized structures for municipal political oversight and functional assignments (the Municipal Structures Act), the modernization of municipal planning and administrative systems (the Municipal Systems Act) and the fundamental reform of municipal budgeting financial management practices (the Municipal Financial Management Act).

By 2003, a significant restructuring of both subnational government and associated resource flows had occurred, and a (controversial) macroeconomic adjustment programme had restored public fiscal health to the point that subnational resource allocations were poised for significant growth. Strengthened subnational capacity, as well as some experience of the effectiveness of central and subnational service delivery systems, resulted in a second round of reform efforts. At the local government level, these focussed on deepening the devolution of functions to municipalities, particularly for water services. Funding for local infrastructure delivery, previously administered through asset transfers and/or a plethora of small sectoral infrastructure grants was consolidated into a single, formula-based Municipal Infrastructure Grant (MIG). Conversely, at the provincial level it was agreed that social safety functions, such as the payment of social grants, required consolidation and centralized management, which was introduced in agreement with provincial governments through the formation of the South African Social Security Agency.

By 2008, the stage was set for a significant growth in resources to subnational governments. Importantly, much of this growth happened as government was seeking to ramp up public investment in infrastructure and prepare for the 2010 FIFA World Cup. The latter, for local government in the host cities in particular, provided a significant inflexion point. Unlike the resources that had been provided through the MIG in the past, specific-purpose, project-based grants were introduced specifically to fund World Cup stadia and associated Bus Rapid Transit Systems.

However, while attention was focussed on the significant delivery challenges associated with hosting the World Cup, there was growing concern that other investment programmes – such as the MIG – were delivering declining returns. In particular, there was concern that there had been significant central administrative clawback of the autonomy of local governments in investment selection and execution that was granted through the MIG, which had originated from a concern over delivery capacity by the weakest municipalities. Additionally, there was growing concern that larger urban municipalities were failing to invest adequately in infrastructure renewal and extension, despite having largely succeeded in meeting historical backlogs to basic services.

These concerns laid the foundation for increasing fiscal differentiation among local governments. This sought to provide a more prescriptive, sector-based framework for infrastructure investment in more rural municipalities that were perceived to have weaker capacity. In large, more urban municipalities (and particularly metropolitan municipalities) it sought to provide significantly greater certainty over allocations and reduced central administrative interference in investment selection and execution, in order to promote more integrated, locally led development. Importantly, these arguments for differentiation focussed largely on the needs of larger and more urban municipalities and were accompanied by associated efforts to effect functional and operational reforms. In more rural municipalities a far less programmatic approach was evident, with the change in approach being driven through the proliferation of sector-based, specific-purpose grant programmes and a resurgence of in-kind (asset) transfers to municipalities.

Most recently, from 2012 the National Treasury has led a broad process to review the fiscal framework for municipal infrastructure investment, focussing both on the role of grants and on opportunities to expand the scope for sustainable and responsible borrowing by creditworthy municipalities. A key finding of this review, beyond the ongoing need for differentiation, has been the need to focus investment on supporting infrastructure renewal and expansion as a central municipal contribution to faster and more inclusive economic growth. For large and more urban municipalities, the emphasis has been on providing greater incentives for improved performance in both the self-financing of infrastructure (and thus a reduction in the proportion of investments financed through grants), and in the developmental outcomes of these expenditures. While the current national programme of fiscal consolidation has begun to reduce the real value of transfers to urban municipalities, the alignment and introduction of performance-based measures in grant programmes for urban municipalities has supported a programme of intra-urban spatial targeting of public infrastructure investments designed to alter the urban spatial form of South African cities, which is considered to have a significant negative impact on long-term economic growth prospects.

4. PHASES OF REFORM

The intergovernmental transfer system in South Africa has been subject to ongoing reform and fine-tuning since the introduction of the new Constitution in 1996 (see Figure 16.3 for the historical evolution). With hindsight it is now possible to identify various phases of reform, as well as to reflect on the various countervailing pressures that have constrained or altered the impacts of reform initiatives over time.

a) Characterization of Phases of Reform

Establishment (consolidation and stabilization)
The first phase of intergovernmental fiscal reform in South Africa was associated with the establishment of governance and fiscal systems required by the new constitutional dispensation. The legacy of the apartheid period had provided a deeply fragmented and highly centralized system of governance that was mirrored in associated fiscal arrangements. Subnational authorities were deeply fragmented on racial lines, and national government transfers were both inequitably distributed between racially defined subnational authorities and structured into a complex series of specific-purpose operating and capital grants.

The 1996 Constitution introduced a comparatively clearer set of functional and fiscal assignments between spheres of government, along with a constitutional requirement for an unconditional 'equitable share of nationally raised revenue' for both provinces and municipalities. The respective equitable shares were initially funded from the consolidation of the majority of existing specific-purpose operating transfers and inter-agency agreements, and then progressively expanded, and were distributed by formulae.

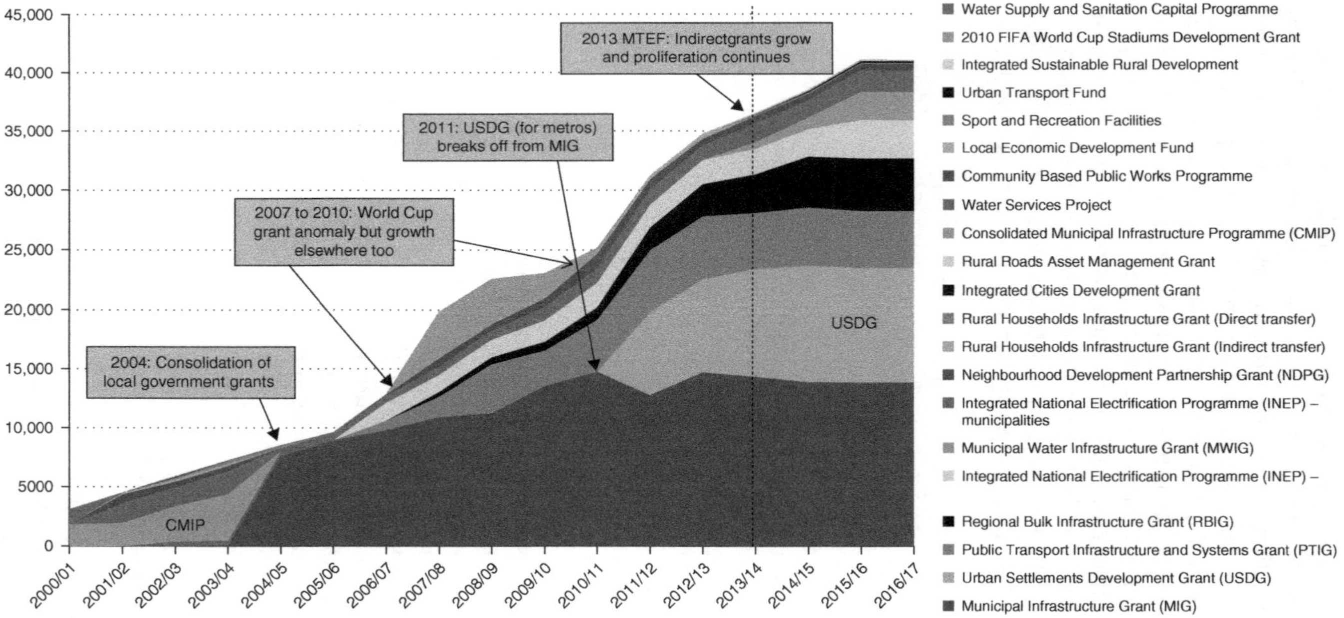
45,000
40,000
35,000
30,000
25,000
20,000
15,000
10,000
5000
0
2000/01
2001/02
2002/03
2003/04
2004/05
2005/06
2006/07
2007/08
2008/09
2009/10
2010/11
2011/12
2012/13
2013/14
2014/15
2015/16
2016/17
CMIP
USDG
2004: Consolidation of local government grants
2007 to 2010: World Cup grant anomaly but growth elsewhere too
2011: USDG (for metros) breaks off from MIG
2013 MTEF: Indirectgrants grow and proliferation continues
Water Supply and Sanitation Capital Programme
2010 FIFA World Cup Stadiums Development Grant
Integrated Sustainable Rural Development
Urban Transport Fund
Sport and Recreation Facilities
Local Economic Development Fund
Community Based Public Works Programme
Water Services Project
Consolidated Municipal Infrastructure Programme (CMIP)
Rural Roads Asset Management Grant
Integrated Cities Development Grant
Rural Households Infrastructure Grant (Direct transfer)
Rural Households Infrastructure Grant (Indirect transfer)
Neighbourhood Development Partnership Grant (NDPG)
Integrated National Electrification Programme (INEP) – municipalities
Municipal Water Infrastructure Grant (MWIG)
Integrated National Electrification Programme (INEP) –
Regional Bulk Infrastructure Grant (RBIG)
Public Transport Infrastructure and Systems Grant (PTIG)
Urban Settlements Development Grant (USDG)
Municipal Infrastructure Grant (MIG)

Source: National Treasury (2014).

Figure 16.3 The historical evolution of infrastructure grants

Various minor amendments were made to the formulae in this period, of which three were most significant for the local government sphere. Firstly, transition arrangements were introduced to progressively consolidate remaining operating transfers into the mechanism, specifically in the case of certain settlements in former homeland areas (known as R293 towns) that were almost entirely funded by special purpose transfers and stood to lose from the new formula. Secondly, a specific variable was introduced to fund the cost of allowances for municipal councillors. Finally, in 1999 government sought to clarify that the equitable share should primarily be used for the provision of free basic services to poor households.

The process for the consolidation of infrastructure grants to local government took a similar but somewhat longer route. In the initial period, a range of sector-based specific-purpose transfers emerged to fund national programmes that sought to address national backlogs in access to basic services. These transfers were made both in cash and as asset transfers, managed by respective central government departments. By 1998 it had become clear that the proliferation of small transfer programmes was largely ineffective. The system was criticized for having high transaction costs (individual administrative and reporting requirements), being unresponsive to local development priorities and development plans, making inappropriate and expensive technology choices, and failing to address the long-term operating costs of infrastructure investments. The National Treasury proposed a consolidated MIG to address these issues, to be managed cooperatively among departments, distributed by formula and funded through the consolidation of existing programmes.

The MIG proposals were met with considerable resistance by national departments, who stood to lose direct control of funding and infrastructure programmes. This resistance was ultimately overcome through a two-track approach of:

a) Prolonged negotiations on the management approach to the new programme, including an agreement to establish a jointly controlled special purpose vehicle to manage the MIG.

b) The exclusion of the bulk of transfers for housing and public transport, which were transferred through provincial governments due to concurrency in the functional assignment.

c) A progressive tightening of the regulatory requirements in the DoRA that governed existing programmes, specifically through requiring the publication of rolling three-year allocations to individual municipalities of all transfers and the written consent of receiving municipalities for all asset transfers prior to the commencement of construction.

The MIG was formally introduced in 2003, and quickly expanded through additional allocations to become the largest single infrastructure funding source for most municipalities.

Differentiation
The foundation for a greater recognition of the significant contextual variations between urban and rural local governments was introduced with the reform of municipal financial management legislation that was introduced in 2003. It had long been understood that there were marked variations in the demographic trajectories, economies, service delivery requirements and development pressures, institutional and fiscal capabilities and fiscal risks associated with larger urban municipalities and their rural counterparts. However, the initial reforms to the regulatory and fiscal framework largely treated all municipalities alike (although the two-tier structure of district and local municipalities was dispensed with in the largest metropolitan areas).

The Municipal Financial Management Act (2003) built extensively on new Public Management-style reforms to modernize public financial management, but also introduced key elements of the capital financing framework for municipalities. Importantly, this included an emphasis on market-based borrowing for infrastructure investment by creditworthy municipalities, without any central government guarantees. In order to provide a framework to deal effectively with municipal fiscal distress that might lead to debt default, a specific regime for interventions was also introduced. The National Treasury also took direct responsibility for the oversight of the largest municipalities that presented the greatest national fiscal risks and opportunities, while delegating the remainder for oversight by Provincial Treasuries.

As early as 2007, it became clear that the Department of Provincial and Local Government would not administer the MIG in conformity with the finally agreed proposals. In particular, it failed to establish a special purpose vehicle for programme administration (relying instead on a joint committee to oversee allocations) and introduced complex project registration mechanisms before municipalities could proceed with project implementation. While the latter was notionally intended to facilitate the tracking of investments it had the effect of requiring central government approval of individual investments. This led to growing concern from larger, more urban municipalities that the MIG was constraining their ability to respond to urbanization in a timely and integrated manner.

In response, the National Treasury commissioned research on the efficacy of municipal infrastructure investment programmes which found that:

a) Considerable progress had been made in eliminating backlogs in access to basic services, but that there remained severe underinvestment in asset maintenance and renewal, as well as expansion of infrastructure to accommodate economic growth and urbanization.

b) A one-size-fits-all approach to municipal financing was failing to adequately differentiate between the funding requirements of urban and rural settlement types and the fiscal and institutional capacity of their associated municipalities.

c) Larger urban municipalities, in particular, were constrained in responding to urban growth pressures through ongoing concurrency in housing and public transport functions which complicated the integrated management of the urban built environment. This functional and fiscal fragmentation was evident in both poor planning alignment and investment outcomes, with patterns of urban development continuing to reinforce the low-density, fragmented, exclusionary and fiscally costly spatial form inherited from apartheid.

d) The financing of infrastructure was becoming progressively more dependent on grants from central government, proportionately squeezing out local sources of capital finance from local revenues and municipal borrowing and threatening the long-term fiscal sustainability of urban local governments.

South Africa won the bid to host the 2010 FIFA World Cup and initiated a large-scale programme to build or refurbish football stadia and associated public transport infrastructure in host cities across the country. This programme was funded through two specific-purpose grants, for stadia and public transport networks respectively. It was the latter, which favoured the construction of Bus Rapid Transit Systems, that was to have a more lasting effect on the fiscal system. Thus, countervailing pressures had emerged to consolidate and decentralize funding to municipalities, while simultaneously to expand specific-purpose transfers to support national priority investments.

The initial fiscal response to this was to remove metropolitan municipalities from the MIG programme to release them from the need for detailed compliance with grant registration requirements. This initially took the form of a new grant called the MIG-2. This was later converted into the Urban Settlements Development Grant (USDG), with its administration moved to the Department of Human Settlements, and the consolidation of a portion of existing housing subsidies for metros into the grant.

The USDG was a significant advance over previous funding arrangements, not only in the greater discretion granted to metros in investment selection, but also in a much closer link to the investment planning process that was introduced, through a requirement that they develop results-oriented, integrated Built Environment Performance Plans (BEPPs) that outlined their expenditure programmes across all sectors and sources of finance, and eventually also included investments by other spheres of government and public entities within their jurisdictions.

Towards performance
By 2012, the tensions in the fiscal system, particularly for large urban municipalities, remained unresolved. One the one hand, the USDG had consolidated and decentralized a significant portion of grant finance for infrastructure investment, while funding for housing top structures (housing subsidies) and public transport investment remained centralized, project driven and fragmented. Moreover, there was growing evidence that the growth of the municipal borrowing market was stagnating with municipalities becoming increasingly reliant on grants as their primary source of capital finance.

A review of infrastructure grant arrangements confirmed the original basic principles of the intergovernmental fiscal framework, emphasizing the need to respect constitutional mandates, provide stable and predictable financing, encourage transparency, simplicity and accountability, integrated funding sources, differentiation between jurisdictions, and be focussed on supporting inclusive growth and poverty reduction. The National Treasury committed to a grant reform programme that would:

a)   Improve grant structures, particularly through consolidation of grants and differentiation between municipalities;
b)   Emphasize the importance of asset management and maintenance;
c)   Improve the overall management and efficiency of the grant system and individual grant programmes, through clarifying roles for national departments, and rationalizing reporting requirements to enable measurement of actual performance.

While this process is ongoing and incremental, the current emphasis of reform implementation has been on:

a)   The development of an effective non-financial outcomes measurement system for the built environment, which can form the basis of both an outcomes-led planning system and the provision of performance-based grants in the future. This has required extensive technical investment and consultation;
b)   The gradual reduction of project-based approvals associated with certain grants, in favour of programmatic oversight (for instance, in

the implementation of overall public transport strategies rather than a specific bus route); and

c) The introduction of performance-based grants, or grant components, based on specific eligibility requirements and objective performance variables. This has taken the form of a small dedicated performance grant (the Integrated City Development Grant) and a performance component introduced into the Public Transport Network Grant.

5. RESULTS OF REFORMS TO THE LOCAL GOVERNMENT FISCAL FRAMEWORK

This characterization of the periods of reform to the intergovernmental fiscal system in South Africa highlights the close connection between the design of the transfer system and the nature of the development challenges facing subnational authorities. At the introduction of the system, the development focus was on universalizing access to basic services, while simultaneously strengthening the governance systems that would sustain the services delivered on the back of new infrastructure assets. The fiscal system was thus designed to drive largely sectoral, project-based asset creation, often through asset transfers. This approach drove a rapid expansion in access to basic services, but rapidly generated its own challenges. Unit costs of connecting households to infrastructure networks rose as central agencies pursued even larger regional investment programmes, with little concern for long-term operating cost implications. Asset maintenance suffered as municipalities often found the assets too technically complex to operate and maintain, or were unwilling to take transfer of the assets due to the absence of sustainable revenues. Prospects of repeated central investments to rehabilitate or replace failing infrastructure created perverse incentives for municipalities to abandon preventive maintenance programmes, or budget adequately for infrastructure depreciation. This led to growing concerns with the sustainability of centrally driven investment programmes.

Following the establishment and stabilization of the local government system, significant impetus developed to align the functional and fiscal responsibility for infrastructure investment at the local government level. As the national fiscal position stabilized providing scope for additional grants to local government, and local government capacity was improved, the transfer system was consolidated and decentralized, particularly through the introduction of the MIG. However, this occurred in an undifferentiated manner, accounting neither for variations in context of capability across municipalities. Moreover, it provided no clear signals to municipalities on national development priorities to follow after the universalization of basic services access, nor adequate guidance on responsibilities for asset maintenance and renewal.

However, despite efforts to differentiate the approach to intergovernmental transfers, many of these issues remained unresolved. This led to a proliferation of new grant instruments, both to reintroduce centrally driven, project-based investments in weak capacity municipalities, and to drive national spending priorities in larger urban centres (particularly related to the World Cup). Yet neither of these approaches managed to address the core issues of weak capacity or national developmental priorities effectively. In the case of institutionally weaker municipalities, simply reintroducing project-based approaches did little to strengthen capacity, nor stem growing evidence of ineffective resource use or corruption. In larger urban centres, project-based grants promoted fiscally unsustainable investment choices, generating large-scale fiscal commitments that may yet threaten the sustainability of larger urban municipalities.

The consensus on the need for differentiation did, however, open the door to the ongoing programme of reforms to the intergovernmental fiscal system. It has led to the progressive introduction of performance-based funding instruments (albeit still small scale and fragmented), which has reasserted the importance of co-locating functional and fiscal responsibility, and strengthening planning and project preparation practices in municipalities. The current programme of national fiscal consolidation, and associated reductions to grants to municipalities, is likely to accelerate this process and encourage municipalities to leverage private finance more aggressively to fund their investment needs.

Reforms to the intergovernmental fiscal system in South Africa have gone through periods of rapid and radical change, hiatus and incremental progress. A few key features of the reform process stand out:

a) Grants have seldom been reformed for their own sake. Periods of rapid change have been as part of a broader reform to the intergovernmental system, whether through the restructuring of the local government system, or the introduction of a broader differentiated approach to metropolitan municipalities, focussed on improved integrated planning and delivery.

b) Reforms have not been linear. While the National Treasury has maintained a consistent approach to the management of the intergovernmental fiscal system and the role of grants within it, there have always been countervailing pressures and perspectives and pressures that have disrupted or contested the reform trajectory. Some of these pressures have been rooted in legitimate concerns about the capacity of subnational governments. However, others reflected often powerful vested interests in sector departments seeking to maximize their own control, or established rent-seeking coalitions that are resisting disruption to their activities.

c) The quality of grant design and management is often weak, undermining reform efforts. The experience of the MIG, MIG-2 and USDG all reveal problems in the quality of grant design and the effectiveness of implementation. Inadequate quality at entry, the absence of credible and regular review and adjustment to design, and a lack of investment in grant administration capacity have all weakened and delayed reform efforts, creating justifications for central administrative clawback.

d) The quality of spending must remain the ultimate goal. Although competing perspectives on the design of the fiscal system are inevitable, reform programmes must respond to changing contexts in order to improve the quality of life of citizens as their ultimate beneficiaries. Spending performance, in both financial and non-financial terms – is ultimately essential to the design of robust fiscal transfer systems and individual transfer programmes.

6.   CROSS-CUTTING ISSUES

There are a number of cross-cutting issues that are evident from this brief review of the intergovernmental fiscal system and its reform in South Africa:

a) *Addressing coordination failures:* much of the debate over the structure of the fiscal transfer system has sought to trade off the pursuit of national development priorities with functional assignments in the Constitution. Historically, sector departments have expressed a preference for centrally managed, project-based transfers, rather than integrated local-level determination of priorities through the planning system. More recently, efforts to 'align' national and local priorities and plans have placed increasing emphasis on improved intergovernmental coordination and alignment through the planning system. While significant progress has been made in this regard, 'joined up planning' comes with significant transaction costs itself and does not necessarily align incentives or actual investment practices. It may in reality merely seek to play down the costs of not abiding by – or adjusting – the system of functional assignments in the first place.

b) *Capacity and accountability:* concerns over expenditure performance, particularly in terms of value for money and fiduciary issues have been a key driver of efforts to recentralize the transfer system, and to differentiate it. This has revealed a presumption that central authorities have both greater planning and execution capacity, and sufficient capability for oversight than is necessarily the case. What has been missing in this system is the perspectives and role of non-state parties in being able to address both capacity and accountability concerns. Private financiers will have a direct interest in the maintenance of assets and associated revenue streams, and thus also in the quality of project design. Citizens themselves will have direct interests that go beyond confirming investment needs (through participatory planning processes) but also in the co-production of services and the oversight of performance (through various social accountability tools, such as social audits). For non-state actors, a key starting point for their involvement is much greater information of, and sense of ownership of, intergovernmental resource flows.

c) *The role of incentives:* recent efforts to expand performance incentives offer a promising new direction for a differentiated fiscal transfer system. However, performance-based systems require careful construction of objective and measurable indicators and targets which can take significant effort to develop, negotiate and manage. Moreover, simple cash-based rewards are not the only form of incentive to which organizations respond. Greater discretion over resource use, for example, may provide a greater incentive at the margin than simply more money with strings attached.

d) *Project finance and fiscal transfers:* the push towards consolidated, formula-based transfers must pay careful attention to the needs of larger investment projects and programmes. In the first instance these may demand very lumpy expenditures that are not well suited to an annual grant allocation. However, large infrastructure projects also pose significant risks that require careful mitigation in the project preparation process, and may offer significant opportunities to leverage private finance, for which grant allocations are typically poorly designed.

7.   IMPLICATIONS FOR OTHER COUNTRIES

The trajectory of the intergovernmental fiscal system in South Africa remains unique to its own changing context. There are, however, three broad lessons from this experience that could be considered to be universal:

a) *Monitoring and oversight:* all transfer systems require monitoring and oversight, which in turn requires regular, useful and verifiable information flows. These are typically easier to establish in relation to purely financial matters, rather than actual outputs and impacts. Considerable, complementary investment in management information systems, which provides a critical feedback loop to planning and budgeting systems, is thus a long-term priority for any system of intergovernmental transfers and should be central to any reform efforts. The government has struggled to improve verifiable flows of both financial and non-financial information. While the South African case demonstrates the financial information can easily be improved, this is of limited value if not accompanied by relevant service output data associated with financing arrangements.

b) *Incentives and triggers for reform:* any reform to the system of intergovernmental transfers will generate winners and losers, both in terms of administrative authority and in terms of opportunities provided for rent-seeking. In many cases this will lead to ongoing resistance to efforts at reform, which can be expressed through blocking of proposals, poor design or application of new approaches, or outright efforts to block project level implementation. Addressing these obstacles requires reformers to pay far closer attention to the political-economy of reform, and particularly to the design and execution of the reform process itself.

   Systemic reforms to the transfer system are often easier in times of more systemic reforms (for example, to the local government system as a whole), and in times of fiscal crisis when few other options are available, not least as the authority required to execute reforms is often more clearly established. Yet even in these cases the momentum of reform needs to be established and maintained into implementation. Regulatory tools (as were used in the DoRA) and more positive efforts to strengthen collaboration most often need to work in tandem to achieve this.

c) *Strengthening accountability:* intergovernmental transfers, by their nature, create accountability challenges for both transferring and receiving authorities. Famously, those who 'pay the piper, call the tune' and an excessive reliance on central transfers will ultimately weaken the downward accountability of the receiving authority to its citizens. Addressing this fundamental challenge is often posited as a choice between local state discretion and central state control, with the latter perspective most often argued for in terms of an absence of local state capacity.

However, both these perspectives ignore the central role of non-state actors in strengthening downward accountability for results. Ultimately, citizens are the intended beneficiaries of these resources and can play an important local role in advising on resource allocations, co-producing services, monitoring outputs and assessing value for money. Limited, obscure, complicated and outdated information all undermine the capacity of citizens to engage with resource allocation and programme execution processes. Much greater innovation in, and basic standards for, citizen engagement are a critical gap that South Africa has yet to address in the design of its intergovernmental fiscal systems.

REFERENCES

National Treasury (2014), *Review of Local Government Infrastructure Grants: Recommendations for Reform*. Draft Report to Budget Forum, September 2014. Accessed online on 1 February 2019 at www.ffc.co.za/. . ./804-review-of-local-government-infrastructure-grants-recommendat.
National Treasury (2019), *Budget Review 2019, 20 February 2019*. Government Printers, Pretoria.
Statistics South Africa (2017), *General Household Survey 2017*. Statistical Release P0318. Accessed online on 1 February 2019 at www.statssa.gov.za/?page_id=1854&PPN=P0318.

Index